BENCHMARK SERIES

MICROSOFT
ACCESS 2013
LEVEL 1

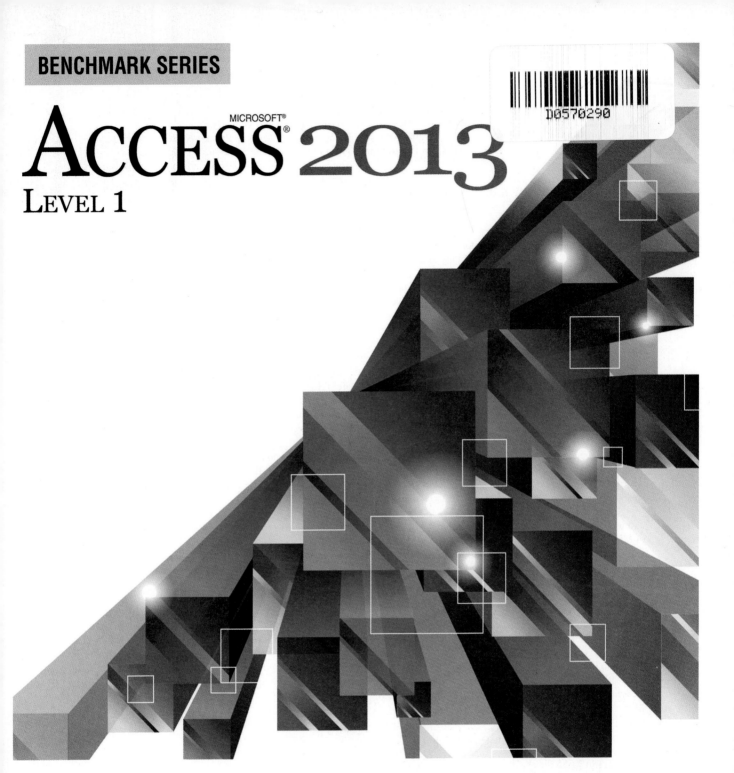

NITA RUTKOSKY
Pierce College at Puyallup
Puyallup, Washington

AUDREY ROGGENKAMP
Pierce College at Puyallup
Puyallup, Washington

IAN RUTKOSKY
Pierce College at Puyallup
Puyallup, Washington

Paradigm PUBLISHING

St. Paul

Managing Editor	Christine Hurney
Director of Production	Timothy W. Larson
Production Editor	Sarah Kearin
Cover and Text Designers	Leslie Anderson and Jaana Bykonich
Copy Editors	Communicáto, Ltd.; Nan Brooks, Abshier House
Desktop Production	Jaana Bykonich, Julie Johnston, Valerie King, Timothy W. Larson, Jack Ross, and Sara Schmidt Boldon
Indexer	Terry Casey
VP & Director of Digital Projects	Chuck Bratton
Digital Projects Manager	Tom Modl

Acknowledgements: The authors, editors, and publisher thank the following instructors for their helpful suggestions during the planning and development of the books in the Benchmark Office 2013 Series: Olugbemiga Adekunle, Blue Ridge Community College, Harrisonburg, VA; Letty Barnes, Lake WA Institute of Technology, Kirkland, WA; Erika Nadas, Wilbur Wright College, Chicago, IL; Carolyn Walker, Greenville Technical College, Greenville, SC; Carla Anderson, National College, Lynchburg, VA; Judy A. McLaney, Lurleen B. Wallace Community College, Opp, AL; Sue Canter, Guilford Technical Community College, Jamestown, NC; Reuel Sample, National College, Knoxville, TN; Regina Young, Wiregrass Georgia Technical College, Valdosta, GA; William Roxbury, National College, Stow, OH; Charles Adams, II, Danville Community College, Danville, VA; Karen Spray, Northeast Community College, Norfolk, NE; Deborah Miller, Augusta Technical College, Augusta, GA; Wanda Stuparits, Lanier Technical College, Cumming, GA; Gale Wilson, Brookhaven College, Farmers Branch, TX; Jocelyn S. Pinkard, Arlington Career Institute, Grand Prairie, TX; Ann Blackman, Parkland College, Champaign, IL; Fathia Williams, Fletcher Technical Community College, Houma, LA; Leslie Martin, Gaston College, Dallas, NC; Tom Rose, Kellogg Community College, Battle Creek, MI; Casey Thompson, Wiregrass Georgia Technical College, Douglas, GA; Larry Bush, University of Cincinnati, Clermont College, Amelia, OH; Tim Ellis, Schoolcraft College, Liconia, MI; Miles Cannon, Lanier Technical College, Oakwood, GA; Irvin LaFleur, Lanier Technical College, Cumming, GA; Patricia Partyka, Schoolcraft College, Prudenville, MI.

The authors and publishing team also thanks the following individuals for their contributions to this project: checking the accuracy of the instruction and exercises—Brienna McWade, Traci Post, and Janet Blum, Fanshawe College, London, Ontario; creating annotated model answers and developing lesson plans—Ann Mills, Ivy Tech Community College, Evansville, Indiana; developing rubrics—Marjory Wooten, Laneir Techncial College, Cumming, Georgia.

Trademarks: Access, Excel, Internet Explorer, Microsoft, PowerPoint, and Windows are trademarks or registered trademarks of Microsoft Corporation in the United States and/or other countries. Some of the product names and company names included in this book have been used for identification purposes only and may be trademarks or registered trade names of their respective manufacturers and sellers. The authors, editors, and publisher disclaim any affiliation, association, or connection with, or sponsorship or endorsement by, such owners.

We have made every effort to trace the ownership of all copyrighted material and to secure permission from copyright holders. In the event of any question arising as to the use of any material, we will be pleased to make the necessary corrections in future printings. Thanks are due to the aforementioned authors, publishers, and agents for permission to use the materials indicated.

Paradigm Publishing is independent from Microsoft Corporation, and not affiliated with Microsoft in any manner. While this publication may be used in assisting individuals to prepare for a Microsoft Office Specialist certification exam, Microsoft, its designated program administrator, and Paradigm Publishing do not warrant that use of this publication will ensure passing a Microsoft Office Specialist certification exam.

ISBN 978-0-76385-350-1 (Text)
ISBN 978-0-76385-393-8 (Text + CD)
ISBN 978-0-76385-372-3 (ebook via email)
ISBN 978-0-76385-415-7 (ebook via mail)

© 2014 by Paradigm Publishing, Inc.
875 Montreal Way
St. Paul, MN 55102
Email: educate@emcp.com
Website: www.emcp.com

Printed in the United States of America

22 21 20 19 18 17 16 15 14 13   2 3 4 5 6 7 8 9 10

Contents

Microsoft Access 2013 Level 1

Benchmark Series Microsoft Access 2013 is designed for students who want to learn how to use this feature-rich data management tool to track, report, and share information. No prior knowledge of database management systems is required. After successfully completing a course using this textbook, students will be able to

- Create database tables to organize business or personal records
- Modify and manage tables to ensure that data is accurate and up to date
- Perform queries to assist with decision making
- Plan, research, create, revise, and publish database information to meet specific communication needs
- Given a workplace scenario requiring the reporting and analysis of data, assess the information requirements and then prepare the materials that achieve the goal efficiently and effectively

In addition to mastering Access skills, students will learn the essential features and functions of computer hardware, the Windows 8 operating system, and Internet Explorer 10. Upon completing the text, they can expect to be proficient in using Access to organize, analyze, and present information.

Well-designed textbook pedagogy is important, but students learn technology skills from practice and problem solving. Technology provides opportunities for interactive learning as well as excellent ways to quickly and accurately assess student performance. To this end, this textbook is supported with SNAP, Paradigm Publishing's web-based training and assessment learning management system. Details about SNAP as well as additional student courseware and instructor resources can be found on page xiv.

Achieving Proficiency in Access 2013 ■■■■■■

Since its inception several Office versions ago, the Benchmark Series has served as a standard of excellence in software instruction. Elements of the book function individually and collectively to create an inviting, comprehensive learning environment that produces successful computer users. The following visual tour highlights the text's features.

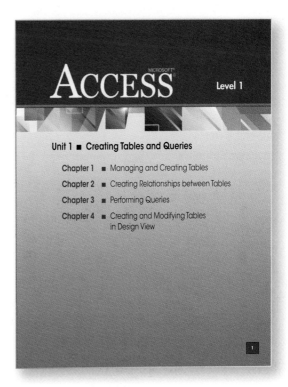

UNIT OPENERS display the unit's four chapter titles. Each level has two units, which conclude with a comprehensive unit performance assessment.

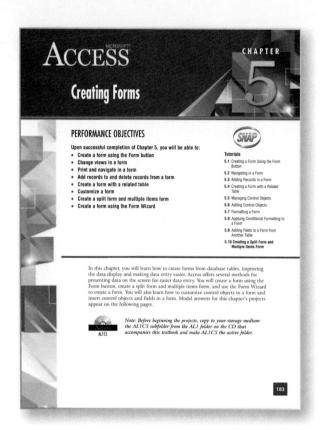

CHAPTER OPENERS present the performance objectives and an overview of the skills taught.

SNAP interactive tutorials are available to support chapter-specific skills at snap2013.emcp.com.

DATA FILES are provided for each chapter. A prominent note reminds students to copy the appropriate chapter data folder and make it active.

PROJECT APPROACH: Builds Skill Mastery within Realistic Context

MODEL ANSWERS provide a preview of the finished chapter projects and allow students to confirm they have created the materials accurately.

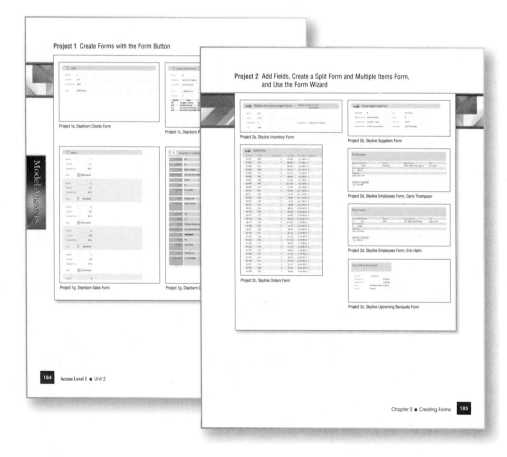

MULTIPART PROJECTS provide a framework for the instruction and practice on software features. A project overview identifies tasks to accomplish and key features to use in completing the work.

Between project parts, the text presents instruction on the features and skills necessary to accomplish the next section of the project.

Project 1   Create Forms with the Form Button   7 Parts

You will use the Form button to create forms with fields in the Clients, Representatives, and Sales tables. You will also add, delete, and print records and use buttons in the FORM LAYOUT TOOLS FORMAT tab to apply formatting to control objects in the forms.

Creating Forms ■■■■■■■■■■■■■■■■■■■■■■■■■■■■■■

HINT
A form allows you to focus on a single record at a time.

HINT
Save a form before making changes or applying formatting to it.

Access offers a variety of options for presenting data in a clear and attractive format. For instance, you can view, add, or edit data in a table in Datasheet view. When you enter data in a table in Datasheet view, you will see multiple records at the same time. If a record contains several fields, you may not be able to view all of the fields within the record at the same time. If you create a form, however, all of the fields for a record are generally visible on the screen.

A *form* is an object you can use to enter and edit data in a table or query. It is a user-friendly interface for viewing, adding, editing, and deleting records. A form is also useful in helping to prevent incorrect data from being entered and it can be used to control access to specific data.

Several methods are available for creating forms. In this chapter, you will learn how to create forms using the Form, Split Form, and Multiple Items buttons as well as the Form Wizard.

Creating a Form with the Form Button

Quick Steps
Create a Form with the Form Button
1. Click desired table.
2. Click CREATE tab.
3. Click Form button.

The simplest method for creating a form is to click a table in the Navigation pane, click the CREATE tab, and then click the Form button in the Forms groups. Figure 5.1 shows the form you will create in Project 1a with the Sales table in AL1-C5-Dearborn.accdb. Access creates the form using all fields in the table in a vertical layout and displays the form in Layout view with the FORM LAYOUT TOOLS DESIGN tab active.

Changing Views

Form

Form View

Layout View

When you click the Form button to create a form, the form displays in Layout view. This is one of three views for working with forms. Use the Form view to enter and manage records. Use the Layout view to view the data and modify the appearance and contents of the form. Use the Design view to view the structure of the form and modify the form. Change views with the View button in the Views group on the FORM LAYOUT TOOLS DESIGN tab or with buttons in the view area located at the right side of the Status bar.

You can open an existing form in Layout view. To do this, right-click the form name in the Navigation pane and then click *Layout View* at the shortcut menu.

Printing a Form

Print all of the records in a form by clicking the FILE tab, clicking the *Print* option, and then clicking the Quick Print button. If you want to print a specific record in a form, click the FILE tab, click the *Print* option, and then click the Pr...

Adding and Deleting Records

Add a new record to the form by clicking the New (blank) record button (contains a right-pointing arrow and a yellow asterisk) that displays on the Record Navigation bar along the bottom of the form. You can also add a new record to a form by clicking the HOME tab and then clicking the New button in the Records group. To delete a record, display the record, click the HOME tab, click the Delete button arrow in the Records group, and then click *Delete Record* at the drop-down list. At the message telling you that the record will be deleted permanently, click Yes. Add records to or delete records from the table from which the form was created and the form will reflect the additions or deletions. Also, if you make additions or deletions to the form, the changes are reflected in the table on which the form was created.

Quick Steps
Add a Record
Click New (blank) record button on Record Navigation bar.
OR
1. Click HOME tab.
2. Click New button.
Delete a Record
1. Click HOME tab.
2. Click Delete button arrow.
3. Click *Delete Record*.
4. Click Yes.

New (blank) record   Delete

Sorting Records

Sort data in a form by clicking in the field containing data on which you want to sort and then clicking the Ascending button or Descending button in the Sort & Filter group on the HOME tab. Click the Ascending button to sort text in alphabetic order from A to Z or numbers from lowest to highest or click the Descending button to sort text in alphabetic order from Z to A or numbers from highest to lowest.

STEP-BY-STEP INSTRUCTIONS guide students to the desired outcome for each project part. Screen captures illustrate what the student's screen should look like at key points.

Project 1b   Adding and Deleting Records in a Form   Part 2 of 7

1. Open the Sales table (not the form) and add a new record by completing the following steps:
   a. Click the New (blank) record button located in the Record Navigation bar.

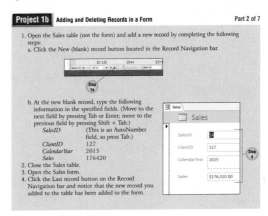

   b. At the new blank record, type the following information in the specified fields. (Move to the next field by pressing Tab or Enter; move to the previous field by pressing Shift + Tab.)
      SalesID   (This is an AutoNumber field, so press Tab.)
      ClientID   127
      CalendarYear   2015
      Sales   176420
2. Close the Sales table.
3. Open the Sales form.
4. Click the Last record button on the Record Navigation bar and notice that the new record you added to the table has been added to the form.

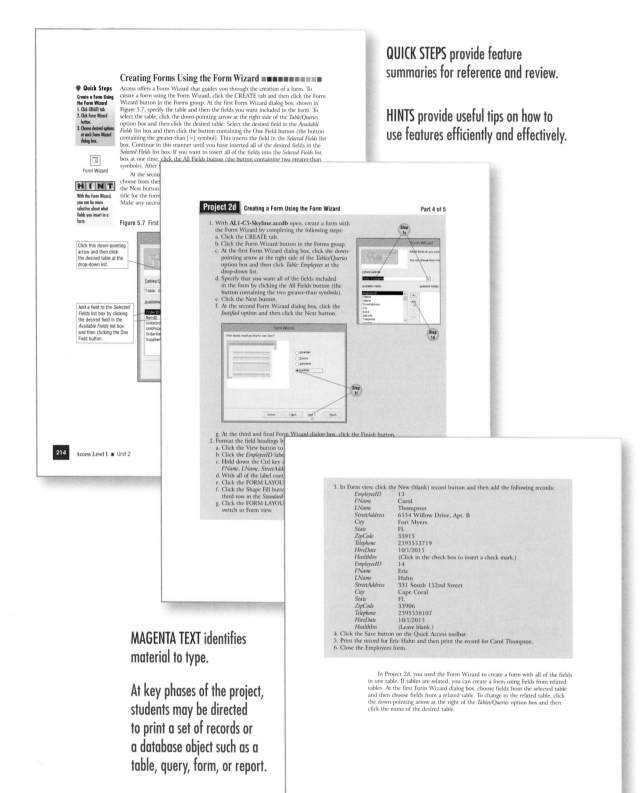

QUICK STEPS provide feature
summaries for reference and review.

HINTS provide useful tips on how to
use features efficiently and effectively.

MAGENTA TEXT identifies
material to type.

At key phases of the project,
students may be directed
to print a set of records or
a database object such as a
table, query, form, or report.

CHAPTER REVIEW ACTIVITIES: A Hierarchy of Learning Assessments

Chapter Summary

- Microsoft Access is a database management system software program that can organize, store, maintain, retrieve, sort, and print all types of business data.
- In Access, open an existing database by clicking the Open Other Files hyperlink at the Access 2013 opening screen. At the Open backstage area, double-click your SkyDrive or the Computer option. At the Open dialog box, navigate to the location of the database and then double-click the desired database.
- Some common objects found in a database include tables, queries, forms, and reports.
- The Navigation pane displays at the left side of the Access screen and displays the objects that are contained in the database.
- Open a database object by double-clicking the object in the Navigation pane. Close an object by clicking the Close button that displays in the upper right corner of the work area.
- When a table is open, the Record Navigation bar displays at the bottom of the screen and contains buttons for displaying records in the table.
- Insert a new record in a table by clicking the New button in the Records group on the HOME tab or by clicking the New [record] button on the Record Navigation bar. Delete a record by clicking [in the record you want to] delete, clicking the Delete button arrow [in the Records group, and then clicking] *Delete Record* at the drop-down list.
- To add a column to a table, click the first [column] heading and then type the desired data. T[o move a column, click the column heading] and then use the mouse to drag a thick, b[lack line (representing the] column) to the desired location. To delete [a column, click the column heading,] click the Delete button arrow, and then cl[ick].
- Data you enter in a table is automatically [saved. Changes to the layout of] a table are not automatically saved.
- Hide, unhide, freeze, and unfreeze colum[ns with options at the More button] drop-down list. Display this list by clickin[g the More button in the Records] group on the HOME tab.
- Adjust the width of a column (or selected [columns) to accommodate the] longest entry by double-clicking the colu[mn boundary. You can also adjust the] width of a column by dragging the colum[n boundary.]
- Rename a table by right-clicking the tab[le name in the Navigation pane,] clicking *Rename*, and then typing the new [name. You can also right-click] the table name in the Navigation pane a[nd].
- Print a table by clicking the FILE tab, cli[cking the Print option, and then] clicking the Quick Print button. You can [preview a table before printing by] clicking the Print Preview button at the P[rint backstage area.]
- With buttons and option on the PRINT [PREVIEW tab you can change the] page size, orientation, and margins.
- The first principle in database design is t[o reduce redundant data because] redundant data increases the amount of [data entry required, increases the] chances for errors, and takes up additiona[l].
- A data type defines the type of data Acce[ss will allow in the field. Assign a data] type to a field with buttons in the Add & [Delete].

CHAPTER SUMMARY captures the purpose and execution of key features.

FIELDS tab, by clicking an option from the column heading drop-down list, or with options at the More button drop-down list.
- Rename a column heading by right-clicking the heading, clicking *Rename Field* at the shortcut menu, and then typing the new name.
- Type a name, caption, and description for a column with options at the Enter Field Properties dialog box.
- Use options in the *Quick Start* category in the More Fields button drop-down list to define a data type and assign a field name to a group of related fields.
- Insert a default value in a column with the Default Value button and assign a field size with the *Field Size* text box in the Properties group on the TABLE TOOLS FIELDS tab.
- Use the *Data Type* option box in the Formatting group on the TABLE TOOLS FIELDS tab to change the AutoNumber data type for the first column in a table.

Commands Review

FEATURE	RIBBON TAB, GROUP/OPTION	BUTTON, OPTION	KEYBOARD SHORTCUT
close Access		✕	Alt + F4
close database	FILE, *Close*		
create table	CREATE, Tables		
Currency data type	TABLE TOOLS FIELDS, Add & Delete		
Date & Time data type	TABLE TOOLS FIELDS, Add & Delete		
delete column	HOME, Records	✕ *Delete Column*	
delete record	HOME, Records	✕ *Delete Record*	
Enter Field Properties dialog box	TABLE TOOLS FIELDS, Properties		
Expression Builder dialog box	TABLE TOOLS FIELDS, Proper[ties]		
freeze column	HOME, Records		
hide column	HOME, Records		
landscape orientation	FILE, *Print*		
new record	HOME, Records		
next field			
Number data type	TABLE TOOLS FIELDS, Add & [Delete]		
Page Setup dialog box	FILE, *Print*		

COMMANDS REVIEW summarizes visually the major features and command options.

Concepts Check   Test Your Knowledge   SNAP

records in one table that have no matching records in the other related table.

Completion: In the space provided at the right, indicate the correct term, symbol, or command.

1. The Query Design button is located in the Queries group on this tab.
2. Click the Query Design button and the query window displays with this dialog box open.
3. To establish a criterion for a query, click in this row in the column containing the desired field name and then type the criterion.
4. This is the term used for the results of the query.
5. This is the symbol Access automatically inserts before and after a date when writing a criterion for the query.
6. Use this symbol to indicate a wildcard character when writing a query criterion.
7. This is the criterion you would type to return field values greater than $500.
8. This is the criterion you would type to return field values that begin with the letter *L*.
9. This is the criterion you would type to return field values that are not in Oregon.
10. You can sort a field in a query in ascending order or in this order.
11. Multiple criteria entered in the *Criteria* row in the query design grid become this type of statement.
12. This wizard guides you through the steps for preparing a query.
13. This type of query calculates aggregate functions, in which field values are grouped by two fields.
14. Use this type of query to compare two tables and produce a list of the records in one table that have no matching records in the other table.

CONCEPTS CHECK questions assess knowledge recall. Students enrolled in SNAP can complete the concepts check online. SNAP automatically scores student work.

Skills Check   Assess Your Performance

Assessment

1 DESIGN QUERIES IN A LEGAL SERVICES DATABASE

1. Display the Open dialog box with the AL1C3 folder on your storage medium the active folder.
2. Open **AL1-C3-WarrenLegal.accdb** and enable the contents.
3. Design a query that extracts information from the Billing table with the following specifications:
   a. Include the fields *BillingID, ClientID,* and *CategoryID* in the query.
   b. Ex...
      fie...
      Ac...
   c. Sa...
   d. Pr...
4. Desi...
   follo...
   a. In...
   b. Ex...
      an...
   c. Sa...
   d. Pr...
5. Desi...
   follo...
   a. In...
   b. Ex...
   c. Sa...
   d. Pr...
6. Desi...
   speci...
   a. In...
      tal...
   b. In...
   c. Ex...
   d. Sa...
   e. Pr...
7. Desi...
   speci...
   a. In...
   b. In...
   c. In...
   d. Ex...
   e. Sa...
   f. Pr...
8. Desi...
   speci...
   a. In...
   b. In...
   c. In...

SKILLS CHECK exercises ask students to develop both standard and customized kinds of database elements. Versions of the activities marked with a SNAP Grade It icon are available for automatic scoring in SNAP.

Assessment

4 CREATE AND CUSTOMIZE AN EMPLOYEES FORM

1. Open **AL1-C5-Griffin.accdb** from the AL1C5 folder on your storage medium and enable the contents.
2. Suppose you want to create a form for entering employee information but you do not want to include the employees' salaries, since that is confidential information and accessible only to the account manager. Use the Form Wizard to create an Employees form that includes all fields *except* the *AnnualSalary* field and name the form *Employees*.
3. Type a new record with the following information in the specified fields:

EmpID	1099
LastName	Williamson
FirstName	Carrie
BirthDate	6/24/1986
HireDate	8/1/2014
DeptID	RD

4. Switch to layout view, apply the Slice theme, change the theme colors to *Blue Warm,* and change the theme fonts to *Franklin Gothic*.
5. Print the new record you typed.
6. Close the Employees form.

Visual Benchmark   Demonstrate Your Proficiency

CREATE AND FORMAT A PROPERTIES FORM

1. Open **AL1-C5-SunProperties.accdb** located in the AL1C5 folder on your storage medium and enable the contents.
2. Create a form with the Properties table and format the form so it appears similar to the form in Figure 5.8 using the following specifications:
   a. Apply the Facet theme and apply the Paper theme colors.
   b. Insert the logo, title...
      the figure. (Insert th...
      title control object a...
   c. Select all of the obj...
      to Maroon 5 (sixth...
   d. Select the first colu...
      Background 2, Dark...
      Theme Colors section...
      column, sixth row i...
      alignment to Align...

VISUAL BENCHMARK assessments test students' problem-solving skills and mastery of program features.

Case Study   Apply Your Skills

Part 1 You are the office manager at the Lewis Vision Care Center and your center is switching over to Access to manage files. You have already created four basic tables and now need to create relationships and enter data. Open **AL1-C5-LewisCenter.accdb** and then create the following relationships between tables (enforce referential integrity and cascade fields and records):

Field Name	"One" Table	"Many" Table
PatientID	Patients	Billing
ServiceID	Services	Billing
DoctorID	Doctors	Billing

Save and then print the relationships.

Part 2 Before entering data in the tables, create a form for each table and apply a theme of your choosing. Enter data in the forms in the order in which it appears in Figure 5.10 on the next page. Apply any additional formatting to enhance the visual appearance of each form. After entering the information in the forms, print the first record of each form.

Part 3 Apply the following conditions to fields in forms:
   • In the Patients form, apply the condition that the city *Tulsa* displays in red and the city *Broken Arrow* displays in blue in the *City* field. Print the first record of the Patients form and then close the form.
   • In the Billing form, apply the condition that amounts in the *Fee* field over $99 display in green. Print the second record of the Billing form and then close the form.
   Close **AL1-C5-LewisCenter.accdb**.

Part 4 Your center has a procedures manual that describes workplace processes and procedures. Open Word and then create a document for the procedures manual that describes the formatting and conditions you applied to the forms in **AL1-C5-LewisCenter.accdb**. Save the completed document and name it **AL1-C5-CS-Manual**. Print and then close **AL1-C5-CS-Manual.docx**.

CASE STUDY requires analyzing a workplace scenario and then planning and executing multipart projects.

Students strengthen their analytical and writing skills by using Microsoft Word to describe best uses of Access features or to explain the decisions they made in completing the Case Study.

UNIT PERFORMANCE ASSESSMENT: Cross-Disciplinary, Comprehensive Evaluation

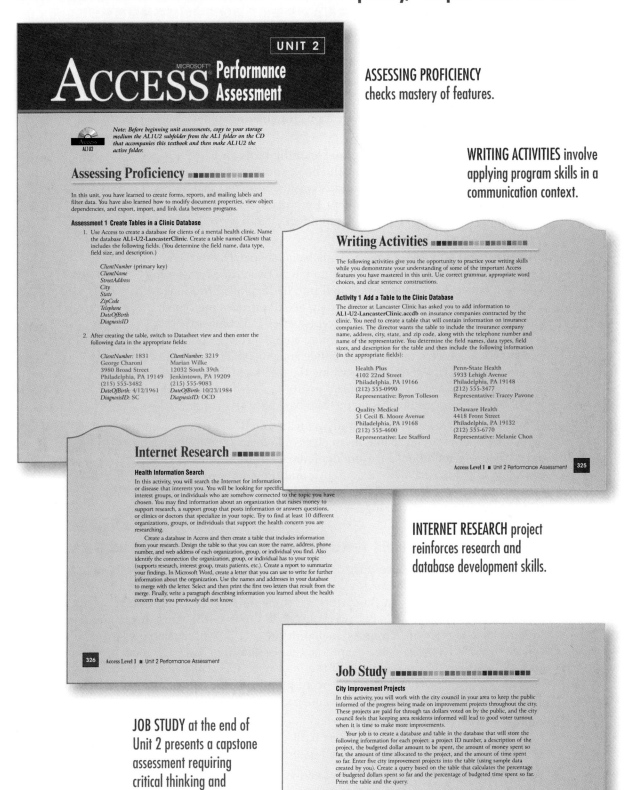

ASSESSING PROFICIENCY checks mastery of features.

WRITING ACTIVITIES involve applying program skills in a communication context.

INTERNET RESEARCH project reinforces research and database development skills.

JOB STUDY at the end of Unit 2 presents a capstone assessment requiring critical thinking and problem solving.

UNIT 2

ACCESS Performance Assessment

Note: Before beginning unit assessments, copy to your storage medium the AL1U2 subfolder from the AL1 folder on the CD that accompanies this textbook and then make AL1U2 the active folder.

Assessing Proficiency

In this unit, you have learned to create forms, reports, and mailing labels and filter data. You have also learned how to modify document properties, view object dependencies, and export, import, and link data between programs.

Assessment 1 Create Tables in a Clinic Database

1. Use Access to create a database for clients of a mental health clinic. Name the database **AL1-U2-LancasterClinic**. Create a table named *Clients* that includes the following fields. (You determine the field name, data type, field size, and description.)

   ClientNumber (primary key)
   ClientName
   StreetAddress
   City
   State
   ZipCode
   Telephone
   DateOfBirth
   DiagnosisID

2. After creating the table, switch to Datasheet view and then enter the following data in the appropriate fields:

   ClientNumber: 1831   ClientNumber: 3219
   George Charoni   Marian Wilke
   3980 Broad Street   12032 South 39th
   Philadelphia, PA 19149   Jenkintown, PA 19209
   (215) 555-3482   (215) 555-9083
   DateOfBirth: 4/12/1961   DateOfBirth: 10/23/1984
   DiagnosisID: SC   DiagnosisID: OCD

Writing Activities

The following activities give you the opportunity to practice your writing skills while you demonstrate your understanding of some of the important Access features you have mastered in this unit. Use correct grammar, appropriate word choices, and clear sentence constructions.

Activity 1 Add a Table to the Clinic Database

The director at Lancaster Clinic has asked you to add information to **AL1-U2-LancasterClinic.accdb** on insurance companies contracted by the clinic. You need to create a table that will contain information on insurance companies. The director wants the table to include the insurance company name, address, city, state, and zip code, along with the telephone number and name of the representative. You determine the field names, data types, field sizes, and description for the table and then include the following information (in the appropriate fields):

Health Plus   Penn-State Health
4102 22nd Street   5933 Lehigh Avenue
Philadelphia, PA 19166   Philadelphia, PA 19148
(212) 555-0990   (212) 555-3477
Representative: Byron Tolleson Representative: Tracey Pavone

Quality Medical   Delaware Health
51 Cecil B. Moore Avenue   4418 Front Street
Philadelphia, PA 19168   Philadelphia, PA 19132
(212) 555-4600   (212) 555-6770
Representative: Lee Stafford   Representative: Melanie Chon

Internet Research

Health Information Search

In this activity, you will search the Internet for information or disease that interests you. You will be looking for specific interest groups, or individuals who are somehow connected to the topic you have chosen. You may find information about an organization that raises money to support research, a support group that posts information or answers questions, or clinics or doctors that specialize in your topic. Try to find at least 10 different organizations, groups, or individuals that support the health concern you are researching.

Create a database in Access and then create a table that includes information from your research. Design the table so that you can store the name, address, phone number, and web address of each organization, group, or individual you find. Also identify the connection the organization, group, or individual has to your topic (supports research, interest group, treats patients, etc.). Create a report to summarize your findings. In Microsoft Word, create a letter that you can use to write for further information about the organization. Use the names and addresses in your database to merge with the letter. Select and then print the first two letters that result from the merge. Finally, write a paragraph describing information you learned about the health concern that you previously did not know.

Job Study

City Improvement Projects

In this activity, you will work with the city council in your area to keep the public informed of the progress being made on improvement projects throughout the city. These projects are paid for through tax dollars voted on by the public, and the city council feels that keeping area residents informed will lead to good voter turnout when it is time to make more improvements.

Your job is to create a database and table in the database that will store the following information for each project: a project ID number, a description of the project, the budgeted dollar amount to be spent, the amount of money spent so far, the amount of time allocated to the project, and the amount of time spent so far. Enter five city improvement projects into the table (using sample data created by you). Create a query based on the table that calculates the percentage of budgeted dollars spent so far and the percentage of budgeted time spent so far. Print the table and the query.

Student Courseware ■■■■■■■■■■■■■■■■■■■■■■■■■■■■■■

Student Resources CD Each Benchmark Series textbook is packaged with a Student Resources CD containing the data files required for completing the projects and assessments. A CD icon and folder name displayed on the opening page of chapters reminds students to copy a folder of files from the CD to the desired storage medium before beginning the project exercises. Directions for copying folders are printed on the inside back cover.

Internet Resource Center Additional learning tools and reference materials are available at the book-specific website at www.paradigmcollege.net/BenchmarkAccess13. Students can access the same files that are on the Student Resources CD along with study aids, web links, and tips for using computers effectively in academic and workplace settings.

SNAP Training and Assessment Available at snap2013.emcp.com, SNAP is a web-based program offering an interactive venue for learning Microsoft Office 2013, Windows 8, and Internet Explorer 10. Along with a web-based learning management system, SNAP provides multimedia tutorials, performance skill items, Concepts Check matching activities, Grade It Skills Check Assessment activities, comprehensive performance evaluations, a concepts test bank, an online grade book, and a set of course planning tools. A CD of tutorials teaching the basics of Office, Windows, and Internet Explorer is also available if instructors wish to assign additional SNAP tutorial work without using the web-based SNAP program.

eBook For students who prefer studying with an eBook, the texts in the Benchmark Series are available in an electronic form. The web-based, password-protected eBooks feature dynamic navigation tools, including bookmarking, a linked table of contents, and the ability to jump to a specific page. The eBook format also supports helpful study tools, such as highlighting and note taking.

Instructor Resources ■■■■■■■■■■■■■■■■■■■■■■■■■■■■■■

Instructor's Guide and Disc Instructor support for the Benchmark Series includes an *Instructor's Guide and Instructor Resources Disc* package. This resource includes planning information, such as Lesson Blueprints, teaching hints, and sample course syllabi; presentation resources, such as PowerPoint slide shows with lecture notes and audio support; and assessment resources, including an overview of available assessment venues, live model answers for chapter activities, and live and PDF model answers for end-of-chapter exercises. Contents of the *Instructor's Guide and Instructor Resources Disc* package are also available on the password-protected section of the Internet Resource Center for this title at www.paradigmcollege.net/BenchmarkAccess13.

Computerized Test Generator Instructors can use the ExamView® Assessment Suite and test banks of multiple-choice items to create customized web-based or print tests.

Blackboard Cartridge This set of files allows instructors to create a personalized Blackboard website for their course and provides course content, tests, and the mechanisms for establishing communication via e-discussions and online group conferences. Available content includes a syllabus, test banks, PowerPoint presentations with audio support, and supplementary course materials. Upon request, the files can be available within 24–48 hours. Hosting the site is the responsibility of the educational institution.

System Requirements ■■■■■■■■■■■■■■■■■■■■■■■■■■■

This text is designed for the student to complete projects and assessments on a computer running a standard installation of Microsoft Office Professional Plus 2013 and the Microsoft Windows 8 operating system. To effectively run this suite and operating system, your computer should be outfitted with the following:

- 1 gigahertz (GHz) processor or higher; 1 gigabyte (GB) of RAM (32 bit) or 2 GB of RAM (64 bit)
- 3 GB of available hard-disk space
- .NET version 3.5, 4.0, or 4.5
- DirectX 10 graphics card
- Minimum 1024 × 576 resolution (or 1366 × 768 to use Windows Snap feature)
- Computer mouse, multi-touch device, or other compatible pointing device

Office 2013 will also operate on computers running the Windows 7 operating system.

Screen captures in this book were created using a screen resolution display setting of 1600 × 900. Refer to the *Customizing Settings* section of *Getting Started in Office 2013* following this preface for instructions on changing your monitor's resolution. Figure G.9 on page 10 shows the Microsoft Office Word ribbon at three resolutions for comparison purposes. Choose the resolution that best matches your computer; however, be aware that using a resolution other than 1600 × 900 means that your screens may not match the illustrations in this book.

About the Authors ■■■■■■■■■■■■■■■■■■■■■■■■■■■

Nita Rutkosky began teaching business education courses at Pierce College in Puyallup, Washington, in 1978. Since then she has taught a variety of software applications to students in postsecondary Information Technology certificate and degree programs. In addition to *Benchmark Office 2013,* she has co-authored *Marquee Series: Microsoft Office 2013, 2010, 2007,* and *2003; Signature Series: Microsoft Word 2013, 2010, 2007,* and *2003; Using Computers in the Medical Office: Microsoft Word, Excel, and PowerPoint 2010, 2007* and *2003;* and *Computer and Internet Essentials: Preparing for IC³.* She has also authored textbooks on keyboarding, WordPerfect, desktop publishing, and voice recognition for Paradigm Publishing, Inc.

Audrey Roggenkamp has been teaching courses in the Business Information Technology department at Pierce College in Puyallup since 2005. Her courses have included keyboarding, skill building, and Microsoft Office programs. In addition to this title, she has co-authored *Marquee Series: Microsoft Office 2013, 2010,* and *2007; Signature Series: Microsoft Word 2013, 2010,* and *2007; Using Computers in the Medical Office: Microsoft Word, Excel, and PowerPoint 2010, 2007,* and *2003;* and *Computer and Internet Essentials: Preparing for IC³* for Paradigm Publishing, Inc.

Ian Rutkosky teaches Business Technology courses at Pierce College in Puyallup, Washington. In addition to this title, he has coauthored *Computer and Internet Essentials: Preparing for IC³, Marquee Series: Microsoft Office 2013,* and *Using Computers in the Medical Office: Microsoft Word, Excel, and PowerPoint 2010.* He is also a co-author and consultant for Paradigm's SNAP training and assessment software.

Getting Started in Office 2013

In this textbook, you will learn to operate several computer programs that combine to make the Microsoft Office 2013 application suite. The programs you will learn are known as *software*, and they contain instructions that tell the computer what to do. Some of the application programs in the suite include Word, a word processing program; Excel, a spreadsheet program; Access, a database program; and PowerPoint, a presentation program.

Identifying Computer Hardware ■■■■■■■■■■■■■■■■

The computer equipment you will use to operate the Microsoft Office suite is referred to as *hardware*. You will need access to a computer system that includes a CPU, monitor, keyboard, printer, drives, and mouse. If you are not sure what equipment you will be operating, check with your instructor. The computer system shown in Figure G.1 consists of six components. Each component is discussed separately in the material that follows.

Figure G.1 Computer System

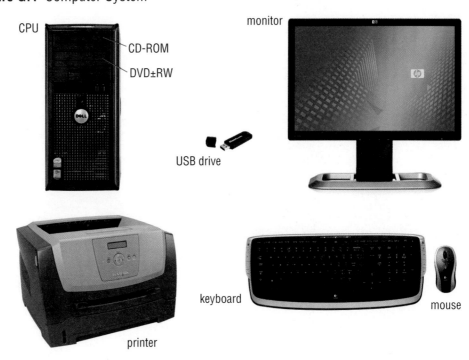

CPU
CD-ROM
DVD±RW
USB drive
monitor
printer
keyboard
mouse

CPU

The *central processing unit (CPU)* is the brain of the computer and is where all processing occurs. Silicon chips, which contain miniaturized circuitry, are placed on boards that are plugged into slots within the CPU. Whenever an instruction is given to the computer, it is processed through the circuitry in the CPU.

Monitor

A computer *monitor* looks like a television screen. It displays the information in a program and the text you input using the keyboard. The quality of display for monitors varies depending on the type of monitor and the level of resolution. Monitors can also vary in size—generally from 13 inches to 26 inches or larger.

Keyboard

The *keyboard* is used to input information into the computer. The number and location of the keys on a keyboard can vary. In addition to letters, numbers, and symbols, most computer keyboards contain function keys, arrow keys, and a numeric keypad. Figure G.2 shows an enhanced keyboard.

The 12 keys at the top of the keyboard, labeled with the letter F followed by a number, are called *function keys*. Use these keys to perform functions within each of the Office programs. To the right of the regular keys is a group of *special* or *dedicated keys*. These keys are labeled with specific functions that will be performed when you press the key. Below the special keys are arrow keys. Use these keys to move the insertion point in the document screen.

Some keyboards include mode indicator lights. When you select certain modes, a light appears on the keyboard. For example, if you press the Caps Lock key, which disables the lowercase alphabet, a light appears next to Caps Lock. Similarly, pressing the Num Lock key will disable the special functions on the numeric keypad, which is located at the right side of the keyboard.

Figure G.2 Keyboard

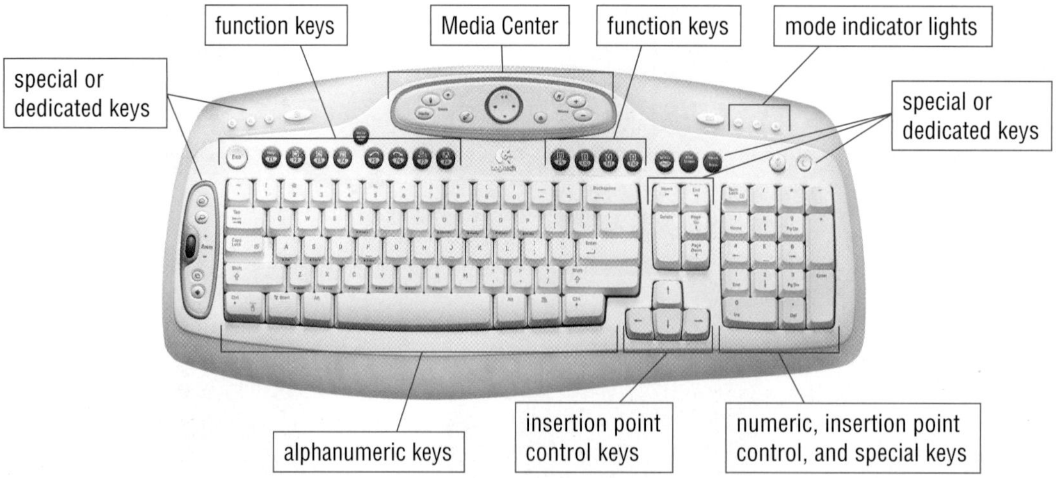

special or dedicated keys | function keys | Media Center | function keys | mode indicator lights | special or dedicated keys

alphanumeric keys | insertion point control keys | numeric, insertion point control, and special keys

Drives and Ports

Depending on the computer system you are using, Microsoft Office 2013 is installed on a hard drive or as part of a network system. Either way, you will need to have a CD or DVD drive to complete the projects and assessments in this book. If you plan to use a USB drive as your storage medium, you will also need a USB port. You will insert the CD that accompanies this textbook into the CD or DVD drive and then copy folders from the disc to your storage medium. You will also save documents you create to folders on your storage medium.

Printer

An electronic version of a file is known as a *soft copy*. If you want to create a *hard copy* of a file, you need to print it. To print documents you will need to access a printer, which will probably be either a laser printer or an ink-jet printer. A *laser printer* uses a laser beam combined with heat and pressure to print documents, while an *ink-jet printer* prints a document by spraying a fine mist of ink on the page.

Mouse or Touchpad

Most functions and commands in the Microsoft Office suite are designed to be performed using a mouse or a similar pointing device. A *mouse* is an input device that sits on a flat surface next to the computer. You can operate a mouse with your left or right hand. Moving the mouse on the flat surface causes a corresponding pointer to move on the screen, and clicking the left or right mouse buttons allows you to select various objects and commands. Figure G.1 contains an image of a mouse.

If you are working on a laptop computer, you may use a touchpad instead of a mouse. A *touchpad* allows you to move the mouse pointer by moving your finger across a surface at the base of the keyboard. You click by using your thumb to press the button located at the bottom of the touchpad.

Using the Mouse

The programs in the Microsoft Office suite can be operated with the keyboard and a mouse. The mouse generally has two buttons on top, which you press to execute specific functions and commands. A mouse may also contain a wheel, which can be used to scroll in a window or as a third button. To use the mouse, rest it on a flat surface or a mouse pad. Put your hand over it with your palm resting on top of the mouse, your wrist resting on the table surface, and your index finger resting on the left mouse button. As you move your hand, and thus the mouse, a corresponding pointer moves on the screen.

When using the mouse, you should understand four terms — point, click, double-click, and drag. When operating the mouse, you may need to point to a specific command, button, or icon. To *point* means to position the mouse pointer on the desired item. With the mouse pointer positioned on the desired item, you may need to click a button on the mouse to select the item. To *click* means to quickly tap a button on the mouse once. To complete two steps at one time, such as choosing and then executing a function, double-click the mouse button. To *double-click* means to tap the left mouse button twice in quick succession. The term *drag* means to press and hold the left mouse button, move the mouse pointer to a specific location, and then release the button.

Using the Mouse Pointer

The mouse pointer will look different depending on where you have positioned it and what function you are performing. The following are some of the ways the mouse pointer can appear when you are working in the Office suite:

- The mouse pointer appears as an I-beam (called the *I-beam pointer*) when you are inserting text in a file. The I-beam pointer can be used to move the insertion point or to select text.
- The mouse pointer appears as an arrow pointing up and to the left (called the *arrow pointer*) when it is moved to the Title bar, Quick Access toolbar, ribbon, or an option in a dialog box, among other locations.
- The mouse pointer becomes a double-headed arrow (either pointing left and right, pointing up and down, or pointing diagonally) when you perform certain functions such as changing the size of an object.
- In certain situations, such as when you move an object or image, the mouse pointer displays with a four-headed arrow attached. The four-headed arrow means that you can move the object left, right, up, or down.
- When a request is being processed or when a program is being loaded, the mouse pointer may appear as a moving circle. The moving circle means "please wait." When the process is completed, the circle is replaced with a normal arrow pointer.
- When the mouse pointer displays as a hand with a pointing index finger, it indicates that more information is available about an item. The mouse pointer also displays as a hand with a pointing index finger when you hover the mouse over a hyperlink.

Choosing Commands

Once a program is open, you can use several methods in the program to choose commands. A *command* is an instruction that tells the program to do something. You can choose a command using the mouse or the keyboard. When a program such as Word or PowerPoint is open, the ribbon contains buttons and options for completing tasks, as well as tabs you can click to display additional buttons and options. To choose a button on the Quick Access toolbar or on the ribbon, position the tip of the mouse arrow pointer on the button and then click the left mouse button.

The Office suite provides *accelerator keys* you can press to use a command in a program. Press the Alt key on the keyboard to display KeyTips that identify the accelerator key you can press to execute a command. For example, if you press the Alt key in a Word document with the HOME tab active, KeyTips display as shown in Figure G.3. Continue pressing accelerator keys until you execute the desired command. For example, to begin spell checking a document, press the Alt key, press the R key on the keyboard to display the REVIEW tab, and then press the letter S on the keyboard.

Figure G.3 Word HOME Tab KeyTips

Choosing Commands from Drop-Down Lists

To choose a command from a drop-down list with the mouse, position the mouse pointer on the desired option and then click the left mouse button. To make a selection from a drop-down list with the keyboard, type the underlined letter in the desired option.

Some options at a drop-down list may appear in gray (dimmed), indicating that the option is currently unavailable. If an option at a drop-down list displays preceded by a check mark, it means the option is currently active. If an option at a drop-down list displays followed by an ellipsis (...), clicking that option will display a dialog box.

Choosing Options from a Dialog Box

A **dialog box** contains options for applying formatting or otherwise modifying a file or data within a file. Some dialog boxes display with tabs along the top that provide additional options. For example, the Font dialog box shown in Figure G.4 contains two tabs — the Font tab and the Advanced tab. The tab that displays in the front is the active tab. To make a tab active using the mouse, position the arrow pointer on the desired tab and then click the left mouse button. If you are using the keyboard, press Ctrl + Tab or press Alt + the underlined letter on the desired tab.

Figure G.4 Word Font Dialog Box

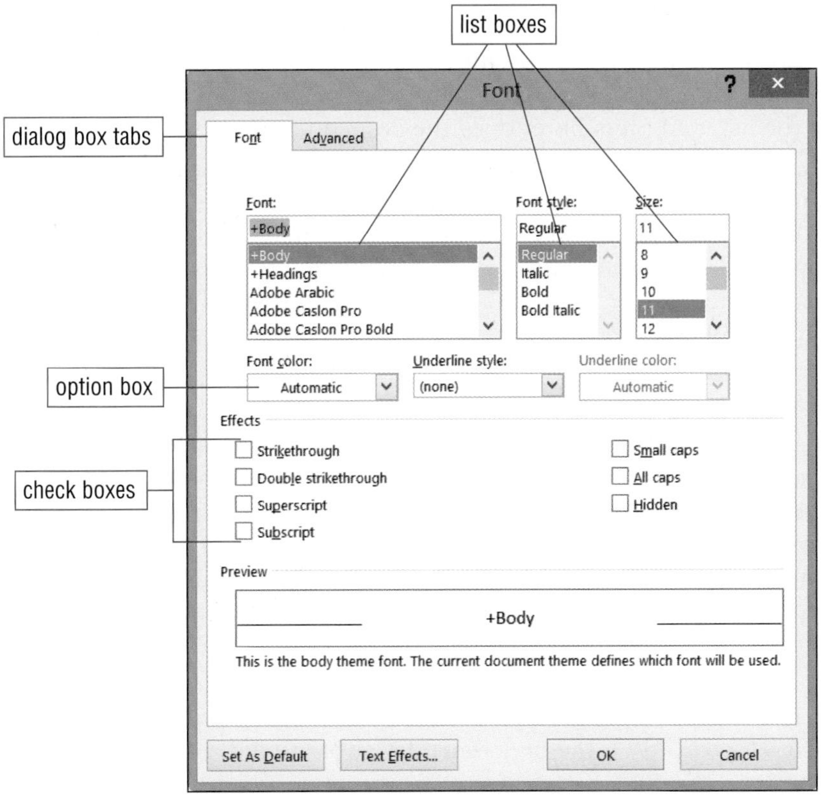

To choose options from a dialog box with the mouse, position the arrow pointer on the desired option and then click the left mouse button. If you are using the keyboard, press the Tab key to move the insertion point forward from option to option. Press Shift + Tab to move the insertion point backward from option to option. You can also hold down the Alt key and then press the underlined letter of the desired option. When an option is selected, it displays with a blue background or surrounded by a dashed box called a *marquee*. A dialog box contains one or more of the following elements: list boxes, option boxes, check boxes, text boxes, option buttons, measurement boxes, and command buttons.

List Boxes and Option Boxes

The fonts below the *Font* option in the Font dialog box in Figure G.4 are contained in a *list box*. To make a selection from a list box with the mouse, move the arrow pointer to the desired option and then click the left mouse button.

Some list boxes may contain a scroll bar. This scroll bar will display at the right side of the list box (a vertical scroll bar) or at the bottom of the list box (a horizontal scroll bar). Use a vertical scroll bar or a horizontal scroll bar to move through the list if the list is longer (or wider) than the box. To move down a list using a vertical scroll bar, position the arrow pointer on the down-pointing arrow and hold down the left mouse button. To scroll up through the list, position the arrow pointer on the up-pointing arrow and hold down the left mouse button. You can also move the arrow pointer above the scroll box and click the left mouse button to scroll up the list or move the arrow pointer below the scroll box and click the left mouse button to move down the list. To navigate a list with a horizontal scroll bar, click the left-pointing arrow to scroll to the left of the list or click the right-pointing arrow to scroll to the right of the list.

To use the keyboard to make a selection from a list box, move the insertion point into the box by holding down the Alt key and pressing the underlined letter of the desired option. Press the Up and/or Down Arrow keys on the keyboard to move through the list, and press Enter once the desired option is selected.

In some dialog boxes where there is not enough room for a list box, lists of options are contained in a drop-down list box called an *option box*. Option boxes display with a down-pointing arrow. For example, in Figure G.4, the font color options are contained in an option box. To display the different color options, click the down-pointing arrow at the right of the *Font color* option box. If you are using the keyboard, press Alt + C.

Check Boxes

Some dialog boxes contain options preceded by a box. A check mark may or may not appear in the box. The Word Font dialog box shown in Figure G.4 displays a variety of check boxes within the *Effects* section. If a check mark appears in the box, the option is active (turned on). If the check box does not contain a check mark, the option is inactive (turned off). Any number of check boxes can be active. For example, in the Word Font dialog box, you can insert a check mark in several of the boxes in the *Effects* section to activate the options.

To make a check box active or inactive with the mouse, position the tip of the arrow pointer in the check box and then click the left mouse button. If you are using the keyboard, press Alt + the underlined letter of the desired option.

Text Boxes

Some options in a dialog box require you to enter text. For example, the boxes below the *Find what* and *Replace with* options at the Excel Find and Replace dialog box shown in Figure G.5 are text boxes. In a text box, you type text or edit existing text. Edit text in a text box in the same manner as normal text. Use the Left and Right Arrow keys on the keyboard to move the insertion point without deleting text and use the Delete key or Backspace key to delete text.

Option Buttons

The Word Insert Table dialog box shown in Figure G.6 contains options in the *AutoFit behavior* section preceded by **option button**s. Only one option button can be selected at any time. When an option button is selected, a blue or black circle displays in the button. To select an option button with the mouse, position the tip of the arrow pointer inside the option button or on the option and then click the left mouse button. To make a selection with the keyboard, hold down the Alt key and then press the underlined letter of the desired option.

Measurement Boxes

Some options in a dialog box contain measurements or amounts you can increase or decrease. These options are generally located in a **measurement box**. For example, the Word Insert Table dialog box shown in Figure G.6 contains the *Number of columns* and *Number of rows* measurement boxes. To increase a number in a measurement box, position the tip of the arrow pointer on the up-pointing arrow at the right of the desired option and then click the left mouse button. To decrease the number, click the down-pointing arrow. If you are using the keyboard, press and hold down Alt + the underlined letter of the desired option and then press the Up Arrow key to increase the number or the Down Arrow key to decrease the number.

Command Buttons

The buttons at the bottom of the Excel Find and Replace dialog box shown in Figure G.5 are called **command buttons**. Use a command button to execute or cancel a command. Some command buttons display with an ellipsis (...), which means another dialog box will open if you click that button. To choose a command button with the mouse, position the arrow pointer on the desired button and then click the left mouse button. To choose a command button with the keyboard, press the Tab key until the desired command button is surrounded by a marquee and then press the Enter key.

Figure G.5 Excel Find and Replace Dialog Box

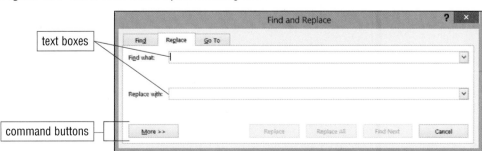

Choosing Commands with Keyboard Shortcuts

Applications in the Office suite offer a variety of keyboard shortcuts you can use to execute specific commands. Keyboard shortcuts generally require two or more keys. For example, the keyboard shortcut to display the Open dialog box in an application is Ctrl + F12. To use this keyboard shortcut, hold down the Ctrl key, press the F12 function on the keyboard, and then release the Ctrl key. For a list of keyboard shortcuts, refer to the Help files.

Choosing Commands with Shortcut Menus

The software programs in the Office suite include shortcut menus that contain commands related to different items. To display a shortcut menu, position the mouse pointer over the item for which you want to view more options, and then click the right mouse button or press Shift + F10. The shortcut menu will appear wherever the insertion point is positioned. For example, if the insertion point is positioned in a paragraph of text in a Word document, clicking the right mouse button or pressing Shift + F10 will cause the shortcut menu shown in Figure G.7 to display in the document screen (along with the Mini toolbar).

To select an option from a shortcut menu with the mouse, click the desired option. If you are using the keyboard, press the Up or Down Arrow key until the desired option is selected and then press the Enter key. To close a shortcut menu without choosing an option, click anywhere outside the shortcut menu or press the Esc key.

Figure G.6 Word Insert Table Dialog Box

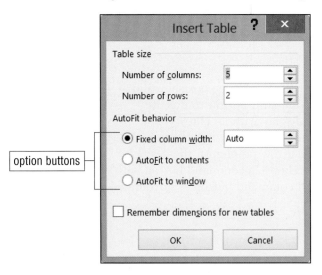

Figure G.7 Word Shortcut Menu

Working with Multiple Programs ▪▪▪▪▪▪▪▪▪▪▪▪▪▪▪▪▪▪

As you learn the various programs in the Microsoft Office suite, you will notice many similarities between them. For example, the steps to save, close, and print are virtually the same whether you are working in Word, Excel, or PowerPoint. This consistency between programs greatly enhances a user's ability to transfer knowledge learned in one program to another within the suite. Another benefit to using Microsoft Office is the ability to have more than one program open at the same time and to integrate content from one program with another. For example, you can open Word and create a document, open Excel and create a spreadsheet, and then copy the Excel spreadsheet into Word.

When you open a program, a button containing an icon representing the program displays on the Taskbar. If you open another program, a button containing an icon representing that program displays to the right of the first program button on the Taskbar. Figure G.8 on the next page, shows the Taskbar with Word, Excel, Access, and PowerPoint open. To move from one program to another, click the Taskbar button representing the desired program.

Figure G.8 Taskbar with Word, Excel, Access, and PowerPoint Open

Customizing Settings ▪▪▪▪▪▪▪▪▪▪▪▪▪▪▪▪▪▪▪▪▪▪▪▪▪▪

Before beginning computer projects in this textbook, you may need to customize your monitor's settings and turn on the display of file extensions. Projects in the chapters in this textbook assume that the monitor display is set at 1600 x 900 pixels and that the display of file extensions is turned on.

Before you begin learning the applications in the Microsoft Office 2013 suite, take a moment to check the display settings on the computer you are using. Your monitor's display settings are important because the ribbon in the Microsoft Office suite adjusts to the screen resolution setting of your computer monitor. A computer monitor set at a high resolution will have the ability to show more buttons in the ribbon than will a monitor set to a low resolution. The illustrations in this textbook were created with a screen resolution display set at 1600 × 900 pixels. In Figure G.9 on the next page, the Word ribbon is shown three ways: at a lower screen resolution (1366 × 768 pixels), at the screen resolution featured throughout this textbook, and at a higher screen resolution (1920 × 1080 pixels). Note the variances in the ribbon in all three examples. If possible, set your display to 1600 × 900 pixels to match the illustrations you will see in this textbook.

Figure G.9 Monitor Resolution

1366 × 768 screen resolution

1600 × 900 screen resolution

1920 × 1080 screen resolution

Project 1 Setting Monitor Display to 1600 by 900

1. At the Windows 8 desktop, right-click a blank area of the screen.
2. At the shortcut menu, click the *Screen resolution* option.
3. At the Screen Resolution window, click the *Resolution* option box. (This displays a slider bar. Your slider bar may display differently than what you see in the image at the right.)
4. Drag the button on the slider bar until *1600 × 900* displays to the right of the slider bar.
5. Click in the Screen Resolution window to remove the slider bar.
6. Click the Apply button.
7. Click the Keep Changes button.
8. Click the OK button.

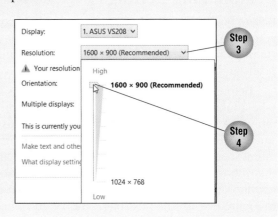

Project 2   Displaying File Extensions

1. At the Windows 8 desktop, position the mouse pointer in the lower left corner of the Taskbar until the Start screen thumbnail displays and then click the right mouse button.
2. At the pop-up list, click the *File Explorer* option.
3. At the Computer window, click the View tab on the ribbon and then click the *File name extensions* check box in the Show/hide group to insert a check mark.
4. Close the Computer window.

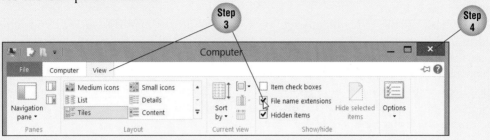

Completing Computer Projects ▪▪▪▪▪▪▪▪▪▪▪▪▪▪▪▪▪▪▪▪

Some projects in this textbook require that you open an existing file. Project files are saved on the Student Resources CD in individual chapter folders. Before beginning a chapter, copy the necessary folder from the CD to your storage medium (such as a USB flash drive or your SkyDrive) using the Computer window. To maximize storage capacity, delete previous chapter folders before copying a new chapter folder onto your storage medium.

Project 3   Copying a Folder from the Student Resources CD to a USB Flash Drive

1. Insert the CD that accompanies this textbook into your computer's CD/DVD drive.
2. Insert your USB flash drive into an available USB port.
3. At the Windows 8 Start screen, click the Desktop tile.
4. Open File Explorer by clicking the File Explorer button on the Taskbar.
5. Click *Computer* in the Navigation pane at the left side of the File Explorer window.
6. Double-click the CD/DVD drive that displays with the name *BM13StudentResources* preceded by the drive letter.
7. Double-click **StudentDataFiles** in the Content pane.
8. Double-click the desired program folder name (and level number, if appropriate) in the Content pane.
9. Click once on the desired chapter (or unit performance assessment) folder name to select it.
10. Click the Home tab and then click the Copy button in the Clipboard group.
11. Click your USB flash drive that displays in the Navigation pane at the left side of the window.
12. Click the Home tab and then click the Paste button in the Clipboard group.
13. Close the File Explorer window by clicking the Close button located in the upper right corner of the window.

Project 4 Copying a Folder from the Student Resources CD to your SkyDrive Account

Note: SkyDrive is updated periodically, so the steps to create folders and upload files may vary from the steps below.
1. Insert the CD that accompanies this textbook into your computer's CD/DVD drive.
2. At the Windows 8 Start screen, click the Desktop tile.
3. Open Internet Explorer by clicking the Internet Explorer button on the Taskbar.
4. At the Internet Explorer home page, click in the Address bar, type **www.skydrive.com**, and then press Enter.
5. At the Microsoft SkyDrive login page, type your Windows Live ID (such as your email address).
6. Press the Tab key, type your password, and then press Enter.
7. Click the Documents tile in your SkyDrive.
8. Click the Create option on the SkyDrive menu bar and then click *Folder* at the drop-down list.
9. Type the name of the folder that you want to copy from the Student Resources CD and then press the Enter key.
10. Click the folder tile you created in the previous step.
11. Click the Upload option on the menu bar.
12. Click the CD/DVD drive that displays in the Navigation pane at the left side of the Choose File to Upload dialog box.
13. Open the chapter folder on the CD that contains the required student data files.
14. Select all of the files in the folder by pressing Ctrl + A and then click the Open button.

Project 5 Deleting a Folder

Note: Check with your instructor before deleting a folder.
1. Insert your storage medium (such as a USB flash drive) into your computer's USB port.
2. At the Windows desktop, open File Explorer by right-clicking the Start screen thumbnail and then clicking *File Explorer* at the shortcut menu.
3. Double-click the drive letter for your storage medium (the drive containing your USB flash drive, such as *Removable Disk (F:)*).
4. Click the chapter folder in the Content pane.
5. Click the Home tab and then click the Delete button in the Organize group.
6. At the message asking if you want to delete the folder, click the Yes button.
7. Close the Computer window by clicking the Close button located in the upper right corner of the window.

Using Windows 8

A computer requires an operating system to provide necessary instructions on a multitude of processes including loading programs, managing data, directing the flow of information to peripheral equipment, and displaying information. Windows 8 is an operating system that provides functions of this type (along with much more) in a graphical environment. Windows is referred to as a *graphical user interface* (GUI—pronounced *gooey*) that provides a visual display of information with features such as icons (pictures) and buttons. In this introduction, you will learn these basic features of Windows 8:

- Use the Start screen to launch programs
- Use desktop icons and the Taskbar to launch programs and open files or folders
- Organize and manage data, including copying, moving, creating, and deleting files and folders; and create a shortcut
- Explore the Control Panel and personalize the desktop
- Use the Windows Help and Support features
- Use search tools
- Customize monitor settings

Before using the software programs in the Microsoft Office suite, you will need to start the Windows 8 operating system. To do this, turn on the computer. Depending on your computer equipment configuration, you may also need to turn on the monitor and printer. If you are using a computer that is part of a network system or if your computer is set up for multiple users, a screen will display showing the user accounts defined for your computer system. At this screen, click your user account name; if necessary, type your password; and then press the Enter key. The Windows 8 operating system will start and, after a few moments, the Windows 8 Start screen will display as shown in Figure W.1. (Your Windows 8 Start screen may vary from what you see in Figure W.1.)

Exploring the Start Screen and Desktop ■■■■■■■■■■■■

When Windows is loaded, the Windows 8 Start screen displays. This screen contains tiles that open various applications. Open an application by clicking an application's tile or display the Windows 8 desktop by clicking the Desktop tile. Click the Desktop tile and the screen displays as shown in Figure W.2. Think of the desktop in Windows as the top of a desk in an office. A businessperson places necessary tools—such as pencils, pens, paper, files, calculator—on the desktop to perform functions. Like the tools that are located on a desk, the Windows 8 desktop contains tools for operating the computer. These tools are logically grouped and placed in dialog boxes or panels that you can display using icons on the desktop. The desktop contains a variety of features for using your computer and applications installed on the computer.

Figure W.1 Windows 8 Start Screen

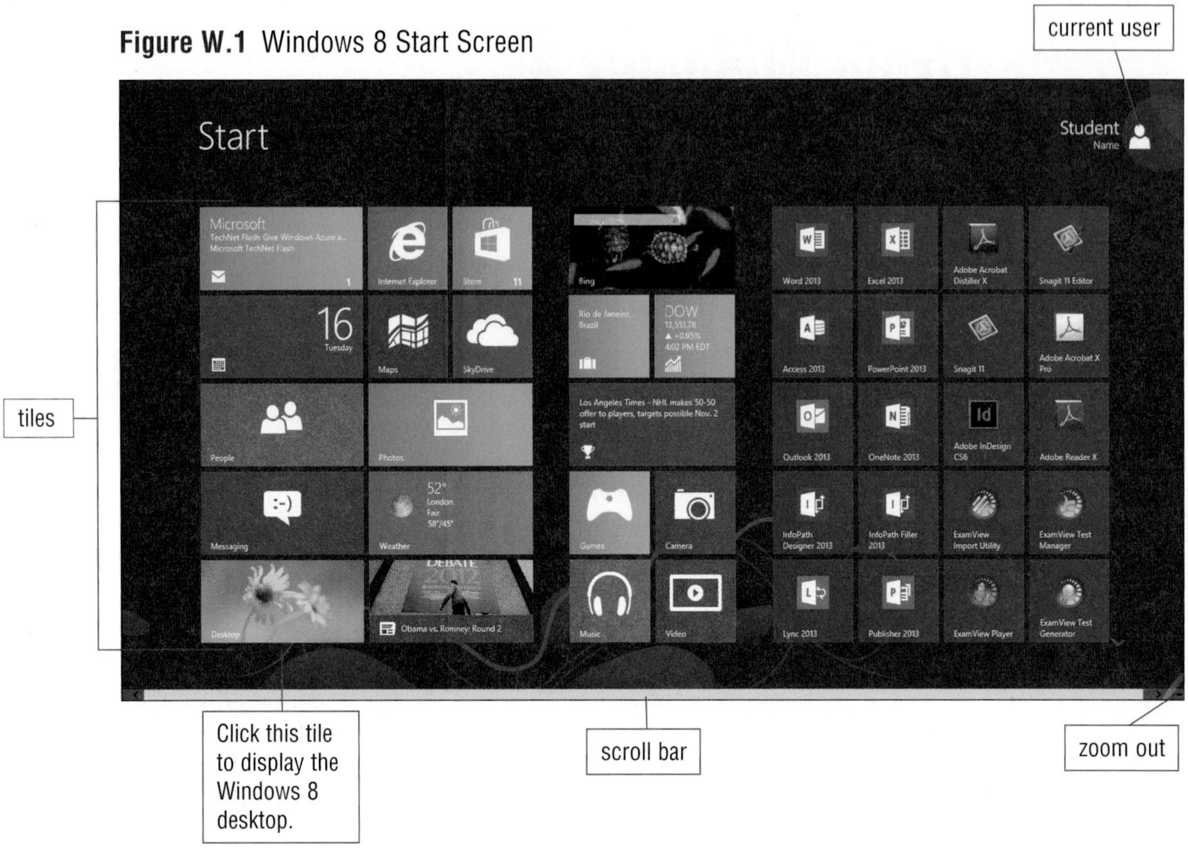

current user

Start

Student
Name

tiles

Click this tile
to display the
Windows 8
desktop.

scroll bar

zoom out

Figure W.2 Windows 8 Desktop

Recycle Bin icon

Position the mouse pointer here
to access the Start screen.

Taskbar

Using Icons

Icons are visual symbols that represent programs, files, or folders. Figure W.2 identifies the Recycle Bin icon on the Windows desktop. The Windows desktop on your computer may contain additional icons. Applications that have been installed on your computer may be represented by an icon on the desktop. Icons that represent files or folders may also display on your desktop. Double-click an icon and the application, file, or folder it represents opens on the desktop.

Using the Taskbar

The bar that displays at the bottom of the desktop (see Figure W.2) is called the *Taskbar*. The Taskbar, shown in Figure W.3, contains the Start screen area (a spot where you point to access the Start screen), pinned items, a section that displays task buttons representing active tasks, the notification area, and the Show desktop button.

Position the mouse pointer in the lower left corner of the Taskbar to display the Start screen thumbnail. When the Start screen thumbnail displays, click the left mouse button to access the Windows 8 Start screen, shown in Figure W.1. (Your Start screen may look different.) You can also display the Start screen by pressing the Windows key on your keyboard or by pressing Ctrl + Esc. The left side of the Start menu contains tiles you can click to access the most frequently used applications. The name of the active user (the person who is currently logged on) displays in the upper right corner of the Start screen.

To open an application from the Start screen, drag the arrow pointer to the desired tile (referred to as *pointing*) and then click the left mouse button. When a program is open, a task button representing the program appears on the Taskbar. If multiple programs are open, each program will appear as a task button on the Taskbar (a few specialized tools may not).

Figure W.3 Windows 8 Taskbar

Manipulating Windows ■■■■■■■■■■■■ ■■■■■■■■■■■■■■

When you open a program, a defined work area known as a *window* displays on the screen. A Title bar displays at the top of the window and contains buttons at the right side for minimizing, maximizing, and restoring the size of the window, as well as for closing it. You can open more than one window at a time and the open windows can be cascaded or stacked. Windows 8 contains a Snap feature that causes a window to "stick" to the edge of the screen when the window is moved to the left or right side of the screen. Move a window to the top of the screen and the window is automatically maximized. If you drag down a maximized window, the window is automatically restored down (returned to its previous smaller size).

In addition to moving and sizing a window, you can change the display of all open windows. To do this, position the mouse pointer on the Taskbar and then click the right mouse button. At the pop-up menu that displays, you can choose to cascade all open windows, stack all open windows, or display all open windows side by side.

Project 1 — Opening Programs, Switching between Programs, and Manipulating Windows

1. Open Windows 8. (To do this, turn on the computer and, if necessary, turn on the monitor and/or printer. If you are using a computer that is part of a network system or if your computer is set up for multiple users, you may need to click your user account name, type your password, and then press the Enter key. Check with your instructor to determine if you need to complete any additional steps.)

2. When the Windows 8 Start screen displays, open Microsoft Word by positioning the mouse pointer on the *Word 2013* tile and then clicking the left mouse button. (You may need to scroll to the right to display the Word 2013 tile.)

3. When the Microsoft Word program is open, notice that a task button representing Word displays on the Taskbar.

4. Open Microsoft Excel by completing the following steps:
   a. Position the arrow pointer in the lower left corner of the Taskbar until the Start screen thumbnail displays and then click the left mouse button.
   b. At the Start screen, position the mouse pointer on the *Excel 2013* tile and then click the left mouse button.

5. When the Microsoft Excel program is open, notice that a task button representing Excel displays on the Taskbar to the right of the task button representing Word.

6. Switch to the Word program by clicking the Word task button on the Taskbar.

7. Switch to the Excel program by clicking the Excel task button on the Taskbar.

8. Restore down the Excel window by clicking the Restore Down button that displays immediately left of the Close button in the upper right corner of the screen. (This reduces the Excel window so it displays along the bottom half of the screen.)

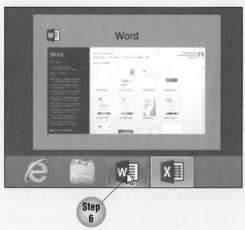

9. Restore down the Word window by clicking the Restore Down button located immediately left of the Close button in the upper right corner of the screen.

10. Position the mouse pointer at the top of the Word window screen, hold down the left mouse button, drag to the left side of the screen until an outline of the window displays in the left half of the screen, and then release the mouse button. (This "sticks" the window to the left side of the screen.)

11. Position the mouse pointer at the top of the Excel window screen, hold down the left mouse button, drag to the right until an outline of the window displays in the right half of the screen, and then release the mouse button.

12. Minimize the Excel window by clicking the Minimize button that displays in the upper right corner of the Excel window screen.

13. Hover your mouse over the Excel button on the Taskbar and then click the Excel window thumbnail that displays. (This displays the Excel window at the right side of the screen.)

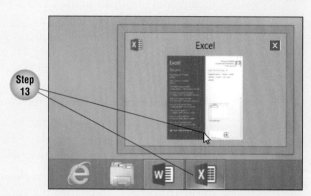

14. Cascade the Word and Excel windows by positioning the arrow pointer in an empty area of the Taskbar, clicking the right mouse button, and then clicking *Cascade windows* at the shortcut menu.

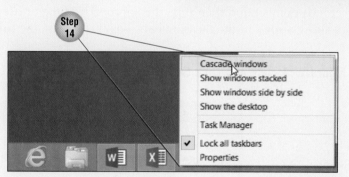

15. After viewing the windows cascaded, display them stacked by right-clicking an empty area of the Taskbar and then clicking *Show windows stacked* at the shortcut menu.

16. Display the desktop by right-clicking an empty area of the Taskbar and then clicking *Show the desktop* at the shortcut menu.

17. Display the windows stacked by right-clicking an empty area of the Taskbar and then clicking *Show open windows* at the shortcut menu.

18. Position the mouse pointer at the top of the Word window screen, hold down the left mouse button, drag the window to the top of the screen, and then release the mouse button. This maximizes the Word window so it fills the screen.

19. Close the Word window by clicking the Close button located in the upper right corner of the window.

20. At the Excel window, click the Maximize button located immediately left of the Close button in the upper right corner of the Excel window.

21. Close the Excel window by clicking the Close button located in the upper right corner of the window.

Using the Pinned Area

The icons that display immediately right of the Start screen area represent *pinned applications*. Clicking an icon opens the application associated with the icon. Click the first icon to open the Internet Explorer web browser and click the second icon to open a File Explorer window containing Libraries.

Exploring the Notification Area

The notification area is located at the right side of the Taskbar and contains icons that show the status of certain system functions such as a network connection or battery power. The notification area contains icons for managing certain programs and Windows 8 features, as well as the system clock and date. Click the time or date in the notification area and a window displays with a clock and a calendar of the current month. Click the Change date and time settings hyperlink that displays at the bottom of the window and the Date and Time dialog box displays. To change the date and/or time, click the Change date and time button and the Date and Time Settings dialog box displays, similar to the dialog box shown in Figure W.4. (If a dialog box displays telling you that Windows needs your permission to continue, click the Continue button.)

Change the month and year by clicking the left-pointing or right-pointing arrow at the top of the calendar. Click the left-pointing arrow to display the previous month(s) and click the right-pointing arrow to display the next month(s).

To change the day, click the desired day in the monthly calendar that displays in the dialog box. To change the time, double-click either the hour, minute, or seconds number and then type the appropriate time or use the up- and down-pointing arrows in the measurement boxes to adjust the time.

Figure W.4 Date and Time Settings Dialog Box

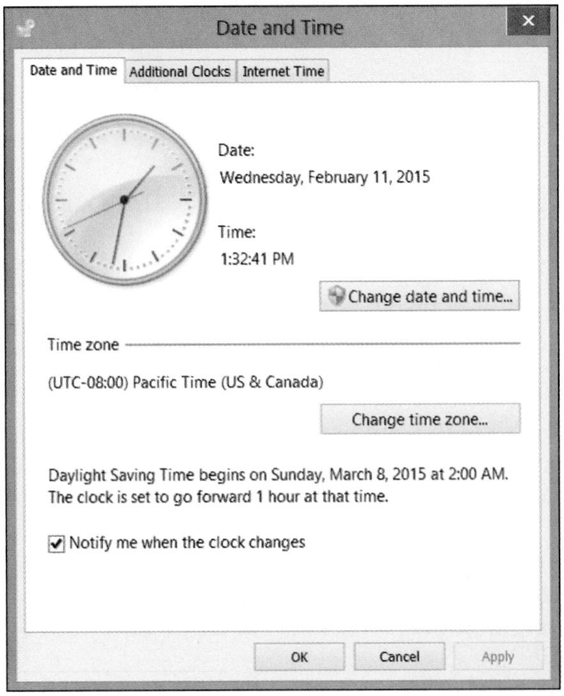

Some applications, when installed, will add an icon to the notification area of the Taskbar. To determine the name of an icon, position the mouse pointer on the icon and, after approximately one second, its label will display. If more icons have been inserted in the notification area than can be viewed at one time, an up-pointing arrow button displays at the left side of the notification area. Click this up-pointing arrow to display the remaining icons.

Setting Taskbar Properties

Customize the Taskbar with options at the Taskbar shortcut menu. Display this menu by right-clicking in an empty portion of the Taskbar. The Taskbar shortcut menu contains options for turning on or off the display of specific toolbars, specifying the display of multiple windows, displaying the Start Task Manager dialog box, locking or unlocking the Taskbar, and displaying the Taskbar Properties dialog box.

With options in the Taskbar Properties dialog box, shown in Figure W.5, you can change settings for the Taskbar. Display this dialog box by right-clicking an empty area on the Taskbar and then clicking *Properties* at the shortcut menu.

Each Taskbar property is controlled by a check box or an option box. If a property's check box contains a check mark, that property is active. Click the check box to remove the check mark and make the option inactive. If an option is inactive, clicking the check box will insert a check mark and turn on the option (make it active). A property option box displays the name of the currently active option. Click the option box to select a different option from the drop-down list.

Figure W.5 Taskbar Properties Dialog Box

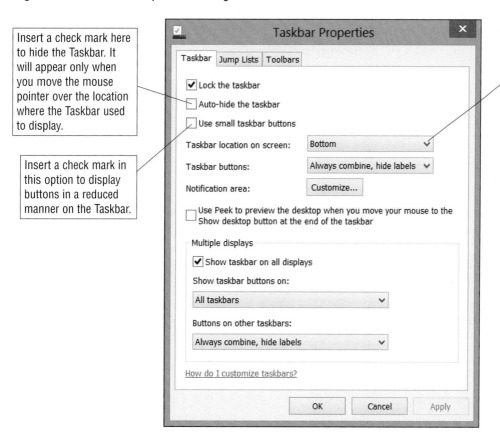

Insert a check mark here to hide the Taskbar. It will appear only when you move the mouse pointer over the location where the Taskbar used to display.

Insert a check mark in this option to display buttons in a reduced manner on the Taskbar.

Use this option box to change the location of the Taskbar from the bottom of the desktop to the left side, right side, or top of the desktop.

1. Make sure the Windows 8 desktop displays.
2. Change the Taskbar properties by completing the following steps:
    a. Position the arrow pointer in an empty area of the Taskbar and then click the right mouse button.
    b. At the shortcut menu that displays, click *Properties*.
    c. At the Taskbar Properties dialog box, click the *Auto-hide the taskbar* check box to insert a check mark.
    d. Click the *Use small taskbar buttons* check box to insert a check mark.
    e. Click the option box (contains the word *Bottom*) that displays at the right side of the *Taskbar location on screen:* option and then click *Right* at the drop-down list.
    f. Click OK to close the dialog box.

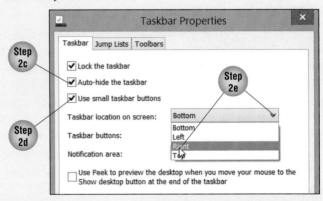

3. Since the *Auto-hide the taskbar* check box contains a check mark, the Taskbar does not display. Display the Taskbar by moving the mouse pointer to the right side of the screen. Notice that the buttons on the Taskbar are smaller than they were before.
4. Return to the default Taskbar properties by completing the following steps:
    a. Move the mouse pointer to the right side of the screen to display the Taskbar.
    b. Right-click an empty area of the Taskbar and then click *Properties* at the shortcut menu.
    c. Click the *Auto-hide the taskbar* check box to remove the check mark.
    d. Click the *Use small taskbar buttons* check box to remove the check mark.
    e. Click the *Taskbar location on screen* option box (displays with the word *Right*) and then click *Bottom* at the drop-down list.
    f. Click OK to close the dialog box.

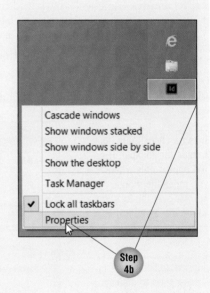

Using the Charm Bar ▪▪▪▪▪▪▪▪▪▪▪▪▪▪▪▪▪▪▪▪▪▪▪▪▪▪▪▪▪

Windows 8 contains a new feature called the ***Charm bar***. The Charm bar is a bar that displays when you position the mouse pointer in the upper or lower right corner of the screen. Use the buttons on the Charm bar, shown in Figure W.6, to access certain features or tools. Use the Search button to search the computer for applications, files, folders and settings. With the Share button, you can share information with others via email or social networks. Clicking the Start button displays the Windows 8 Start screen. Access settings for various devices such as printers, monitors, and so on with the Devices button. The Settings button gives you access to common computer settings and is also used to power down the computer.

Figure W.6 Charm Bar

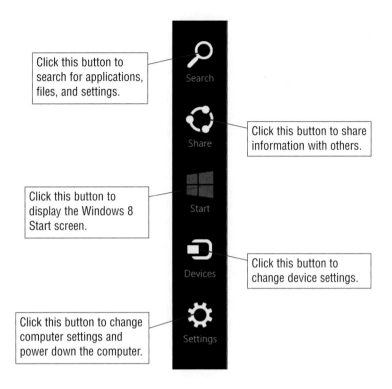

Click this button to search for applications, files, and settings.

Click this button to share information with others.

Click this button to display the Windows 8 Start screen.

Click this button to change device settings.

Click this button to change computer settings and power down the computer.

Powering Down the Computer ▪▪▪▪▪▪▪▪▪▪▪▪▪▪▪▪▪▪▪▪▪▪▪

If you want to shut down Windows, first close any open programs and then display the Charm bar. Click the Settings button on the Charm bar, click the Power tile, and then click the *Shut down* option. The Power tile also contains options for restarting the computer or putting the computer to sleep. Restarting the computer may be useful when installing new applications or if Windows 8 stops working properly. In sleep mode, Windows saves files and information about applications and then powers down the computer to a low-power state. To "wake up" the computer, press the computer's power button.

In a multi-user environment, you can sign out of or lock your account so that no one can tamper with your work. To access these features, display the Windows 8 Start screen and then click your user account tile in the upper right corner. This displays a shortcut menu with three options. The *Lock* option locks the computer, which means that it is still powered on but requires a user password in order to access any applications or files that were previously opened. (To unlock the computer, click the icon on the login screen representing your account, type your password, and then press Enter.) Use the *Sign out* option to sign out of your user account while still keeping the computer turned on so that others may log on to it. Click the *Change account picture* option if you want to change the picture associated with your user account.

Managing Files and Folders ■■■■■■■■■■■■■■■■■■■■■■■■■■■■

As you begin working with programs in Windows 8, you will create files in which data (information) is saved. A file might be a Word document, an Excel workbook, an Access database, or a PowerPoint presentation. As you begin creating files, consider creating folders in which to store these files. Complete file management tasks such as creating a folder or moving a file at the Computer window. To display the Computer window, shown in Figure W.7, position your mouse pointer in the lower left corner of the screen to display the Start screen thumbnail, click the right mouse button, and then click *File Explorer* at the shortcut menu. The various components of the Computer window are identified in Figure W.7.

In the Content pane of the Computer window, icons display representing each hard disk drive and removable storage medium (such as a CD, DVD, or USB device) connected to your computer. Next to each storage device icon, Windows displays the amount of storage space available as well as a bar with the amount of used space shaded with color. This visual cue allows you to see at a glance the amount of space available relative to the capacity of the device. Double-click a device icon in the Content pane to change the display to show the contents stored on the device. Display contents from another device or folder using the Navigation pane or the Address bar on the Computer window.

Figure W.7 Computer Window

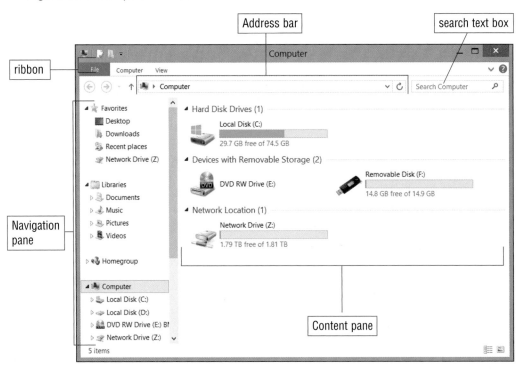

Copying, Moving, and Deleting Files and Folders

File and folder management activities include copying and moving files and folders from one folder or drive to another, as well as deleting files and folders. The Computer window offers a variety of methods for performing these actions. This section will provide you with steps for copying, moving, and deleting files and folders using options from the Home tab (shown in Figure W.8) and the shortcut menu (shown in Figure W.9).

To copy a file to another folder or drive, first display the file in the Content pane. If the file is located in the Documents folder, click the *Documents* folder in the *Libraries* section of the Navigation pane and then, in the Content pane, click the name of the file you want to copy. Click the Home tab on the ribbon and then click the Copy button in the Clipboard group. Use the Navigation pane to navigate to the location where you want to paste the file. Click the Home tab and then click the Paste button in the Clipboard group. Complete similar steps to copy and paste a folder to another location.

If the desired file is located on a storage medium such as a CD, DVD, or USB device, double-click the device in the section of the Content pane labeled *Devices with Removable Storage*. (Each removable device is assigned an alphabetic drive letter by Windows, usually starting at E or F and continuing through the alphabet depending on the number of removable devices that are currently in use.) After double-clicking the storage medium in the Content pane, navigate to the desired folder and then click the file to select it. Click the Home tab on the ribbon and then click the Copy button in the Clipboard group. Navigate to the desired folder, click the Home tab, and then click the Paste button in the Clipboard group.

To move a file, click the desired file in the Content pane, click the Home tab on the ribbon, and then click the Cut button in the Clipboard group. Navigate to the desired location, click the Home tab, and then click the Paste button in the Clipboard group.

To delete a file or folder, click the file or folder in the Content pane in the Computer window. Click the Home tab and then click the Delete button in the Organize group. At the message asking if you want to move the file or folder to the Recycle Bin, click the Yes button.

Figure W.8 File Explorer Home tab

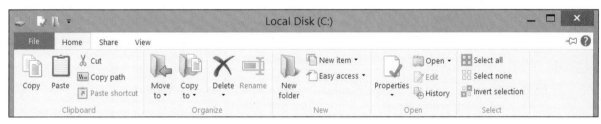

Figure W.9 Shortcut Menu

Project 3   Copying a File and Folder and Deleting a File

1. Insert the CD that accompanies this textbook into the appropriate drive.
2. Insert your storage medium (such as a USB flash drive) into the appropriate drive.
3. At the Windows 8 desktop, position the mouse pointer in the lower left corner of the Taskbar to display the Start screen thumbnail, click the right mouse button, and then click *File Explorer* at the shortcut menu.
4. Copy a file from the CD that accompanies this textbook to the drive containing your storage medium by completing the following steps:
   a. In the Content pane, double-click the drive into which you inserted the CD that accompanies this textbook.
   b. Double-click the *StudentDataFiles* folder in the Content pane.
   c. Double-click the *Windows8* folder in the Content pane.
   d. Click ***WordDocument01.docx*** in the Content pane.
   e. Click the Home tab and then click *Copy* in the Clipboard group.

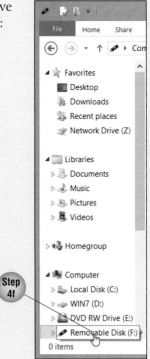

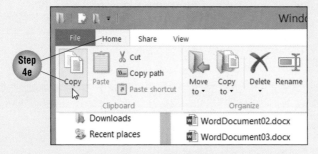

   f. In the Computer section in the Navigation pane, click the drive containing your storage medium. (You may need to scroll down the Navigation pane.)
   g. Click the Home tab and then click the Paste button in the Clipboard group.
5. Delete ***WordDocument01.docx*** from your storage medium by completing the following steps:
   a. Make sure the contents of your storage medium display in the Content pane in the Computer window.

b. Click *WordDocument01.docx* in the Content pane to select it.

c. Click the Home tab and then click the Delete button in the Organize group.

d. At the message asking if you want to permanently delete the file, click the Yes button.

6. Copy the Windows8 folder from the CD to your storage medium by completing the following steps:

a. With the Computer window open, click the drive in the *Computer* section in the Navigation pane that contains the CD that accompanies this book.

b. Double-click *StudentDataFiles* in the Content pane.

c. Click the *Windows8* folder in the Content pane.

d. Click the Home tab and then click the Copy button in the Clipboard group.

e. In the *Computer* section in the Navigation pane, click the drive containing your storage medium.

f. Click the Home tab and then click the Paste button in the Clipboard group.

7. Close the Computer window by clicking the Close button located in the upper right corner of the window.

In addition to options on the Home tab, you can use options in a shortcut menu to copy, move, and delete files or folders. To use a shortcut menu, select the desired file(s) or folder(s), position the mouse pointer on the selected item, and then click the right mouse button. At the shortcut menu that displays, click the desired option, such as *Copy*, *Cut*, or *Delete*.

Selecting Files and Folders

You can move, copy, or delete more than one file or folder at the same time. Before moving, copying, or deleting files or folders, select the desired files or folders. To make selecting easier, consider displaying the files in the Content pane in a list or detailed list format. To change the display, click the View tab on the ribbon and then click *List* or *Details* in the Layout group.

To select adjacent files or folders, click the first file or folder, hold down the Shift key, and then click the last file or folder. To select nonadjacent files or folders, click the first file or folder, hold down the Ctrl key, and then click the other files or folders you wish to select.

Project 4 **Copying and Deleting Files**

1. At the Windows 8 desktop, position the mouse pointer in the lower left corner of the Taskbar to display the Start screen thumbnail, click the right mouse button, and then click *File Explorer* at the shortcut menu.

2. Copy files from the CD that accompanies this textbook to the drive containing your storage medium by completing the following steps:

a. Make sure the CD that accompanies this textbook and your storage medium are inserted in the appropriate drives.

b. Double-click the CD drive in the Content pane in the Computer window.

c. Double-click the *StudentDataFiles* folder in the Content pane.

d. Double-click the *Windows8* folder in the Content pane.

e. Change the display to List by clicking the View tab and then clicking *List* in the Layout group list box.

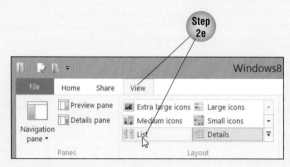

Step 2e

f. Click **WordDocument01.docx** in the Content pane.

g. Hold down the Shift key, click **WordDocument05.docx**, and then release the Shift key. (This selects five documents.)

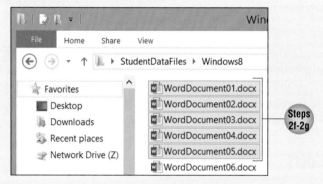

Steps 2f-2g

h. Click the Home tab and then click the Copy button in the Clipboard group.

i. In the *Computer* section of the Navigation pane, click the drive containing your storage medium.

j. Click the Home tab and then click the Paste button in the Clipboard group.

3. Delete the files you just copied to your storage medium by completing the following steps:

a. Change the display by clicking the View tab and then clicking *List* in the Layout group.

b. Click **WordDocument01.docx** in the Content pane.

c. Hold down the Shift key, click **WordDocument05.docx**, and then release the Shift key.

d. Position the mouse pointer on any selected file, click the right mouse button, and then click *Delete* at the shortcut menu.

e. At the message asking if you are sure you want to permanently delete the files, click Yes.

4. Close the Computer window by clicking the Close button located in the upper right corner of the window.

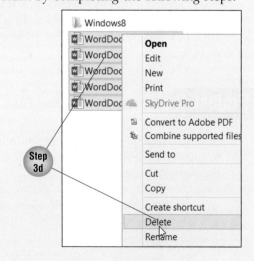

Step 3d

Manipulating and Creating Folders

As you begin working with and creating multiple files, consider creating folders in which you can logically group and store the files. To create a folder, display the Computer window and then display the drive or folder where you want to create the folder in the Content pane. To create the new folder, click the New folder button in the New group on the Home tab; click the New folder button on the Quick Access toolbar; or click in a blank area in the Content pane, click the right mouse button, point to *New* in the shortcut menu, and then click *Folder* at the side menu. Any of the three methods inserts a folder icon in the Content pane and names the folder *New folder*. Type the desired name for the new folder and then press Enter.

Project 5 — Creating a New Folder

1. At the Windows 8 desktop, open the Computer window.
2. Create a new folder by completing the following steps:
   a. In the Content pane, double-click the drive that contains your storage medium.
   b. Double-click the *Windows8* folder in the Content pane. (This opens the folder.)
   c. Click the View tab and then click *List* in the Layout group.
   d. Click the Home tab and then click the New folder button in the New group.
   e. Type SpellCheckFiles and then press Enter. (This changes the name from *New folder* to *SpellCheckFiles*.)

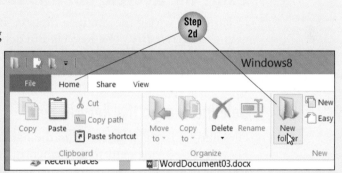

Step 2d

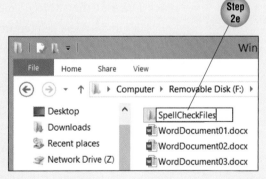

Step 2e

3. Copy **WordSpellCheck01.docx**, **WordSpellCheck02.docx**, and **WordSpellCheck03.docx** into the SpellCheckFiles folder you just created by completing the following steps:
   a. Click the View tab and then click *List* in the Layout group. (Skip this step if *List* is already selected.)
   b. Click ***WordSpellCheck01.docx*** in the Content pane.
   c. Hold down the Shift key, click ***WordSpellCheck03.docx***, and then release the Shift key. (This selects three documents.)
   d. Click the Home tab and then click the Copy button in the Clipboard group.
   e. Double-click the *SpellCheckFiles* folder in the Content pane.
   f. Click the Home tab and then click the Paste button in the Clipboard group.

4. Delete the SpellCheckFiles folder and its contents by completing the following steps:
   a. Click the Back button (contains a left-pointing arrow) located at the left side of the Address bar.
   b. With the SpellCheckFiles folder selected in the Content pane, click the Home tab and then click the Delete button in the Organize group.
   c. At the message asking you to confirm the deletion, click Yes.
5. Close the window by clicking the Close button located in the upper right corner of the window.

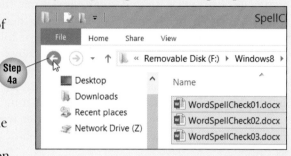

Using the Recycle Bin

Deleting the wrong file can be a disaster, but Windows 8 helps protect your work with the *Recycle Bin*. The Recycle Bin acts just like an office wastepaper basket; you can "throw away" (delete) unwanted files, but you can also "reach in" to the Recycle Bin and take out (restore) a file if you threw it away by accident.

Deleting Files to the Recycle Bin

Files and folders you delete from the hard drive are sent automatically to the Recycle Bin. If you want to permanently delete files or folders from the hard drive without first sending them to the Recycle Bin, select the desired file(s) or folder(s), right-click one of the selected files or folders, hold down the Shift key, and then click *Delete* at the shortcut menu.

Files and folders deleted from a USB flash drive or disc are deleted permanently. (Recovery programs are available, however, that will help you recover deleted files or folders. If you accidentally delete a file or folder from a USB flash drive or disc, do not do anything more with the USB flash drive or disc until you can run a recovery program.)

You can delete files in the manner described earlier in this section and you can also delete a file by dragging the file icon to the Recycle Bin. To do this, click the desired file in the Content pane in the Computer window, drag the file icon to the Recycle Bin icon on the desktop until the text *Move to Recycle Bin* displays, and then release the mouse button.

Restoring Files from the Recycle Bin

To restore a file from the Recycle Bin, double-click the Recycle Bin icon on the desktop. This opens the Recycle Bin window, shown in Figure W.10. (The contents of the Recycle Bin will vary.) To restore a file, click the file you want restored, click the Recycle Bin Tools Manage tab and then click the Restore the selected items button in the Restore group. This removes the file from the Recycle Bin and returns it to its original location. You can also restore a file by positioning the mouse pointer on the file, clicking the right mouse button, and then clicking *Restore* at the shortcut menu.

Figure W.10 Recycle Bin Window

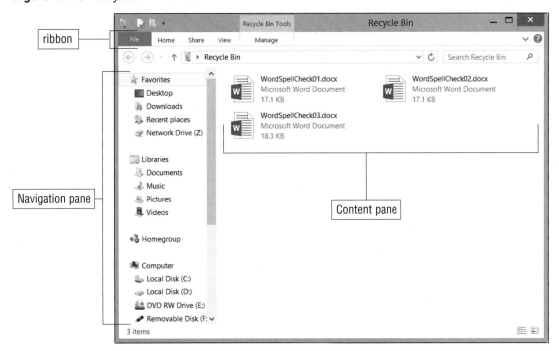

Project 6 Deleting Files to and Restoring Files from the Recycle Bin

Before beginning this project, check with your instructor to determine if you can copy files to the hard drive.

1. At the Windows 8 desktop, open the Computer window.
2. Copy files from your storage medium to the Documents folder on your hard drive by completing the following steps:
   a. In the Content pane, double-click the drive containing your storage medium.
   b. Double-click the *Windows8* folder in the Content pane.
   c. Click the View tab and then click *List* in the Layout group. (Skip this step if *List* is already selected.)
   d. Click *WordSpellCheck01.docx* in the Content pane.
   e. Hold down the Shift key, click *WordSpellCheck03.docx*, and then release the Shift key.
   f. Click the Home tab and then click the Copy button in the Clipboard group.
   g. Click the *Documents* folder in the *Libraries* section of the Navigation pane.
   h. Click the Home tab and then click the Paste button in the Clipboard group.

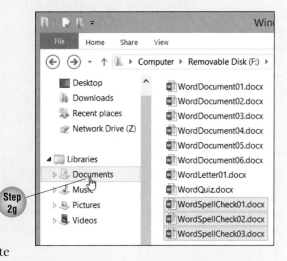

Step 2g

3. With **WordSpellCheck01.docx** through **WordSpellCheck03.docx** selected in the Content pane, click the Home tab and then click the Delete button in the Organize group to delete the files to the Recycle Bin.
4. Close the Computer window.
5. At the Windows 8 desktop, display the contents of the Recycle Bin by double-clicking the Recycle Bin icon.
6. Restore the files you just deleted by completing the following steps:
   a. Select **WordSpellCheck01.docx** through **WordSpellCheck03.docx** in the Recycle Bin Content pane. (If these files are not visible, you will need to scroll down the list of files in the Content pane.)
   b. Click the Recycle Bin Tools Manage tab and then click the Restore the selected items button in the Restore group.

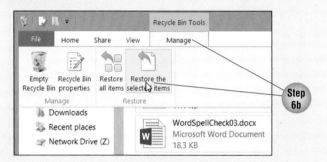

7. Close the Recycle Bin by clicking the Close button located in the upper right corner of the window.
8. Display the Computer window.
9. Click the *Documents* folder in the *Libraries* section of the Navigation pane.
10. Delete the files you restored.
11. Close the Computer window.

Emptying the Recycle Bin

Just like a wastepaper basket, the Recycle Bin can get full. To empty the Recycle Bin, position the arrow pointer on the Recycle Bin icon on the desktop and then click the right mouse button. At the shortcut menu that displays, click the *Empty Recycle Bin* option. At the message asking if you want to permanently delete the items, click Yes. You can also empty the Recycle Bin by displaying the Recycle Bin window and then clicking the Empty Recycle Bin button in the Manage group on the Recycle Bin Tools Manage tab. At the message asking if you want to permanently delete the items, click Yes. To delete a specific file from the Recycle Bin window, click the desired file in the Recycle Bin window, click the Home tab, and then click the Delete button in the Organize group. At the message asking if you want to permanently delete the file, click Yes. When you empty the Recycle Bin, the files cannot be recovered by the Recycle Bin or by Windows 8. If you have to recover a file, you will need to use a file recovery program.

Project 7 | Emptying the Recycle Bin

Note: Before beginning this project, check with your instructor to determine if you can delete files/folders from the Recycle Bin.

1. At the Windows 8 desktop, double-click the Recycle Bin icon.
2. At the Recycle Bin window, empty the contents by clicking the Empty Recycle Bin button in the Manage group on the Recycle Bin Tools Manage tab.
3. At the message asking you if you want to permanently delete the items, click Yes.
4. Close the Recycle Bin by clicking the Close button located in the upper right corner of the window.

Creating a Shortcut ▪▪▪▪▪▪▪▪▪▪▪▪▪▪▪▪▪▪▪▪▪▪▪▪▪▪▪▪▪▪▪▪▪

If you use a file or application on a consistent basis, consider creating a shortcut to the file or application. A *shortcut* is a specialized icon that points the operating system to an actual file, folder, or application. If you create a shortcut to a Word document, the shortcut icon is not the actual document but a very small file that contains the path to the document. Double-click the shortcut icon and Windows 8 opens the document in Word.

One method for creating a shortcut is to display the Computer window and then make active the drive or folder where the file is located. Right-click the desired file, point to *Send to*, and then click *Desktop (create shortcut)*. You can easily delete a shortcut icon from the desktop by dragging the shortcut icon to the Recycle Bin icon. This deletes the shortcut icon but does not delete the file to which the shortcut pointed.

Project 8 | Creating a Shortcut

1. At the Windows 8 desktop, display the Computer window.
2. Double-click the drive containing your storage medium.
3. Double-click the *Windows8* folder in the Content pane.
4. Change the display of files to a list by clicking the View tab and then clicking *List* in the Layout group. (Skip this step if *List* is already selected.)
5. Create a shortcut to the file named **WordQuiz.docx** by right-clicking **WordQuiz.docx**, pointing to *Send to*, and then clicking *Desktop (create shortcut)*.
6. Close the Computer window.

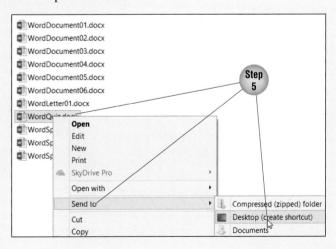

7. Open Word and **WordQuiz.docx** by double-clicking the *WordQuiz.docx* shortcut icon on the desktop.
8. After viewing the file in Word, close Word by clicking the Close button that displays in the upper right corner of the window.
9. Delete the *WordQuiz.docx* shortcut icon by completing the following steps:
   a. At the desktop, position the mouse pointer on the *WordQuiz.docx* shortcut icon.
   b. Hold down the left mouse button, drag the icon on top of the Recycle Bin icon, and then release the mouse button.

Step 7

Exploring the Control Panel

The Control Panel, shown in Figure W.11, contains a variety of icons for customizing the appearance and functionality of your computer as well as accessing and changing system settings. Display the Control Panel by right-clicking the Start screen thumbnail and then clicking *Control Panel* at the shortcut menu. The Control Panel organizes settings into categories to make them easier to find. Click a category icon and the Control Panel displays lower-level categories and tasks within each of them.

Hover your mouse over a category icon in the Control Panel and a ScreenTip displays with an explanation of what options are available. For example, if you hover the mouse over the Appearance and Personalization icon, a ScreenTip displays with information about the tasks available in the category, such as changing the appearance of desktop items, applying a theme or screen saver to your computer, or customizing the Taskbar.

If you click a category icon in the Control Panel, the Control Panel displays all of the available subcategories and tasks in the category. Also, the categories display in text form at the left side of the Control Panel. For example, if you click the Appearance and Personalization icon, the Control Panel displays as shown in Figure W.12. Notice how the Control Panel categories display at the left side of the Control Panel and options for changing the appearance and personalizing your computer display in the middle of the Control Panel.

By default, the Control Panel displays categories of tasks in what is called *Category* view. You can change this view to display large or small icons. To change the view, click the down-pointing arrow that displays at the right side of the text *View by* that displays in the upper right corner of the Control Panel, and then click the desired view at the drop-down list (see Figure W.11).

Figure W.11 The Control Panel

Click a category icon or hyperlink to display all of the category's options.

Use this option to change views.

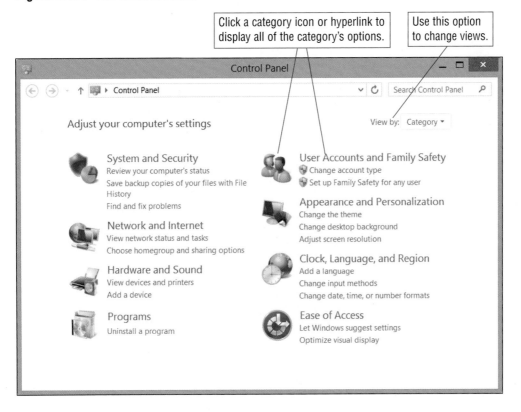

Figure W.12 Appearance and Personalization Window

Click this option to return to the main Control Panel.

lower-level categories

task hyperlinks

Click a category to display category options.

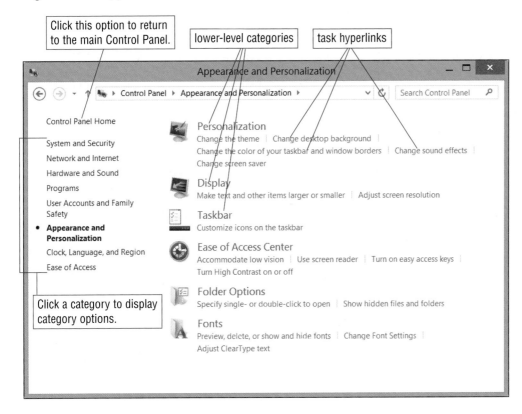

1. At the Windows 8 desktop, right-click the Start screen thumbnail and then click *Control Panel* at the shortcut menu.
2. At the Control Panel, click the Appearance and Personalization icon.

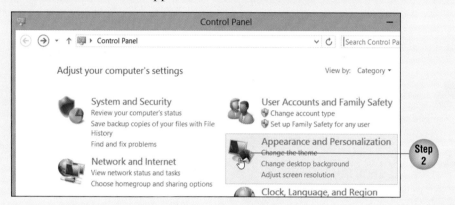

3. Click the <u>Change the theme</u> hyperlink that displays below *Personalization* in the panel at the right in the Control Panel.
4. At the window that displays with options for changing visuals and sounds on your computer, click *Earth* in the *Windows Default Themes* section.

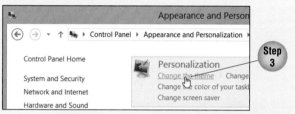

5. Click the <u>Desktop Background</u> hyperlink that displays in the lower left corner of the panel.
6. Click the button that displays below the text *Change picture every* and then click *10 Seconds* at the drop-down list. (This tells Windows to change the picture on your desktop every 10 seconds.)
7. Click the Save changes button that displays in the lower right corner of the Control Panel.
8. Click the Close button located in the upper right corner to close the Control Panel.
9. Look at the picture that displays as the desktop background. Wait for 10 seconds and then look at the second picture that displays.
10. Right-click the Start screen thumbnail and then click *Control Panel* at the shortcut menu.
11. At the Control Panel, click the Appearance and Personalization icon.
12. Click the <u>Change the theme</u> hyperlink that displays below *Personalization* in the panel at the right.

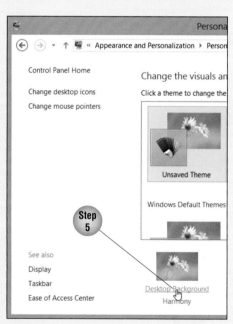

13. At the window that displays with options for changing visuals and sounds on your computer, click *Windows* in the *Windows Default Themes* section. (This is the default theme.)
14. Click the Close button located in the upper right corner of the Control Panel.

Searching in the Control Panel

The Control Panel contains a large number of options for customizing the appearance and functionality of your computer. If you want to customize a feature and are not sure where the options for the feature are located, search for the feature. To do this, display the Control Panel and then type the name of the desired feature. By default, the insertion point is positioned in the *Search Control Panel* text box. When you type the feature name in the text box, options related to the feature display in the Control Panel.

Project 10 | Customizing the Mouse

1. Right-click the Start screen thumbnail and then click *Control Panel*.
2. At the Control Panel, type **mouse**. (The insertion point is automatically located in the *Search Control Panel* text box when you open the Control Panel. When you type *mouse*, features for customizing the mouse display in the Control Panel.)
3. Click the Mouse icon that displays in the Control Panel.
4. At the Mouse Properties dialog box, notice the options that display. (The *Switch primary and secondary buttons* option might be useful, for example, if you are left-handed and want to switch the buttons on the mouse.)
5. Click the Cancel button to close the dialog box.
6. At the Control Panel, click the Change the mouse pointer display or speed hyperlink.

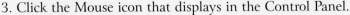

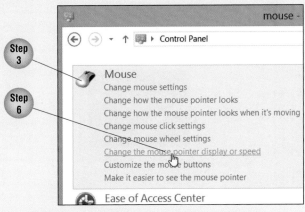

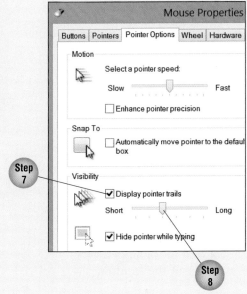

7. At the Mouse Properties dialog box with the Pointer Options tab selected, click the *Display pointer trails* check box in the *Visibility* section to insert a check mark.
8. Drag the button on the slider bar (located below the *Display pointer trails* check box) approximately to the middle of the bar.
9. Click OK to close the dialog box.
10. Close the Control Panel.
11. Move the mouse pointer around the screen to see the pointer trails.

Displaying Personalize Options with a Shortcut Command

In addition to the Control Panel, display customization options with a command from a shortcut menu. Display a shortcut menu by positioning the mouse pointer in the desired position and then clicking the right mouse button. For example, display a shortcut menu with options for customizing the desktop by positioning the mouse pointer in an empty area of the desktop and then clicking the right mouse button. At the shortcut menu that displays, click the desired shortcut command.

Project 11   Customizing with a Shortcut Command

1. At the Windows 8 desktop, position the mouse pointer in an empty area on the desktop, click the right mouse button, and then click *Personalize* at the shortcut menu.
2. At the Control Panel Appearance and Personalization window that displays, click the <u>Change mouse pointers</u> hyperlink that displays at the left side of the window.

Step 2

3. At the Mouse Properties dialog box, click the Pointer Options tab.
4. Click in the *Display pointer trails* check box to remove the check mark.
5. Click OK to close the dialog box.
6. At the Control Panel Appearance and Personalization window, click the <u>Screen Saver</u> hyperlink that displays in the lower right corner of the window.
7. At the Screen Saver Settings dialog box, click the option button below the *Screen saver* option and then click *Ribbons* at the drop-down list.
8. Check the number in the *Wait* measurement box. If a number other than *1* displays, click the down-pointing arrow at the right side of the measurement box until *1* displays. (This tells Windows to display the screen saver after one minute of inactivity.)
9. Click OK to close the dialog box.
10. Close the Control Panel by clicking the Close button located in the upper right corner of the window.

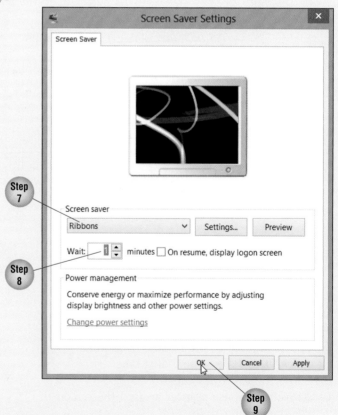

Step 7

Step 8

Step 9

11. Do not touch the mouse or keyboard and wait over one minute for the screen saver to display. After watching the screen saver, move the mouse. (This redisplays the desktop.)
12. Right-click in an empty area of the desktop and then click *Personalize* at the shortcut menu.
13. At the Control Panel Appearance and Personalization window, click the Screen Saver hyperlink.
14. At the Screen Saver Settings dialog box, click the option button below the *Screen saver* option and then click *(None)* at the drop-down list.
15. Click OK to close the dialog box.
16. Close the Control Panel Appearance and Personalization window.

Exploring Windows Help and Support ▪▪▪▪▪▪▪▪▪▪▪▪▪▪▪

Windows 8 includes an on-screen reference guide providing information, explanations, and interactive help on learning Windows features. Get help at the Windows Help and Support window, shown in Figure W.13. Display this window by clicking the Start screen thumbnail to display the Windows 8 Start screen. Right-click a blank area of the Start screen, click the All apps button, and then click the *Help and Support* tile in the Windows System group. Use options in the Windows Help and Support window to search for help on a specific feature; display the opening Windows Help and Support window; print the current information; and display information on getting started with Windows 8, setting up a network, and protecting your computer.

Figure W.13 Windows Help and Support Window

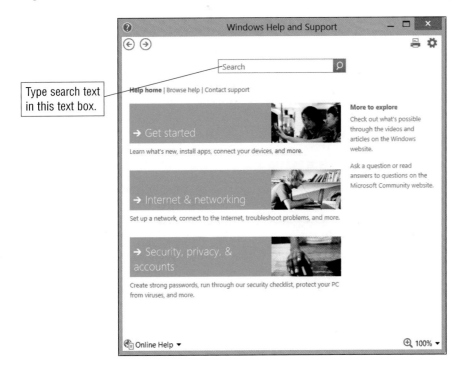

Type search text in this text box.

1. Display the Windows 8 Help and Support window by following these steps:
   a. At the Windows 8 desktop, position the mouse pointer in the lower left corner of the screen and then click the Start screen thumbnail.
   b. Position the mouse in a blank area of the Windows 8 Start screen and then click the right mouse button.
   c. Click the All apps button that appears in the lower right corner of the Start screen and then scroll to the right of the Start screen.
   d. Click the *Help and Support* tile located in the *Windows System* category.

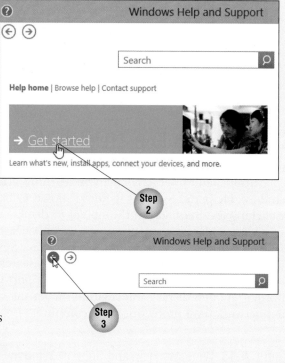

2. At the Windows Help and Support window, click the Get started hyperlink.
3. Click a hyperlink that interests you, read the information, and then click the Back button. (The Back button is located in the upper left corner of the window.)
4. Click another hyperlink that interests you and then read the information.
5. Click the Help home hyperlink that displays below the search text box. (This returns you to the opening Windows Help and Support window.)
6. Click in the search text box, type **delete files**, and then press Enter.
7. Click the How to work with files and folders hyperlink that displays in the window.
8. Read the information that displays about working with files or folders and then click the Print button located in the upper right corner of the Windows Help and Support window.
9. At the Print dialog box, click the Print button.
10. Click the Close button to close the Windows Help and Support window.

Using Search Tools ■■■■■■■■■■■ ■■■■■■■■■■■ ■■■■■■■

The Charm bar contains a search tool you can use to quickly find an application or file on your computer. To use the search tool, display the Charm bar, click the Search button and then type in the search text box the first few characters of the application or file for which you are searching. As you type characters in the text box, a list displays with application names or file names that begin with the characters. As you continue typing characters, the search tool refines the list.

You can also search for programs or files with the search text box in the Computer window. The search text box displays in the upper right corner of the Computer window at the right side of the Address bar. If you want to search a specific folder, make that folder active in the Content pane and then type the search text in the text box.

When conducting a search, you can use the asterisk (*) as a wildcard character in place of any letters, numbers, or symbols within a file name. For example, in the following project you will search for file names containing *check* by typing **check** in the search text box. The asterisk indicates that the file name can start with any letter but it must contain the letters *check* somewhere in the file name.

Project 13   Searching for Programs and Files

1. At the Windows 8 desktop, display the Charm bar and then click the Search button.
2. With the insertion point positioned in the search text box, type **paint**. (Notice as you type the letters that Windows displays applications that begin with the same letters you are typing or that are associated with the same letters in a keyword. Notice that the Paint program displays below the heading *Apps* at the top of the list. Depending on the contents stored in the computer you are using, additional items may display below Paint.)

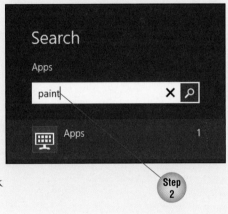

3. Click *Paint* that displays below the *Apps* heading.
4. Close the Paint window.
5. Right-click the Start screen thumbnail and then click *File Explorer*.
6. At the Computer window, double-click the icon representing your storage medium.
7. Double-click the *Windows8* folder.
8. Click in the search text box located at the right of the Address bar and then type **document**. (As you begin typing the letters, Windows filters the list of files in the Content pane to those that contain the letters you type. Notice that the Address bar displays *Search Results in Windows8* to indicate that the files that display matching your criteria are limited to the current folder.)

9. Select the text *document* that displays in the search text box and then type **check**. (Notice that the Content pane displays file names containing the letters *check* no matter how the file name begins.)
10. Double-click ***WordSpellCheck02.docx*** to open the document in Word.
11. Close the document and then close Word by clicking the Close button located in the upper right corner of the window.
12. Close the Computer window.

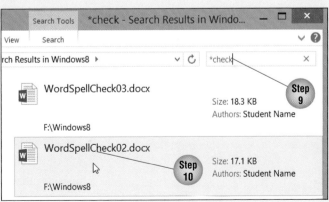

Browsing the Internet Using Internet Explorer 10

Microsoft Internet Explorer 10 is a web browser with options and features for displaying sites as well as navigating and searching for information on the Internet. The **Internet** is a network of computers connected around the world. Users access the Internet for several purposes: to communicate using instant messaging and/or email, to subscribe to newsgroups, to transfer files, to socialize with other users around the globe on social websites, and to access virtually any kind of information imaginable.

Using the Internet, people can find a phenomenal amount of information for private or public use. To use the Internet, three things are generally required: an **Internet Service Provider (ISP)**, software to browse the Web (called a **web browser**), and a **search engine**. In this section, you will learn how to:

- Navigate the Internet using URLs and hyperlinks
- Use search engines to locate information
- Download web pages and images

You will use the Microsoft Internet Explorer web browser to locate information on the Internet. A **Uniform Resource Locator**, referred to as a **URL**, identifies a location on the Internet. The steps for browsing the Internet vary but generally include opening Internet Explorer, typing the URL for the desired site, navigating the various pages of the site, navigating to other sites using links, and then closing Internet Explorer.

To launch Internet Explorer 10, click the Internet Explorer icon on the Taskbar at the Windows desktop. Figure IE.1 identifies the elements of the Internet Explorer 10 window. The web page that displays in your Internet Explorer window may vary from what you see in Figure IE.1.

If you know the URL for a desired website, click in the Address bar, type the URL, and then press Enter. The website's home page displays in a tab within the Internet Explorer window. The format of a URL is *http://server-name.path*. The first part of the URL, *http*, stands for HyperText Transfer Protocol, which is the protocol or language used to transfer data within the World Wide Web. The colon and slashes separate the protocol from the server name. The server name is the second component of the URL. For example, in the URL http://www.microsoft.com, the server name is *microsoft*. The last part of the URL specifies the domain to which the server belongs. For example, *.com* refers to "commercial" and establishes that the URL is a commercial company. Examples of other domains include *.edu* for "educational," *.gov* for "government," and *.mil* for "military."

Internet Explorer 10 has been streamlined to provide users with more browsing space and reduced clutter. By default, Microsoft has turned off many features in Internet Explorer 10 such as the Menu bar, Command bar, and Status bar. You can turn these features on by right-clicking the empty space above the Address bar and to the right of the new tab button (see Figure IE.1) and then clicking the desired option at the drop-down list that displays. For example, if you want to turn on the Menu bar (the bar that contains File, Edit, and so on), right-click the empty space above the Address bar and then click *Menu bar* at the drop-down list. (This inserts a check mark next to *Menu bar*.)

Figure IE.1 Internet Explorer Window

Project 1 Browsing the Internet Using URLs

1. Make sure you are connected to the Internet through an Internet Service Provider and that the Windows 8 desktop displays. (Check with your instructor to determine if you need to complete steps for accessing the Internet such as typing a user name and password to log on.)
2. Launch Microsoft Internet Explorer by clicking the Internet Explorer icon located at the left side of the Windows Taskbar, which is located at the bottom of the Windows desktop.
3. Turn on the Command bar by right-clicking the empty space above the Address bar or to the right of the new tab button (see Figure IE.1) and then clicking *Command bar* at the drop-down list.
4. At the Internet Explorer window, explore the website for Yosemite National Park by completing the following steps:
   a. Click in the Address bar, type **www.nps.gov/yose**, and then press Enter.
   b. Scroll down the home page for Yosemite National Park by clicking the down-pointing arrow on the vertical scroll bar located at the right side of the Internet Explorer window.

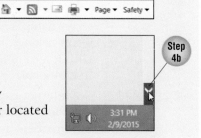

c. Print the home page by clicking the Print button located on the Command bar. (Note that some websites have a printer-friendly button you can click to print the page.)

5. Explore the website for Glacier National Park by completing the following steps:

   a. Click in the Address bar, type **www.nps.gov/glac**, and then press Enter.

   b. Print the home page by clicking the Print button located on the Command bar.

6. Close Internet Explorer by clicking the Close button (contains an X) located in the upper right corner of the Internet Explorer window.

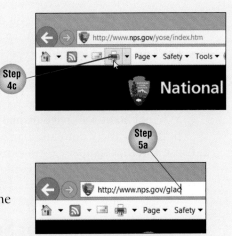

Navigating Using Hyperlinks ■■■■■■■■■■■■■■■■■■■■■■

Most web pages contain *hyperlinks* that you click to connect to another page within the website or to another site on the Internet. Hyperlinks may display in a web page as underlined text in a specific color or as images or icons. To use a hyperlink, position the mouse pointer on the desired hyperlink until the mouse pointer turns into a hand and then click the left mouse button. Use hyperlinks to navigate within and between sites on the Internet. The Internet Explorer window contains a Back button (see Figure IE.1) that, when clicked, takes you to the previous web page viewed. If you click the Back button and then want to return to the previous page, click the Forward button. You can continue clicking the Back button to back your way out of several linked pages in reverse order since Internet Explorer maintains a history of the websites you visit.

Project 2   Navigating Using Hyperlinks

1. Make sure you are connected to the Internet and then click the Internet Explorer icon on the Windows Taskbar.

2. At the Internet Explorer window, display the White House web page and navigate in the page by completing the following steps:

   a. Click in the Address bar, type **whitehouse.gov**, and then press Enter.

   b. At the White House home page, position the mouse pointer on a hyperlink that interests you until the pointer turns into a hand and then click the left mouse button.

   c. At the linked web page, click the Back button. (This returns you to the White House home page.)

   d. At the White House home page, click the Forward button to return to the previous web page viewed.

   e. Print the web page by clicking the Print button on the Command bar.

3. Display the website for Amazon.com and navigate in the site by completing the following steps:

Step 3a

a. Click in the Address bar, type **www.amazon.com**, and then press Enter.

b. At the Amazon.com home page, click a hyperlink related to books.

c. When a book web page displays, click the Print button on the Command bar.

4. Close Internet Explorer by clicking the Close button (contains an X) located in the upper right corner of the Internet Explorer window.

Searching for Specific Sites ■■■■■■■■■■■■■■■■■■■■■■

If you do not know the URL for a specific site or you want to find information on the Internet but do not know what site to visit, complete a search with a search engine. A *search engine* is software created to search quickly and easily for desired information. A variety of search engines are available on the Internet, each offering the opportunity to search for specific information. One method for searching for information is to click in the Address bar, type a keyword or phrase related to your search, and then press Enter. Another method for completing a search is to visit the website for a search engine and use options at the site.

Bing is Microsoft's online search portal and is the default search engine used by Internet Explorer. Bing organizes search results by topic category and provides related search suggestions.

Project 3 **Searching for Information by Topic**

1. Start Internet Explorer.
2. At the Internet Explorer window, search for sites on bluegrass music by completing the following steps:
   a. Click in the Address bar.
   b. Type **bluegrass music** and then press Enter.
   c. When a list of sites displays in the Bing results window, click a site that interests you.
   d. When the page displays, click the Print button.

Step 2b

3. Use the Yahoo! search engine to find sites on bluegrass music by completing the following steps:
   a. Click in the Address bar, type **www.yahoo.com**, and then press Enter.
   b. At the Yahoo! website, with the insertion point positioned in the search text box, type **bluegrass music** and then press Enter. (Notice that the sites displayed vary from sites displayed in the earlier search.)

Step 3b

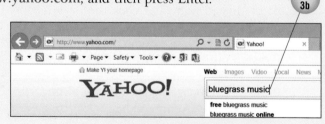

c. Click hyperlinks until a website displays that interests you.

d. Print the page.

4. Use the Google search engine to find sites on jazz music by completing the following steps:

   a. Click in the Address bar, type **www.google.com**, and then press Enter.

   b. At the Google website, with the insertion point positioned in the search text box, type **jazz music** and then press Enter.

   c. Click a site that interests you.

   d. Print the page.

5. Close Internet Explorer.

Using a Metasearch Engine

Bing, Yahoo!, and Google are search engines that search the Web for content and display search results. In addition to individual search engines, you can use a metasearch engine, such as Dogpile, that sends your search text to other search engines and then compiles the results in one list. With a metasearch engine, you type the search text once and then access results from a wider group of search engines. The Dogpile metasearch engine provides search results from Google, Yahoo!, and Yandex.

Project 4   **Searching with a Metasearch Search Engine**

1. Start Internet Explorer.

2. Click in the Address bar.

3. Type **www.dogpile.com** and then press Enter.

4. At the Dogpile website, type **jazz music** in the search text box and then press Enter.

5. Click a hyperlink that interests you.

6. Close the Internet Explorer window. If a message displays asking if you want to close all tabs, click the Close all tabs button.

Completing Advanced Searches for Specific Sites

The Internet contains an enormous amount of information. Depending on what you are searching for on the Internet and the search engine you use, some searches can result in several thousand "hits" (sites). Wading through a large number of sites can be very time-consuming and counterproductive. Narrowing a search to very specific criteria can greatly reduce the number of hits for a search. To narrow a search, use the advanced search options offered by the search engine.

Project 5   Narrowing a Search

1. Start Internet Explorer.
2. Search for sites on skydiving in Oregon by completing the following steps:
   a. Click in the Address bar, type **www.yahoo.com**, and then press Enter.
   b. At the Yahoo! home page, click the Search button next to the search text box.
   c. Click the More hyperlink located above the search text box and then click *Advanced Search* at the drop-down list.
   d. At the Advanced Web Search page, click in the search text box next to *all of these words*.
   e. Type **skydiving Oregon tandem static line**. (This limits the search to web pages containing all of the words typed in the search text box.)
   f. Click the Yahoo! Search button.
   g. When the list of websites displays, click a hyperlink that interests you.
   h. Click the Back button until the Yahoo! Advanced Web Search page displays.
   i. Click in the *the exact phrase* text box and then type **skydiving in Oregon**.
   j. Click the *Only .com domains* option in the *Site/Domain* section.
   k. Click the Yahoo! Search button.
   l. When the list of websites displays, click a hyperlink that interests you.
   m. Print the page.
3. Close Internet Explorer.

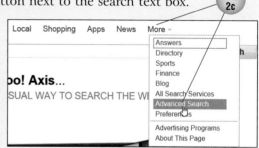

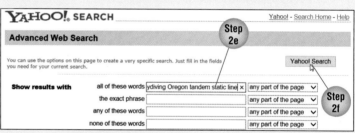

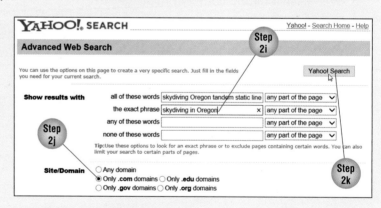

Downloading Images, Text, and Web Pages
from the Internet ▪■▪■▪■▪■▪■ ▪■▪■▪■▪■▪■▪■

The image(s) and/or text that display when you open a web page, as well as the web page itself, can be saved as a separate file. This separate file can be viewed, printed, or inserted in another file. The information you want to save in a separate file is downloaded from the Internet by Internet Explorer and saved in a folder of your choosing with the name you specify. Copyright laws protect much of the information on the Internet. Before using information downloaded from the Internet, check the site for restrictions. If you do use information, make sure you properly cite the source.

Project 6 | Downloading Images and Web Pages

1. Start Internet Explorer.
2. Download a web page and image from Banff National Park by completing the following steps:
   a. Search for websites related to Banff National Park.
   b. From the list of sites that displays, choose a site that contains information about Banff National Park and at least one image of the park.
   c. Make sure the Command bar is turned on. (If the Command bar is turned off, turn it on by right-clicking the empty space above the Address bar or to the right of the new tab button and then clicking *Command bar* at the drop-down list.)

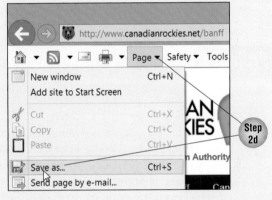

   d. Save the web page as a separate file by clicking the Page button on the Command bar and then clicking *Save as* at the drop-down list.
   e. At the Save Webpage dialog box, type **BanffWebPage**.
   f. Click the down-pointing arrow for the *Save as type* option and then click *Web Archive, single file (*.mht)*.
   g. Navigate to the drive containing your storage medium and then click the Save button.

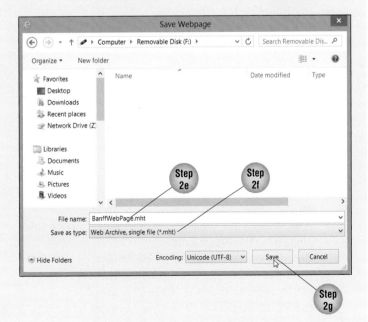

3. Save an image file by completing the following steps:
   a. Right-click an image that displays at the website.
   b. At the shortcut menu that displays, click *Save picture as*.

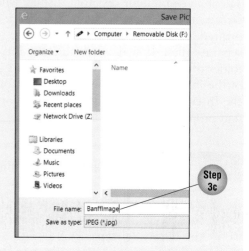

Step 3b

Step 3c

   c. At the Save Picture dialog box, type **BanffImage** in the *File name* text box.
   d. Navigate to the drive containing your storage medium and then click the Save button.
4. Close Internet Explorer.

Project 7   Opening the Saved Web Page and Image in a Word Document

1. Open Microsoft Word by positioning the mouse pointer in the lower left corner of the Taskbar, clicking the Start screen thumbnail, and then clicking the *Word 2013* tile in the Windows 8 Start screen. At the Word opening screen, click the *Blank document* template.
2. With Microsoft Word open, insert the image in a document by completing the following steps:
   a. Click the INSERT tab and then click the Pictures button in the Illustrations group.
   b. At the Insert Picture dialog box, navigate to the drive containing your storage medium and then double-click *BanffImage.jpg*.

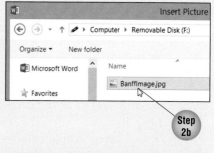

Step 2b

   c. When the image displays in the Word document, print the document by pressing Ctrl + P and then clicking the Print button.
   d. Close the document by clicking the FILE tab and then clicking the *Close* option. At the message asking if you want to save the changes, click the Don't Save button.
3. Open the **BanffWebPage.mht** file by completing the following steps:
   a. Click the FILE tab and then click the *Open* option.
   b. Double-click the *Computer* option.
   c. At the Open dialog box, navigate to the drive containing your storage medium and then double-click *BanffWebPage.mht*.

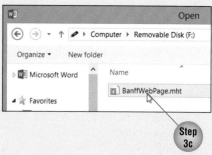

Step 3c

   d. Preview the web page(s) by pressing Ctrl + P. At the Print backstage area, preview the page shown at the right side of the backstage area.
4. Close Word by clicking the Close button (contains an X) that displays in the upper right corner of the screen.

MICROSOFT
ACCESS®

Level 1

Unit 1 ■ Creating Tables and Queries

MICROSOFT®
ACCESS®

CHAPTER 1

Managing and Creating Tables

PERFORMANCE OBJECTIVES

Upon successful completion of Chapter 1, you will be able to:

- **Open and close objects in a database**
- **Insert, delete, and move rows and columns in a table**
- **Hide, unhide, freeze, and unfreeze columns**
- **Adjust table column width**
- **Preview and print a table**
- **Design and create a table**
- **Rename column headings**
- **Insert a column name, caption, and description**
- **Insert Quick Start fields**
- **Assign a default value and field size**

SNAP

Tutorials

1.1 Opening and Closing an Access Database and Table
1.2 Using the Recent List
1.3 Navigating in Objects
1.4 Adding Records in a Table
1.5 Deleting Records in a Table
1.6 Adjusting Column Width
1.7 Previewing and Printing a Table
1.8 Creating a New Database; Creating a Table in Datasheet View
1.9 Creating a Table Using Quick Start Fields
1.10 Modifying Field Size, Caption, and Default Value Properties

Managing information is an integral part of operating a business. Information can come in a variety of forms, such as data about customers, including names, addresses, and telephone numbers; product data; and purchasing and buying data. Most companies today manage data using a system software program. Microsoft Office Professional Plus includes a database management system software program named *Access*. With Access, you can organize, store, maintain, retrieve, sort, and print all types of business data.

This chapter contains just a few ideas on how to manage data with Access. With a properly designed and maintained database management system, a company can operate smoothly with logical, organized, and useful information. Model answers for this chapter's projects appear on the following pages.

Access
AL1C1

Note: Before beginning the projects, copy to your storage medium the AL1C1 subfolder from the AL1 folder on the CD that accompanies this textbook. Make sure you have copied the files from the CD to your storage medium. Open all database files from your removable storage device and not directly from the CD since Access database files on the CD are read-only. Steps on how to copy a folder are presented on the inside of the back cover of this textbook. Do this every time you start a chapter's projects.

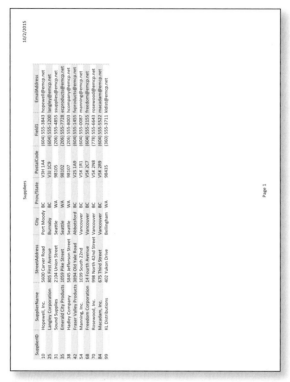

Suppliers Table

10/2/2015

Suppliers

SupplierID	SupplierName	StreetAddress	City	Prov/State	PostalCode	Field1	EmailAddress
10	Hopewell, Inc.	5600 Carver Road	Port Moody	BC	V3H 1A4	(604) 555-3843	hopewell@emcp.net
25	Langley Corporation	805 First Avenue	Burnaby	BC	V3J 1C9	(604) 555-1200	langley@emcp.net
31	Sound Supplies	2104 Union Street	Seattle	WA	98105	(206) 555-4855	ssupplies@emcp.net
35	Emerald City Products	1059 Pike Street	Seattle	WA	98102	(206) 555-7728	ecproducts@emcp.net
38	Hadley Company	5845 Jefferson Street	Seattle	WA	98107	(206) 555-8003	hcompany@emcp.net
42	Fraser Valley Products	3894 Old Yale Road	Abbotsford	BC	V2S 1A9	(604) 555-1455	fvproducts@emcp.net
54	Manning, Inc.	1039 South 22nd	Vancouver	BC	V5K 1R1	(604) 555-0087	manning@emcp.net
68	Freedom Corporation	14 Fourth Avenue	Vancouver	BC	V5K 2C7	(604) 555-2155	freedom@emcp.net
70	Rosewood, Inc.	998 North 42nd Street	Vancouver	BC	V5K 2N8	(778) 555-6643	rosewood@emcp.net
84	Macadam, Inc.	675 Third Street	Vancouver	BC	V5K 2R9	(604) 555-5532	macadam@emcp.net
99	KL Distributions	402 Yukon Drive	Bellingham	WA	98435	(360) 555-3711	kldist@emcp.net

Page 1

Products Table, Page 1

10/2/2015

Products

ProductID	Product	SupplierID	UnitsInStock	UnitsOnOrder	ReorderLevel
101-51B	SL 0-degrees down sleeping bag, black	54	16	0	15
101-51R	SL 0-degrees down sleeping bag, red	54	17	0	15
101-52B	SL 15-degrees synthetic sleeping bag, blac	54	21	0	15
101-52R	SL 15-degrees synthetic sleeping bag, red	54	12	15	15
101-53B	SL 20-degrees synthetic sleeping bag, blac	54	4	15	15
101-53R	SL 20-degrees synthetic sleeping bag, red	54	4	10	10
209-L	Gordon wool ski hat, L	68	21	25	25
209-XL	Gordon wool ski hat, XL	68	14	25	25
209-XXL	Gordon wool ski hat, XXL	68	10	20	20
210-L	Tech-lite ski hat, L	68	17	25	25
210-M	Tech-lite ski hat, M	68	6	15	15
210-XL	Tech-lite ski hat, XL	68	22	15	20
299-M1	HT waterproof hiking boots, MS13	31	8	0	10
299-M2	HT waterproof hiking boots, MS12	31	2	10	10
299-M3	HT waterproof hiking boots, MS11	31	6	10	10
299-M4	HT waterproof hiking boots, MS10	31	7	0	10
299-M5	HT waterproof hiking boots, MS9	31	9	10	10
299-W1	HT waterproof hiking boots, WS11	31	5	8	8
299-W2	HT waterproof hiking boots, WS10	31	9	0	8
299-W3	HT waterproof hiking boots, WS9	31	3	10	10
299-W4	HT waterproof hiking boots, WS8	31	2	10	10
299-W5	HT waterproof hiking boots, WS7	31	10	10	10
299-W6	HT waterproof hiking boots, WS6	31	11	0	10
371-L	Lite-tech ski gloves, ML	68	3	10	10
371-M	Lite-tech ski gloves, MM	68	5	10	10
371-XL	Lite-tech ski gloves, MXL	68	3	10	10
371-XXL	Lite-tech ski gloves, MXXL	68	12	0	10
375-L	Lite-tech ski gloves, WL	68	22	0	20
375-M	Lite-tech ski gloves, WM	68	6	20	20
375-S	Lite-tech ski gloves, WS	68	6	20	20
442-1A	Polar backpack, 1500RW	42	12	0	10
442-1B	Polar backpack, 1500W	42	9	10	10
443-1A	Polar backpack, 2500R	42	14	0	15
443-1B	Polar backpack, 2500RW	42	6	15	15
558-C	ICE snow goggles, clear	68	18	0	15
559-B	ICE snow goggles, bronze	68	22	0	20

Page 1

Products Table, Page 2

10/2/2015

Products

ProductID	Product	SupplierID	UnitsInStock	UnitsOnOrder	ReorderLevel
602-XR	Binoculars, 8 x 42	35	3	5	5
602-XT	Binoculars, 10.5 x 45	35	5	0	4
602-XX	Binoculars, 10 x 50	35	7	0	5
647-1	Two-person dome tent	99	10	15	15
648-2	Three-person dome tent	99	5	0	10
651-1	K-2 one-person tent	99	8	0	10
652-2	K-2 two-person tent	99	12	0	10
804-50	AG freestyle snowboard, X50	70	7	0	10
804-60	AG freestyle snowboard, X60	70	8	0	5
897-L	Lang blunt snowboard	70	8	0	7
897-W	Lang blunt snowboard, wide	70	4	0	3
901-S	Solar battery pack	38	16	0	15
917-S	Silo portable power pack	38	8	0	10

Page 2

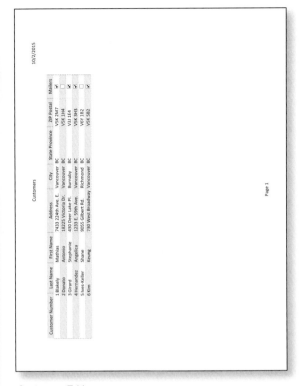

Customers Table

Orders Table

Project 1 — Explore an Access Database   1 Part

You will open a database and open and close objects in the database, including tables, queries, forms, and reports.

Exploring a Database ■■■■■■■■■■■■■■■■■■■■■■■

A *database* is comprised of a series of objects (such as tables, queries, forms, and reports) that you use to enter, manage, view, and print data. Data in a database is organized into tables, which contain information for related items (such as customers, employees, orders, and products). To view the various objects in a database, you will open a previously created database and then navigate in the database and open objects.

To create a new database or open a previously created database, click the Access 2013 tile at the Windows 8 Start screen. (This step may vary depending on your system configuration.) This displays the Access 2013 opening screen, as shown in Figure 1.1. At this opening screen, you can open a recently opened database, a blank database, a database from the Open backstage area, or a database based on a template.

To create a new blank database, click the Blank desktop database template. At the Blank desktop database window that displays, type a name for the database in the *File Name* text box, and then click the Create button. If you want to save the database in a particular location, click the Browse button at the right side of the *File Name* text box. At the File New Database dialog box that displays, navigate to the desired location or folder, type the database name in the *File name* text box, and then click OK.

▼ Quick Steps

Create a New Database
1. Open Access.
2. Click Blank desktop database template.
3. Type database name.
4. Click Create button.

Create

Figure 1.1 Access 2013 Opening Screen

Click this template to create a blank database.

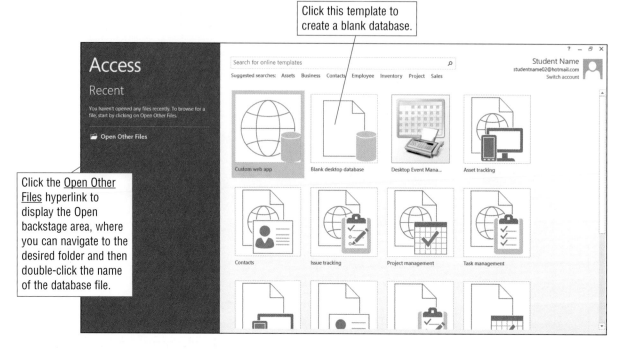

Click the Open Other Files hyperlink to display the Open backstage area, where you can navigate to the desired folder and then double-click the name of the database file.

Opening a Database

▼ Quick Steps

Open a Database
1. Open Access.
2. Click Open Other Files hyperlink.
3. Double-click SkyDrive or *Computer* option.
4. Navigate to desired location.
5. Double-click database.

To open an existing Access database, click the Open Other Files hyperlink that displays in the left panel at the Access 2013 opening screen. This displays the Open backstage area. You can also display the Open backstage area with the keyboard shortcut Ctrl + O or by inserting an Open button on the Quick Access toolbar and clicking that button. At the Open backstage area, click the desired location, such as your SkyDrive or the *Computer* option, and then click the Browse button. (If you are opening a database from your computer or USB flash drive, double-click the *Computer* option.) At the Open dialog box that displays, navigate to the desired folder and then double-click the desired database name in the Content pane.

If you are opening a database from your SkyDrive, Access requires you to save a copy of the database to a location such as your computer's hard drive or a USB flash drive. Any changes you make to the database will be saved to the local copy of the database but not the database on your SkyDrive. If you want to save the database back to your SkyDrive, you will need to upload the database by opening a web browser, going to skydrive.com, logging in to your SkyDrive account, and then clicking the Upload link. Microsoft constantly updates the skydrive.com website, so these steps may vary.

When you click your SkyDrive or the *Computer* option at the Open backstage area, a list of the most recently accessed folders displays in the Recent Folders list in the *Computer* section. Open a folder from this list by clicking the folder name.

At the Open backstage area with *Recent* selected in the middle panel, a list of the most recently opened databases displays in the Recent list. Open a database from this list by clicking the database name. When you open a database, the Access screen displays, as shown in Figure 1.2. Refer to Table 1.1 for descriptions of the Access screen elements.

Figure 1.2 Access Screen

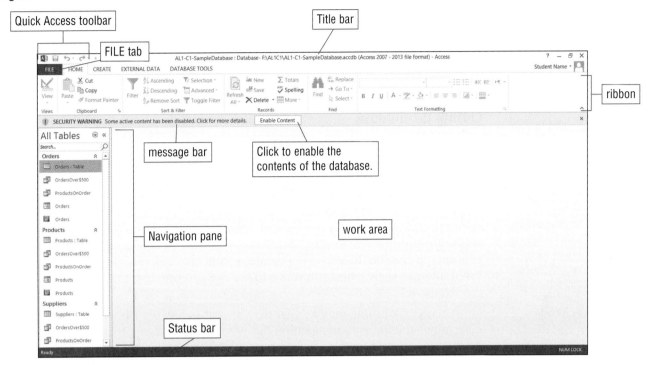

Table 1.1 Access Screen Elements

Feature	Description
FILE tab	When clicked, displays the backstage area that contains options for working with and managing databases.
message bar	Displays security alerts if the database being opened contains potentially unsafe content.
Navigation pane	Displays the names of objects within the database grouped by categories.
Quick Access toolbar	Contains buttons for commonly used commands.
ribbon	Contains the tabs with commands and buttons divided into groups.
Status bar	Displays messages, the current view, and view buttons.
tabs	Contain commands and features organized into groups.
Title bar	Displays the database name followed by the program name.
work area	Displays opened objects.

Pinning a Database File or Folder to the Recent List

If you want a database to remain in the Recent list at the Open backstage area, "pin" the database to the list. To do this, position the mouse pointer over the desired database file name and then click the small, left-pointing stick pin that displays at the right side of the list. When you click the stick pin, it changes to a down-pointing stick pin. The next time you display the Open backstage area, the database file name you pinned displays at the top of the Recent list.

You can also pin a folder name to the Recent Folders list in the same manner as you pin a database file name. The Recent Folders list displays at the Open backstage area when you click the SkyDrive or *Computer* option. You can pin more than one database file name to the Recent list or more than one folder name to the Recent Folders list. To "unpin" a database or folder name, click the stick pin to change it from a down-pointing pin to a left-pointing pin.

Closing a Database

Close

To close a database, click the FILE tab and then click the *Close* option. Close Access by clicking the Close button that displays in the upper right corner of the screen or with the keyboard shortcut Alt + F4.

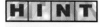

The active database is saved automatically on a periodic basis and when you make another record active, close the table, or close the database.

Only one Access database can be open at a time. If you open a new database in the current Access window, the existing database closes. You can, however, open multiple instances of Access and open a database in each instance. In other applications in the Microsoft Office suite, you have to save a revised file after you edit data in the file. In an Access database, any changes you make to data are saved automatically when you move to the next record, close the table, or close the database.

A security warning message bar may appear below the ribbon if Access determines the file you are opening did not originate from a trusted location on your computer and may have viruses or other security hazards. This often occurs when you copy a file from another medium (such as a CD or the Web). Active content in the file is disabled until you click the Enable Content button. The message bar closes when you identify the database as a trusted source. Before making any changes to the database, you must click the Enable Content button.

The Navigation pane at the left side of the Access screen displays the objects contained in the database. Some common objects found in a database include tables, queries, forms, and reports. Refer to Table 1.2 for descriptions of these four types of objects.

Opening and Closing Objects

Database objects display in the Navigation pane. Control what displays in the pane by clicking the menu bar at the top of the Navigation pane and then clicking the desired option at the drop-down list or by clicking the button on the menu bar containing the down-pointing triangle. (The name of this button changes

Table 1.2 Database Objects

Object Type	Description
table	Organizes data in fields (columns) and records (rows). A database must contain at least one table. The table is the base upon which other objects are created.
query	Displays data from a table or related tables that meets a conditional statement and/or performs calculations. For example, all records from a specific month can be displayed or only those records containing a specific city.
form	Allows fields and records to be presented in a layout different from the datasheet. Used to facilitate data entry and maintenance.
report	Prints data from tables or queries.

depending on what is selected.) For example, to display a list of all saved objects in the database, click the *Object Type* option at the drop-down list. This view displays the objects grouped by type: *Tables*, *Queries*, *Forms*, and *Reports*. To open an object, double-click the object in the Navigation pane. The object opens in the work area and a tab displays with the object name at the left side of the object.

To view more of an object, consider closing the Navigation pane by clicking the Shutter Bar Open/Close Button located in the upper right corner of the Navigation pane or by using the keyboard shortcut F11. Click the button or press F11 again to reopen the Navigation pane. You can open more than one object in the work area. Each object opens with a visible tab. Navigate to objects by clicking the object tab. To close an object, click the Close button that displays in the upper right corner of the work area or use the keyboard shortcut Ctrl + F4.

HINT

Hide the Navigation pane by clicking the Shutter Bar Open/Close Button or by pressing F11.

Shutter Bar Open/Close Button

Project 1 Opening and Closing a Database and Objects in a Database   Part 1 of 1

1. Open Access by clicking the Access 2013 tile at the Windows 8 Start screen.
2. At the Access 2013 opening screen, click the <u>Open Other Files</u> hyperlink that displays in the left panel.
3. At the Open backstage area, click the desired location in the middle panel of the backstage area. (For example, click your SkyDrive if you are using your SkyDrive account or click the *Computer* option if you are opening a database from your computer's hard drive or a USB flash drive.)
4. Click the Browse button (or click *AL1C1* if it displays in the Recent Folders list).
5. At the Open dialog box, navigate to the AL1C1 folder on your storage medium and then double-click *AL1-C1-SampleDatabase.accdb*. (This database contains data on orders, products, and suppliers for a specialty hiking and backpacking outfitters store named Pacific Trek.)
6. Click the Enable Content button in the message bar if a security warning message appears. (The message bar will display immediately below the ribbon.)
7. With the database open, click the Navigation pane menu bar and then click *Object Type* at the drop-down list. (This option displays the objects grouped by type: *Tables*, *Queries*, *Forms*, and *Reports*.)

Step 7

8. Double-click *Suppliers* in the Tables group in the Navigation pane. This opens the Suppliers table in the work area, as shown in Figure 1.3.
9. Close the Suppliers table by clicking the Close button in the upper right corner of the work area.
10. Double-click *OrdersOver$500* in the Queries group in the Navigation pane. A query displays data that meets a conditional statement. This query displays orders that meet the criterion of being more than $500.
11. Close the query by clicking the Close button in the upper right corner of the work area.
12. Double-click *SuppliersNotVancouver* in the Queries group in the Navigation pane and notice that the query displays information about suppliers but excludes those located in Vancouver.

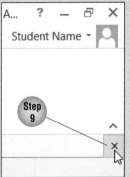

Step 9

13. Click the Close button in the work area.
14. Double-click *Orders* in the Forms group in the Navigation pane. This displays an order form. A form is used to view and edit data in a table one record at a time.
15. Click the Close button in the work area.
16. Double-click *Orders* in the Reports group in the Navigation pane. This displays a report with information about orders and order amounts.
17. Close the Navigation pane by clicking the Shutter Bar Open/Close Button located in the upper right corner of the pane.
18. After viewing the report, click the Shutter Bar Open/Close Button again to open the Navigation pane.
19. Click the Close button in the work area to close the report.
20. Close the database by clicking the FILE tab and then clicking the *Close* option.
21. Close Access by clicking the Close button (contains an X) that displays in the upper right corner of the screen.

Figure 1.3 Open Suppliers Table

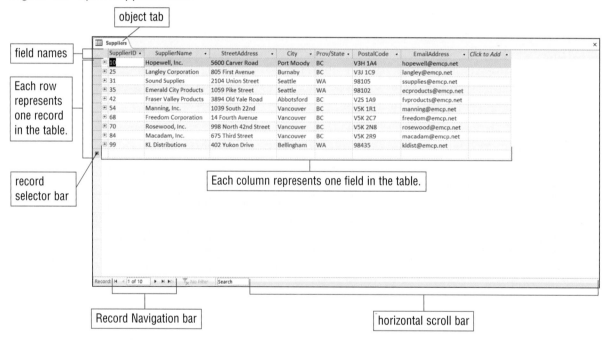

Project 2 **Manage Tables in a Database** 7 Parts

Pacific Trek is an outfitting store specializing in hiking and backpacking gear. Information about the store, including suppliers and products, is contained in a database. You will open the database and then insert and delete records; insert, move, and delete fields; preview and print tables; rename and delete a table; and create two new tables for the database.

Managing Tables ■■■■■■■■■■■■■■■■■■■■■■■■

In a new database, tables are the first objects created, since all other database objects rely on a table as the source for their data. Managing the tables in the database is important for keeping the database up to date and may include inserting or deleting records, inserting or deleting fields, renaming fields, creating a hard copy of the table by printing the table, and renaming and deleting tables.

Inserting and Deleting Records

When you open a table, it displays in Datasheet view in the work area. The Datasheet view displays the contents of a table in a column and row format similar to an Excel worksheet. Columns contain the field data, with the field names in the header row at the top of the table, and rows contain the records. A Record Navigation bar displays at the bottom of the screen just above the Status bar and contains buttons to navigate in the table. Figure 1.4 identifies the buttons and other elements on the Record Navigation bar.

To add a new record to the open table, make sure the HOME tab is active and then click the New button in the Records group. This moves the insertion point to the first field in the blank row at the bottom of the table and the *Current Record* box on the Record Navigation bar indicates what record you are creating (or editing). You can also create a new record by clicking the New (blank) record button on the Record Navigation bar.

When working in a table, press the Tab key to make the next field active or press Shift + Tab to make the previous field active. You can also click in the desired field using the mouse. When you begin typing data for the first field in the record, another row of cells is automatically inserted below the current row and a pencil icon displays in the record selector bar at the beginning of the current record. The pencil icon indicates that the record is being edited and that the changes to the data have not been saved. When you enter the data in the last field in the record and then move the insertion point out of the field, the pencil icon is removed, indicating that the data is saved.

When managing a table, you may need to delete a record when you no longer want the data in the record. One method for deleting a record is to click in one of the fields in the record, make sure the HOME tab is active, click the Delete button arrow, and then click *Delete Record* at the drop-down list. At the message that displays asking if you want to delete the record, click the Yes button. When you click in a field in a record, the Delete button displays in a dimmed manner unless specific data is selected.

When you are finished entering data in a record in a table, the data is automatically saved. Changes to the layout of a table, however, are not automatically saved. For example, if you delete a column in a table, when you close the table you will be asked if you are sure you want to delete the selected field.

▼ Quick Steps

Add a New Record
1. Open table.
2. Click New button on HOME tab.
3. Type data.
OR
1. Open table.
2. Click New (blank) record button on Record Navigation bar.
3. Type data.

Delete a Record
1. Open table.
2. Click Delete button arrow on HOME tab.
3. Click *Delete Record*.
4. Click Yes button.

New

Delete

Figure 1.4 Record Navigation Bar

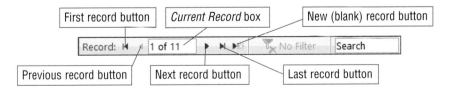

1. Open Access.
2. At the Access 2013 opening screen, click the <u>Open Other Files</u> hyperlink.
3. At the Open backstage area, double-click the *Computer* option or your SkyDrive (depending on where your AL1C1 folder is located).
4. At the Open dialog box, navigate to the AL1C1 folder on your storage medium or SkyDrive and then double-click *AL1-C1-PacTrek.accdb*.
5. Click the Enable Content button in the message bar if a security warning message appears. (The message bar will display immediately below the ribbon.)
6. With the database open, make sure the Navigation pane displays object types. (If it does not, click the Navigation pane menu bar and then click *Object Type* at the drop-down list.)
7. Double-click *Suppliers* in the Tables group in the Navigation pane. (This opens the table in Datasheet view.)

8. With the Suppliers table open and the HOME tab active, create a new record by completing the following steps:
   a. Click the New button in the Records group on the HOME tab. (This moves the insertion point to the first field in the blank record at the bottom of the table and the *Current Record* box in the Record Navigation bar indicates what record you are creating or editing.)
   b. Type 38. (This inserts *38* in the field immediately below *99*.)
   c. Press the Tab key (to make the next field active) and then type **Hadley Company**.
   d. Press the Tab key and then type **5845 Jefferson Street**.
   e. Press the Tab key and then type **Seattle**.
   f. Press the Tab key and then type **WA**.
   g. Press the Tab key and then type **98107**.
   h. Press the Tab key and then type **hcompany@emcp.net**.
   i. Press the Tab key and then type **Jurene Miller**.

SupplierID	SupplierName	StreetAddres	City	Prov/State	PostalCode	EmailAddres	Contact	Click to Add
10	Hopewell, Inc.	5600 Carver Ro	Port Moody	BC	V3H 1A4	hopewell@emc	Jacob Hopewel	
25	Langley Corporation	805 First Avenu	Burnaby	BC	V3J 1C9	langley@emcp.	Mandy Shin	
31	Sound Supplies	2104 Union Str	Seattle	WA	98105	ssupplies@emc	Regan Levine	
35	Emerald City Products	1059 Pike Stree	Seattle	WA	98102	ecproducts@er	Howard Greer	
42	Fraser Valley Products	3894 Old Yale F	Abbotsford	BC	V2S 1A9	fvproducts@en	Layla Adams	
54	Manning, Inc.	1039 South 22n	Vancouver	BC	V5K 1R1	manning@emc	Jack Silverstein	
68	Freedom Corporation	14 Fourth Aven	Vancouver	BC	V5K 2C7	freedom@emc	Opal Northwoc	
70	Rosewood, Inc.	998 North 42nc	Vancouver	BC	V5K 2N8	rosewood@em	Clint Rivas	
84	Macadam, Inc.	675 Third Stree	Vancouver	BC	V5K 2R9	macadam@em	Hans Reiner	
99	KL Distributions	402 Yukon Driv	Bellingham	WA	98435	kldist@emcp.n	Noland Dannisc	
38	Hadley Company	5845 Jefferson	Seattle	WA	98107	hcompany@en	Jurene Miller	

Steps 8b-8i

9. Close the Suppliers table by clicking the Close button in the work area.
10. Open the Products table by double-clicking *Products* in the Tables group in the Navigation pane. (This opens the table in Datasheet view.)
11. Insert two new records by completing the following steps:
    a. Click the New button in the Records group and then enter the data for a new record as shown in Figure 1.5. (See the record that begins with *901-S*.)

b. After you type the last field entry in the record for product number 901-S, press the Tab key. This moves the insertion point to the blank field below *901-S*.

c. Type the new record as shown in Figure 1.5. (See the record that begins with *917-S*.)

12. With the Products table open, delete a record by completing the following steps:

a. Click in the field containing the data *780-2*.

b. Click the Delete button arrow in the Records group (notice that the button displays in a dimmed manner) and then click *Delete Record* at the drop-down list.

c. At the message asking if you want to delete the record, click the Yes button.

13. Close the Products table by clicking the Close button in the work area.

Figure 1.5 Project 2a, Step 11

ProductID	Product	SupplierID	UnitsInStock	UnitsOnOrder	ReorderLevel	Click to Add
559-B	ICE snow goggles, bronze	68	22	0	20	
602-XR	Binoculars, 8 x 42	35	3	5	5	
602-XT	Binoculars, 10.5 x 45	35	5	0	4	
602-XX	Binoculars, 10 x 50	35	7	0	5	
647-1	Two-person dome tent	99	10	15	15	
648-2	Three-person dome tent	99	5	0	10	
651-1	K-2 one-person tent	99	8	0	10	
652-2	K-2 two-person tent	99	12	0	10	
780-2	Two-person tent	99	17	10	20	
804-50	AG freestyle snowboard, X50	70	7	0	10	
804-60	AG freestyle snowboard, X60	70	8	0	5	
897-L	Lang blunt snowboard	70	8	0	7	
897-W	Lang blunt snowboard, wide	70	4	0	3	
901-S	Solar battery pack	38	16	0	15	
917-S	Silo portable power pack	38	8	0	10	

Step 11

Inserting, Moving, and Deleting Fields

When managing a database, you may determine that you need to add additional information to a table. For example, you might decide that you want to insert a field for contact information, a field for cell phone numbers, or a field for the number of items in stock. To insert a new field in a table, open the table in Datasheet view and then click in the first field below the *Click to Add* heading. Type the desired data in the field for the first record, press the Down Arrow key to make the field below active, and then type the desired data for the second record. Continue in this manner until you have entered data in the new field for all records in the table. Instead of pressing the Down Arrow key to move the

Quick Steps

Insert a New Field
1. Open table.
2. Click in first field below *Click to Add* heading.
3. Type desired data.

Move a Field Column
1. Select column.
2. Position mouse pointer on heading.
3. Hold down left mouse button.
4. Drag to desired location.
5. Release mouse button.

Delete a Field Column
1. Click in field.
2. Click Delete button arrow on HOME tab.
3. Click *Delete Column.*
4. Click Yes button.

insertion point down to the next field, you can click in the desired field using the mouse or you can press the Tab key until the desired field is active.

A new field is added to the right of existing fields. Move a field by positioning the mouse pointer on the field heading until the pointer displays as a down-pointing black arrow and then clicking the left mouse button. This selects the entire column. With the field column selected, position the mouse pointer on the heading; hold down the left mouse button; drag to the left or right until a thick, black vertical line displays in the desired location; and then release the mouse button. The thick, black vertical line indicates where the field column will be positioned when you release the mouse button. In addition, the pointer displays with the outline of a gray box attached to it, indicating that you are performing a move operation.

Delete a field column in a manner similar to deleting a row. Click in one of the fields in the column, make sure the HOME tab is active, click the Delete button arrow, and then click *Delete Column* at the drop-down list. At the message that displays asking if you want to delete the column, click the Yes button.

Project 2b **Inserting, Moving, and Deleting Fields**   **Part 2 of 7**

1. With **AL1-C1-PacTrek.accdb** open, you decide to add a new field to the Suppliers table. Do this by completing the following steps:
   a. Double-click *Suppliers* in the Tables group in the Navigation pane.
   b. Click in the field immediately below the heading *Click to Add.*
   c. Type **(604) 555-3843** and then press the Down Arrow key on your keyboard.
   d. Type the remaining telephone numbers as shown at the right.

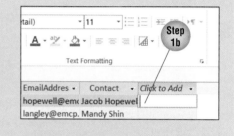

2. Move the field column so it is positioned immediately left of the *EmailAddress* field by completing the following steps:
   a. Position the mouse pointer on the heading *Field1* until the pointer displays as a down-pointing black arrow and then click the left mouse button. (This selects the column.)
   b. Position the mouse pointer on the heading. (The pointer displays as the normal, white arrow pointer.) Hold down the left mouse button; drag to the left until the thick, black vertical line displays immediately left of the *EmailAddress* field; and then release the mouse button.

3. You realize that you no longer need the supplier contact information so you decide to delete the field. Do this by completing the following steps:
   a. Position the mouse pointer on the heading *Contact* until the pointer displays as a down-pointing black arrow and then click the left mouse button. (This selects the column.)

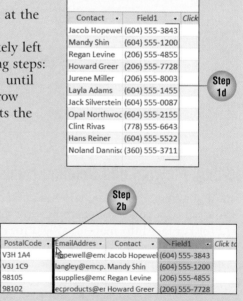

b. Click the Delete button arrow in the Records group and then click *Delete Column* at the drop-down list.

c. At the message asking if you want to permanently delete the selected fields, click the Yes button.

4. Close the Suppliers table. At the message that displays asking if you want to save the changes to the layout of the table, click the Yes button.

Hiding, Unhiding, Freezing, and Unfreezing Column Fields

You can hide columns of data in a table if you do not want the data visible or you want to make it easier to view two nonadjacent columns containing data you want to compare. To hide a column, click in any field in the column you want to hide, click the More button in the Records group on the HOME tab, and then click *Hide Fields* at the drop-down list. Hide adjacent columns by selecting the columns, clicking the More button in the Records group, and then clicking *Hide Fields* at the drop-down list. To unhide columns, click the More button and then click *Unhide Fields*. At the Unhide Columns dialog box that displays, insert a check mark in the check boxes for those columns you want to be visible.

More

Another method for comparing column fields side by side is to freeze a column. Freezing a column is also helpful when not all of the columns of data are visible at one time. To freeze a column, click in any field in the column you want to freeze, click the More button, and then click *Freeze Fields* at the drop-down list. To freeze adjacent columns, select the columns first, click the More button, and then click *Freeze Fields* at the drop-down list. To unfreeze all columns in a table, click the More button and then click *Unfreeze All Fields* at the drop-down list.

Changing Column Width

When entering data in the Suppliers and Products table, did you notice that not all of the data was visible? To remedy this, you can adjust the widths of columns so that all data is visible. You can adjust the width of one column in a table to accommodate the longest entry in the column by positioning the arrow pointer on the column boundary at the right side of the column until the pointer turns into a left-and-right-pointing arrow with a vertical line in the middle and then double-clicking the left mouse button.

Adjust the widths of adjacent columns by selecting the columns first and then double-clicking on one of the selected column boundaries. To select adjacent columns, position the arrow pointer on the first column heading until the pointer turns into a down-pointing black arrow, hold down the left mouse button, drag to the last column you want to adjust, and then release the mouse button. With the columns selected, double-click one of the column boundaries.

You can also adjust the width of a column by dragging the boundary to the desired position. To do this, position the arrow pointer on the column boundary until it turns into a left-and-right-pointing arrow with a vertical line in the middle, hold down the left mouse button, drag until the column is the desired width, and then release the mouse button.

▼ **Quick Steps**

Change a Table Column Width
Double-click column boundary.
OR
Select columns and then double-click column boundary.
OR
Drag column boundary to desired position.

Automatically adjust column widths in an Access table in the same manner as adjusting column widths in an Excel worksheet.

1. With **AL1-C1-PacTrek.accdb** open, open the Suppliers table.
2. Hide the *PostalCode* column by clicking in any field in the *PostalCode* column, clicking the More button in the Records group on the HOME tab, and then clicking *Hide Fields* at the drop-down list.
3. Unhide the column by clicking the More button and then clicking *Unhide Fields* at the drop-down list. At the Unhide Columns dialog box, click in the *PostalCode* check box to insert a check mark, and then click the Close button.

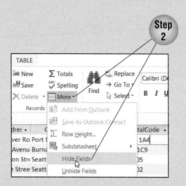

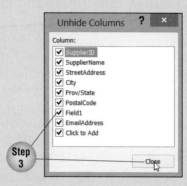

4. Adjust the width of the *SupplierID* column by positioning the arrow pointer on the column boundary at the right side of the *SupplierID* column until it turns into a left-and-right-pointing arrow with a vertical line in the middle and then double-clicking the left mouse button.

5. Adjust the width of the remaining columns by completing the following steps:
   a. Position the arrow pointer on the *SupplierName* heading until the pointer turns into a down-pointing black arrow, hold down the left mouse button, drag to the *EmailAddress* heading, and then release the mouse button.
   b. With the columns selected, double-click one of the column boundaries.
   c. Click in any field in the table to deselect the columns.
6. Increase the width of the *EmailAddress* column by positioning the arrow pointer on the column boundary at the right side of the *EmailAddress* column until it turns into a left-and-right-pointing arrow with a vertical line in the middle, holding down the left mouse button while dragging all of the way to the right side of the screen, and then releasing the mouse button. (Check the horizontal scroll bar located toward the bottom of the table and notice that the scroll bar contains a scroll box.)
7. Position the mouse pointer on the scroll box on the horizontal scroll bar and then drag to the left until the *SupplierID* field is visible.
8. Freeze the *SupplierID* column by clicking in any field in the *SupplierID* column, clicking the More button in the Records group, and then clicking *Freeze Fields* at the drop-down list.

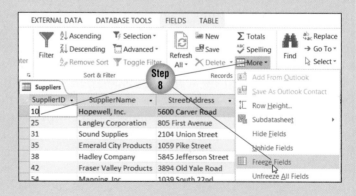

9. Using the mouse, drag the scroll box along the horizontal scroll to the right and then to the left and notice that the *SupplierID* column remains visible on the screen.
10. Unfreeze the column by clicking the More button in the Records group and then clicking *Unfreeze All Fields* at the drop-down list.
11. Double-click on the column boundary at the right side of the *EmailAddress* column.
12. Close the Suppliers table and click the Yes button at the message that asks if you want to save the changes to the layout.
13. Open the Products table and then complete steps similar to those in Step 5 to select and then adjust the column widths.
14. Close the Products table and click the Yes button at the message that asks if you want to save the changes to the layout.

Renaming and Deleting a Table

Managing tables might include actions such as renaming and deleting a table. Rename a table by right-clicking the table name in the Navigation pane, clicking *Rename* at the shortcut menu, typing the new name, and then pressing Enter. Delete a table from a database by right-clicking the table name in the Navigation pane, clicking the Delete button in the Records group on the HOME tab, and then clicking the Yes button at the message asking if you want to permanently delete the table. Another method is to right-click the table in the Navigation pane, click *Delete* at the shortcut menu, and then click the Yes at the message. If you are deleting a table from your computer's hard drive, the message asking if you want to permanently delete the table will not display. This is because Access automatically sends the deleted table to the Recycle Bin, where it can be retrieved if necessary.

▼ **Quick Steps**

Rename a Table
1. Right-click table name in Navigation pane.
2. Click *Rename*.
3. Type new name.
4. Press Enter

Delete a Table
1. Right-click table name in Navigation pane.
2. Click *Delete*.
3. Click Yes, if necessary.

Printing Tables ■■■■■■■■■■■■■■■■■■■■■■■■■■■■■■■

In some situations, you may want to print a table. To do this, open the table, click the FILE tab, and then click the *Print* option. This displays the Print backstage area, as shown in Figure 1.6. Click the Quick Print button to send the table directly to the printer without making any changes to the printer setup or the table formatting. Click the Print button to display the Print dialog box, where you can specify the printer, page range, and specific records to print. Click OK to close the dialog box and send the table to the printer. By default, Access prints a table on letter-size paper in portrait orientation.

▼ **Quick Steps**

Print a Table
1. Click FILE tab.
2. Click *Print* option.
3. Click Quick Print button.
OR
1. Click FILE tab.
2. Click *Print* option.
3. Click Print button.
4. Click OK.

Figure 1.6 Print Backstage Area

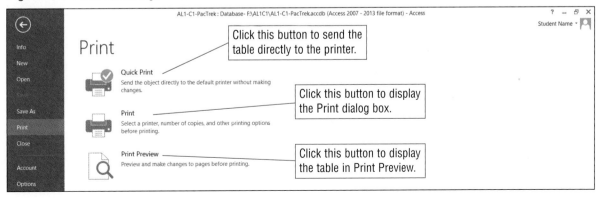

Previewing a Table

Quick Steps

Preview a Table
1. Click FILE tab.
2. Click *Print* option.
3. Click Print Preview button.

Print Preview

Print

Close Print Preview

Size

Margins

Before printing a table, you may want to display the table in Print Preview to see how the table will print on the page. To display a table in Print Preview, as shown in Figure 1.7, click the Print Preview button at the Print backstage area.

Use options in the Zoom group on the PRINT PREVIEW tab to increase or decrease the size of the page display. You can also change the size of the page display using the Zoom slider bar located at the right side of the Status bar. If your table spans more than one page, use buttons on the Navigation bar to display the next or previous page.

Print a table from Print Preview by clicking the Print button located at the left side of the PRINT PREVIEW tab. Click the Close Print Preview button if you want to close Print Preview and continue working in the table without printing it.

Changing Page Size and Margins

By default, Access prints a table in standard letter size (8.5 inches wide and 11 inches tall). Click the Size button in the Page Size group on the PRINT PREVIEW tab and a drop-down list displays with options for changing the page size to legal, executive, envelope, and so on. Access uses default top, bottom, left, and right margins of 1 inch. Change these default margins by clicking the Margins button in the Page Size group and then clicking one of the predesigned margin options.

Figure 1.7 Print Preview

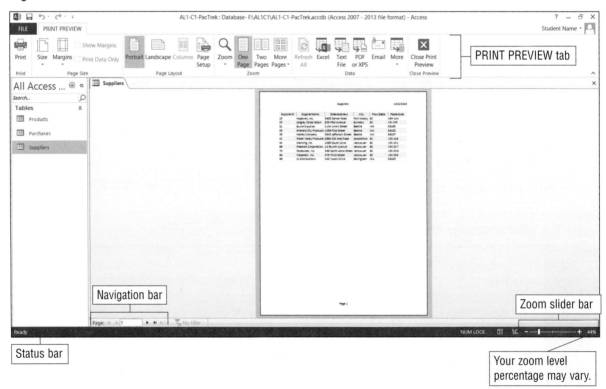

Changing Page Layout

The PRINT PREVIEW tab contains the Page Layout group with buttons for controlling how data is printed on the page. By default, Access prints a table in portrait orientation, which prints the text on the page so that it is taller than it is wide (like a page in this textbook). If a table contains a number of columns, changing to landscape orientation allows more columns to fit on a page. Landscape orientation rotates the printout to be wider than it is tall. To change from the default portrait orientation to landscape orientation, click the Landscape button in the Page Layout group on the PRINT PREVIEW tab.

Landscape

Click the Page Setup button in the Page Layout group and the Page Setup dialog box displays as shown in Figure 1.8. At the Page Setup dialog box with the Print Options tab selected, notice that the default margins are 1 inch. Change these defaults by typing a different number in the desired margin text box. By default, the table name prints at the top center of the page and the current date prints in the upper right corner of the page. In addition, the word *Page* followed by the page number prints at the bottom of the page. If you do not want the name of the table, date, and page number to print, remove the check mark from the *Print Headings* option at the Page Setup dialog box with the Print Options tab selected.

▼ Quick Steps

Display Page Setup Dialog Box
1. Click FILE tab.
2. Click *Print* option.
3. Click Print Preview button.
4. Click Page Setup button.

Page Setup

Click the Page tab at the Page Setup dialog box and the dialog box displays as shown in Figure 1.9. Change the orientation with options in the *Orientation* section and change the paper size with options in the *Paper* section. Click the *Size* option box arrow and a drop-down list displays with paper sizes similar to the options available at the *Size* button drop-down list in the Page Size group on the PRINT PREVIEW tab. Specify the printer with options in the *Printer for (table name)* section of the dialog box.

Figure 1.8 Page Setup Dialog Box with Print Options Tab Selected

Figure 1.9 Page Setup Dialog Box with Page Tab Selected

Enter measurements in these boxes to change the page margins.

Click this option to change the page orientation to landscape.

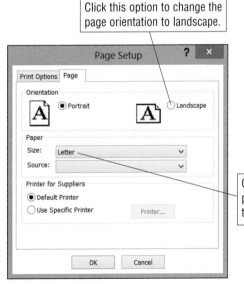

Change the paper size with this option.

Remove the check mark from this check box if you do not want the table name, date, and page number printed.

1. With **AL1-C1-PacTrek.accdb** open, open the Suppliers table.
2. Preview and then print the Suppliers table in landscape orientation by completing the following steps:

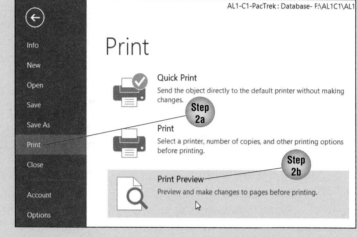

   a. Click the FILE tab and then click the *Print* option.
   b. At the Print backstage area, click the Print Preview button.
   c. Click the Two Pages button in the Zoom group on the PRINT PREVIEW tab. (This displays two pages of the table.)
   d. Click the Zoom button arrow in the Zoom group on the PRINT PREVIEW tab and then click *75%* at the drop-down list.

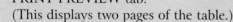

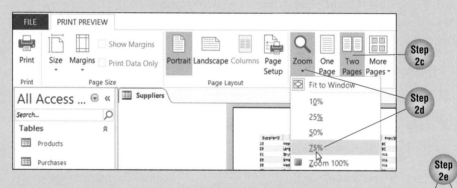

   e. Position the arrow pointer on the Zoom slider bar button that displays at the right side of the Status bar, hold down the left mouse button, drag to the right until *100%* displays at the right of the Zoom slider bar, and then release the mouse button.
   f. Return the display to a full page by clicking the One Page button in the Zoom group on the PRINT PREVIEW tab.
   g. Click the Margins button in the Page Size group on the PRINT PREVIEW tab and then click the *Narrow* option at the drop-down list. (Notice how the data will print on the page with the narrow margins.)
   h. Change the margins back to the default by clicking the Margins button in the Page Size group and then clicking the *Normal* option at the drop-down list.
   i. Change to landscape orientation by clicking the Landscape button in the Page Layout group. (Check the Next Page button on the Record Navigation bar and notice that it is dimmed. This indicates that the table will print on only one page.)

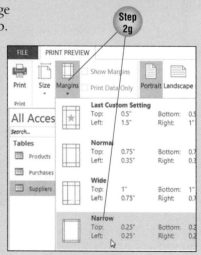

j. Print the table by clicking the Print button located at the left side of the PRINT PREVIEW tab and then clicking the OK button at the Print dialog box.

3. Close the Suppliers table.

4. Open the Products table and then print the table by completing the following steps:

   a. Click the FILE tab and then click the *Print* option.

   b. At the Print backstage area, click the Print Preview button.

   c. Click the Page Setup button in the Page Layout group on the PRINT PREVIEW tab. (This displays the Page Setup dialog box with the Print Options tab selected.)

   d. At the Page Setup dialog box, click the Page tab.

   e. Click the *Landscape* option.

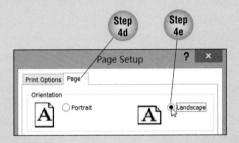

   f. Click the Print Options tab.

   g. Select the current measurement in the *Top* text box and then type 0.5.

   h. Select the current measurement in the *Bottom* text box and then type 0.5.

   i. Select the current measurement in the *Left* text box and then type 1.5.

   j. Click OK to close the dialog box.

   k. Click the Print button on the PRINT PREVIEW tab and then click the OK button at the Print dialog box. (This table will print on two pages.)

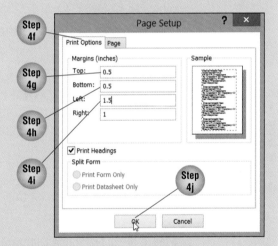

5. Close the Products table.

6. Rename the Purchases table by right-clicking *Purchases* in the Navigation pane, clicking *Rename* at the shortcut menu, typing **Orders**, and then pressing Enter.

7. Delete the Orders table by right-clicking *Orders* in the Navigation pane and then clicking *Delete* at the shortcut menu. If a message displays asking if you want to permanently delete the table, click Yes.

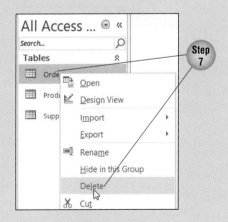

Designing a Table ■■■■■■■■■■■■■■■■■■■■■■■■■■■■■■

Tables are the first objects created in a new database and all other objects in a database rely on tables for data. Designing a database involves planning the number of tables needed and the fields that will be included in each table. Each table in a database should contain information about only one subject. For example, the Suppliers table in the AL1-C1-PacTrek.accdb database contains data only about suppliers and the Products table contains data only about products.

Database designers often create a visual representation of the database's structure in a diagram similar to the one shown in Figure 1.10. Each table is represented by a box with the table name at the top. Within each box, the fields that will be stored in the table are listed with the field names that will be used when the table is created.

Notice that one field in each table has an asterisk next to its name. The field with the asterisk is called the ***primary key***. A primary key holds data that uniquely identifies each record in a table and is usually an identification number. The lines drawn between each table in Figure 1.10 are called ***join lines,*** and they represent links established between tables (called ***relationships***) so that data can be extracted from one or more tables. Notice the join lines point to a common field name included in each table that is to be linked. (You will learn how to join, or relate, tables in Chapter 2.) A database with related tables is called a ***relational database***.

Notice the join line in the database diagram that connects the *SupplierID* field in the Suppliers table with the *SupplierID* field in the Products table and another join line that connects the *SupplierID* field in the Suppliers table with the *SupplierID* field in the Orders table. In the database diagram, a join line connects the *ProductID* field in the Products table with the *ProductID* field in the Orders table.

Organize data in tables to minimize or eliminate duplication.

When designing a database, you need to consider certain design principles. The first principle is to reduce redundant (duplicate) data, for several reasons. Redundant data increases the amount of data entry required, increases the chances for errors and inconsistencies, and takes up additional storage space. The Products table contains a *SupplierID* field and that field reduces the redundant

Figure 1.10 Database Diagram

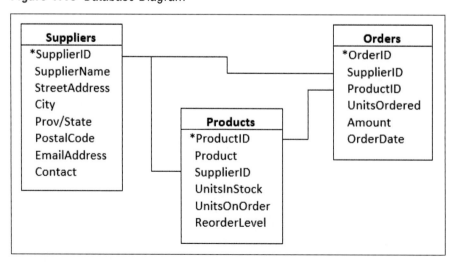

data needed in the table. For example, rather than typing the supplier information in the Suppliers table *and* the Products table, you type the information once in the Suppliers table and then "join" the tables with the connecting field *SupplierID*. If you need information on suppliers as well as specific information about products, you can draw the information into one object, such as a query or report using data from both tables. When you create the Orders table, you will use the *SupplierID* field and the *ProductID* field rather than typing all of the information for the suppliers and the product description. Typing a two-letter unique identifier number for a supplier greatly reduces the amount of typing required to create the Orders table. Inserting the *ProductID* field in the Orders table eliminates the need to type the product description for each order; instead, you type a unique five-, six-, or seven-digit identifier number.

Creating a Table

Creating a new table generally involves determining fields, assigning a data type to each field, modifying properties, designating the primary key, and naming the table. This process is referred to as ***defining the table structure***.

The first step in creating a table is to determine the fields. A ***field***, commonly called a column, is one piece of information about a person, place, or item. Each field contains data about one aspect of the table subject, such as a company name or product number. All fields for one unit, such as a customer or product, are considered a ***record***. For example, in the Suppliers table in the AL1-C1-PacTrek.accdb database, a record is all of the information pertaining to one supplier. A collection of records becomes a ***table***.

When designing a table, determine fields for information to be included on the basis of how you plan to use the data. When organizing fields, be sure to consider not only current needs for the data but also any future needs. For example, a company may need to keep track of customer names, addresses, and telephone numbers for current mailing lists. In the future, the company may want to promote a new product to customers who purchase a specific type of product. For this information to be available at a later date, a field that identifies product type must be included in the database. When organizing fields, consider all potential needs for the data but also try to keep the fields logical and manageable.

You can create a table in Access in Datasheet view or in Design view. To create a table in Datasheet view, open the desired database (or create a new database), click the CREATE tab, and then click the Table button in the Tables group. This inserts a blank table in the work area with the tab labeled *Table1*, as shown in Figure 1.11. Notice the column with the field name *ID* has been created automatically. Access creates *ID* as an AutoNumber field in which the field value is assigned automatically by Access as you enter each record. In many tables, you can use this AutoNumber field to create the unique identifier for the table. For example, in Project 2e, you will create an Orders table and use the ID AutoNumber field to assign automatically a number to each order, since each order must contain a unique number.

Table

When creating a new field (column), determine the type of data you will insert in the field. For example, one field might contain text such as a name or product description, another field might contain an amount of money, and another might contain a date. The data type defines the type of information Access will allow to be entered into the field. For example, Access will not allow alphabetic

Figure 1.11 Blank Table

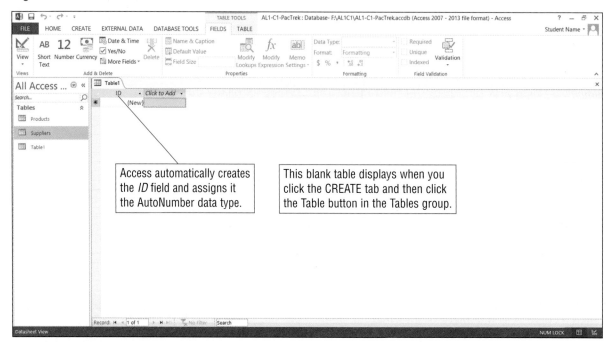

Access automatically creates the *ID* field and assigns it the AutoNumber data type.

This blank table displays when you click the CREATE tab and then click the Table button in the Tables group.

More Fields

characters to be entered into a field with a data type set to Date & Time. The Add & Delete group on the TABLE TOOLS FIELDS tab contains five buttons for assigning data types plus a More Fields button. Descriptions of the five data types assigned by the buttons are provided in Table 1.3.

Table 1.3 Data Types

Data Type Button	Description
Short Text	Alphanumeric data up to 255 characters in length—for example, a name, an address, or a value such as a telephone number or social security number that is used as an identifier and not for calculating.
Number	Positive or negative values that can be used in calculations; not to be used for values that will calculate monetary amounts (see Currency).
Currency	Values that involve money; Access will not round off during calculations.
Date & Time	Used to ensure dates and times are entered and sorted properly.
Yes/No	Data in the field will be either *Yes* or *No*; *True* or *False*, *On* or *Off*.

In Project 2e, you will create the Orders table, as shown in Figure 1.12. Looking at the diagram in Figure 1.10, you will assign the following data types to the columns:

OrderID: AutoNumber (Access automatically assigns this data type to the first column)

SupplierID: Short Text (the supplier numbers are identifiers, not numbers for calculating)

ProductID: Short Text (the product numbers are identifiers, not numbers for calculating)

UnitsOrdered: Number (the unit numbers are values for calculating)

Amount: Currency

OrderDate: Date & Time

When you click a data type button, Access inserts a field to the right of the *ID* field and selects the field heading *Field1*. Type a name for the field; press the Enter key; and Access selects the next field column, named *Click to Add*, and displays a drop-down list of data types. This drop-down list contains the same five data types as the buttons in the Add & Delete group as well as additional data types. Click the desired data type at the drop-down list, type the desired field name, and then press Enter. Continue in this manner until you have entered all field names for the table. When naming a field, consider the following guidelines:

- Each field must have a unique name.
- The name should describe the contents of the field.
- A field name can contain up to 64 characters.
- A field name can contain letters and numbers. Some symbols are permitted but others are excluded, so avoid using symbols other than the underscore (to separate words) and the number symbol (to indicate an identifier number).
- Do not use spaces in field names. Although a space is an accepted character, most database designers avoid using spaces in field names and object names. Use field compound words for field names or the underscore character as a word separator. For example, a field name for a person's last name could be named *LastName*, *Last_Name*, or *LName*.
- Abbreviate field names so that they are as short as possible but still easily understood. For example, a field such as *CompanyName* could be shortened to *CoName* and a field such as *EmailAddress* could be shortened to *Email*.

Avoid using spaces in field names.

Project 2e   **Creating a Table and Entering Data**   **Part 5 of 7**

1. With **AL1-C1-PacTrek.accdb** open, create a new table and specify data types and column headings by completing the following steps:
   a. Click the CREATE tab.
   b. Click the Table button in the Tables group.
   c. Click the Short Text button in the Add & Delete group.

d. With the *Field1* column heading selected, type **SupplierID** and then press the Enter key. (This displays a drop-down list of data types below the *Click to Add* heading.)

e. Click the *Short Text* option at the drop-down list.

f. Type **ProductID** and then press Enter.

g. Click *Number* at the drop-down list, type **UnitsOrdered**, and then press Enter.

h. Click *Currency* at the drop-down list, type **Amount**, and then press Enter.

i. Click *Date & Time* at the drop-down list and then type **OrderDate**. (Do not press the Enter key since this is the last column in the table.)

2. Enter the first record in the table, as shown in Figure 1.12, by completing the following steps:

a. Click twice in the first field below the *SupplierID* column heading. (The first time you click the mouse button, the row is selected. Clicking the second time makes active only the field below *SupplierID*.)

b. Type the data in the fields as shown in Figure 1.12. Press the Tab key to move to the next field or press Shift + Tab to move to the previous field. Access will automatically insert the next number in the sequence in the first column (the *ID* column). When typing the money amounts in the *Amount* column, you do not need to type the dollar sign or the comma. Access will automatically insert them when you make the next field active.

3. When the 14 records have been entered, click the Save button on the Quick Access toolbar.

4. At the Save As dialog box, type **Orders** and then press the Enter key. (This saves the table with the name *Orders*.)

5. Close the Orders table by clicking the Close button located in the upper right corner of the work area.

Figure 1.12 Project 2e

ID	SupplierID	ProductID	UnitsOrdered	Amount	OrderDate	Click to Add
1	54	101-S3	10	$1,137.50	1/5/2015	
2	68	209-L	25	$173.75	1/5/2015	
3	68	209-XL	25	$180.00	1/5/2015	
4	68	209-XXL	20	$145.80	1/5/2015	
5	68	210-M	15	$97.35	1/5/2015	
6	68	210-L	25	$162.25	1/5/2015	
7	31	299-M2	10	$887.90	1/19/2015	
8	31	299-M3	10	$887.90	1/19/2015	
9	31	299-M5	10	$887.90	1/19/2015	
10	31	299-W1	8	$602.32	1/19/2015	
11	31	299-W3	10	$752.90	1/19/2015	
12	31	299-W4	10	$752.90	1/19/2015	
13	31	299-W5	10	$752.90	1/19/2015	
14	35	602-XR	5	$2,145.00	1/19/2015	
*	(New)		0	$0.00		

Renaming a Field Heading

When you click a data type button or click a data type at the data type drop-down list, the default heading (such as *Field1*) is automatically selected. You can type a name for the field heading that takes the place of the selected text. If you create a field heading and then decide to change the name, right-click the heading, click *Rename Field* at the shortcut menu (which selects the current column heading), and then type the new name.

Inserting a Name, Caption, and Description

When you create a table that others will use, consider providing additional information so users understand the fields in the table and what should be entered in each one. Along with the field heading name, you can provide a caption and description for each field with options at the Enter Field Properties dialog box, shown in Figure 1.13. Display this dialog by clicking the Name & Caption button in the Properties group on the TABLE TOOLS FIELDS tab.

Name & Caption

At the Enter Field Properties dialog box, type the desired name for the field heading in the *Name* text box. If you want a more descriptive name for the field heading, type the heading in the *Caption* text box. The text you type will display as the field heading but the actual field name will still be part of the table structure. Creating a caption is useful if you abbreviate a field name or want to show spaces between words in a field name. A caption also provides more information for others using the database. The name is what Access uses for the table and the caption is what displays to users.

The *Description* text box is another source for providing information about the field to others using the database. Type information in the text box that specifies what should be entered in the field. The text you type in the *Description* text box displays at the left side of the Status bar when a field in the column is active. For example, if you type *Enter the total amount of the order* in the *Description* text box for the *Amount* field column, that text will display at the left side of the Status bar when a field in the column is active.

Figure 1.13 Enter Field Properties Dialog Box

Type in the *Caption* text box a more descriptive name for the field heading.

Type information in the *Description* text box that specifies what should be entered in the field.

Enter Field Properties	?	×
Name	SupplierID	
Caption		
Description		
	OK	Cancel

1. With **AL1-C1-PacTrek.accdb** open, open the Orders table.
2. Access automatically named the first field *ID*. You want to make the heading more descriptive so you decide to rename the heading. To do this, right-click the *ID* heading and then click *Rename Field* at the drop-down list.
3. Type **OrderID** and then press the Enter key.
4. To provide more information for others using the table, you decide to add information for the *SupplierID* field by creating a caption and description. To do this, complete the following steps:
   a. Click the *SupplierID* field heading. (This selects the entire column.)
   b. Click the TABLE TOOLS FIELDS tab.
   c. Click the Name & Caption button in the Properties group. (At the Enter Field Properties dialog box, notice that *SupplierID* is already inserted in the *Name* text box.)
   d. At the Enter Field Properties dialog box, click in the *Caption* text box and then type **Supplier Number**.
   e. Click in the *Description* text box and then type **Supplier identification number**.
   f. Click OK to close the dialog box. (Notice that the field name now displays as *Supplier Number*. The field name is still *SupplierID* but what displays is *Supplier Number*.)

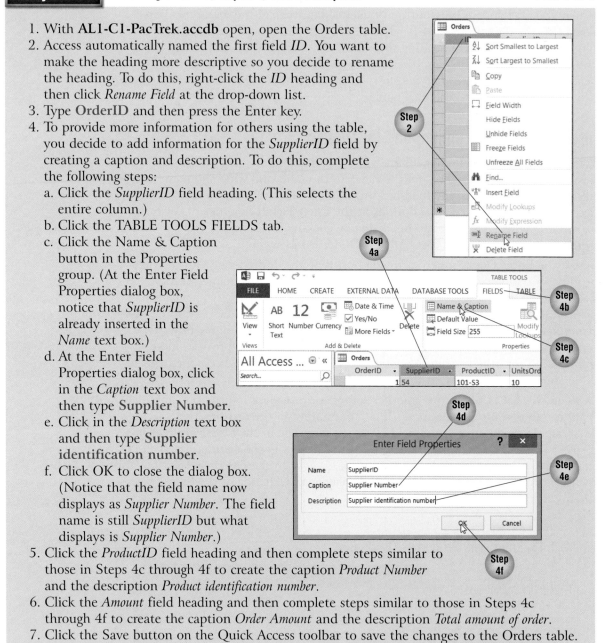

5. Click the *ProductID* field heading and then complete steps similar to those in Steps 4c through 4f to create the caption *Product Number* and the description *Product identification number*.
6. Click the *Amount* field heading and then complete steps similar to those in Steps 4c through 4f to create the caption *Order Amount* and the description *Total amount of order*.
7. Click the Save button on the Quick Access toolbar to save the changes to the Orders table.
8. Close the Orders table.

Inserting Quick Start Fields

Short Text

The Add & Delete group on the TABLE TOOLS FIELDS tab contains buttons for specifying data types. You used the Short Text button to specify the data type for the *SupplierID* field when you created the Orders table. You also used the field heading drop-down list to choose a data type. In addition to these two methods, you can specify a data type by clicking the More Fields button in the Add & Delete group on the TABLE TOOLS FIELDS tab. When you click this button, a drop-down list displays with data types grouped into categories such as *Basic Types*, *Number*, *Date and Time*, *Yes/No*, and *Quick Start*.

The options in the *Quick Start* category not only define a data type but also assign a field name. Additionally, with options in the *Quick Start* category, you can add a group of related fields in one step. For example, if you click the *Name* option in the *Quick Start* category, Access inserts the *LastName* field in one column and the *FirstName* field in the next column. Both fields are automatically assigned a short text data type. If you click the *Address* option in the *Quick Start* category, Access inserts five fields, including *Address*, *City*, *StateProvince*, *ZIPPostal*, and *CountryRegion*—all with the short text data type assigned.

Assigning a Default Value

The Properties group on the TABLE TOOLS FIELDS tab contains additional buttons for defining field properties in a table. If most records in a table are likely to contain the same field value in a column, consider inserting that value by default. Do this by clicking the Default Value button in the Properties group. At the Expression Builder dialog box, type the desired default value and then click OK.

Default Value

For example, in Project 2g, you will create a new table in the AL1-C1-PacTrek database containing information on customers, most of whom live in Vancouver, British Columbia. You will create a default value of *Vancouver* for the *City* field and a default value of *BC* for the *Prov/State* field. You can replace the default value with different text, so if a customer lives in Abbotsford instead of Vancouver, simply type *Abbotsford* in the *City* field instead.

Assigning a Field Size

The default field size property varies depending on the data type. For example, if you assign a short text data type to a field, the maximum length of the data you can enter in the field is 255 characters. You can decrease this number depending on what data will be entered in the field. You can also change the field size number to control how much data is entered and help reduce errors. For example, if you have a field for states and you want a two-letter state abbreviation inserted in each field in the column, you can assign a field size of 2 characters. If someone entering data into the table tries to type more than two letters, Access will not accept the additional text. To change field size, click in the *Field Size* text box in the Properties group on the TABLE TOOLS FIELDS tab and then type the desired number.

Changing the AutoNumber Field

Access automatically applies the AutoNumber data type to the first field in a table and assigns a unique number to each record in the table. In many cases, letting Access automatically assign a number to a record is a good idea. Some situations may arise, however, when you want the unique value in the first field to be something other than a number.

If you try to change the AutoNumber data type in the first column by clicking one of the data type buttons in the Add & Delete group on the TABLE TOOLS FIELDS tab, Access creates another field. To change the AutoNumber data type for the first field, click the down-pointing arrow at the right side of the *Data Type* option box in the Formatting group on the TABLE TOOLS FIELDS tab and then click the desired data type at the drop-down list.

1. The owners of Pacific Trek have decided to publish a semiannual product catalog and have asked customers who want to receive the catalog to fill out a form and include on the form whether or not they want to receive notices of upcoming sales in addition to the catalog. Create a table to store the data for customers by completing the following steps:

   a. With **AL1-C1-PacTrek.accdb** open, click the CREATE tab.
   b. Click the Table button in the Tables group.
   c. With the *Click to Add* field heading active, click the More Fields button in the Add & Delete group on the TABLE TOOLS FIELDS tab.
   d. Scroll down the drop-down list and then click *Name* located in the *Quick Start* category. (This inserts the *Last Name* and *First Name* field headings in the table.)
   e. Click the *Click to Add* field heading that displays immediately right of the *First Name* field heading. (The data type drop-down list displays. You are going to use the More Fields button rather than the drop-down list to create the next fields.)
   f. Click the More Fields button, scroll down the drop-down list, and then click *Address* in the *Quick Start* category. (This inserts five more fields in the table.)
   g. Scroll to the right in the table to display the *Click to Add* field heading that follows the *Country Region* column heading. (You can scroll in the table using the horizontal scroll bar that displays to the right of the Record Navigation bar.)
   h. Click the *Click to Add* field heading and then click *Yes/No* at the drop-down list.

   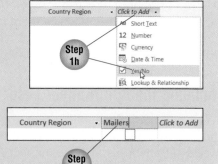

   i. With the name *Field1* selected, type **Mailers**. (When entering records in the table, you will insert a check mark in the field check box if a customer wants to receive sales promotion mailers. If a customer does not want to receive the mailers, you will leave the check box blank.)
2. Rename and create a caption and description for the *ID* column heading by completing the following steps:
   a. Scroll to the beginning of the table and then click the *ID* column heading. (You can scroll in the table using the horizontal scroll bar that displays to the right of the Record Navigation bar.)
   b. Click the Name & Caption button in the Properties group on the TABLE TOOLS FIELDS tab.

c. At the Enter Field Properties dialog box, select the text *ID* that displays in the *Name* text box and then type **CustomerID**.

d. Press the Tab key and then type **Customer Number** in the *Caption* text box.

e. Press the Tab key and then type **Access will automatically assign the record the next number in the sequence.**

f. Click OK to close the Enter Field Properties dialog box. (Notice the description that displays at the left side of the Status bar.)

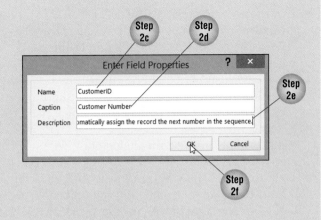

3. Add a description to the *Last Name* column by completing the following steps:

a. Click the *Last Name* column heading.

b. Click the Name & Caption button in the Properties group.

c. At the Enter Field Properties dialog box notice that Access named the field *LastName* but provided the caption *Last Name*. You do not want to change the name and caption so press the Tab key twice to make the *Description* text box active and then type **Customer last name.**

d. Click OK to close the dialog box.

4. You know that a customer's last name will not likely exceed 30 characters, so you decide to limit the field size. To do this, click in the *Field Size* text box in the Properties group (this selects *255*), type **30**, and then press the Enter key.

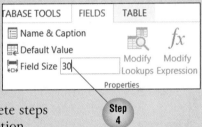

5. Click the *First Name* column heading and then complete steps similar to those in Steps 3 and 4 to create the description *Customer first name* and change the field size to 30 characters.

6. Since most of Pacific Trek's customers live in the city of Vancouver, you decide to make it the default field value. To do this, complete the following steps:

a. Click the *City* column heading.

b. Click the Default Value button in the Properties group.

c. At the Expression Builder dialog box, type **Vancouver**.

d. Click the OK button to close the dialog box.

7. Change the name of the *State Province* field name and insert a default value by completing the following steps:

a. Right-click the *State Province* column heading and then click *Rename Field* at the shortcut menu.

b. Type **Province**.

c. Click the Default Value button in the Properties group.

d. Type **BC** in the Expression Builder dialog box and then click the OK button.

8. Click the *ZIP Postal* column heading and then limit the field size to 7 characters by clicking

in the *Field Size* text box (which selects *255*), typing 7, and then pressing the Enter key.

9. Since most customers want to be sent the sales promotional mailers, you decide to insert a check mark as the default value in the check boxes in the *Yes/No* column. To do this, complete the following steps:
   a. Click the *Mailers* field heading.
   b. Click the Default Value button in the Properties group.
   c. At the Expression Builder dialog box, press the Backspace key two times to delete *No* and then type Yes.
   d. Click OK to close the dialog box.

10. Delete the *Country Region* field by clicking the *Country Region* field heading and then clicking the Delete button in the Add & Delete group.

11. Save the table by completing the following steps:
    a. Click the Save button on the Quick Access toolbar.
    b. At the Save As dialog box, type Customers and then press Enter.

12. Enter the six records in the table shown in Figure 1.14. To remove a check mark in the *Mailers* column, press the spacebar.

13. Adjust the column widths to accommodate the longest entry in each column by completing the following steps:
    a. Position the arrow pointer on the *Customer Number* field heading until the pointer turns into a down-pointing black arrow, hold down the left mouse button, drag to the *Mailers* field heading, and then release the mouse button.
    b. With the columns selected, double-click one of the column boundaries.

14. Click the Save button to save the Customers table.

15. Print the Customers table by completing the following steps:
    a. Click the FILE tab and then click the *Print* option.
    b. At the Print backstage area, click the Print Preview button.
    c. Click the Landscape button in the Page Layout group on the PRINT PREVIEW tab.
    d. Click the Print button that displays at the left side of the PRINT PREVIEW tab.
    e. At the Print dialog box, click OK.

16. Close the Customers table.

17. Open the Orders table.

18. Automatically adjust the column widths to accommodate the longest entry in each column.

19. Click the Save button to save the Orders table.

20. Print the table in landscape orientation (refer to Step 15) and then close the table.

21. Close **AL1-C1-PacTrek.accdb**.

Figure 1.14 Project 2g

Customer Number	Last Name	First Name	Address	City	State Province	ZIP Postal	Mailers
1	Blakely	Mathias	7433 224th Ave. E.	Vancouver	BC	V5K 2M7	✔
2	Donato	Antonio	18225 Victoria Dr.	Vancouver	BC	V5K 1H4	
3	Girard	Stephanie	430 Deer Lake Pl.	Burnaby	BC	V3J 1E4	✔
4	Hernandez	Angelica	1233 E. 59th Ave.	Vancouver	BC	V5K 3H3	✔
5	Ives-Keller	Shane	9055 Gilbert Rd.	Richmond	BC	V6Y 1B2	
6	Kim	Keung	730 West Broadway	Vancouver	BC	V5K 5B2	✔
* (New)				Vancouver	BC		✔

Chapter Summary

- Microsoft Access is a database management system software program that can organize, store, maintain, retrieve, sort, and print all types of business data.

- In Access, open an existing database by clicking the Open Other Files hyperlink at the Access 2013 opening screen. At the Open backstage area, double-click your SkyDrive or the *Computer* option. At the Open dialog box, navigate to the location of the database and then double-click the desired database.

- Some common objects found in a database include tables, queries, forms, and reports.

- The Navigation pane displays at the left side of the Access screen and displays the objects that are contained in the database.

- Open a database object by double-clicking the object in the Navigation pane. Close an object by clicking the Close button that displays in the upper right corner of the work area.

- When a table is open, the Record Navigation bar displays at the bottom of the screen and contains buttons for displaying records in the table.

- Insert a new record in a table by clicking the New button in the Records group on the HOME tab or by clicking the New (blank) record button in the Record Navigation bar. Delete a record by clicking in a field in the record you want to delete, clicking the Delete button arrow on the HOME tab, and then clicking *Delete Record* at the drop-down list.

- To add a column to a table, click the first field below the *Click to Add* column heading and then type the desired data. To move a column, select the column and then use the mouse to drag a thick, black, vertical line (representing the column) to the desired location. To delete a column, click the column heading, click the Delete button arrow, and then click *Delete Column* at the drop-down list.

- Data you enter in a table is automatically saved while changes to the layout of a table are not automatically saved.

- Hide, unhide, freeze, and unfreeze columns with options at the More button drop-down list. Display this list by clicking the More button in the Records group on the HOME tab.

- Adjust the width of a column (or selected columns) to accommodate the longest entry by double-clicking the column boundary. You can also adjust the width of a column by dragging the column boundary.

- Rename a table by right-clicking the table name in the Navigation pane, clicking *Rename*, and then typing the new name. Delete a table by right-clicking the table name in the Navigation pane and then clicking *Delete*.

- Print a table by clicking the FILE tab, clicking the *Print* option, and then clicking the Quick Print button. You can also preview a table before printing by clicking the Print Preview button at the Print backstage area.

- With buttons and option on the PRINT PREVIEW tab, you can change the page size, orientation, and margins.

- The first principle in database design is to reduce redundant data, because redundant data increases the amount of data entry required, increases the chances for errors, and takes up additional storage space.

- A data type defines the type of data Access will allow in the field. Assign a data type to a field with buttons in the Add & Delete group on the TABLE TOOLS

FIELDS tab, by clicking an option from the column heading drop-down list, or with options at the More button drop-down list.

- Rename a column heading by right-clicking the heading, clicking *Rename Field* at the shortcut menu, and then typing the new name.
- Type a name, caption, and description for a column with options at the Enter Field Properties dialog box.
- Use options in the *Quick Start* category in the More Fields button drop-down list to define a data type and assign a field name to a group of related fields.
- Insert a default value in a column with the Default Value button and assign a field size with the *Field Size* text box in the Properties group on the TABLE TOOLS FIELDS tab.
- Use the *Data Type* option box in the Formatting group on the TABLE TOOLS FIELDS tab to change the AutoNumber data type for the first column in a table.

Commands Review

FEATURE	RIBBON TAB, GROUP/OPTION	BUTTON, OPTION	KEYBOARD SHORTCUT
close Access		⊠	Alt + F4
close database	FILE, *Close*		
create table	CREATE, Tables	▦	
Currency data type	TABLE TOOLS FIELDS, Add & Delete	▣	
Date & Time data type	TABLE TOOLS FIELDS, Add & Delete	▦	
delete column	HOME, Records	⊠, *Delete Column*	
delete record	HOME, Records	⊠, *Delete Record*	
Enter Field Properties dialog box	TABLE TOOLS FIELDS, Properties	▤	
Expression Builder dialog box	TABLE TOOLS FIELDS, Properties	▦	
freeze column	HOME, Records	▦, *Freeze Fields*	
hide column	HOME, Records	▦, *Hide Fields*	
landscape orientation	FILE, *Print*	Print Preview, ▧	
new record	HOME, Records	▦	Ctrl + +
next field			Tab
Number data type	TABLE TOOLS FIELDS, Add & Delete	12	
Page Setup dialog box	FILE, *Print*	Print Preview, ▧	

FEATURE	RIBBON TAB, GROUP/OPTION	BUTTON, OPTION	KEYBOARD SHORTCUT
page size	FILE, *Print*	Print Preview,	
page margins	FILE, *Print*	Print Preview,	
portrait orientation	FILE, *Print*	Print Preview,	
previous field			Shift + Tab
Print backstage area	FILE, *Print*		
Print dialog box	FILE, *Print*	Print	Ctrl + P
Print Preview	FILE, *Print*	Print Preview	
Short Text data type	TABLE TOOLS FIELDS, Add & Delete	AB	
unfreeze column	HOME, Records	, *Unfreeze Fields*	
unhide column	HOME, Records	, *Unhide Fields*	
Yes/No data type	TABLE TOOLS FIELDS, Add & Delete	☑	

Concepts Check   Test Your Knowledge

Completion: In the space provided at the right, indicate the correct term, symbol, or command.

1. Click this template at the Access 2013 opening screen to create a new database. _____

2. This toolbar contains buttons for commonly used commands. _____

3. This displays the names of objects within a database grouped by categories. _____

4. When you open a table, it displays in this view. _____

5. Use buttons on this bar to navigate in a table. _____

6. To add a new record, click the New button in this group on the HOME tab. _____

7. At the Print backstage area, click this button to send the table directly to the printer. _____

8. The Landscape button is located in this group on the PRINT PREVIEW tab. _____

9. All fields for one unit, such as an employee or customer, are considered to be this. _____

10. Assign this data type to values that involve money. _____

11. Click this button in the Properties group on the TABLE TOOLS FIELDS tab to display the Enter Field Properties dialog box. _____

12. With options in this category in the More Fields button drop-down list, you can define a data type and also assign a field name. _____

13. If you want to assign the same field value to a column, click this button to display the Expression Builder dialog box and then type the desired value. _____

Skills Check   Assess Your Performance

The database designer for Griffin Technologies has created the database diagram shown in Figure 1.15 to manage data about company employees. You will open the Griffin database and maintain and create tables that follow the diagram.

Figure 1.15 Griffin Technologies Database Diagram

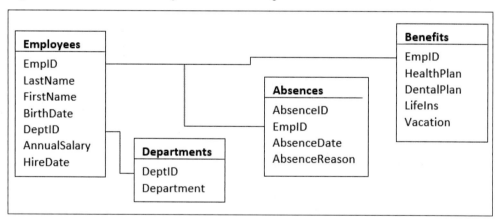

Assessment

1 INSERTING AND DELETING ROWS AND COLUMNS

1. In Access, open **AL1-C1-Griffin.accdb** from the AL1C1 folder on your storage medium and enable the contents.
2. Double-click *Employees* in the Tables group in the Navigation pane.
3. Delete the record for Scott Jorgensen (employee number 1025).
4. Delete the record for Leanne Taylor (employee number 1060).

5. Insert the following records:

EmpID: **1010**
LastName: **Harrington**
FirstName: **Tyler**
Birthdate: **9/7/1976**
AnnualSalary: **$53,350**
HireDate: **10/1/2010**

EmpID: **1052**
LastName: **Reeves**
FirstName: **Carrie**
Birthdate: **12/4/1978**
AnnualSalary: **$38,550**
HireDate: **10/1/2012**

6. Close the Employees table.
7. Looking at the database diagram in Figure 1.15, you realize that the Employees table includes a *DeptID* field. Open the Employees table, insert the new field in the Employees table, and name it *DeptID*. Change the field size to 2 characters (since department abbreviations are only one or two letters in length). At the message telling you that some data may be lost, click the Yes button. Type the department identification for each record as shown below (the records are listed from left to right):

1001: HR	1002: RD	1003: IT	1005: DP	1010: DP
1013: RD	1015: HR	1020: A	1023: IT	1030: PR
1033: A	1040: DP	1043: HR	1045: RD	1050: IT
1052: PR	1053: HR	1063: DP	1065: DP	1080: IT
1083: HR	1085: PR	1090: RD	1093: A	1095: RD

8. Move the *DeptID* column so it is positioned between the *BirthDate* column and the *AnnualSalary* column.
9. Automatically adjust the widths of the columns.
10. Save the table.
11. Display the table in Print Preview, change the top margin to 1.5 inches, change the left margin to 1.25 inches, and then print the table.
12. Close the Employees table.

Assessment

2 CREATE A DEPARTMENTS TABLE

SNAP Grade It

1. You entered a one- or two-letter abbreviation representing each department within the company. Creating the abbreviations saved you from having to type the entire department name for each record. You need to create the Departments table that will provide the department name for each abbreviation. Create a new table in the **AL1-C1-Griffin.accdb** database with the column headings and data shown in Figure 1.16 by completing the following steps:
   a. Click the CREATE tab and then click the Table button.
   b. Click the *ID* column heading, click the down-pointing arrow at the right side of the *Data Type* option box in the Formatting group, and then click *Short Text* at the drop-down list.
   c. Limit the field size to 2 characters and rename the heading as *DeptID*.
   d. Click the *Click to Add* column heading, click *Short Text* at the drop-down list, and then type **Department**.
   e. Type the data in the fields as shown in Figure 1.16 on the next page.
   f. Automatically adjust the widths of the columns.
2. Save the table and name it *Departments*.
3. Print and then close the table.

Figure 1.16 Departments Table

DeptID	Department	Click to Add
A	Accounting	
DP	Design and Production	
HR	Human Resources	
IT	Information Technology Services	
PR	Public Relations	
RD	Research and Development	

Assessment

3 CREATE A BENEFITS TABLE

1. Create a new table in **AL1-C1-Griffin.accdb** with the data shown in Figure 1.17 and with the following specifications:
   a. Name the fields as shown in the Benefits table in the diagram in Figure 1.15 and create the caption names for the fields as shown in Figure 1.17. (For example, name the life insurance field *LifeIns* and create the caption *Life Insurance*.)
   b. For the first column (EmpID), click the *ID* column heading, click the down-pointing arrow at the right side of the *Data Type* option box in the Formatting group, and then click *Short Text* at the drop-down list. Limit the field size to 4 characters and rename the field as *EmpID*.
   c. Apply the Yes/No data type to the second column, make the default value a check mark (by typing **Yes** at the Expression Builder dialog box), and provide the description *A check mark indicates the employee has signed up for the health plan.*

Figure 1.17 Benefits Table

EmployeeID	Health Plan	Dental Plan	Life Insurance	Vacation	Click to Add
103	✔	✔	$100,000.00	4 weeks	
105	✔	✔	$200,000.00	3 weeks	
106		✔	$150,000.00	3 weeks	
109	✔	✔	$200,000.00	3 weeks	
110	✔	✔	$185,000.00	4 weeks	
112		✔	$200,000.00	3 weeks	
117			$100,000.00	3 weeks	
120	✔	✔	$200,000.00	4 weeks	
122			$75,000.00	2 weeks	
125	✔	✔	$125,000.00	3 weeks	
128	✔	✔	$200,000.00	3 weeks	
130	✔	✔	$200,000.00	3 weeks	
132			$50,000.00	2 weeks	
138	✔		$125,000.00	2 weeks	
141	✔	✔	$85,000.00	3 weeks	
143	✔	✔	$175,000.00	3 weeks	
149	✔		$100,000.00	2 weeks	
152	✔	✔	$150,000.00	2 weeks	
153	✔	✔	$200,000.00	2 weeks	
155		✔	$150,000.00	1 week	
159	✔		$75,000.00	1 week	
163	✔	✔	$125,000.00	1 week	
165	✔		$150,000.00	1 week	
170		✔	$185,000.00	1 week	
173	✔	✔	$125,000.00	1 week	
	✔	✔			

d. Apply the Yes/No data type to the third column, make the default value a check mark (by typing **Yes** at the Expression Builder dialog box), and provide the description *A check mark indicates the employee has signed up for the dental plan.*

e. Apply the Currency data type to the fourth column.

f. Apply the Short Text data type to the fifth column and limit the field size to 8 characters.

g. Type the data in each record as shown in Figure 1.17.

h. Automatically adjust the column widths.

i. Save the table and name it *Benefits*.

2. Display the table in Print Preview, change the top and left margins to 1.5 inches, and then print the table.

3. Close the Benefits table.

Assessment

4 SORT DATA

1. With **AL1-C1-Griffin.accdb** open, open the Employees table.

2. Experiment with the buttons in the Sort & Filter group on the HOME tab and determine how to sort columns of data in ascending and descending order.

3. Sort the records in the Employees table in ascending order by last name.

4. Save, print, and then close the Employees table.

5. Open the Benefits table and then sort the records in descending order by life insurance amounts.

6. Save, print, and then close the Benefits table.

Visual Benchmark Demonstrate Your Proficiency

CREATE AN ABSENCES TABLE

1. With **AL1-C1-Griffin.accdb** open, create the Absences table shown in Figure 1.18 (using the field names as shown in Figure 1.15 on page 36) with the following specifications:

a. Use the default AutoNumber data type for column 1. Apply the appropriate data type to the other columns.

b. Create an appropriate caption and description for the *EmpID*, *AbsenceDate*, and *AbsenceReason* columns.

c. Apply the default value of Sick Day to the *AbsenceReason* column. (You will need to type "**Sick Day**" in the Expression Builder dialog box.)

2. Save the table and name it *Absences*.

3. Print the table in landscape orientation with top and left margins of 1.5 inches.

4. Close the Absences table and then close **AL1-C1-Griffin.accdb**.

Figure 1.18 Visual Benchmark

AbsenceID	EmpID	Absent Date	Absent Reason	Click to Add
1	141	1/2/2015	Sick Day	
2	141	1/5/2015	Sick Day	
3	105	1/6/2015	Sick Day	
4	163	1/9/2015	Sick Day	
5	125	1/9/2015	Bereavement	
6	125	1/12/2015	Bereavement	
7	125	1/12/2015	Bereavement	
8	117	1/13/2015	Sick Day	
9	170	1/14/2015	Personal Day	
10	153	1/16/2015	Sick Day	
11	153	1/19/2015	Sick Day	
12	103	1/19/2015	Personal Day	
13	109	1/20/2015	Sick Day	
14	109	1/22/2015	Sick Day	
15	167	1/23/2015	Personal Day	
16	138	1/29/2015	Sick Day	
17	159	1/30/2015	Sick Day	
* (New)			Sick Day	

Case Study Apply Your Skills

You are the office manager for Elite Limousines, and your company is switching over to Access for managing company data. The database designer has provided you with the database diagram in Figure 1.19. She wants you to follow the diagram when creating the database.

Figure 1.19 Elite Limousines Database Diagram

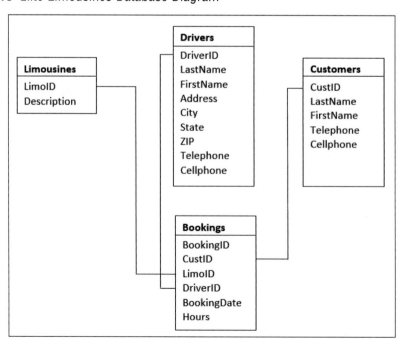

Part 1

Create a new database named **AL1-C1-Elite.accdb** and then create the Limousines table shown in the database diagram in Figure 1.19. The database designer has asked you to include an appropriate caption and description for each field and to change the field size for the *LimoID* field. Type the following records in the table:

LimoID: 01
Description: 2011 White stretch

LimoID: 02
Description: 2011 Black stretch

LimoID: 04
Description: 2012 Black minibus

LimoID: 06
Description: 2012 Black standard

LimoID: 08
Description: 2014 Black SUV stretch

LimoID: 10
Description: 2015 Black stretch

Part 2

With **AL1-C1-Elite.accdb** open, create the Drivers table shown in the database diagram shown in Figure 1.19. Include appropriate captions and descriptions for each field and change the field sizes where appropriate. Type the following records in the table:

DriverID#: 101
LastName: Brennan
FirstName: Andrea
Address: 4438 Gowan Rd.
City: Las Vegas
State: NV
ZIP: 89115
Telephone: (702) 555-3481
Cellphone: (702) 555-1322

DriverID: 114
LastName: Gould
FirstName: Randall
Address: 330 Aura Ave.
City: Las Vegas
State: NV
ZIP: 89052
Telephone: (702) 555-1239
Cellphone: (702) 555-7474

DriverID: 120
LastName: Martinelli
FirstName: Albert
Address: 107 Cameo Dr.
City: Las Vegas
State: NV
ZIP: 89138
Telephone: (702) 555-0349
Cellphone: (702) 555-6649

DriverID: 125
LastName: Nunez
FirstName: Frank
Address: 4832 Helena St.
City: Las Vegas
State: NV
ZIP: 89129
Telephone: (702) 555-3748
Cellphone: (702) 555-2210

Part 3

With **AL1-C1-Elite.accdb** open, create the Customers table shown in the database diagram in Figure 1.19. Include appropriate captions and descriptions for the fields and change the field sizes where appropriate. Type the following records in the table:

CustID: 1001
LastName: Spencer
FirstName: Maureen
Telephone: (513) 555-3943
Cellphone: (513) 555-4884

CustID: 1002
LastName: Tsang
FirstName: Lee
Telephone: (702) 555-4775
Cellphone: (702) 555-4211

CustID: 1028
LastName: Gabriel
FirstName: Nicholas
Telephone: (612) 555-7885
Cellphone: (612) 555-7230

CustID: 1031
LastName: Marshall
FirstName: Patricia
Telephone: (702) 555-6410
Cellphone: (702) 555-0137

CustID: 1010
LastName: Chavez
FirstName: Blake
Telephone: (206) 555-3774
Cellphone: (206) 555-3006

CustID: 1044
LastName: Vanderhage
FirstName: Vernon
Telephone: (213) 555-8846
Cellphone: (213) 555-4635

Part 4

With **AL1-C1-Elite.accdb** open, create the Bookings table shown in the database diagram in Figure 1.19. Include appropriate captions and descriptions for the fields and change the field sizes where appropriate. Type the following records in the table:

BookingID: (AutoNumber)
CustID: 1044
LimoID: 02
DriverID: 114
BookingDate: 7/1/2015
Hours: 6

BookingID: (AutoNumber)
CustID: 1001
LimoID: 10
DriverID: 120
BookingDate: 7/1/2015
Hours: 8

BookingID: (AutoNumber)
CustID: 1002
LimoID: 04
DriverID: 101
BookingDate: 7/6/2015
Hours: 8

BookingID: (AutoNumber)
CustID: 1028
LimoID: 02
DriverID: 125
BookingDate: 7/6/2015
Hours: 4

BookingID: (AutoNumber)
CustID: 1010
LimoID: 06
DriverID: 125
BookingDate: 7/3/2015
Hours: 3

BookingID: (AutoNumber)
CustID: 1031
LimoID: 08
DriverID: 120
BookingDate: 7/7/2015
Hours: 5

Automatically adjust the column widths of each table to accommodate the longest entry in each column. Print each table so all records fit on one page.

MICROSOFT®
ACCESS®
Creating Relationships between Tables

PERFORMANCE OBJECTIVES

Upon successful completion of Chapter 2, you will be able to:

- Define a primary key in a table
- Create a one-to-many relationship
- Specify referential integrity
- Print, edit, and delete relationships
- Create a one-to-one relationship
- View and edit a subdatasheet

Tutorials

2.1 Defining a Primary Key

2.2 Deleting a Relationship; Printing a Relationships Report

2.3 Creating a Relationship between Two Tables in a Database

2.4 Creating a One-to-One Relationship between Tables

2.5 Editing a Relationship; Enforcing Referential Integrity; Viewing a Subdatasheet

Access is a relational database program you can use to create tables that are related or connected within the same database. When a relationship is established between tables, you can view and edit records in related tables with a subdatasheet. In this chapter, you will learn how to identify a primary key in a table that is unique to that table, how to join tables by creating a relationship between them, and how to view and edit subdatasheets. Model answers for this chapter's projects appear on the following pages.

AL1C2

Note: Before beginning the projects, copy the AL1C2 subfolder from the AL1 folder on the CD that accompanies this textbook to your storage medium and make AL1C2 the active folder.

Project 1 Establish Relationships between Tables

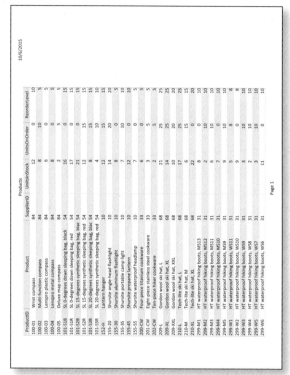

Products Table, Page 1

Orders (10/6/2015)

OrderID	OrderDate	ProductID	UnitsOrdered	Amount
1001	1/5/2015	101-S2R	15	$1,945.25
1002	1/5/2015	202-CW	5	$124.25
1003	1/5/2015	201-CW	5	$99.75
1004	1/5/2015	100-05	5	$129.75
1005	1/5/2015	101-S3R	10	$1,199.50
1006	1/5/2015	101-S3B	10	$1,137.50
1007	1/5/2015	100-02	10	$45.95
1008	1/19/2015	590-TL	5	$196.25
1009	1/19/2015	602-XR	5	$2,145.00
1010	1/19/2015	299-W5	10	$752.90
1011	1/19/2015	299-W4	10	$752.90
1012	1/19/2015	299-W3	10	$752.90
1013	1/19/2015	299-W1	8	$602.32
1014	1/19/2015	560-TL	20	$397.00
1015	2/2/2015	299-M5	10	$887.90
1016	2/2/2015	299-M3	10	$887.90
1017	2/2/2015	442-1B	10	$1,495.00
1018	2/2/2015	443-1B	15	$2,397.75
1019	2/2/2015	780-2	10	$1,288.50
1020	2/2/2015	299-M2	10	$887.90
1021	2/2/2015	647-1	15	$2,999.85
1022	2/16/2015	209-XXL	20	$145.80
1023	2/16/2015	152-H	15	$44.85
1024	2/16/2015	210-L	25	$162.25
1025	2/16/2015	210-M	15	$97.35
1026	2/16/2015	375-S	20	$199.00
1027	2/16/2015	375-M	20	$199.00
1028	2/16/2015	371-L	10	$129.50
1029	2/16/2015	209-L	25	$173.75
1030	2/16/2015	209-XL	25	$180.00
1031	2/16/2015	155-35	10	$199.50
1032	2/16/2015	155-20	15	$104.25
1033	2/15/2015	185-10	10	$310.90

Page 1

Orders Table

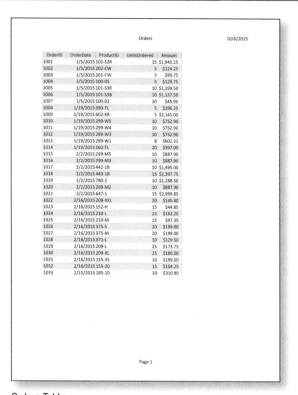

Products (10/6/2015)

ProductID	Product	SupplierID	UnitsInStock	UnitsOnOrder	ReorderLevel
100-01	Wrist compass	84	12	0	5
100-02	Multi-function compass	84	8	0	5
100-03	Lenspro plastic compass	84	6	0	5
100-04	Lenspro metal compass	84	2	5	15
100-05	Deluxe map compass	84	10	0	15
101-S1B	SL 0-degrees down sleeping bag, black	54	16	0	15
101-S1R	SL 0-degrees down sleeping bag, red	54	17	0	15
101-S2B	SL 15-degrees synthetic sleeping bag, blac	54	21	0	15
101-S2R	SL 15-degrees synthetic sleeping bag, red	54	12	15	10
101-S3B	SL 20-degrees synthetic sleeping bag, blac	54	8	15	15
101-S3R	SL 20-degrees synthetic sleeping bag, red	54	4	15	10
152-H	Lantern hanger	10	12	10	20
155-20	Shursite angle-head flashlight	10	14	20	10
155-30	Shursite aluminum flashlight	10	9	0	10
155-35	Shursite portable camp light	10	7	10	10
155-45	Shursite propane lantern	10	12	0	5
155-55	Shursite waterproof headlamp	10	7	0	5
200-CW	Four-piece titanium cookware	33	6	5	25
201-CW	Eight-piece stainless steel cookware	33	3	5	25
202-CW	Ten-piece hiker cookware	33	21	25	25
209-L	Gordon wool ski hat, L	68	14	25	20
209-XL	Gordon wool ski hat, XL	68	10	20	20
209-XXL	Gordon wool ski hat, XXL	68	17	25	25
210-L	Tech-lite ski hat, L	68	6	15	20
210-M	Tech-lite ski hat, M	68	22	0	20
210-XL	Tech-lite ski hat, XL	68	8	0	10
299-M1	HT waterproof hiking boots, MS13	31	2	10	10
299-M2	HT waterproof hiking boots, MS12	31	6	10	10
299-M3	HT waterproof hiking boots, MS11	31	6	0	10
299-M4	HT waterproof hiking boots, MS10	31	7	0	10
299-M5	HT waterproof hiking boots, MS9	31	9	0	5
299-W1	HT waterproof hiking boots, WS11	31	5	10	8
299-W2	HT waterproof hiking boots, WS10	31	9	8	8
299-W3	HT waterproof hiking boots, WS9	31	9	0	10
299-W4	HT waterproof hiking boots, WS8	31	3	10	10
299-W5	HT waterproof hiking boots, WS7	31	2	10	10
299-W6	HT waterproof hiking boots, WS6	31	11	0	10

Page 1

Products Table, Page 1

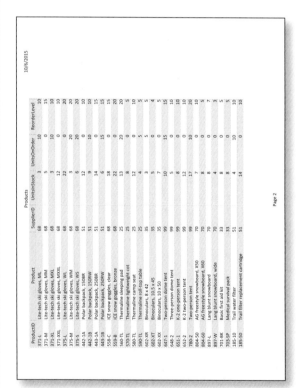

Products (10/6/2015)

ProductID	Product	SupplierID	UnitsInStock	UnitsOnOrder	ReorderLevel
371-L	Lite-tech ski gloves, ML	68	3	0	10
371-M	Lite-tech ski gloves, MM	68	5	0	15
371-XL	Lite-tech ski gloves, MXL	68	3	10	10
371-XXL	Lite-tech ski gloves, MXXL	68	12	0	10
375-L	Lite-tech ski gloves, WL	68	22	0	20
375-M	Lite-tech ski gloves, WM	68	4	20	10
375-S	Lite-tech ski gloves, WS	68	6	20	20
442-1A	Polar backpack, 1508R	51	12	0	20
442-1B	Polar backpack, 1508W	51	9	10	15
443-1A	Polar backpack, 2508R	51	14	0	15
443-1B	Polar backpack, 2508W	51	6	15	15
558-C	ICE snow goggles, clear	68	18	0	20
559-B	ICE snow goggles, bronze	68	22	20	20
560-TL	Thermaline sleeping pad	25	13	0	10
570-TL	Thermaline lightweight cot	25	8	0	5
580-TL	Thermaline camp seat	25	12	5	4
590-TL	Thermaline roll-top table	25	4	5	15
602-XR	Binoculars, 8 x 42	35	3	0	15
602-XT	Binoculars, 10.5 x 45	35	4	5	10
602-XX	Binoculars, 10 x 50	35	5	0	10
647-1	Two-person dome tent	99	10	15	20
648-2	Three-person dome tent	99	5	0	10
651-1	K-2 one-person tent	99	8	0	20
652-2	K-2 two-person tent	99	12	0	10
780-2	Two-person tent	99	17	10	20
804-50	AG freestyle snowboard, X50	70	7	0	5
804-60	AG freestyle snowboard, X60	70	8	0	7
897-L	Lang blunt snowboard	70	4	0	5
897-W	Lang blunt snowboard, wide	70	4	0	5
701-BK	Basic first aid kit	33	8	0	5
703-SP	Medical survival pack	33	8	10	10
185-10	Trail water filter	51	4	0	10
185-50	Trail filter replacement cartridge	51	14	0	10

Page 2

Products Table, Page 2

Suppliers (10/6/2015)

SupplierID	SupplierName	StreetAddress	City	Prov/State	PostalCode	Telephone	EmailAddress
10	Hopewell, Inc.	5600 Carver Road	Port Moody	BC	V3H 1A4	(604) 555-3843	hopewell@emcp.net
25	Langley Corporati	805 First Avenue	Burnaby	BC	V3J 1C9	(604) 555-1200	langley@emcp.net
31	Sound Supplies	2104 Union Street	Seattle	WA	98105	(206) 555-4855	ssupplies@emcp.net
33	Bayside Supplies	6705 North Street	Bellingham	WA	98432	(360) 555-6005	bside@emcp.net
35	Emerald City Produ	1059 Pike Street	Seattle	WA	98102	(206) 555-7728	ecproducts@emcp.n
51	Fraser Valley Prod	3894 Old Yale Roa	Abbotsford	BC	V2S 1A9	(604) 555-1455	fvproducts@emcp.net
54	Manning, Inc.	1039 South 22nd	Vancouver	BC	V5K 1R1	(604) 555-0087	manning@emcp.net
68	Freedom Corporati	14 Fourth Avenue	Vancouver	BC	V5K 2C7	(604) 555-2155	freedom@emcp.net
70	Rosewood, Inc.	998 North 42nd St	Vancouver	BC	V5K 2N8	(778) 555-6643	rosewood@emcp.net
84	Macadam, Inc.	675 Third Street	Vancouver	BC	V5K 2R9	(604) 555-5522	macadam@emcp.net
99	KL Distributions	402 Yukon Drive	Bellingham	WA	98435	(360) 555-3711	kldist@emcp.net
16	Olympic Suppliers	1773 50th Avenue	Seattle	WA	98101	(206) 555-9488	olysuppliers@emcp.
28	Gorman Company	543 26th Street	Vancouver	BC	V5K 3C5	(778) 555-4550	gormanco@emcp.ne

Suppliers Table

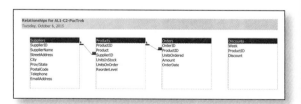

Relationships for ALL1-C2-PacTrek
Tuesday, October 6, 2015

Relationships Report

Project 2 Create Relationships and Display Subdatasheets in a Database

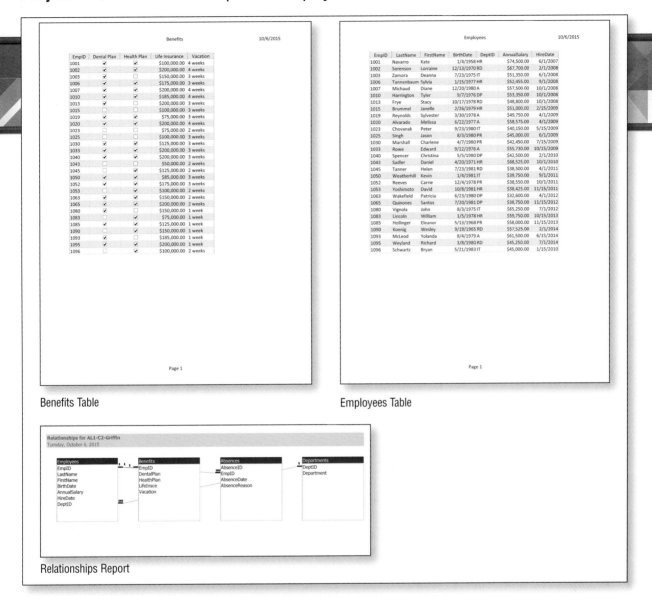

Benefits Table

Employees Table

Relationships Report

You will specify primary keys in tables, establish one-to-many relationships between tables, specify referential integrity, and print the relationships. You will also edit and delete a relationship.

Creating Related Tables ■■■■■■■■■■■■■■■■■■■■■

Generally, a database management system fits into one of two categories: a file management system (also sometimes referred to as a *flat file database*) or a relational database management system. A flat file management system stores all data in a single directory and cannot contain multiple tables. This type of management system is a simple way to store data but becomes more inefficient as more data is added. In a

relational database management system, like Access, relationships are defined between sets of data, allowing greater flexibility in manipulating data and eliminating data redundancy (entering the same data in more than one place).

In Project 1, you will define relationships between tables in the AL1-C2-PacTrek.accdb database. Because the tables in the database will be related, information on the same product does not need to be repeated in a table on orders. If you used a flat file management system to maintain product information, you would need to repeat the product description for each order.

Determining Relationships

Taking time to plan a database is extremely important. Creating a database with related tables takes even more consideration. You need to determine how to break down the required data and what tables to create to eliminate redundancies. One idea to help you determine what tables are necessary in a database is to think of the word *about*. For example, the Pacific Trek store needs a table *about* products, another *about* suppliers, and another *about* orders. A table should be about only one subject, such as products, suppliers, or orders.

Along with determining the necessary tables for a database, you need to determine the relationship between tables. The ability to relate, or "join," tables is what makes Access a relational database system. As you learned in Chapter 1, database designers often create a visual representation of the database's structure in a diagram. Figure 2.1 displays the database diagram for the AL1-C2-PacTrek.accdb database. (Some of the fields in the tables have been slightly modified from the database you used in Chapter 1.)

Defining the Primary Key

A database table can contain two different types of keys: a primary key and a foreign key. In the database diagram in Figure 2.1, notice that one field in each table contains an asterisk. The asterisk indicates a *primary key field*, which is a field that holds data that uniquely identifies each record in a table. For example,

Figure 2.1 AL1-C2-PacTrek.accdb Database Diagram

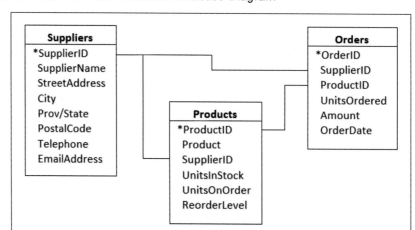

the *SupplierID* field in the Suppliers table contains a unique supplier number for each record in the table and the *ProductID* field in the Products table contains a unique product number for each product. A table can have only one primary key field and it is the field by which the table is sorted whenever the table is opened.

When a new record is added to a table, Access checks to ensure that there is no existing record with the same data in the primary key. If there is, Access displays an error message indicating there are duplicate values and does not allow the record to be saved. When adding a new record to a table, the primary key field cannot be left blank. Access expects a value in each record in the table and this is referred to as ***entity integrity***. If a value is not entered in a field, Access actually enters a null value. A null value cannot be given to a primary key field. Access will not let you close a database containing a primary key field with a null value.

By default, Access includes the *ID* field as the first field in a table, assigns the AutoNumber data type, and identifies the field as the primary key. The AutoNumber data type assigns the first record a field value of *1* and each new record is assigned the next sequential number. You can use this default field as the primary key or define your own. To determine what field is the primary key or to define a primary key field, you must display the table in Design view. To do this, open the table and then click the View button located at the left side of the HOME tab. You can also display the table in Design view by clicking the View button arrow and then clicking *Design View* at the drop-down list. To add or remove a primary key from a field, click the desired field in the *Field Name* column and then click the Primary Key button in the Tools group on the TABLE TOOLS DESIGN tab. A key icon is inserted in the field selector bar (the blank column to the left of the field names) for the desired field. Figure 2.2 displays the Products table in Design view with the *ProductID* field identified as the primary key.

▼ **Quick Steps**

Define a Primary Key
1. Open table.
2. Click View button.
3. Click desired field.
4. Click Primary Key button.
5. Click Save button.

Primary Key

Figure 2.2 Products Table in Design View

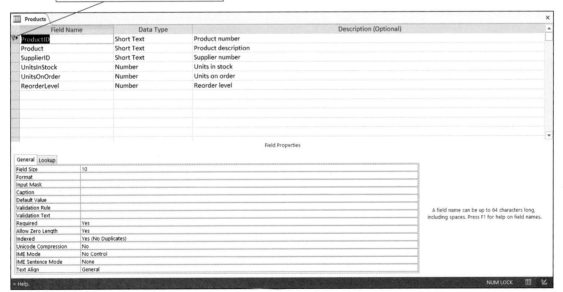

A key icon in the field selector bar specifies the primary key field.

Typically, a primary key field in one table becomes the *foreign key field* in a related table. For example, the primary key field *SupplierID* in the Suppliers table is considered the foreign key field in the Orders table. In the Suppliers table, each entry in the *SupplierID* field must be unique since it is the primary key field but the same supplier number may appear more than once in the *SupplierID* field in the Orders table (for instance, in a situation when more than one product is ordered from the same supplier).

Data in the foreign key field must match data in the primary key field of the related table. For example, any supplier number you enter in the *SupplierID* field in the Orders table must be contained in the Suppliers table. In other words, you would not make an order to a supplier that does not exist in the Suppliers table. Figure 2.3 identifies the primary and foreign keys in the tables in the AL1-C2-PacTrek.accdb database. Primary keys are identified with *(PK)* and foreign keys are identified with *(FK)* in the figure.

Figure 2.3 AL1-C2-PacTrek.accdb Database Diagram with Primary and Foreign Keys Identified

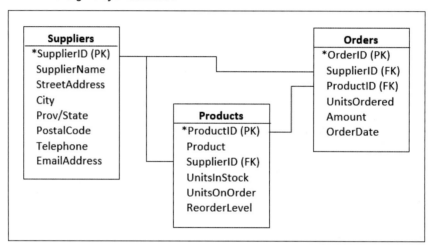

Project 1a **Defining a Primary Key Field**   **Part 1 of 4**

1. Open Access.
2. At the Access 2013 opening screen, click the <u>Open Other Files</u> hyperlink that displays at the left side of the screen.
3. At the Open backstage area, double-click the *Computer* option or your SkyDrive (depending on where your student data files are located).
4. At the Open dialog box, navigate to the AL1C2 folder on your storage medium and then double-click the database ***AL1-C2-PacTrek.accdb***.
5. Click the Enable Content button in the message bar if the security warning message appears. (The message bar will display immediately below the ribbon.)
6. Open the Products table.
7. View the primary key field by completing the following steps:
   a. Click the View button located at the left side of the HOME tab. (This displays the table in Design view.)

b. In Design view, notice the *Field Name*, *Data Type*, and *Description* columns and notice the information that displays for each field. The first field, *ProductID* is the primary key field and is identified by the key icon that displays in the field selector bar.

c. Click the View button to return to the Datasheet view.

d. Close the Products table.

8. Open the Suppliers table, click the View button to display the table in Design view, and then notice the *SupplierID* field is defined as the primary key field.

9. Click the View button to return to Datasheet view and then close the table.

10. Open the Orders table. (The first field in the Orders table has been changed from the AutoNumber field automatically assigned by Access in the AL1-C2-PacTrek.accdb database to a Short Text data type field.)

11. Define the *OrderID* field as the primary key field by completing the following steps:

a. Click the View button located at the left side of the HOME tab.

b. With the table in Design view and the *OrderID* field selected in the *Field Name* column, click the Primary Key button located in the Tools group on the TABLE TOOLS DESIGN tab.

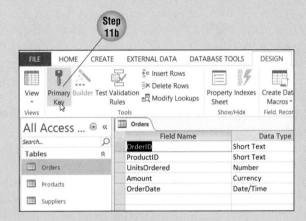

c. Click the Save button on the Quick Access toolbar.

d. Click the View button to return the table to Datasheet view.

12. Move the *OrderDate* field by completing the following steps:

a. Click the *OrderDate* field heading. (This selects the column.)

b. Position the mouse pointer on the heading; hold down the left mouse button; drag to the left until the thick, black vertical line displays immediately left of the *ProductID* field; and then release the mouse button.

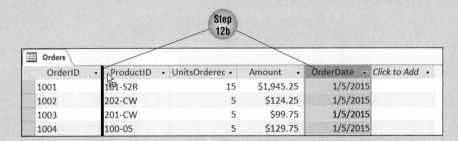

13. Automatically adjust the column widths.

14. Save and then close the Orders table.

Relating Tables in a One-to-Many Relationship

In Access, one table can be related to another, which is generally referred to as performing a *join*. When tables with a common field are joined, data can be extracted from both tables as if they were one large table. Relate tables to ensure the integrity of the data. For example, in Project 1b, you will create a relationship between the Suppliers table and the Products table. The relationship you establish will ensure that a supplier number cannot be entered in the Products table without first being entered in the Suppliers table. This type of relationship is called a *one-to-many relationship*, which means that one record in the Suppliers table will match zero, one, or many records in the Products table.

In a one-to-many relationship, the table containing the "one" is referred to as the *primary table* and the table containing the "many" is referred to as the *related table*. Access follows a set of rules that provide *referential integrity*, which enforces consistency between related tables. These rules are enforced when data is updated in related tables. The referential integrity rules ensure that a record added to a related table has a matching record in the primary table.

To create a one-to-many relationship, open the database containing the tables to be related. Click the DATABASE TOOLS tab and then click the Relationships button in the Relationships group. This displays the Show Table dialog box, as shown in Figure 2.4. At the Show Table dialog box, each table that will be related must be added to the Relationships window. To do this, click the first table name to be included and then click Add (or double-click the desired table). Continue in this manner until all necessary table names have been added to the Relationships window and then click the Close button.

At the Relationships window, such as the one shown in Figure 2.5, use the mouse to drag the common field from the primary table's field list box (the "one") to the related table's field list box (the "many"). This causes the Edit Relationships dialog box to display, as shown in Figure 2.6. At the Edit Relationships dialog box, check to make sure the correct field name displays in the *Table/Query* and *Related Table/Query* list boxes and the relationship type at the bottom of the dialog box displays as *One-To-Many*.

Specify the relationship options by choosing *Enforce Referential Integrity*, as well as *Cascade Update Related Fields* and/or *Cascade Delete Related Records*, and then click the Create button. This causes the Edit Relationships dialog box to close and the Relationships window to display showing the relationship between the tables.

▼ **Quick Steps**

Create a One-to-Many Relationship
1. Click DATABASE TOOLS tab.
2. Click Relationships button.
3. At Show Table dialog box, add tables.
4. In Relationships window, drag "one" field from primary table to "many" field in related table.
5. At Edit Relationships dialog box, enforce referential integrity.
6. Click Create button.
7. Click Save button.

Relationships

Figure 2.4 Show Table Dialog Box

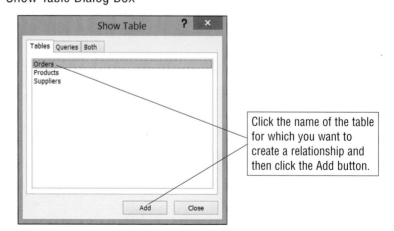

Figure 2.5 Relationships Window

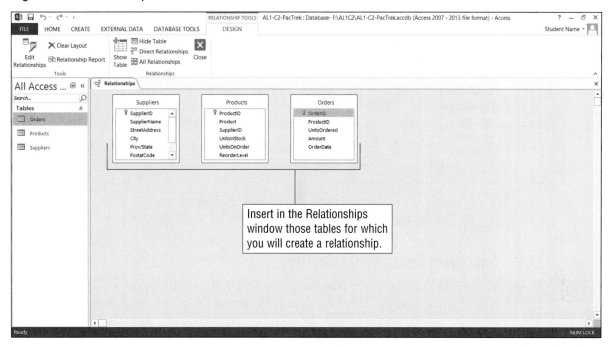

Figure 2.6 Edit Relationships Dialog Box

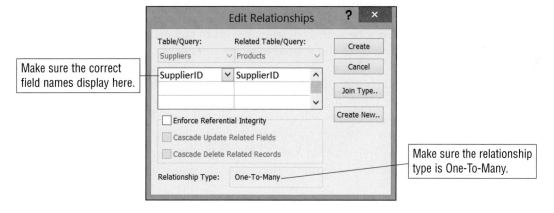

In Figure 2.7, the *Suppliers* field list box displays with a black line attached along with the number *1* (signifying the "one" side of the relationship). The black line is connected to the *Products* field list box along with the infinity symbol, ∞ (signifying the "many" side of the relationship). The black line, called the *join line*, is thick at both ends if the *Enforce Referential Integrity* option is chosen. If this option is not chosen, the line is thin at both ends. Click the Save button on the Quick Access toolbar to save the relationship. Close the Relationships window by clicking the Close button located in the upper right corner of the window.

Figure 2.7 One-to-Many Relationship

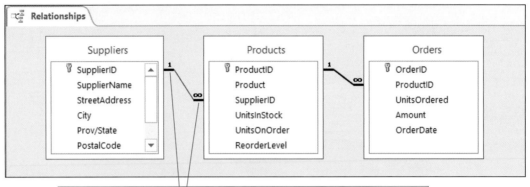

This is an example of a one-to-many relationship, where 1 identifies the "one" side of the relationship and the infinity symbol (∞) identifies the "many" side.

Specifying Referential Integrity

Referential integrity ensures that a record exists in the "one" table before the record can be entered in the "many" table.

Choose *Enforce Referential Integrity* at the Edit Relationships dialog box to ensure that the relationships between records in related tables are valid. Referential integrity can be set if the field from the primary table is a primary key and the related fields have the same data type. When referential integrity is established, a value for the primary key must first be entered in the primary table before it can be entered in the related table.

If you select only *Enforce Referential Integrity* and the related table contains a record, you will not be able to change a primary key field value in the primary table. You will not be able to delete a record in the primary table if its key value equals a foreign key in the related table. If you choose *Cascade Update Related Fields*, you will be able to change a primary key field value in the primary table and Access will automatically update the matching value in the related table. Choose *Cascade Delete Related Records* and you will be able to delete a record in the primary table and Access will delete any related records in the related table.

In Project 1b, you will create a one-to-many relationship between tables in the AL1-C2-PacTrek.accdb database. Figure 2.8 displays the Relationships window with the relationships identified that you will create in the project.

Figure 2.8 Relationships in the AL1-C2-PacTrek Database

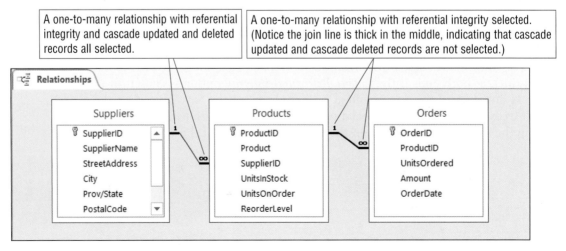

Printing Relationships

You can print a report displaying the relationships between tables. To do this, display the Relationships window and then click the Relationship Report button in the Tools group. This displays the relationships report in Print Preview. Click the Print button in the Print group on the PRINT PREVIEW tab and then click OK at the Print dialog box. After printing the relationships report, click the Close button to close the relationships report.

▼ **Quick Steps**

Print a Relationship
1. Click DATABASE TOOLS tab.
2. Click Relationships button.
3. Click Relationships Report button.
4. Click Print button.
5. Click OK.
6. Click Close button.

Relationship
Report

Project 1b **Creating Relationships between Tables**   **Part 2 of 4**

1. With **AL1-C2-PacTrek.accdb** open, click the DATABASE TOOLS tab and then click the Relationships button in the Relationships group. (The Show Table dialog box should display in the Relationships window. If it does not display, click the Show Table button in the Relationships group on the RELATIONSHIP TOOLS DESIGN tab.)

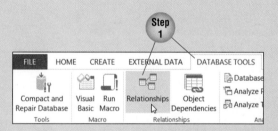

2. At the Show Table dialog box with the Tables tab selected, add the Suppliers, Products, and Orders tables to the Relationships window by completing the following steps:
   a. Click *Suppliers* in the list box and then click the Add button.
   b. Click *Products* in the list box and then click the Add button.
   c. Click *Orders* in the list box and then click the Add button.
3. Click the Close button to close the Show Table dialog box.

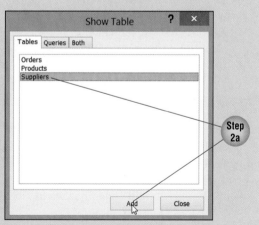

4. At the Relationships window, drag the *SupplierID* field from the *Suppliers* field list box to the *Products* field list box by completing the following steps:

   a. Position the arrow pointer on the *SupplierID* field that displays in the *Suppliers* field list box.

   b. Hold down the left mouse button, drag the arrow pointer (with a field icon attached) to the *SupplierID* field in the *Products* field list box, and then release the mouse button. (This causes the Edit Relationships dialog box to display.)

5. At the Edit Relationships dialog box, make sure *SupplierID* displays in the *Table/Query* and *Related Table/Query* list boxes and the relationship type at the bottom of the dialog box displays as *One-To-Many*.

6. Enforce the referential integrity of the relationship by completing the following steps:

   a. Click the *Enforce Referential Integrity* check box to insert a check mark. (This makes the other two options available.)

   b. Click the *Cascade Update Related Fields* check box to insert a check mark.

   c. Click the *Cascade Delete Related Records* check box to insert a check mark.

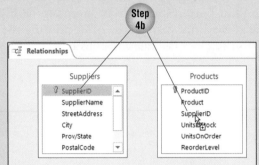

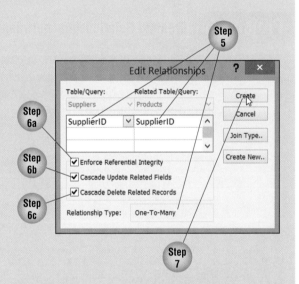

7. Click the Create button. (This causes the Edit Relationships dialog box to close and the Relationships window to display, showing a black line (thick on the ends and thin in the middle) connecting the *SupplierID* field in the *Suppliers* field list box to the *SupplierID* field in the *Products* field list box. A *1* appears at the Suppliers table side and an infinity symbol (∞) appears at the Products table side of the black line.)

8. Click the Save button on the Quick Access toolbar to save the relationship.

9. Create a one-to-many relationship between the Products table and the Orders table with the *ProductID* field by completing the following steps:

   a. Position the arrow pointer on the *ProductID* field that displays in the *Products* field list box.

   b. Hold down the left mouse button, drag the arrow pointer (with a field icon attached) to the *ProductID* field in the *Orders* field list box, and then release the mouse button.

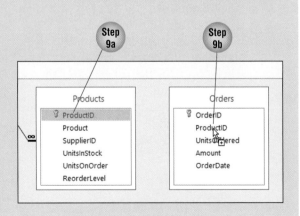

c. At the Edit Relationships dialog box, make sure *ProductID* displays in the *Table/Query* and *Related Table/Query* list boxes and the relationship type displays as *One-To-Many*.

d. Click the *Enforce Referential Integrity* check box. (Do not insert check marks in the other two check boxes.)

e. Click the Create button.

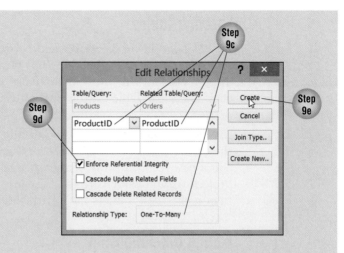

10. Click the Save button on the Quick Access toolbar to save the relationships.

11. Print the relationships by completing the following steps:

a. At the Relationships window, click the Relationship Report button in the Tools group. This displays the relationships report in Print Preview. (If a security notice displays, click the Open button.)

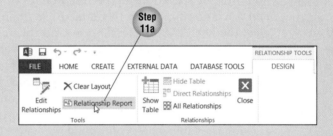

b. Click the Print button in the Print group at the left side of the PRINT PREVIEW tab.

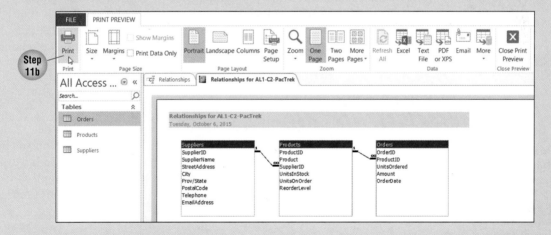

c. Click OK at the Print dialog box.

d. Close the report by clicking the Close button that displays in the upper right corner of the work area.

e. At the message asking if you want to save changes to the design of the report, click No.

12. Close the Relationships window by clicking the Close button that displays in the upper right corner of the work area.

Showing Tables

Show Table

Once a relationship is established between tables and the Relationships window is closed, clicking the Relationships button causes the Relationships window to display without the Show Table dialog box. To display the Show Table dialog box, click the Show Table button in the Relationships group.

Pacific Trek offers a discount on one product each week. You want to keep track of this information so you decide to create a Discounts table that includes the discount item for each week of the first three months of the year. (You will add a new record to this field each week when the discount item is chosen.) In Project 1c, you will create the Discounts table shown in Figure 2.9 on page 59 and then relate the Products table with the Discounts table using the *ProductID* field.

Editing a Relationship

▼ **Quick Steps**

Edit a Relationship
1. Click DATABASE TOOLS tab.
2. Click Relationships button.
3. Click Edit Relationships button.
4. Make desired changes at Edit Relationships dialog box.
5. Click OK.

Edit
Relationships

You can edit a relationship between tables or delete the relationship altogether. To edit a relationship, open the database containing the tables with the relationship, click the DATABASE TOOLS tab, and then click the Relationships button in the Relationships group. This displays the Relationships window with the related tables. Click the Edit Relationships button located in the Tools group to display the Edit Relationships dialog box. The dialog box will be similar to the one shown in Figure 2.6 on page 51. Identify the relationship you want to edit by clicking the down-pointing arrow at the right side of the *Table/Query* option box and then clicking the table name containing the "one" field. Click the down-pointing arrow at the right side of the *Related Table/Query* option box and then click the table name containing the "many" field.

To edit a specific relationship, position the arrow pointer on the middle portion of the black line that connects the related tables and then click the right mouse button. At the shortcut menu that displays, click the *Edit Relationship* option. This displays the Edit Relationships dialog box with the specific related field in both list boxes.

Deleting a Relationship

▼ **Quick Steps**

Delete a Relationship
1. Click DATABASE TOOLS tab.
2. Click Relationships button.
3. Right-click black line connecting related tables.
4. Click *Delete*.
5. Click Yes.

To delete a relationship between tables, display the related tables in the Relationships window. Position the arrow pointer on the middle portion of the black line connecting the related tables and then click the right mouse button. At the shortcut menu that displays, click *Delete*. At the message asking if you are sure you want to permanently delete the selected relationship from your database, click Yes.

1. With **AL1-C2-PacTrek.accdb** open, create the Discounts table shown in Figure 2.9 on page 59 by completing the following steps:
   a. Click the CREATE tab.
   b. Click the Table button in the Tables group.
   c. Click the Short Text button in the Add & Delete group. (This creates and then selects the *Field1* heading that displays to the right of the *ID* column.)

   d. Type **ProductID** and then press Enter.
   e. Click the *Short Text* option at the drop-down list and then type **Discount**.
   f. Click the *ID* heading (the first column), click the down-pointing arrow at the right side of the *Data Type* option box in the Formatting group, and then click *Date/Time* at the drop-down list.

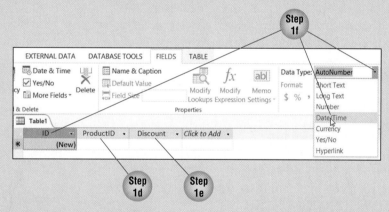

   g. Right-click the *ID* heading, click *Rename Field* at the shortcut menu, type **Week**, and then press Enter.
   h. Type the 13 records in the Discounts table shown in Figure 2.9 on page 59.
2. After typing the records, save the table by completing the following steps:
   a. Click the Save button on the Quick Access toolbar.
   b. At the Save As dialog box, type **Discounts** and then press Enter.
3. Close the Discounts table.
4. Create a relationship from the Products table to the Discounts table by completing the following steps:
   a. Click the DATABASE TOOLS tab and then click the Relationships button in the Relationships group.
   b. Display the Show Table dialog box by clicking the Show Table button in the Relationships group.
   c. At the Show Table dialog box, double-click the Discounts table.
   d. Click the Close button to close the Show Table dialog box.

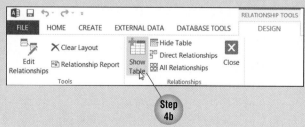

5. At the Relationships window, create a one-to-many relationship between the Products table and the Discounts table with the *ProductID* field by completing the following steps:

a. Drag the *ProductID* field from the *Products* field list box to the *ProductID* field in the *Discounts* field list box.

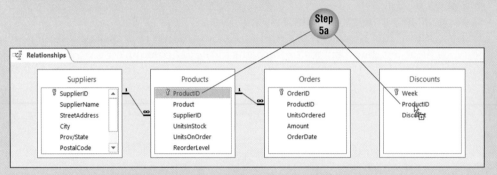

b. At the Edit Relationships dialog box, make sure *ProductID* displays in the *Table/Query* and *Related Table/Query* list boxes and the relationship type at the bottom of the dialog box displays as *One-To-Many*.

c. Click the *Enforce Referential Integrity* check box.

d. Click the *Cascade Update Related Fields* check box.

e. Click the *Cascade Delete Related Records* check box.

f. Click the Create button. (At the Relationships window, notice the join line that displays between the Products table and the Discounts table. If a message occurs telling you that the relationship cannot be created, click the Cancel button. Open the Discounts table, check to make sure the product numbers are entered correctly in the *ProductID* field, and then close the Discounts table. Try again to create the relationship.)

6. Edit the one-to-many relationship between the *ProductID* field in the Products table and the Orders table and specify that you want to cascade updated and related fields and cascade and delete related records by completing the following steps:

a. Click the Edit Relationships button located in the Tools group on the RELATIONSHIP TOOLS DESIGN tab.

b. At the Edit Relationships dialog box, click the down-pointing arrow at the right side of the *Table/Query* option box and then click *Products* at the drop-down list.

c. Click the down-pointing arrow at the right side of the *Related Table/Query* option box and then click *Orders* at the drop-down list.

d. Click the *Cascade Update Related Fields* check box.

e. Click the *Cascade Delete Related Records* check box.

f. Click the OK button.

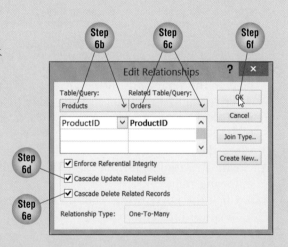

7. Click the Save button on the Quick Access toolbar to save the relationship.

8. Print the relationships by completing the following steps:

a. Click the Relationship Report button in the Tools group.

b. Click the Print button in the Print group.

c. Click OK at the Print dialog box.

d. Close the report by clicking the Close button that displays in the upper right corner of the work area.

e. At the message asking if you want to save changes to the design of the report, click No.

9. Delete the relationship between the Products table and the Discounts table by completing the following steps:

a. Position the arrow pointer on the thin portion of the black line connecting the *ProductID* field in the *Products* field list box with the *ProductID* field in the *Discounts* field list box and then click the right mouse button.

b. Click the *Delete* option at the shortcut menu.

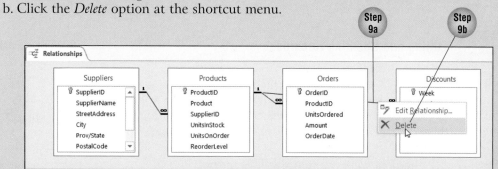

c. At the message asking if you are sure you want to permanently delete the selected relationship from your database, click Yes.

10. Click the Save button on the Quick Access toolbar to save the relationship.

11. Print the relationships by completing the following steps:

a. Click the RELATIONSHIP TOOLS DESIGN tab and then click the Relationship Report button in the Tools group.

b. Click the Print button in the Print group.

c. Click OK at the Print dialog box.

d. Close the report by clicking the Close button that displays in the upper right corner of the work area.

e. At the message asking if you want to save changes to the design of the report, click No.

12. Close the Relationships window by clicking the Close button that displays in the upper right corner of the work area.

Figure 2.9 Discounts Table

Week	ProductID	Discount	Click to Add
1/5/2015	155-45	20%	
1/12/2015	652-2	15%	
1/19/2015	443-1A	20%	
1/26/2015	202-CW	15%	
2/2/2015	804-60	10%	
2/9/2015	652-2	15%	
2/16/2015	101-S1B	5%	
2/23/2015	560-TL	20%	
3/2/2015	652-2	20%	
3/9/2015	602-XX	15%	
3/16/2015	100-05	10%	
3/23/2015	652-2	15%	
3/30/2015	202-CW	15%	

Inserting and Deleting Records in Related Tables

In the relationship established in Project 1b, a record must first be added to the Suppliers table before a related record can be added to the Products table. This is because you chose the *Enforce Referential Integrity* option at the Edit Relationships dialog box. Because you chose the two options *Cascade Update Related Fields* and *Cascade Delete Related Records*, records in the Suppliers table (the primary table) can be updated or deleted and related records in the Products table (the related table) are automatically updated or deleted.

Project 1d **Editing and Updating Records** Part 4 of 4

1. With **AL1-C2-PacTrek.accdb** open, open the Suppliers table.
2. Change two supplier numbers in the Suppliers table (Access will automatically change them in the Products table and the Orders table) by completing the following steps:
   a. Double-click the field value *15* that displays in the *SupplierID* field.
   b. Type 33.
   c. Double-click the field value *42* that displays in the *SupplierID* field.
   d. Type 51.
   e. Click the Save button on the Quick Access toolbar.
   f. Close the Suppliers table.
   g. Open the Products table and notice that supplier number *15* changed to *33* and supplier number *42* changed to *51*.
   h. Close the Products table.

   Step 2b
   Step 2d

Suppliers	
SupplierID	SupplierName
⊞ 10	Hopewell, Inc.
⊞ 33	Bayside Supplies
⊞ 25	Langley Corporatio
⊞ 31	Sound Supplies
⊞ 35	Emerald City Produ
⊞ 38	Hadley Company
⊞ 51	Fraser Valley Produ
⊞ 54	Manning, Inc.
⊞ 68	Freedom Corporatio
⊞ 70	Rosewood, Inc.
⊞ 84	Macadam, Inc.
⊞ 99	KL Distributions

3. Open the Suppliers table and then add the following records:

   SupplierID: 16
   SupplierName: Olympic Suppliers
   StreetAddress: 1773 50th Avenue
   City: Seattle
   Prov/State: WA
   PostalCode: 98101
   Telephone: (206) 555-9488
   EmailAddress: olysuppliers@emcp.net

   SupplierID: 28
   SupplierName: Gorman Company
   StreetAddress: 543 26th Street
   City: Vancouver
   Prov/State: BC
   PostalCode: V5K 3C5
   Telephone: (778) 555-4550
   EmailAddress: gormanco@emcp.net

Suppliers								
SupplierID	SupplierName	StreetAddress	City	Prov/State	PostalCode	Telephone	EmailAddress	Click to Add
⊞ 10	Hopewell, Inc.	5600 Carver Road	Port Moody	BC	V3H 1A4	(604) 555-3843	hopewell@emcp.net	
⊞ 25	Langley Corporatio	805 First Avenue	Burnaby	BC	V3J 1C9	(604) 555-1200	langley@emcp.net	
⊞ 31	Sound Supplies	2104 Union Street	Seattle	WA	98105	(206) 555-4855	ssupplies@emcp.net	
⊞ 33	Bayside Supplies	6705 North Street	Bellingham	WA	98432	(360) 555-6005	bside@emcp.net	
⊞ 35	Emerald City Produ	1059 Pike Street	Seattle	WA	98102	(206) 555-7728	ecproducts@emcp.ne	
⊞ 38	Hadley Company	5845 Jefferson Stre	Seattle	WA	98107	(206) 555-8003	hcompany@emcp.net	
⊞ 51	Fraser Valley Produ	3894 Old Yale Roa(	Abbotsford	BC	V2S 1A9	(604) 555-1455	fvproducts@emcp.ne	
⊞ 54	Manning, Inc.	1039 South 22nd	Vancouver	BC	V5K 1R1	(604) 555-0087	manning@emcp.net	
⊞ 68	Freedom Corporatio	14 Fourth Avenue	Vancouver	BC	V5K 2C7	(604) 555-2155	freedom@emcp.net	
⊞ 70	Rosewood, Inc.	998 North 42nd Str	Vancouver	BC	V5K 2N8	(778) 555-6643	rosewood@emcp.net	
⊞ 84	Macadam, Inc.	675 Third Street	Vancouver	BC	V5K 2R9	(604) 555-5522	macadam@emcp.net	
⊞ 99	KL Distributions	402 Yukon Drive	Bellingham	WA	98435	(360) 555-3711	kldist@emcp.net	
⊞ 16	Olympic Suppliers	1773 50th Avenue	Seattle	WA	98101	(206) 555-9488	olysuppliers@emcp.ne	
⊞ 28	Gorman Company	543 26th Street	Vancouver	BC	V5K 3C5	(778) 555-4550	gormanco@emcp.net	

   Step 3

4. Delete the record for supplier number 38 (Hadley Company). At the message telling you that relationships that specify cascading deletes are about to cause records in this table and related tables to be deleted, click Yes.
5. Display the table in Print Preview, change to landscape orientation, and then print the table.
6. Close the Suppliers table.
7. Open the Products table and then add the following records to the table:

ProductID: 701-BK
Product: Basic first aid kit
SupplierID: 33
UnitsInStock: 8
UnitsOnOrder: 0
ReorderLevel: 5

ProductID: 703-SP
Product: Medical survival pack
SupplierID: 33
UnitsInStock: 8
UnitsOnOrder: 0
ReorderLevel: 5

ProductID: 185-10
Product: Trail water filter
SupplierID: 51
UnitsInStock: 4
UnitsOnOrder: 10
ReorderLevel: 10

ProductID: 185-50
Product: Trail filter replacement cartridge
SupplierID: 51
UnitsInStock: 14
UnitsOnOrder: 0
ReorderLevel: 10

8. Display the Products table in Print Preview, change to landscape orientation, change the top and bottom margins to 0.4 inch and then print the table. (The table will print on two pages.)
9. Close the Products table.
10. Open the Orders table and then add the following record:

OrderID: 1033
OrderDate: 2/15/2015
ProductID: 185-10
UnitsOrdered: 10
Amount: $310.90

11. Print and then close the Orders table.
12. Close **AL1-C2-PacTrek.accdb**.

Project 2 | **Create Relationships and Display Subdatasheets in a Database** | **2 Parts**

You will open a company database and then create one-to-many relationships between tables, as well as a one-to-one relationship. You will also display and edit subdatasheets.

Creating One-to-One Relationships ■■■■■■■■■■■■■■■

You can create a *one-to-one relationship* between tables in which each record in the first table matches only one record in the second table and one record in the second table matches only one record in the first table. A one-to-one relationship is not as common as a one-to-many relationship, since the type of information used to create the relationship can be stored in one table. A one-to-one relationship is generally used when you want to break a large table with many fields into two smaller tables.

The Relationships window displays any relationship you have defined between tables.

In Project 2a, you will create a one-to-one relationship between the Employees table and the Benefits table. Each record in the Employees table and each record in the Benefits table pertains to one employee. These two tables could be merged into one but the data in each table is easier to manage when separated. Figure 2.10 shows the relationships you will define between the tables in AL1-C2-Griffin.accdb. The Benefits table and the Departments table have been moved down so you can more easily see the relationships.

Figure 2.10 AL1-C2-Griffin.accdb Table Relationships

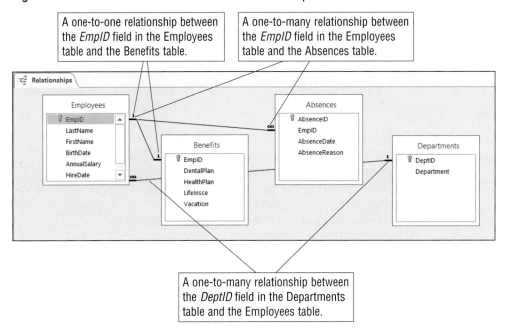

A one-to-one relationship between the *EmpID* field in the Employees table and the Benefits table.

A one-to-many relationship between the *EmpID* field in the Employees table and the Absences table.

A one-to-many relationship between the *DeptID* field in the Departments table and the Employees table.

| **Project 2a** | Creating One-to-Many and One-to-One Relationships | Part 1 of 2 |

1. Open **AL1-C2-Griffin.accdb** and enable the contents.
2. Click the DATABASE TOOLS tab.
3. Click the Relationships button in the Relationships group.
4. At the Show Table dialog box with the Tables tab selected, add all of the tables to the Relationships window by completing the following steps:
   a. Double-click *Employees* in the list box. (This inserts the table in the Relationships window.)
   b. Double-click *Benefits* in the list box.
   c. Double-click *Absences* in the list box.
   d. Double-click *Departments* in the list box.
   e. Click the Close button to close the Show Table dialog box.
5. At the Relationships window, create a one-to-many relationship with the *EmpID* field in the Employees table as the "one" and the *EmpID* field in the Absences table the "many" by completing the following steps:
   a. Position the arrow pointer on the *EmpID* field that displays in the *Employees* field list box.

b. Hold down the left mouse button, drag the arrow pointer (with a field icon attached) to the *EmpID* field in the *Absences* field list box, and then release the mouse button. (This causes the Edit Relationships dialog box to display.)

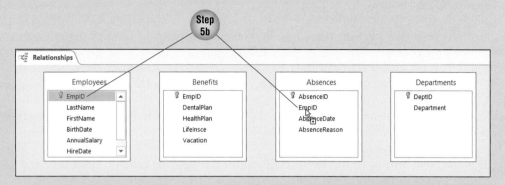

c. At the Edit Relationships dialog box, make sure *EmpID* displays in the *Table/Query* and *Related Table/Query* list boxes and the relationship type at the bottom of the dialog box displays as *One-To-Many*.
d. Click the *Enforce Referential Integrity* check box to insert a check mark.
e. Click the *Cascade Update Related Fields* check box to insert a check mark.
f. Click the *Cascade Delete Related Records* check box to insert a check mark.
g. Click the Create button. (A *1* appears at the *Employees* field list box side and an infinity symbol (∞) appears at the *Absences* field list box side of the black line.)
6. Complete steps similar to those in Step 5 to create a one-to-many relationship with the *DeptID* field in the Departments table the "one" and the *DeptID* field in the Employees table the "many." (You may need to scroll down the Employees field list box to display the *DeptID* field.)
7. Create a one-to-one relationship with the *EmpID* field in the Employees table and the *EmpID* field in the Benefits table by completing the following steps:
a. Position the arrow pointer on the *EmpID* field in the *Employees* field list box.
b. Hold down the left mouse button, drag the arrow pointer to the *EmpID* field in the *Benefits* field list box, and then release the mouse button. (This displays the Edit Relationships dialog box; notice at the bottom of the dialog box that the relationship type displays as *One-To-One*.)
c. Click the *Enforce Referential Integrity* check box to insert a check mark.
d. Click the *Cascade Update Related Fields* check box.
e. Click the *Cascade Delete Related Records* check box.
f. Click the Create button. (Notice that a *1* appears at the side of the *Employees* field list box and at the side of the *Benefits* field list box, indicating a one-to-one relationship.)

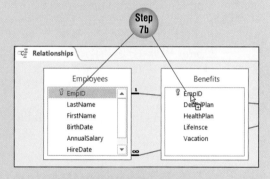

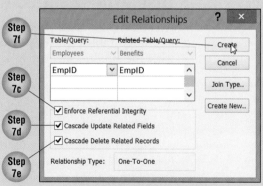

8. Click the Save button on the Quick Access toolbar to save the relationships.
9. Print the relationships by completing the following steps:
   a. Click the Relationship Report button in the Tools group.
   b. Click the Print button in the Print group.
   c. Click OK at the Print dialog box.
   d. Close the report by clicking the Close button that displays in the upper right corner of the work area.
   e. At the message asking if you want to save changes to the design of the report, click No.
10. Close the Relationships window by clicking the Close button that displays in the upper right corner of the work area.
11. Add a record to and delete a record from the Employees and Benefits tables by completing the following steps:
    a. Open the Employees table.
    b. Click the New button in the Records group on the HOME tab and then type the following data in the specified field:
       EmpID: 1096
       LastName: Schwartz
       FirstName: Bryan
       BirthDate: 5/21/1983
       DeptID: IT
       AnnualSalary: $45,000.00
       HireDate: 1/15/2010
    c. Delete the record for Trevor Sargent (employee number 1005). At the message telling you that relationships that specify cascading deletes are about to cause records in this table and related tables to be deleted, click Yes.
    d. Print and then close the Employees table.
12. Open the Benefits table and notice that the record for Trevor Sargent is deleted but the new employee record you entered in the Employees table is not reflected in the Benefits table. Add a new record for Bryan Schwartz with the following information:
    EmpID: 1096
    Dental Plan: (Press spacebar to remove check mark.)
    Health Plan: (Leave check mark.)
    Life Insurance: $100,000.00
    Vacation: 2 weeks
13. Print and then close the Benefits table.

Displaying Related Records in Subdatasheets ■■■■■■■■

When a relationship is established between tables, you can view and edit records in related tables with a *subdatasheet*. Figure 2.11 displays the Employees table with the subdatasheet displayed for employee Kate Navarro. The subdatasheet displays the fields in the Benefits table related to Kate Navarro. Use this sub-datasheet to view and edit information in both the Employees table and Absences table. Changes made to fields in a subdatasheet affect the table and any related table.

Access automatically inserts a plus symbol (referred to as an *expand indicator*) before each record in a table that is joined to another table by a one-to-many relationship. Click the expand indicator and if the table is related to only one other table, a subdatasheet containing fields from the related table displays below the record, as shown in Figure 2.11. To remove the subdatasheet, click the minus sign (referred to as a **collapse indicator**) preceding the record. (The plus symbol turns into the minus symbol when a subdatasheet displays.)

If a table has more than one relationship defined, clicking the expand indicator will display the Insert Subdatasheet dialog box, as shown in Figure 2.12. At this dialog box, click the desired table in the Tables list box and then click OK. You can also display the Insert Subdatasheet dialog box by clicking the More button in the Records group on the HOME tab, pointing to *Subdatasheet*, and then clicking *Subdatasheet*. Display subdatasheets for all records by clicking the More button, pointing to *Subdatasheet*, and then clicking *Expand All*. Remove all subdatasheets by clicking the More button, pointing to *Subdatasheet*, and then clicking *Collapse All*.

If a table is related to two or more tables, specify the desired subdatasheet at the Insert Subdatasheet dialog box. If you decide to display a different subdatasheet, remove the subdatasheet first, before selecting the next subdatasheet. Do this by clicking the More button, pointing to *Subdatasheet*, and then clicking *Remove*.

▼ **Quick Steps**

Display a Subdatasheet
1. Open table.
2. Click expand indicator at left side of desired record.
3. Click desired table at Insert Subdatasheet dialog box.
4. Click OK.

Figure 2.11 Table with Subdatasheet Displayed

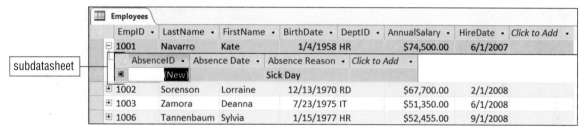

Figure 2.12 Insert Subdatasheet Dialog Box

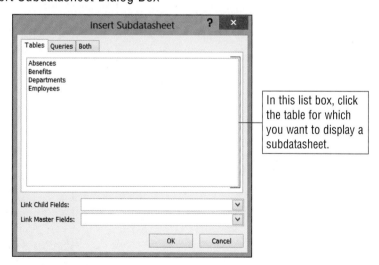

1. With the **AL1-C2-Griffin.accdb** database open, open the Employees table.
2. Display a subdatasheet by clicking the expand indicator (plus symbol) that displays at the left side of the first row (the row for Kate Navarro).

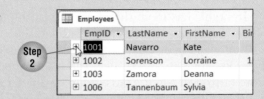

3. Remove the subdatasheet by clicking the collapse indicator (minus sign) that displays at the left side of the record for Kate Navarro.
4. Display subdatasheets for all of the records by clicking the More button in the Records group, pointing to *Subdatasheet*, and then clicking *Expand All*.

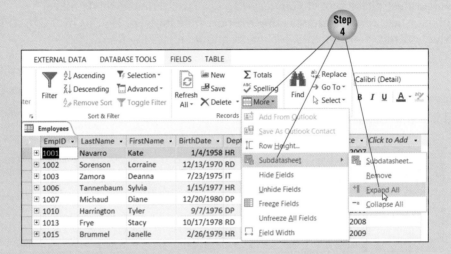

5. Remove the display of all subdatasheets by clicking the More button, pointing to *Subdatasheet*, and then clicking *Collapse All*.
6. Remove the connection between the Employees table and Absences table by clicking the More button, pointing to *Subdatasheet*, and then clicking *Remove*. (Notice that the expand indicators [plus symbols] no longer display before each record.)

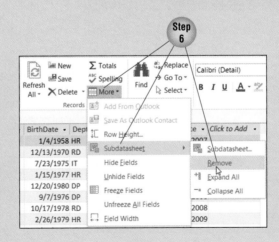

7. Suppose that the employee, Diane Michaud, has moved to a different department and has had an increase in salary. Display the Benefits subdatasheet and make changes to fields in the Employees table and Benefits table by completing the following steps:

a. Click the More button in the Records group, point to *Subdatasheet*, and then click *Subdatasheet* at the side menu.

b. At the Insert Subdatasheet dialog box, click *Benefits* in the list box and then click OK.

c. Change the department ID for the record for *Diane Michaud* from *DP* to *A*.

d. Change the salary from *$56,250.00* to *$57,500.00*.

e. Click the expand indicator (plus symbol) that displays at the left side of the record for Diane Michaud.

f. Insert a check mark in the *Dental Plan* check box and change the vacation from 3 weeks to 4 weeks.

g. Click the collapse indicator (minus symbol) that displays at the left side of the record for Diane Michaud.

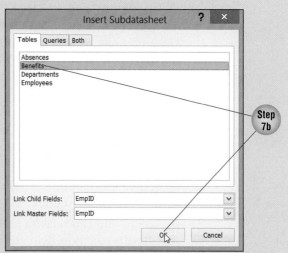

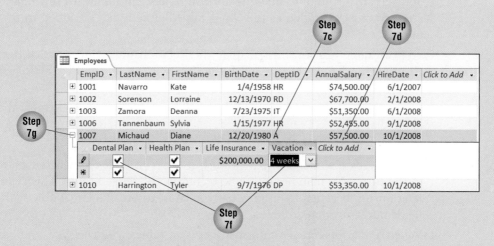

8. Click the Save button on the Quick Access toolbar.
9. Print and then close the Employees table.
10. Open, print, and then close the Benefits table.
11. Close the **AL1-C2-Griffin.accdb** database.

Chapter Summary

- Access is a relational database software program in which you can create tables that are related or connected.

- When planning a table, take time to determine how to break down the required data and what relationships need to be defined to eliminate data redundancies.

- Generally, one field in a table must be unique so that one record can be distinguished from another. A field with a unique value is considered a primary key field.

- A table can have only one primary key field and it is the field by which the table is sorted whenever it is opened.

- In a field defined as a primary key field, duplicate values are not allowed. Access also expects a value in each record in the primary key field.

- Typically, a primary key field in one table becomes the foreign key field in a related table. Data in a foreign key field must match data in the primary key field of the related tables.

- In Access, you can relate a table to another by performing a join. When tables that have a common field are joined, you can extract data from both tables as if they were one large table.

- You can create a one-to-many relationship between tables. In this relationship, a record must be added to the "one" table before it can be added to the "many" table.

- To print table relationships, display the Relationships window, click the Relationship Report button, click the Print button on the PRINT PREVIEW tab, and then click OK at the Print dialog box.

- At the Relationships window, click the Show Table button to display the Show Table dialog box.

- You can edit or delete a relationship between tables.

- You can create a one-to-one relationship between tables in which each record in the first table matches only one record in the related table. This type of relationship is generally used when you want to break a large table with many fields into two smaller tables.

- When a relationship is established between tables, you can view and edit fields in related tables with a subdatasheet.

- To display a subdatasheet for a record, click the expand indicator (plus symbol) that displays to the left of the record. To display subdatasheets for all records, click the More button in the Records group on the HOME tab, point to *Subdatasheet*, and then click *Expand All*.

- Display the Insert Subdatasheet dialog box by clicking the More button in the Reports group on the HOME tab, pointing to *Subdatasheet*, and then clicking *Subdatasheet*.

- Turn off the display of a subdatasheet by clicking the collapse indicator (minus symbol) at the beginning of the record. To turn off the display of subdatasheets for all records, click the More button, point to *Subdatasheet*, and then click *Collapse All*.

Commands Review

FEATURE	RIBBON, GROUP	BUTTON	OPTION
Edit Relationships dialog box	RELATIONSHIP TOOLS DESIGN, Tools		
Insert Subdatasheet dialog box	HOME, Records		Subdatasheet, Subdatasheet
primary key	TABLE TOOLS DESIGN, Tools		
print relationships report	RELATIONSHIP TOOLS DESIGN, Tools		
Relationships window	DATABASE TOOLS, Relationships		
Show Table dialog box	RELATIONSHIP TOOLS DESIGN, Relationships		

Concepts Check   Test Your Knowledge

Completion: In the space provided at the right, indicate the correct term, symbol, or command.

1. In Access, one table can be related to another, which is generally referred to as performing this. _____

2. A database table can contain a foreign key field and this type of key field. _____

3. Open a table, click the View button on the HOME tab, and the table displays in this view. _____

4. In a one-to-many relationship, the table containing the "one" is referred to as this. _____

5. In a one-to-many relationship, the table containing the "many" is referred to as this. _____

6. In a one-to-many relationship, Access follows a set of rules that enforces consistency between related tables and is referred to as this. _____

7. In related tables, this symbol displays near the black line next to the field list box of the related table. _____

8. The black line that connects the field list boxes of related tables is referred to as this. _____

9. Establish this type of relationship between tables in which each record in the first table matches only one record in the second table and only one record in the second table matches each record in the first table.

_____

10. The plus symbol that displays at the beginning of a record in a related table is referred to as this.

_____

11. The minus symbol that displays at the beginning of a record in a related table with a subdatasheet displayed is referred to as this.

_____

12. Display subdatasheets for all records by clicking the More button, pointing to *Subdatasheet*, and then clicking this option.

_____

Skills Check   Assess Your Performance

The database designer for Copper State Insurance has created the database diagram shown in Figure 2.13 to manage company data. You will open the Copper State Insurance database and maintain and create tables that follow the diagram.

Figure 2.13 Copper State Insurance Database Design

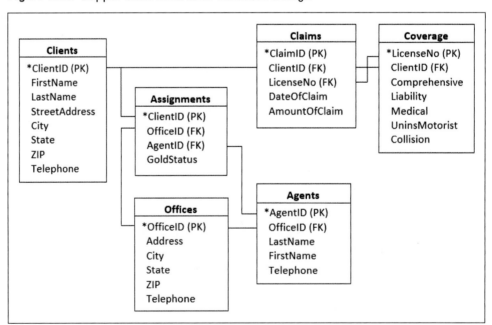

Assessment

1 CREATE RELATIONSHIPS IN AN INSURANCE COMPANY DATABASE

1. Open **AL1-C2-CopperState.accdb** and enable the contents.
2. Open the Claims table.
3. Display the table in Design view, define the *ClaimID* field as the primary key field, click the Save button on the Quick Access toolbar, and then close the Claims table.
4. Display the Relationships window and then insert the Clients, Claims, and Coverage tables.
5. Create a one-to-many relationship with the *ClientID* field in the Clients table the "one" and the *ClientID* field in the Claims table the "many." Enforce referential integrity and cascade fields and records.
6. Create a one-to-many relationship with the *ClientID* field in the Clients table the "one" and the *ClientID* field in the Coverage table the "many." Enforce referential integrity and cascade fields and records.
7. Create a one-to-many relationship with the *LicenseNo* field in the Coverage table the "one" and the *LicenseNo* field in the Claims table the "many." Enforce referential integrity and cascade fields and records.
8. Save and then print the relationships.
9. Close the relationships report without saving it and close the Relationships window.

Assessment

2 CREATE A NEW TABLE AND RELATE THE TABLE

1. With **AL1-C2-CopperState.accdb** open, create the Offices table shown in Figure 2.14. Change the data type of the first column to *Short Text*. (Do this with the *Data Type* option box in the Formatting group on the TABLE TOOLS FIELDS tab.) Change the field size to 2 characters. Change the default value for the *State* field to *AZ*.
2. After typing the records, adjust the column widths to accommodate the longest entry in each column and then save the Offices table.
3. Print and then close the Offices table.
4. Display the Relationships window and then add the Offices table and the Assignments table to the window.
5. Create a one-to-many relationship with the *OfficeID* field in the Offices table the "one" and the *OfficeID* field in the Assignments table the "many." Enforce referential integrity and cascade fields and records.
6. Create a one-to-one relationship with the *ClientID* field in the Clients table and the *ClientID* field in the Assignments table. Enforce referential integrity and cascade fields and records.
7. Save and then print the relationships in landscape orientation. To do this, click the Landscape button in the Page Layout group in Print Preview.
8. Close the relationships report without saving it and then close the Relationships window.

Figure 2.14 Assessment 2 Offices Table

OfficeID	Address	City	State	ZIP	Telephone	Click to Add
GN	North 51st Avenue	Glendale	AZ	85305	(653) 555-8800	
GW	West Bell Road	Glendale	AZ	85312	(623) 555-4300	
PG	Grant Street West	Phoenix	AZ	85003	(602) 555-6200	
PM	McDowell Road	Phoenix	AZ	85012	(602) 555-3800	
SE	East Thomas Road	Scottsdale	AZ	85251	(480) 555-5500	
SN	North 68th Street	Scottsdale	AZ	85257	(480) 555-9000	
*			AZ			

Assessment

3 DELETE AND EDIT RECORDS IN TABLES

1. With **AL1-C2-CopperState.accdb** open, open the Clients table.
2. Delete the record for Harold McDougal (client number 9879). (At the message telling you that relationships that specify cascading deletes are about to cause records in this table and related tables to be deleted, click Yes.)
3. Delete the record for Vernon Cook (client number 7335). (At the message telling you that relationships that specify cascading deletes are about to cause records in this table and related tables to be deleted, click Yes.)
4. Change the client number for Paul Vuong from *4300* to *2560*.
5. Print the Clients table in landscape orientation and then close the table.
6. Open the Claims table, print the table, and then close the table. (The Claims table initially contained two entries for client number 9879 and one entry for 7335. These entries were deleted automatically when you deleted the records in the Clients table.)

Assessment

4 DISPLAY AND EDIT RECORDS IN A SUBDATASHEET

1. With **AL1-C2-CopperState.accdb** open, open the Clients table.
2. Click the expand indicator (plus symbol) that displays at the left side of the record for Erin Hagedorn. At the Insert Subdatasheet dialog box, click *Claims* in the list box and then click OK.
3. Change the amount of the claim from *$1,450.00* to *$1,797.00*, change Erin's street address from *4818 Oakes Boulevard* to *763 51st Avenue*, and change her zip code from *85018* to *85014*.
4. Click the collapse indicator (minus symbol) that displays at the left side of the record for Erin Hagedorn.
5. Remove the connection between the Clients and Claims tables by clicking the More button in the Records group on the HOME tab, pointing to *Subdatasheet*, and then clicking *Remove*.
6. Click the More button in the Records group, point to *Subdatasheet*, and then click *Subdatasheet*.
7. At the Insert Subdatasheet dialog box, click *Coverage* in the list box and then click OK.
8. Expand all records by clicking the More button, pointing to *Subdatasheet*, and then clicking *Expand All*.
9. Change the telephone number for Claire Azevedo (client number 1379) from *480-555-2154* to *480-555-2143* and insert check marks in the *Medical* field and the *UninsMotorist* field.
10. Change the last name of Joanne Donnelly (client number 1574) to *Marquez* and remove the check mark from the *Collision* field.
11. At the record for Brenda Lazzuri (client number 3156), insert check marks in the *UninsMotorist* field and *Collision* field for both vehicles.
12. Click in any field heading and then collapse all records.
13. Remove the connection between the Clients and Coverage tables.
14. Save, print, and then close the Clients table. (Make sure the table displays in landscape orientation.)
15. Open the Coverage table, print the table, and then close the table.
16. Close **AL1-C2-CopperState.accdb**.

Visual Benchmark
Demonstrate Your Proficiency

CREATE A BOOKINGS TABLE

1. Open **AL1-C2-CarefreeTravel.accdb** and then create the Bookings table shown in Figure 2.15. You determine the data types and field sizes. Create a more descriptive caption for each field name and create a description for each field.
2. Save, print, and then close the Bookings table.
3. Create a relationship between the Agents table and Bookings table. You determine what table contains the "one" and what table contains the "many." Enforce referential integrity and cascade fields and records.
4. Create a relationship between the Tours table and Bookings table. You determine what table contains the "one" and what table contains the "many." Enforce referential integrity and cascade fields and records.
5. Save and then print the relationships and then close the Relationships window.
6. Open the Agents table.
7. Change the AgentID for Wayne Postovic from *137* to *115*.
8. Change Jenna Williamson's last name from *Williamson* to *Parr*.
9. Print and then close the Agents table.
10. Open the Bookings table, print the table, and then close the table. (Notice that the *137* AgentID in the Bookings table is changed to *115*. This is because the tables are related and the changes you make in the primary table are made automatically in the related table.)
11. Close **AL1-C2-CarefreeTravel.accdb**.

Figure 2.15 Visual Benchmark Bookings Table

BookingID ▾	BookingDate ▾	TourID ▾	AgentID ▾	NumberPersons ▾	Click to Add ▾
1	6/1/2015	AF02	114	8	
2	6/1/2015	HC01	109	2	
3	6/3/2015	CR02	103	2	
4	6/4/2015	AK01	137	4	
5	6/5/2015	HC01	109	2	
6	6/6/2015	AT02	109	4	
7	6/8/2015	HS02	104	2	
8	6/10/2015	HC01	125	2	
9	6/11/2015	AK01	142	4	
10	6/13/2015	AT01	112	2	
11	6/15/2015	HC03	129	2	
* (New)				0	

Case Study   Apply Your Skills

You are the manager for Gold Star Cleaning Services and your company is switching over to Access for managing company data. The database designer has provided you with the database diagram in Figure 2.17. He wants you to follow the diagram when creating the database.

Figure 2.17 Gold Star Cleaning Services Database Diagram

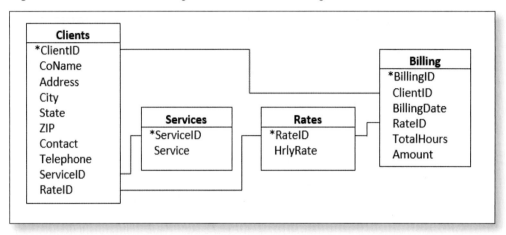

Part 1

Create a new database named **AL1-C2-GoldStar.accdb** and then create the Clients table shown in the database diagram. The database designer has asked you to include an appropriate caption and description for each field. Specify a field size of 3 characters for the *ClientID* field, 4 characters for the *ServiceID* field, and 1 character for the *RateID* field. You determine the field sizes for the *State*, *ZIP*, and *Telephone* fields. The designer also wants you to set the default value for the *City* field to *St. Louis* and the *State* field to *MO*. Type the following records in the table:

ClientID: 101
CoName: Smithson Realty
Address: 492 Papin Street
City: (default value)
State: (default value)
ZIP: 63108
Contact: Danielle Snowden
Telephone: (314) 555-3588
ServiceID: GS-1
RateID: B

*ClientID:*102
CoName: Air-Flow Systems
Address: 1058 Pine Street
City: (default value)
State: (default value)
ZIP: 63186
Contact: Nick Cline
Telephone: (314) 555-9452
ServiceID: GS-3
RateID: A

ClientID: 107
CoName: Mainstreet Mortgage
Address: North 22nd Street
City: (default value)
State: (default value)
ZIP: 63134
Contact: Ted Farrell
Telephone: (314) 555-7744
ServiceID: GS-1
RateID: D

ClientID: 110
CoName: Firstline Finances
Address: 104 Scott Avenue
City: (default value)
State: (default value
ZIP: 63126
Contact: Robert Styer
Telephone: (314) 555-8343
ServiceID: GS-2
RateID: A

ClientID: 112
CoName: GB Construction
Address: 988 Lucas Avenue
City: (default value)
State: (default value)
ZIP: 63175
Contact: Joy Ewing
Telephone: (314) 555-0036
ServiceID: GS-1
RateID: C

ClientID: 115
CoName: Simko Equipment
Address: 1200 Market Street
City: (default value)
State: (default value)
ZIP: 63140
Contact: Dale Aldrich
Telephone: (314) 555-3315
ServiceID: GS-3
RateID: C

Create the Services table shown in the database diagram. Change the *ServiceID* field size to 4 characters. Type the following records in the table:

ServiceID: GS-1
Service: Deep cleaning all rooms and surfaces, garbage removal, recycling, carpet cleaning, disinfecting

ServiceID: GS-2
Service: Deep cleaning all rooms and surfaces, garbage removal, disinfecting

ServiceID: GS-3
Service: Deep cleaning all rooms and surfaces, disinfecting

Create the Rates table shown in the database diagram. Change the *RateID* field size to 1 character. Type the following records in the table:

RateID: A
HrlyRate: $75.50

RateID: B
HrlyRate: $65.00

RateID: C
HrlyRate: $59.75

RateID: D
HrlyRate: $50.50

Create the Billing table shown in the database diagram. Change the *BillingID* field size to 2 characters, the *ClientID* field size to 3 characters, and the *RateID* field size to 1 character. Apply the appropriate data types to the fields. Type the following records in the table:

BillingID: 40
ClientID: 101
BillingDate: 4/1/2015
RateID: B
TotalHours: 26
Amount: $1,690.00

BillingID: 41
ClientID: 102
BillingDate: 4/1/2015
RateID: A
TotalHours: 32
Amount: $2,416.00

BillingID: 42
ClientID: 107
BillingDate: 4/1/2015
RateID: D
TotalHours: 15
Amount: $747.50

BillingID: 43
ClientID: 110
BillingDate: 4/1/2015
RateID: A
TotalHours: 30
Amount: $2,265.00

BillingID: 44
ClientID: 112
BillingDate: 4/1/2015
RateID: C
TotalHours: 20
Amount: $1,195.00

BillingID: 45
ClientID: 115
BillingDate: 4/1/2015
RateID: C
TotalHours: 22
Amount: $1,314.50

Automatically adjust the column widths of each table to accommodate the longest entry in each column and then print each table on one page. *Hint: Check the table in Print Preview and, if necessary, change to landscape orientation and change the margins*.

Part 2

With **AL1-C2-GoldStar.accdb** open, create the one-to-many relationships required to connect the tables. (Refer to Figure 2.17 as a guide.) You will need to increase the size of the Clients field list box to view all of the fields. To do this, position the mouse pointer on the bottom border of the Clients field list box in the Relationships window until the pointer turns into a white arrow pointing up and down. Hold down the left mouse button, drag down to the desired position, and then release the mouse button. Print the relationships report.

Part 3

Open the Services table and then make the following changes to the field values in the *ServiceID* field:

Change *GS-1* to *GS-A*
Change *GS-2* to *GS-B*
Change *GS-3* to *GS-C*

Print and then close the Services table. Open the Clients table, delete the record for client number 112, and then insert the following record:

ClientID: 108
Name: Cedar Ridge Products
Address: 6400 Olive Street
City: (default value)
State: (default value)
ZIP: 63114
Contact: Penny Childers
Telephone: (314) 555-7660
ServiceID: GS-B
RateID: B

Print and then close the Clients table. Open the Billing table, print the table, and then close the table. Close **AL1-C2-GoldStar.accdb**.

MICROSOFT® ACCESS®

CHAPTER 3

Performing Queries

PERFORMANCE OBJECTIVES

Upon successful completion of Chapter 3, you will be able to:
- Design queries to extract specific data from tables
- Modify queries
- Design queries with *Or* and *And* criteria
- Use the Simple Query Wizard to create queries
- Create a calculated field
- Use aggregate functions in queries
- Create crosstab, duplicate, and unmatched queries

One of the primary uses of a database is to extract the specific information needed to answer questions and make decisions. A company might need to know information such as how much inventory is currently on hand, which products have been ordered, which accounts are past due, or which customers live in a particular city. You can extract specific information from a table or multiple tables by completing a query. You will learn how to perform a variety of queries on information in tables in this chapter. Model answers for this chapter's projects appear on the following pages.

Note: Before beginning the projects, copy the AL1C3 subfolder from the AL1 folder on the CD that accompanies this textbook to your storage medium and make AL1C3 the active folder.

Project 1 Design Queries

Project 1a

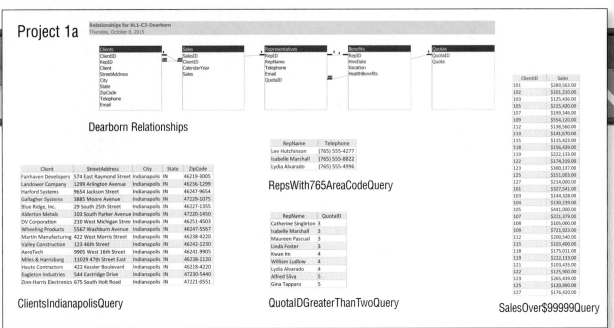

Dearborn Relationships

ClientsIndianapolisQuery

Client	StreetAddress	City	State	ZipCode
Fairhaven Developers	574 East Raymond Street	Indianapolis	IN	46219-3005
Landower Company	1299 Arlington Avenue	Indianapolis	IN	46236-1299
Harford Systems	9654 Jackson Street	Indianapolis	IN	46247-9654
Gallagher Systems	3885 Moore Avenue	Indianapolis	IN	47229-1075
Blue Ridge, Inc.	29 South 25th Street	Indianapolis	IN	46227-1355
Alderton Metals	103 South Parker Avenue	Indianapolis	IN	47220-1450
DV Corporation	210 West Michigan Stree	Indianapolis	IN	46251-4503
Wheeling Products	5567 Washburn Avenue	Indianapolis	IN	46247-5567
Martin Manufacturing	422 West Morris Street	Indianapolis	IN	46238-4220
Valley Construction	123 46th Street	Indianapolis	IN	46242-1230
AeroTech	9905 West 16th Street	Indianapolis	IN	46241-9905
Miles & Harrisburg	11029 47th Street East	Indianapolis	IN	46238-1120
Haute Contractors	422 Kessler Boulevard	Indianapolis	IN	46218-4220
Eagleton Industries	544 Eastridge Drive	Indianapolis	IN	47230-5440
Zinn-Harris Electronics	675 South Holt Road	Indianapolis	IN	47221-0551

RepsWith765AreaCodeQuery

RepName	Telephone
Lee Hutchinson	(765) 555-4277
Isabelle Marshall	(765) 555-8822
Lydia Alvarado	(765) 555-4996

QuotaIDGreaterThanTwoQuery

RepName	QuotaID
Catherine Singleton	3
Isabelle Marshall	3
Maureen Pascual	3
Linda Foster	3
Kwan Im	4
William Ludlow	4
Lydia Alvarado	4
Alfred Silva	5
Gina Tapparo	5

SalesOver$99999Query

ClientID	Sales
101	$289,563.00
102	$101,210.00
103	$125,436.00
105	$215,420.00
107	$199,346.00
109	$554,120.00
112	$138,560.00
113	$141,670.00
115	$115,423.00
118	$156,439.00
119	$222,133.00
122	$174,319.00
123	$300,137.00
125	$151,003.00
127	$214,000.00
101	$327,541.00
103	$144,328.00
104	$130,239.00
105	$441,000.00
107	$221,379.00
108	$105,000.00
109	$721,923.00
112	$200,540.00
115	$103,400.00
118	$175,011.00
119	$222,133.00
121	$103,435.00
122	$125,900.00
123	$265,439.00
125	$120,890.00
127	$176,420.00

Project 1b

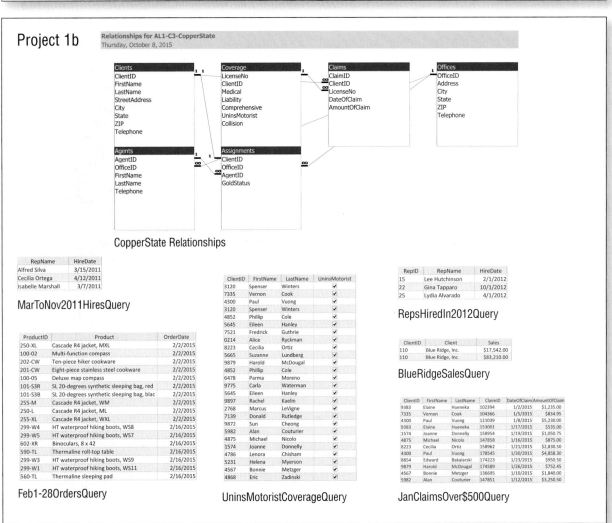

CopperState Relationships

MarToNov2011HiresQuery

RepName	HireDate
Alfred Silva	3/15/2011
Cecilia Ortega	4/12/2011
Isabelle Marshall	3/7/2011

RepsHiredIn2012Query

RepID	RepName	HireDate
15	Lee Hutchinson	2/1/2012
22	Gina Tapparo	10/1/2012
25	Lydia Alvarado	4/1/2012

BlueRidgeSalesQuery

ClientID	Client	Sales
110	Blue Ridge, Inc.	$17,542.00
110	Blue Ridge, Inc.	$83,210.00

Feb1-28OrdersQuery

ProductID	Product	OrderDate
250-XL	Cascade R4 jacket, MXL	2/2/2015
100-02	Multi-function compass	2/2/2015
202-CW	Ten-piece hiker cookware	2/2/2015
201-CW	Eight-piece stainless steel cookware	2/2/2015
100-05	Deluxe map compass	2/2/2015
101-S3R	SL 20-degrees synthetic sleeping bag, red	2/2/2015
101-S3B	SL 20-degrees synthetic sleeping bag, blac	2/2/2015
255-M	Cascade R4 jacket, WM	2/2/2015
250-L	Cascade R4 jacket, ML	2/2/2015
255-XL	Cascade R4 jacket, WXL	2/2/2015
299-W4	HT waterproof hiking boots, WS8	2/16/2015
299-W5	HT waterproof hiking boots, WS7	2/16/2015
602-XR	Binoculars, 8 x 42	2/16/2015
590-TL	Thermaline roll-top table	2/16/2015
299-W3	HT waterproof hiking boots, WS9	2/16/2015
299-W1	HT waterproof hiking boots, WS11	2/16/2015
560-TL	Thermaline sleeping pad	2/16/2015

UninsMotoristCoverageQuery

ClientID	FirstName	LastName	UninsMotorist
3120	Spenser	Winters	✔
7335	Vernon	Cook	✔
4300	Paul	Vuong	✔
3120	Spenser	Winters	✔
4852	Phillip	Cole	✔
5645	Eileen	Hanley	✔
7521	Fredrick	Guthrie	✔
0214	Alice	Ryckman	✔
8223	Cecilia	Ortiz	✔
5665	Suzanne	Lundberg	✔
9879	Harold	McDougal	✔
4852	Phillip	Cole	✔
6478	Parma	Moreno	✔
9775	Carla	Waterman	✔
5645	Eileen	Hanley	✔
9897	Rachel	Kaelin	✔
2768	Marcus	LeVigne	✔
7139	Donald	Rutledge	✔
9872	Sun	Cheong	✔
5982	Alan	Couturier	✔
4875	Michael	Nicolo	✔
1574	Joanne	Donnelly	✔
4786	Lenora	Chisham	✔
5231	Helena	Myerson	✔
4567	Bonnie	Metzger	✔
4868	Eric	Zadinski	✔

JanClaimsOver$500Query

ClientID	FirstName	LastName	ClaimID	DateOfClaim	AmountOfClaim
9383	Elaine	Hueneka	102394	1/2/2015	$1,235.00
7335	Vernon	Cook	104366	1/5/2015	$834.95
4300	Paul	Vuong	121039	1/8/2015	$5,230.00
9383	Elaine	Hueneka	153001	1/17/2015	$535.00
1574	Joanne	Donnelly	158954	1/19/2015	$1,050.75
4875	Michael	Nicolo	147858	1/16/2015	$875.00
8223	Cecilia	Ortiz	158962	1/21/2015	$2,830.50
4300	Paul	Vuong	178545	1/30/2015	$4,858.30
8854	Edward	Bakalarski	174223	1/23/2015	$950.50
9879	Harold	McDougal	174589	1/26/2015	$752.45
4567	Bonnie	Metzger	136695	1/10/2015	$1,840.00
5982	Alan	Couturier	147851	1/12/2015	$3,250.50

Project 1c

ProductID	SupplierID	UnitsOrdered	Amount
442-1B	42	10	$1,495.00
780-2	99	10	$1,288.50
250-XL	60	10	$1,285.00
250-L	60	10	$1,285.00
101-S3R	54	10	$1,199.50
101-S3B	54	10	$1,137.50
299-M3	31	10	$887.90
299-M2	31	10	$887.90
299-M5	31	10	$887.90
299-W4	31	10	$752.90
299-W5	31	10	$752.90
299-W3	31	10	$752.90
299-W1	31	8	$602.32
255-XL	60	5	$599.50
255-M	60	5	$599.50
560-TL	25	20	$397.00
155-35	10	10	$199.50
375-S	68	20	$199.00
375-M	68	20	$199.00
590-TL	25	5	$196.25
209-XL	68	25	$180.00
209-L	68	25	$173.75
210-L	68	25	$162.25
209-XXL	68	20	$145.80
100-05	84	5	$129.75
371-L	68	10	$129.50
202-CW	15	5	$124.25
155-20	10	15	$104.25
201-CW	15	5	$99.75
210-M	68	15	$97.35
100-02	84	10	$45.95
152-H	10	15	$44.85

OrdersLessThan$1500Query

OfficeID	FirstName	LastName
GW	Carlos	Alvarez
GW	Joanne	Donnelly
GW	Cecilia	Ortiz
GW	Donald	Rutledge
GW	Paul	Vuong

GWClientsQuery

RepName	Client	Sales
Andre Kulisek	HE Systems	$721,923.00
Andre Kulisek	HE Systems	$554,120.00
Lee Hutchinson	Harford Systems	$441,000.00
Linda Foster	Bering Company	$327,541.00
Kwan Im	Eagleton Industries	$300,137.00
Linda Foster	Bering Company	$289,563.00
Kwan Im	Eagleton Industries	$265,439.00
Craig Johnson	Miles & Harrisburg	$222,133.00
Craig Johnson	Miles & Harrisburg	$222,133.00
Catherine Singleton	Gallagher Systems	$221,379.00
Lee Hutchinson	Harford Systems	$215,420.00
Catherine Singleton	Zinn-Harris Electronics	$214,000.00
Gina Tapparo	DV Corporation	$200,540.00
Catherine Singleton	Gallagher Systems	$199,346.00
Catherine Singleton	Zinn-Harris Electronics	$176,420.00
David DeBruler	AeroTech	$175,011.00
Jaren Newman	Haute Contractors	$174,319.00
David DeBruler	AeroTech	$156,439.00
Cecilia Ortega	Dover Industries	$151,003.00
Alfred Silva	Clearwater Service	$144,328.00
Catherine Singleton	Franklin Services	$141,670.00
Gina Tapparo	DV Corporation	$138,560.00
Robin Rehberg	Landower Company	$130,239.00
Jaren Newman	Haute Contractors	$125,900.00
Alfred Silva	Clearwater Service	$125,436.00
Cecilia Ortega	Dover Industries	$120,890.00
Craig Johnson	Wheeling Products	$115,423.00
Edward Harris	Karris Supplies	$105,000.00
William Ludlow	Madison Electrics	$103,435.00
Craig Johnson	Wheeling Products	$103,400.00
Kwan Im	Fairhaven Developers	$101,210.00

SalesMoreThan$100000Query

Project 1d

RepName	Client	Sales
William Ludlow	Madison Electrics	$99,450.00
Robin Rehberg	Landower Company	$97,653.00
Kwan Im	Fairhaven Developers	$95,630.00
Isabelle Marshall	Providence, Inc.	$85,628.00
Maureen Pascual	Blue Ridge, Inc.	$83,210.00
Isabelle Marshall	Providence, Inc.	$75,462.00
Catherine Singleton	Franklin Services	$65,411.00
Lydia Alvarado	Martin Manufacturing	$61,539.00
Edward Harris	Karris Supplies	$61,349.00
Jaren Newman	Paragon Corporation	$51,237.00
Alfred Silva	Alderton Metals	$45,230.00
Lydia Alvarado	Martin Manufacturing	$35,679.00
Craig Johnson	Hoosier Corporation	$31,935.00
Kwan Im	Milltown Contractors	$31,230.00
Craig Johnson	Hoosier Corporation	$24,880.00
Lee Hutchinson	Valley Construction	$22,478.00
Jaren Newman	Paragon Corporation	$20,137.00
Maureen Pascual	Blue Ridge, Inc.	$17,542.00
Lee Hutchinson	Valley Construction	$15,248.00
Alfred Silva	Northstar Services	$15,094.00
Alfred Silva	Alderton Metals	$9,547.00
Alfred Silva	Northstar Services	$9,457.00
Kwan Im	Milltown Contractors	$2,356.00

SalesLessThan$100000Query

RepName	Vacation
Alfred Silva	3 weeks
Cecilia Ortega	3 weeks
Isabelle Marshall	3 weeks
Craig Johnson	3 weeks
Gina Tapparo	3 weeks
Edward Harris	3 weeks

RepsWith3WeekVacationsQuery

Project 1e

RepName	Vacation
William Ludlow	4 weeks
Alfred Silva	3 weeks
Cecilia Ortega	3 weeks
Robin Rehberg	4 weeks
Isabelle Marshall	3 weeks
Craig Johnson	3 weeks
Gina Tapparo	3 weeks
Edward Harris	3 weeks

RepsWith3Or4WeekVacationsQuery

Client	City	Sales
Fairhaven Developers	Indianapolis	$101,210.00
Landower Company	Indianapolis	$130,239.00
Harford Systems	Indianapolis	$215,420.00
Harford Systems	Indianapolis	$441,000.00
Gallagher Systems	Indianapolis	$199,346.00
Gallagher Systems	Indianapolis	$221,379.00
DV Corporation	Indianapolis	$138,560.00
DV Corporation	Indianapolis	$200,540.00
Wheeling Products	Indianapolis	$115,423.00
Wheeling Products	Indianapolis	$103,400.00
AeroTech	Indianapolis	$156,439.00
AeroTech	Indianapolis	$175,011.00
Miles & Harrisburg	Indianapolis	$222,133.00
Miles & Harrisburg	Indianapolis	$222,133.00
Haute Contractors	Indianapolis	$174,319.00
Haute Contractors	Indianapolis	$125,900.00
Eagleton Industries	Indianapolis	$300,137.00
Eagleton Industries	Indianapolis	$265,439.00
Zinn-Harris Electronics	Indianapolis	$214,000.00
Zinn-Harris Electronics	Indianapolis	$176,420.00

SalesOver$100000IndianapolisQuery

SupplierID	SupplierName	Product
25	Langley Corporation	Thermaline sleeping pad
25	Langley Corporation	Thermaline light-weight cot
25	Langley Corporation	Thermaline camp seat
25	Langley Corporation	Thermaline roll-top table
31	Sound Supplies	HT waterproof hiking boots, MS13
31	Sound Supplies	HT waterproof hiking boots, MS12
31	Sound Supplies	HT waterproof hiking boots, MS11
31	Sound Supplies	HT waterproof hiking boots, MS10
31	Sound Supplies	HT waterproof hiking boots, MS9
31	Sound Supplies	HT waterproof hiking boots, WS11
31	Sound Supplies	HT waterproof hiking boots, WS10
31	Sound Supplies	HT waterproof hiking boots, WS9
31	Sound Supplies	HT waterproof hiking boots, WS8
31	Sound Supplies	HT waterproof hiking boots, WS7
31	Sound Supplies	HT waterproof hiking boots, WS6
42	Fraser Valley Products	Polar backpack, 150BR
42	Fraser Valley Products	Polar backpack, 150RW
42	Fraser Valley Products	Polar backpack, 250BR
42	Fraser Valley Products	Polar backpack, 250RW

Suppliers25-31-42Query

OrderID	SupplierName	Product	UnitsOrdered
1017	Freedom Corporation	Gordon wool ski hat, L	25
1009	Freedom Corporation	Gordon wool ski hat, XL	25
1008	Freedom Corporation	Gordon wool ski hat, XXL	20
1012	Freedom Corporation	Tech-lite ski hat, L	25
1013	Freedom Corporation	Tech-lite ski hat, M	15
1016	Freedom Corporation	Lite-tech ski gloves, ML	10
1015	Freedom Corporation	Lite-tech ski gloves, WM	20
1014	Freedom Corporation	Lite-tech ski gloves, WS	20

SkiHatsGlovesOnOrderQuery

ProductID	Product	SupplierName
443-1B	Polar backpack, 250RW	Fraser Valley Products
101-S1B	SL 0-degrees down sleeping bag, black	Manning, Inc.
101-S1R	SL 0-degrees down sleeping bag, red	Manning, Inc.
101-S2B	SL 15-degrees synthetic sleeping bag, blac	Manning, Inc.
101-S2R	SL 15-degrees synthetic sleeping bag, red	Manning, Inc.
101-S3B	SL 20-degrees synthetic sleeping bag, blac	Manning, Inc.
101-S3R	SL 20-degrees synthetic sleeping bag, red	Manning, Inc.
299-M1	HT waterproof hiking boots, MS13	Sound Supplies
299-M2	HT waterproof hiking boots, MS12	Sound Supplies
299-M3	HT waterproof hiking boots, MS11	Sound Supplies
299-M4	HT waterproof hiking boots, MS10	Sound Supplies
299-M5	HT waterproof hiking boots, MS9	Sound Supplies
299-W1	HT waterproof hiking boots, WS11	Sound Supplies
299-W2	HT waterproof hiking boots, WS10	Sound Supplies
299-W3	HT waterproof hiking boots, WS9	Sound Supplies
299-W4	HT waterproof hiking boots, WS8	Sound Supplies
299-W5	HT waterproof hiking boots, WS7	Sound Supplies

BootsSleepingBagsBackpacksQuery

FirstName	LastName	Medical	Liability	Comprehensive	UninsMotorist	Collision
Brenda	Lazzuri	☐	✔	☐	☐	☐
Edward	Bakalarski	☐	✔	☐	☐	☐
Brenda	Lazzuri	☐	✔	☐	☐	☐
Bret	Mardock	☐	✔	☐	☐	☐
Carlos	Alvarez	☐	✔	☐	☐	☐

ClientsWithOnlyLiabilityQuery

Project 1f

ClientID	Client	Sales
101	Bering Company	$289,563.00
101	Bering Company	$327,541.00
102	Fairhaven Developers	$101,210.00
102	Fairhaven Developers	$95,630.00
103	Clearwater Service	$125,436.00
103	Clearwater Service	$144,328.00
104	Landower Company	$97,653.00
104	Landower Company	$130,239.00
105	Harford Systems	$215,420.00
105	Harford Systems	$441,000.00
106	Providence, Inc.	$85,628.00
106	Providence, Inc.	$75,462.00
107	Gallagher Systems	$199,346.00
107	Gallagher Systems	$221,379.00
108	Karris Supplies	$61,349.00
108	Karris Supplies	$105,000.00
109	HE Systems	$554,120.00
109	HE Systems	$721,923.00
110	Blue Ridge, Inc.	$17,542.00
110	Blue Ridge, Inc.	$83,210.00
111	Alderton Metals	$9,547.00
111	Alderton Metals	$45,230.00
112	DV Corporation	$138,560.00
112	DV Corporation	$200,540.00
113	Franklin Services	$141,670.00
113	Franklin Services	$65,411.00
114	Milltown Contractors	$2,356.00
114	Milltown Contractors	$31,230.00
115	Wheeling Products	$115,423.00
115	Wheeling Products	$103,400.00
116	Martin Manufacturing	$35,679.00
116	Martin Manufacturing	$61,539.00
117	Valley Construction	$15,248.00
117	Valley Construction	$22,478.00
118	AeroTech	$156,439.00
118	AeroTech	$175,011.00
119	Miles & Harrisburg	$222,133.00
119	Miles & Harrisburg	$222,133.00
120	Paragon Corporation	$51,237.00
120	Paragon Corporation	$20,137.00
121	Madison Electrics	$99,450.00
121	Madison Electrics	$103,435.00
122	Haute Contractors	$174,319.00

ClientSalesQuery, Page 1

ClientID	Client	Sales
122	Haute Contractors	$125,900.00
123	Eagleton Industries	$300,137.00
123	Eagleton Industries	$265,439.00
124	Hoosier Corporation	$24,880.00
124	Hoosier Corporation	$31,935.00
125	Dover Industries	$151,003.00
125	Dover Industries	$120,890.00
126	Northstar Services	$9,457.00
126	Northstar Services	$15,094.00
127	Zinn-Harris Electronics	$214,000.00
127	Zinn-Harris Electronics	$176,420.00

ClientSalesQuery, Page 2

SupplierID	SupplierName	ProductID	Amount
42	Fraser Valley Products	443-1B	$2,397.75
25	Langley Corporation	560-TL	$397.00
25	Langley Corporation	590-TL	$196.25
35	Emerald City Products	602-XR	$2,145.00
99	KL Distributions	647-1	$2,999.85
99	KL Distributions	780-2	$1,288.50
84	Macadam, Inc.	100-02	$45.95
84	Macadam, Inc.	100-05	$129.75
54	Manning, Inc.	101-S2R	$1,945.25
54	Manning, Inc.	101-S3B	$1,137.50
54	Manning, Inc.	101-S3R	$1,199.50
10	Hopewell, Inc.	152-H	$44.85
10	Hopewell, Inc.	155-20	$104.25
10	Hopewell, Inc.	155-35	$199.50
15	Bayside Supplies	201-CW	$99.75
15	Bayside Supplies	202-CW	$124.25
68	Freedom Corporation	209-L	$173.75
68	Freedom Corporation	209-XL	$180.00
68	Freedom Corporation	209-XXL	$145.80
68	Freedom Corporation	210-L	$162.25
68	Freedom Corporation	210-M	$97.35
60	Cascade Gear	250-L	$1,285.00
60	Cascade Gear	250-XL	$1,285.00
60	Cascade Gear	255-M	$599.50
60	Cascade Gear	255-XL	$599.50
31	Sound Supplies	299-M2	$887.90
31	Sound Supplies	299-M3	$887.90
31	Sound Supplies	299-M5	$887.90
31	Sound Supplies	299-W1	$602.32
31	Sound Supplies	299-W3	$752.90
31	Sound Supplies	299-W4	$752.90
31	Sound Supplies	299-W5	$752.90
68	Freedom Corporation	371-L	$129.50
68	Freedom Corporation	375-M	$199.00
68	Freedom Corporation	375-S	$199.00
42	Fraser Valley Products	442-1B	$1,495.00

ProductOrderAmountsQuery

Project 1g

SupplierName	StreetAddress	City	Prov/State	PostalCode
Bayside Supplies	6705 North Street	Bellingham	WA	98432
Hadley Company	5845 Jefferson Street	Seattle	WA	98107
Cascade Gear	540 Broadway	Seattle	WA	98106
Sound Supplies	2104 Union Street	Seattle	WA	98105
Emerald City Products	1059 Pike Street	Seattle	WA	98102
KL Distributions	402 Yukon Drive	Bellingham	WA	96435

SuppliersNotBCQuery

Client	StreetAddress	City	State	ZipCode
Bering Company	4521 East Sixth Street	Muncie	IN	47310-5500
Clearwater Service	10385 North Gavin Street	Muncie	IN	47308-1236
Providence, Inc.	12490 141st Street	Muncie	IN	47306-3410
Paragon Corporation	4500 Meridian Street	Muncie	IN	47302-4338
Dover Industries	4839 Huchins Road	Muncie	IN	47306-4839
Northstar Services	5135 West Second Street	Muncie	IN	47301-7774

ClientsMuncieQuery

ClientID	FirstName	LastName	StreetAddress	City	State	ZIP	ClaimID	AmountOfClaim
7335	Vernon	Cook	1230 South Mesa	Phoenix	AZ	85018	104366	$834.95
1331	Erin	Hagedorn	4818 Oakes Boulevard	Phoenix	AZ	85018	198745	$1,797.00
9879	Harold	McDougal	7115 Elizabeth Lane	Phoenix	AZ	85009	174589	$752.45
9775	Carla	Waterman	3979 19th Avenue	Phoenix	AZ	85031	241485	$4,500.00
6478	Parma	Moreno	610 Sheridan Avenue	Phoenix	AZ	85031	200147	$925.75
4868	Eric	Zadinski	1301 North Meridian	Phoenix	AZ	85031	210369	$2,675.00
9879	Harold	McDougal	7115 Elizabeth Lane	Phoenix	AZ	85009	247823	$775.75

PhoenixClientClaimsOver$500Query

Project 1h

EmpID	FirstName	LastName	AnnualSalary	PensionContribu
101	Joseph	Ammons	$52,350.00	1570.5
102	Walter	Irving	$50,750.00	1522.5
103	Francine	Prescott	$52,500.00	1575
104	Mary	Vanderhoff	$59,750.00	1792.5
105	Corey	Gadeau	$60,150.00	1804.5
106	Stephanie	Wendt	$42,000.00	1260
108	Nathan	Holmes	$53,350.00	1600.5
110	Thomas	Byrnes	$42,500.00	1275
111	Ray	Bannerman	$32,600.00	978
112	Noreen	Blanca	$38,750.00	1162.5
114	Blaine	Kaiser	$64,500.00	1935
115	Sean	O'Callaghan	$52,455.00	1573.65
116	Silas	Workman	$51,000.00	1530
118	Glenn	Ishimoto	$68,525.00	2055.75
119	Lucinda	Larsen	$38,425.00	1152.75
121	Patricia	Ochoa	$59,750.00	1792.5
124	Antonio	Silvestri	$51,350.00	1540.5
125	Debra	Tapparo	$40,150.00	1204.5
126	Michelle	Vincent	$39,750.00	1192.5
127	Kurt	Ziegler	$65,250.00	1957.5
129	Shilo	Alvarado	$45,000.00	1350
130	Norman	Curis	$42,450.00	1273.5
133	Brett	Dupree	$58,550.00	1756.5
134	Sally	Farrell	$58,000.00	1740
135	Dorothy	Griswold	$67,700.00	2031
137	Leslie	Jacobsen	$48,800.00	1464
138	Susan	Masui	$38,500.00	1155
139	Jerry	Prentiss	$57,525.00	1725.75
140	Kathleen	Schreiber	$45,250.00	1357.5

PensionContributionsQuery

EmpID	FirstName	LastName	AnnualSalary	Salary&Pension
101	Joseph	Ammons	$52,350.00	53920.5
102	Walter	Irving	$50,750.00	52272.5
103	Francine	Prescott	$52,500.00	54075
104	Mary	Vanderhoff	$59,750.00	61542.5
105	Corey	Gadeau	$60,150.00	61954.5
106	Stephanie	Wendt	$42,000.00	43260
108	Nathan	Holmes	$53,350.00	54950.5
110	Thomas	Byrnes	$42,500.00	43775
111	Ray	Bannerman	$32,600.00	33578
112	Noreen	Blanca	$38,750.00	39912.5
114	Blaine	Kaiser	$64,500.00	66435
115	Sean	O'Callaghan	$52,455.00	54028.65
116	Silas	Workman	$51,000.00	52530
118	Glenn	Ishimoto	$68,525.00	70580.75
119	Lucinda	Larsen	$38,425.00	39577.75
121	Patricia	Ochoa	$59,750.00	61542.5
124	Antonio	Silvestri	$51,350.00	52890.5
125	Debra	Tapparo	$40,150.00	41354.5
126	Michelle	Vincent	$39,750.00	40942.5
127	Kurt	Ziegler	$65,250.00	67207.5
129	Shilo	Alvarado	$45,000.00	46350
130	Norman	Curis	$42,450.00	43723.5
133	Brett	Dupree	$58,550.00	60306.5
134	Sally	Farrell	$58,000.00	59740
135	Dorothy	Griswold	$67,700.00	69731
137	Leslie	Jacobsen	$48,800.00	50264
138	Susan	Masui	$38,500.00	39655
139	Jerry	Prentiss	$57,525.00	59250.75
140	Kathleen	Schreiber	$45,250.00	46607.5

Salary&PensionQuery

Product	OrderID	UnitsOrdered	Amount	Total
Two-person tent	1001	10	$1,288.50	$12,885.00
HT waterproof hiking boots, MS9	1002	10	$887.90	$8,879.00
HT waterproof hiking boots, MS11	1003	10	$887.90	$8,879.00
Polar backpack, 250RW	1004	15	$2,397.75	$35,966.25
HT waterproof hiking boots, MS12	1005	10	$887.90	$8,879.00
Two-person dome tent	1006	15	$2,999.85	$44,997.75
Polar backpack, 150RW	1007	10	$1,495.00	$14,950.00
Gordon wool ski hat, XXL	1008	20	$145.80	$2,916.00
Gordon wool ski hat, XL	1009	25	$180.00	$4,500.00
Shursite portable camp light	1010	10	$199.50	$1,995.00
Lantern hanger	1011	15	$44.85	$672.75
Tech-lite ski hat, L	1012	25	$162.25	$4,056.25
Tech-lite ski hat, M	1013	15	$97.35	$1,460.25
Lite-tech ski gloves, WS	1014	20	$199.00	$3,980.00
Lite-tech ski gloves, WM	1015	20	$199.00	$3,980.00
Lite-tech ski gloves, ML	1016	10	$129.50	$1,295.00
Gordon wool ski hat, L	1017	25	$173.75	$4,343.75
Shursite angle-head flashlight	1018	15	$104.25	$1,563.75
Cascade R4 jacket, MXL	1019	10	$1,285.00	$12,850.00
Multi-function compass	1020	10	$45.95	$459.50
Ten-piece hiker cookware	1021	5	$124.25	$621.25
Eight-piece stainless steel cookware	1022	5	$99.75	$498.75
Deluxe map compass	1023	5	$129.75	$648.75
SL 20-degrees synthetic sleeping bag, re	1024	10	$1,199.50	$11,995.00
SL 20-degrees synthetic sleeping bag, bla	1025	10	$1,137.50	$11,375.00
Cascade R4 jacket, WM	1026	5	$599.50	$2,997.50
SL 15-degrees synthetic sleeping bag, re	1027	15	$1,945.25	$29,178.75
Cascade R4 jacket, ML	1028	10	$1,285.00	$12,850.00
Cascade R4 jacket, WXL	1029	5	$599.50	$2,997.50
HT waterproof hiking boots, WS8	1030	10	$752.90	$7,529.00
HT waterproof hiking boots, WS7	1031	10	$752.90	$7,529.00
Binoculars, 8 x 42	1032	5	$2,145.00	$10,725.00
Thermaline roll-top table	1033	5	$196.25	$981.25
HT waterproof hiking boots, WS9	1034	10	$752.90	$7,529.00
HT waterproof hiking boots, WS11	1035	8	$602.32	$4,818.56
Thermaline sleeping pad	1036	20	$397.00	$7,940.00

UnitsOrderedTotalQuery

Project 2 Create Aggregate Functions, Crosstab, Find Duplicates, and Find Unmatched Queries

Project 2a

SumOfAmount	AvgOfAmount	MaxOfAmount	MinOfAmount	CountOfAmount
$26,530.27	$736.95	$2,999.85	$44.85	36

AmountsQuery

SumOfAmountOfClaim	AvgOfAmountOfClaim	MaxOfAmountOfClaim	MinOfAmountOfClaim
$38,711.95	$2,037.47	$5,230.00	$535.00

ClaimAmountsQuery

Project 2b

ClientID	SumOfAmountOfClaim	AvgOfAmountOfClaim
1331	$1,797.00	$1,797.00
1574	$2,696.25	$1,348.13
4300	$10,088.30	$5,044.15
4567	$1,840.00	$1,840.00
4868	$2,675.00	$2,675.00
4875	$875.00	$875.00
5982	$3,250.50	$3,250.50
6478	$925.75	$925.75
7335	$834.95	$834.95
8223	$2,830.50	$2,830.50
8854	$3,100.50	$1,550.25
9383	$1,770.00	$885.00
9775	$4,500.00	$4,500.00
9879	$1,528.20	$764.10

SumAvgClaimAmountsQuery

SumOfAmount	AvgOfAmount	SupplierID	SupplierName
$348.60	$116.20	10	Hopewell, Inc.
$224.00	$112.00	15	Bayside Supplies
$593.25	$296.63	25	Langley Corporation
$5,524.72	$789.25	31	Sound Supplies
$2,145.00	$2,145.00	35	Emerald City Products
$3,892.75	$1,946.38	42	Fraser Valley Products
$4,282.25	$1,427.42	54	Manning, Inc.
$3,769.00	$942.25	60	Cascade Gear
$1,286.65	$160.83	68	Freedom Corporation
$175.70	$87.85	84	Macadam, Inc.
$4,288.35	$2,144.18	99	KL Distributions

SupplierAmountsQuery

Project 2c

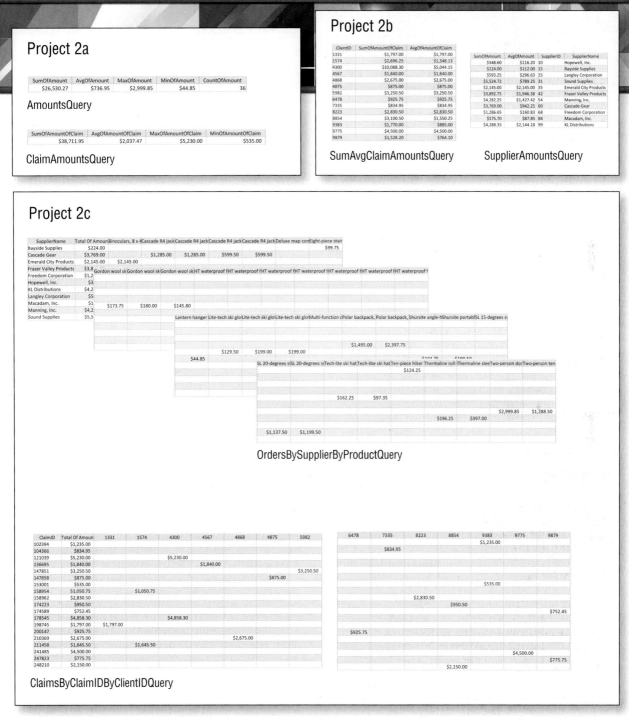

OrdersBySupplierByProductQuery

ClaimsByClaimIDByClientIDQuery

Project 2d

SupplierName	SupplierID	StreetAddress	City	Prov/State	PostalCode	EmailAddress	Telephone
Langley Corporation	25	805 First Avenue	Burnaby	BC	V3J 1C9	langley@emcp.net	(604) 555-1200
Langley Corporation	29	1248 Larson Avenue	Burnaby	BC	V5V 9K2	lc@emcp.net	(604) 555-1200

DuplicateSuppliersQuery

Project 2f

ProductID	Product	SupplierID	UnitsInStock	UnitsOnOrder	ReorderLevel
558-C	ICE snow goggles, clear	68	18	0	15
559-B	ICE snow goggles, bronze	68	22	0	20
570-TL	Thermaline light-weight cot	25	8	0	5
580-TL	Thermaline camp seat	25	12	0	10
602-XT	Binoculars, 10.5 x 45	35	5	0	4
602-XX	Binoculars, 10 x 50	35	7	0	5
648-2	Three-person dome tent	99	5	0	10
651-1	K-2 one-person tent	99	8	0	10
652-2	K-2 two-person tent	99	12	0	10
804-50	AG freestyle snowboard, X50	70	7	0	10
804-60	AG freestyle snowboard, X60	70	8	0	5
897-L	Lang blunt snowboard	70	8	0	7
897-W	Lang blunt snowboard, wide	70	4	0	3
901-S	Solar battery pack	38	16	0	15
917-S	Silo portable power pack	38	8	0	10
100-01	Wrist compass	84	12	0	10
100-03	Lenspro plastic compass	84	6	0	5
100-04	Lenspro metal compass	84	8	0	5
101-S1B	SL 0-degrees down sleeping bag, black	54	16	0	15
101-S1R	SL 0-degrees down sleeping bag, red	54	17	0	15
101-S2B	SL 15-degrees synthetic sleeping bag, blac	54	21	0	15
155-30	Shursite aluminum flashlight	10	8	0	5
155-45	Shursite propane lantern	10	12	0	10
155-55	Shursite waterproof headlamp	10	7	0	5
200-CW	Four-piece titanium cookware	15	6	0	5
210-XL	Tech-lite ski hat, XL	68	22	0	20
250-M	Cascade R4 jacket, MM	60	6	0	5
250-XXL	Cascade R4 jacket, MXXL	60	5	0	0
255-L	Cascade R4 jacket, WL	60	6	0	5
299-M1	HT waterproof hiking boots, MS13	31	8	0	10
299-M4	HT waterproof hiking boots, MS10	31	7	0	10

Products Without Matching Orders

Project 2e

SupplierName Field	NumberOfDups
Bayside Supplies	2
Cascade Gear	4
Fraser Valley Products	2
Freedom Corporation	8
Hopewell, Inc.	3
KL Distributions	2
Langley Corporation	2
Macadam, Inc.	2
Manning, Inc.	3
Sound Supplies	7

SupplierOrdersCountQuery

Project 1   Design Queries   8 Parts

You will design and run a number of queries including queries with fields from one table and queries with fields from more than one table. You will also use the Simple Query Wizard to design queries.

Extracting Data with Queries ■■■■■■■■■■■■■■■■■■■

Being able to extract (pull out) specific data from a table is one of the most important functions of a database. Extracting data in Access is referred to as performing a query. The word *query* means "question" and to perform a query means to ask a question. Access provides several methods for performing a query. You can design your own query, use a simple query wizard, or use complex query wizards. In this chapter, you will learn to design your own query; use the Simple Query Wizard; create a calculated field; use aggregate functions in a query; and use the Crosstab, Find Duplicates, and Unmatched Query wizards.

The first step in designing a query is to choose the fields that you want to display in the query results datasheet.

Query Design

Designing Queries ■■■■■■■■■■■■■■■■■■■■■■■

Designing a query consists of identifying the table from which you are gathering data, the field or fields from which the data will be drawn, and the criteria for selecting the data. To design a query and perform the query, open a database, click the CREATE tab, and then click the Query Design button in the Queries group. This displays a query window in the work area and also displays the Show Table dialog box, as shown in Figure 3.1.

Figure 3.1 Query Window with Show Table Dialog Box

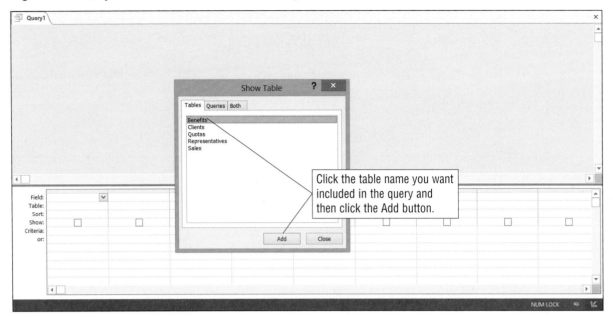

Click the table name in the Show Table dialog box that you want included in the query and then click the Add button or double-click the desired table. This inserts a field list box for the table. Add any other tables required for the query. When all tables have been added, click the Close button. In the query window, click the down-pointing arrow at the right of the first *Field* row field in the query design grid and then click the desired field from the drop-down list. Figure 3.2 displays a sample query window.

To establish a criterion, click inside the *Criteria* row field in the column containing the desired field name in the query design grid and then type the criterion. With the fields and criteria established, click the Run button in the Results group on the QUERY TOOLS DESIGN tab. Access searches the specified tables for records that match the criteria and then displays those records in the query results datasheet. If you plan to use the query in the future, save the query and name it. If you will not need the query again, close the query results datasheet without saving it.

To insert a field in the query design grid, click the down-pointing arrow at the right side of a *Field* row field and then click the desired field at the drop-down list. You can also double-click a field in a table field list box to insert the field in the first available *Field* row field in the query design grid. For example, suppose you want to find out how many purchase orders were issued on a specific date. To do this, double-click *PurchaseOrderID* in the table field list box (which inserts *PurchaseOrderID* in the first *Field* row field in the query design grid) and then double-click *OrderDate* in the table field list box (which inserts *OrderDate* in the second *Field* row field in the query design grid). In this example, both fields are needed, so the purchase order ID is displayed along with the specific order date. After inserting the fields, you insert the criterion. The criterion for this example is something like *#1/15/2015#*. After you insert the criterion, click the Run button in the Results group and the results of the query display in the query results datasheet.

▼ **Quick Steps**

Design a Query
1. Click CREATE tab.
2. Click Query Design button.
3. At Show Table dialog box, click desired table, and then click Add button.
4. Add any additional tables.
5. In query design grid, click down-pointing arrow in *Field* row field and click desired field from drop-down list.
6. Insert criterion.
7. Click Run button.
8. Save query.

Run

Figure 3.2 Query Window

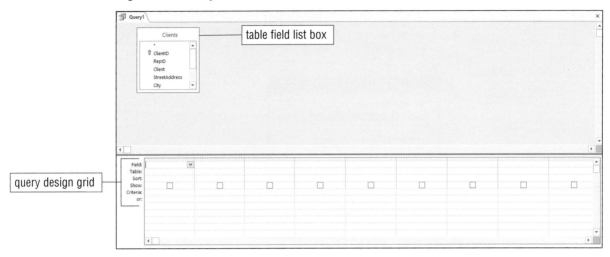

query design grid

table field list box

A third method for inserting a field in the query design grid is to drag a field from the table field list box to the desired field in the query design grid. To do this, position the mouse pointer on the desired field in the table field list box, hold down the left mouse button, drag to the desired *Field* row field in the query design grid, and then release the mouse button.

Establishing Query Criteria

▼ **Quick Steps**

Establish a Query Criterion
1. At query window, click in desired *Criteria* row field in query design grid.
2. Type criterion and then press Enter.
3. Click Run button.

Insert fields in the *Field* row fields in the query design grid in the order in which you want the fields to display in the query results datasheet.

Access inserts quotation marks around text criteria and pound symbols around date criteria.

Performing a query does not require specific criteria to be established. In the example described on the previous page, if the criterion for the date was not included, the query would return all purchase order numbers with the dates. (*Return* is the term used for the results of the query.) While this information may be helpful, you could easily find this information in the table. The value of performing a query is to extract specific information from a table. To do this, you must insert a criterion like the one described in the example.

Access makes writing a criterion fairly simple by inserting the necessary symbols in the criterion. If you type a city name, such as *Indianapolis*, in the *Criteria* row field and then press Enter, Access changes the criterion to "Indianapolis". The quotation marks are inserted by Access and are necessary for the query to run properly. You can either let Access put the proper symbols in the *Criteria* row field, or you can type the criterion with the symbols. Table 3.1 shows some examples of criteria, including what is typed and what is returned.

In the criteria examples, the asterisk is used as a so-called *wildcard character*, or a symbol that can be used to indicate any character. This is consistent with many other software applications. Two of the criteria examples in Table 3.1 use less-than and greater-than symbols. You can use these symbols for fields containing numbers, values, dates, amounts, and so forth. In the next several projects, you will design queries to extract specific information from different tables in databases.

Table 3.1 Criteria Examples

Typing This Criterion	Returns This Result
"Smith"	Field value that matches *Smith*
"Smith" Or "Larson"	Field value that matches either *Smith* or *Larson*
Not "Smith"	Field value that is not *Smith* (the opposite of "Smith")
"s*"	Field value that begins with *S* or *s* and ends in anything
"*s"	Field value that begins with anything and ends in *S* or *s*
"[A-D]*"	Field value that begins with *A, B, C,* or *D* and ends in anything
#01/01/2015#	Field value that matches the date 01/01/2015
<#04/01/2015#	Field value that is less than (before) 04/01/2015
>#04/01/2015#	Field value that is greater than (after) 04/01/2015
Between #01/01/2015# And #03/31/2015#	Field value that is between 01/01/2015 and 03/31/2015

Project 1a Performing Queries on Tables   Part 1 of 8

1. Open **AL1-C3-Dearborn.accdb** from the AL1C3 folder on your storage medium and enable the contents.
2. Create the following relationships and enforce referential integrity (and cascade fields and records) for each relationship:
   a. Create a one-to-many relationship with the *ClientID* field in the *Clients* field list box the "one" and the *ClientID* field in the *Sales* field list box the "many."
   b. Create a one-to-one relationship with the *RepID* field in the *Representatives* field list box the "one" and the *RepID* field in the *Benefits* field list box the "one."
   c. Create a one-to-many relationship with the *RepID* field in the *Representatives* field list box the "one" and the *RepID* field in the *Clients* field list box the "many."
   d. Create a one-to-many relationship with the *QuotaID* field in the *Quotas* field list box the "one" and the *QuotaID* field in the *Representatives* field list box the "many."
3. Click the Save button on the Quick Access toolbar.
4. Print the relationships by completing the following steps:
   a. Click the Relationship Report button in the Tools group on the RELATIONSHIP TOOLS DESIGN tab.
   b. At the relationship report window, click the Landscape button in the Page Layout group on the PRINT PREVIEW tab.
   c. Click the Print button that displays at the left side of the PRINT PREVIEW tab.
   d. At the Print dialog box, click OK.
5. Close the relationship report window without saving the report.
6. Close the Relationships window.

7. Extract records of those clients located in Indianapolis by completing the following steps:
   a. Click the CREATE tab.
   b. Click the Query Design button in the Queries group.

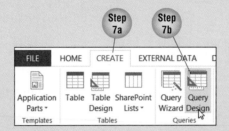

   c. At the Show Table dialog box with the Tables tab selected (see Figure 3.1), click *Clients* in the list box, click the Add button, and then click the Close button.
   d. Insert fields from the *Clients* field list box to the *Field* row fields in the query design grid by completing the following steps:
      1) Click the down-pointing arrow located at the right of the first *Field* row field in the query design grid and then click *Client* in the drop-down list.
      2) Click inside the next *Field* row field (to the right of *Client*) in the query design grid, click the down-pointing arrow, and then click *StreetAddress* in the drop-down list.
      3) Click inside the next *Field* row field (to the right of *StreetAddress*), click the down-pointing arrow, and then click *City* in the drop-down list.
      4) Click inside the next *Field* row field (to the right of *City*), click the down-pointing arrow, and then click *State* in the drop-down list.
      5) Click inside the next *Field* row field (to the right of *State*), click the down-pointing arrow, and then select *ZipCode* in the drop-down list.

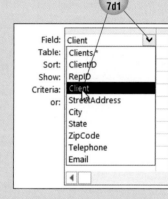

e. Insert the criterion text telling Access to display only those suppliers located in Indianapolis by completing the following steps:

1) Click in the *Criteria* row field in the *City* column in the query design grid. (This positions the insertion point in the field.)

2) Type **Indianapolis** and then press Enter. (This changes the criterion to "Indianapolis".)

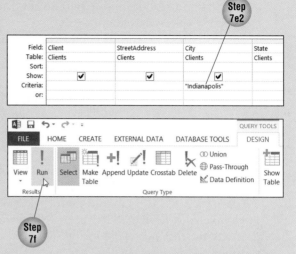

f. Return the results of the query by clicking the Run button in the Results group on the QUERY TOOLS DESIGN tab. (This displays the results in the query results datasheet.)

g. Save the results of the query by completing the following steps:

1) Click the Save button on the Quick Access toolbar.

2) At the Save As dialog box, type **ClientsIndianapolisQuery** and then press Enter or click OK. (See Project 1a query results on page 78.)

h. Print the query results datasheet by clicking the FILE tab, clicking the *Print* option, and then clicking the Quick Print button.

i. Close ClientsIndianapolisQuery.

8. Extract those records with quota identification numbers greater than 2 by completing the following steps:

a. Click the CREATE tab and then click the Query Design button in the Queries group.

b. Double-click *Representatives* in the Show Table dialog box and then click the Close button.

c. In the query window, double-click *RepName*. (This inserts the field in the first *Field* row field in the query design grid.)

d. Double-click *QuotaID*. (This inserts the field in the second *Field* row field in the query design grid.)

e. Insert the query criterion by completing the following steps:

1) Click in the *Criteria* row field in the *QuotaID* column in the query design grid.

2) Type **>2** and then press Enter. (Access will automatically insert quotation marks around *2* since the data type for the field is identified as *Short Text* [rather than *Number*].)

Field:	RepName	QuotaID
Table:	Representatives	Representatives
Sort:		
Show:	✔	✔
Criteria:		>"2"
or:		

Step 8e2

f. Return the results of the query by clicking the Run button in the Results group.

g. Save the query and name it *QuotaIDGreaterThanTwoQuery*. (See Project 1a query results on page 78.)

h. Print and then close the query.

9. Extract those sales greater than $99,999 by completing the following steps:

a. Click the CREATE tab and then click the Query Design button.

b. Double-click *Sales* in the Show Table dialog box and then click the Close button.

c. At the query window, double-click *ClientID*. (This inserts the field in the first *Field* row field in the query design grid.)

d. Insert the *Sales* field in the second *Field* row field.

e. Insert the query criterion by completing the following
   steps:
   1) Click in the *Criteria* row field in the *Sales* column
      in the query design grid.
   2) Type >99999 and then press Enter. (Access will
      not insert quotation marks around *99999* since
      the field is identified as *Currency*.)

Field:	ClientID		Sales	
Table:	Sales		Sales	
Sort:				
Show:		☑		☑
Criteria:			>99999	
or:				

Step
9e2

f. Return the results of the query by clicking the Run
   button in the Results group.
g. Save the query and name it *SalesOver$99999Query*. (See Project 1a query results on
   page 78.)
h. Print and then close the query.
10. Extract records of those representatives with a telephone number that begins with the 765
    area code by completing the following steps:
    a. Click the CREATE tab and then click the Query Design button.
    b. Double-click *Representatives* in the Show Table dialog box and then click the Close button.
    c. Insert the *RepName* field in the first *Field* row field.
    d. Insert the *Telephone* field in the second *Field* row field.
    e. Insert the query criterion by completing the following steps:
       1) Click in the *Criteria* row field in the *Telephone*
          column.
       2) Type "(765*" and then press Enter. (You
          need to type the quotation marks in this
          criterion because the criterion contains a left
          parenthesis.)

Field:	RepName		Telephone	
Table:	Representatives		Representatives	
Sort:				
Show:		☑		☑
Criteria:			Like "(765*"	
or:				

Step
10e2

    f. Return the results of the query by clicking the
       Run button in the Results group.
    g. Save the query and name it *RepsWith765AreaCodeQuery*. (See Project 1a query
       results on page 78.)
    h. Print and then close the query.

In Project 1a, you performed several queries on specific tables. You can also
perform queries on fields from more than one table. In Project 1b, you will perform
queries on related tables.

When completing steps in Project 1b, you will be instructed to open
AL1-C3-CopperState.accdb. Two of the tables in the database contain yes/no
check boxes. When designing a query, you can extract records that contain a check
mark or records that do not contain a check mark. If you want to extract records
that contain a check mark, click in the *Criteria* row field in the desired column
in the query design grid, type a *1*, and then press Enter. When you press the
Enter key, Access changes the *1* to *True*. If you want to extract records that do not
contain a check mark, type *0* in the *Criteria* row field and then press Enter. Access
changes the 0 to *False*.

You can use the Zoom box when entering a criterion in a query to provide a
larger area for typing. To display the Zoom box, press Shift + F2 or right-click in
the desired *Criteria* row field and then click *Zoom* at the shortcut menu. Type the
desired criterion in the Zoom box and then click OK.

1. With **AL1-C3-Dearborn.accdb** open, extract information on representatives hired between March 2011 and November 2011 and include the representatives' names by completing the following steps:

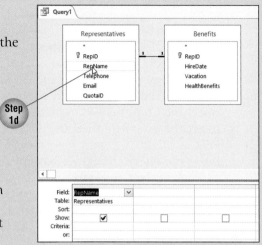

Step 1d

   a. Click the CREATE tab and then click the Query Design button.
   b. Double-click *Representatives* in the Show Table dialog box.
   c. Double-click *Benefits* in the Show Table dialog box and then click the Close button.
   d. At the query window, double-click *RepName* in the *Representatives* field list box.
   e. Double-click *HireDate* in the *Benefits* field list box.
   f. Insert the query criterion in the Zoom box by completing the following steps:
      1) Click in the *Criteria* row field in the *HireDate* column.
      2) Press Shift + F2 to display the Zoom box.
      3) Type **Between 3/1/2011 And 11/30/2011**. (Make sure you type zeros and not capital *O*s.)
      4) Click OK.

Step 1f3   Step 1f4

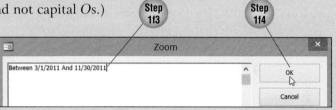

   g. Return the results of the query by clicking the Run button in the Results group.
   h. Save the query and name it *MarToNov2011HiresQuery*. (See Project 1b query results on page 78.)
   i. Print and then close the query.

2. Extract records of those representatives who were hired in 2012 by completing the following steps:
   a. Click the CREATE tab and then click the Query Design button.
   b. Double-click *Representatives* in the Show Table dialog box.
   c. Double-click *Benefits* in the Show Table dialog box and then click the Close button.
   d. At the query window, double-click the *RepID* field in the *Representatives* field list box.
   e. Double-click *RepName* in the *Representatives* field list box.
   f. Double-click *HireDate* in the *Benefits* field list box.
   g. Insert the query criterion by completing the following steps:
      1) Click in the *Criteria* row field in the *HireDate* column.
      2) Type *2012 and then press Enter.

Field:	RepID	RepName	HireDate
Table:	Representatives	Representatives	Benefits
Sort:			
Show:	✔	✔	✔
Criteria:			Like "*2012"
or:			

Step 2g2

   h. Return the results of the query by clicking the Run button in the Results group.
   i. Save the query and name it *RepsHiredIn2012Query*. (See Project 1b query results on page 78.)
   j. Print and then close the query.

3. Suppose you need to determine sales for a company but you can only remember that the company name begins with *Blue*. Create a query that finds the company and identifies the sales by completing the following steps:
   a. Click the CREATE tab and then click the Query Design button.
   b. Double-click *Clients* in the Show Table dialog box.
   c. Double-click *Sales* in the Show Table dialog box and then click the Close button.
   d. At the query window, insert the *ClientID* field from the *Clients* field list box in the first *Field* row field in the query design grid.
   e. Insert the *Client* field from the *Clients* field list box in the second *Field* row field.
   f. Insert the *Sales* field from the *Sales* field list box in the third *Field* row field.
   g. Insert the query criterion by completing the following steps:
      1) Click in the *Criteria* row field in the *Client* column.
      2) Type **Blue*** and then press Enter.
   h. Return the results of the query by clicking the Run button in the Results group.
   i. Save the query and name it *BlueRidgeSalesQuery*. (See Project 1b query results on page 78.)
   j. Print and then close the query.

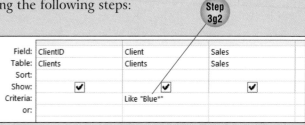

Step 3g2

Field:	ClientID	Client	Sales
Table:	Clients	Clients	Sales
Sort:			
Show:	☑	☑	☑
Criteria:		Like "Blue*"	
or:			

4. Close **AL1-C3-Dearborn.accdb**.
5. Display the Open dialog box with the AL1C3 folder on your storage medium active.
6. Open **AL1-C3-PacTrek.accdb** and enable the contents.
7. Extract information on products ordered between February 1, 2015, and February 28, 2015, by completing the following steps:
   a. Click the CREATE tab and then click the Query Design button.
   b. Double-click *Products* in the Show Table dialog box.
   c. Double-click *Orders* in the Show Table dialog box and then click the Close button.
   d. At the query window, insert the *ProductID* field from the *Products* field list box in the first *Field* row field.
   e. Insert the *Product* field from the *Products* field list box in the second *Field* row field.
   f. Insert the *OrderDate* field from the *Orders* field list box in the third *Field* row field.
   g. Insert the query criterion by completing the following steps:
      1) Click in the *Criteria* row field in the *OrderDate* column.
      2) Type **Between 2/1/2015 And 2/28/2015** and then press Enter. (Make sure you type zeros and not capital *Os*.)
   h. Return the results of the query by clicking the Run button in the Results group.
   i. Save the query and name it *Feb1-28OrdersQuery*. (See Project 1b query results on page 78.)
   j. Print and then close the query.

Field:	ProductID	Product	OrderDate
Table:	Products	Products	Orders
Sort:			
Show:	☑	☑	☑
Criteria:			Between #2/1/2015# An
or:			

Step 7g2

8. Close **AL1-C3-PacTrek.accdb**.
9. Open **AL1-C3-CopperState.accdb** and enable the contents.
10. Display the Relationships window and create the following additional relationships (enforce referential integrity and cascade fields and records):
    a. Create a one-to-many relationship with the *AgentID* field in the Agents field list box the "one" and the *AgentID* field in the Assignments field list box the "many."

b. Create a one-to-many relationship with the *OfficeID* field in the Offices field list box the "one" and the *OfficeID* field in the Assignments field list box the "many."

c. Create a one-to-many relationship with the *OfficeID* field in the Offices field list box the "one" and the *OfficeID* field in the Agents field list box the "many."

11. Save and then print the relationships.

12. Close the relationship report without saving it and then close the Relationships window.

13. Extract records of clients that have uninsured motorist coverage by completing the following steps:
    a. Click the CREATE tab and then click the Query Design button.
    b. Double-click *Clients* in the Show Table dialog box.
    c. Double-click *Coverage* in the Show Table dialog box and then click the Close button.
    d. At the query window, insert the *ClientID* field from the *Clients* field list box in the first *Field* row field.
    e. Insert the *FirstName* field from the *Clients* field list box in the second *Field* row field.
    f. Insert the *LastName* field from the *Clients* field list box in the third *Field* row field.
    g. Insert the *UninsMotorist* field from the *Coverage* field list box in the fourth *Field* row field. (You may need to scroll down the Coverage field list box to display the *UninsMotorist* field.)
    h. Insert the query criterion by clicking in the *Criteria* row field in the *UninsMotorist* column, typing 1, and then pressing the Enter key. (Access changes the *1* to *True*.)

Field:	ClientID	FirstName	LastName	UninsMotorist
Table:	Clients	Clients	Clients	Coverage
Sort:				
Show:	✔	✔		✔
Criteria:			Step 13h	True
or:				

   i. Click the Run button in the Results group.
   j. Save the query and name it *UninsMotoristCoverageQuery*. (See Project 1b query results on page 78.)
   k. Print and then close the query.

14. Extract records of claims in January over $500 by completing the following steps:
    a. Click the CREATE tab and then click the Query Design button.
    b. Double-click *Clients* in the Show Table dialog box.
    c. Double-click *Claims* in the Show Table dialog box and then click the Close button.
    d. At the query window, insert the *ClientID* field from the *Clients* field list box in the first *Field* row field.
    e. Insert the *FirstName* field from the *Clients* field list box in the second *Field* row field.
    f. Insert the *LastName* field from the *Clients* field list box in the third *Field* row field.
    g. Insert the *ClaimID* field from the *Claims* field list box in the fourth *Field* row field.
    h. Insert the *DateOfClaim* field from the *Claims* field list box in the fifth *Field* row field.
    i. Insert the *AmountOfClaim* field from the *Claims* field list box in the sixth *Field* row field.
    j. Click in the *Criteria* row field in the *DateOfClaim* column, type **Between 1/1/2015 And 1/31/2015**, and then press Enter.
    k. With the insertion point positioned in the *Criteria* row field in the *AmountOfClaim* column, type **>500** and then press Enter.

Field:	ClientID	FirstName	LastName	ClaimID	DateOfClaim	AmountOfClaim
Table:	Clients	Clients	Clients	Claims	Claims	Claims
Sort:						
Show:	✔	✔	✔	✔	✔	✔
Criteria:					Between #1/1/2015# An	>500
or:						

Step 14j   Step 14k

   l. Click the Run button in the Results group.
   m. Save the query and name it *JanClaimsOver$500Query*. (See Project 1b query results on page 78.)
   n. Print and then close the query.

Sorting and Showing or Hiding Fields in a Query

**Sort Fields in
a Query**
1. At query window, click
   in *Sort* row field in
   query design grid.
2. Click down arrow in
   Sort row field.
3. Click *Ascending* or
   Descending.

When designing a query, you can specify the sort order of a field or fields. Click inside one of the columns in the *Sort* row field and a down-pointing arrow displays at the right of the field. Click this down-pointing arrow and a drop-down list displays with the choices *Ascending*, *Descending*, and *(not sorted)*. Click *Ascending* to sort from lowest to highest or click *Descending* to sort from highest to lowest. You can hide specific fields in the query result by removing the check mark from the check box in the *Show* row in the design grid for the field you do not want to show.

Arranging Fields in a Query

With buttons in the Query Setup group on the QUERY DESIGN TOOLS tab, you can insert a new field column in the query design grid and delete a field column from the query design grid. To insert a field column, click in a field in the column you want to display immediately right of the new column and then click the Insert Columns button in the Query Setup group on the QUERY DESIGN TOOLS tab. To remove a column, click in a field in the column you want to delete and then click the Delete Columns button in the Query Setup group. Complete similar steps to insert or delete a row in the query design grid.

Insert Columns

Delete Columns

You can also rearrange columns in the query design grid by selecting the desired field column and then dragging the column to the desired position. To select a column in the query design grid, position the mouse pointer at the top of the column until the pointer turns into a small, black, down-pointing arrow and then click the left mouse button. Position the mouse pointer toward the top of the selected column until the mouse displays as a pointer, hold down the left mouse button, drag to the desired position in the design grid, and then release the mouse button. As you drag the column, a thick, black, vertical line displays identifying the location where the column will be inserted.

Project 1c **Performing Queries on Related Tables and Sorting in Field Values** **Part 3 of 8**

1. With **AL1-C3-CopperState.accdb** open, extract information on clients with agents from the West Bell Road Glendale office and sort the information alphabetically by client last name by completing the following steps:
   a. Click the CREATE tab and then click the Query Design button.
   b. Double-click *Assignments* in the Show Table dialog box.
   c. Double-click *Clients* in the Show Table dialog box and then click the Close button.
   d. At the query window, insert the *OfficeID* field from the *Assignments* field list box in the first *Field* row field.
   e. Insert the *AgentID* field from the *Assignments* field list box in the second *Field* row field.
   f. Insert the *FirstName* field from the *Clients* field list box in the third *Field* row field.
   g. Insert the *LastName* field from the *Clients* field list box in the fourth *Field* row field.

h. Click in the *Criteria* row field in the *OfficeID* column, type **GW**, and then press Enter.
i. Sort the *LastName* field in ascending alphabetical order (A–Z) by completing the following steps:
   1) Click in the *Sort* row field in the *LastName* column. (This causes a down-pointing arrow to display at the right side of the field.)
   2) Click the down-pointing arrow at the right side of the *Sort* row field and then click *Ascending*.
j. Specify that you do not want the *AgentID* field to show in the query results by clicking in the check box in the *Show* row field in the *AgentID* column to remove the check mark.

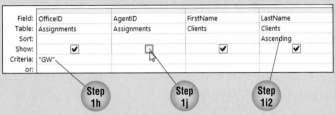

k. Click the Run button in the Results group.
l. Save the query and name it *GWClientsQuery*. (See Project 1c query results on page 79.)
m. Print and then close the query.
2. Close **AL1-C3-CopperState.accdb**.
3. Open **AL1-C3-PacTrek.accdb**.
4. Extract information on orders less than $1,500 by completing the following steps:
   a. Click the CREATE tab and then click the Query Design button.
   b. Double-click *Products* in the Show Table dialog box.
   c. Double-click *Orders* in the Show Table dialog box and then click the Close button.
   d. At the query window, insert the *ProductID* field from the *Products* field list box in the first *Field* row field.
   e. Insert the *SupplierID* field from the *Products* field list box in the second *Field* row field.
   f. Insert the *UnitsOrdered* field from the Orders field list box in the third *Field* row field.
   g. Insert the *Amount* field from the Orders field list box in the fourth *Field* row field.
   h. Insert the query criterion by completing the following steps:
      1) Click in the *Criteria* row field in the *Amount* column.
      2) Type **<1500** and then press Enter. (Make sure you type zeros and not capital *O*s.)

Field:	ProductID	SupplierID	UnitsOrdered	Amount
Table:	Products	Products	Orders	Orders
Sort:				
Show:	✔	✔	✔	✔
Criteria:				<1500
or:				

Step 4h2

   i. Sort the *Amount* field values from highest to lowest by completing the following steps:
      1) Click in the *Sort* row field in the *Amount* column. (This causes a down-pointing arrow to display at the right side of the field.)
      2) Click the down-pointing arrow at the right side of the *Sort* field and then click *Descending*.

Ordered	Amount
rs	Orders
	Descending
✔	Ascending
	Descending
	(not sorted)

Step 4i2

   j. Return the results of the query by clicking the Run button in the Results group.
   k. Save the query and name it *OrdersLessThan$1500Query*. (See Project 1c query results on page 79.)
   l. Print and then close the query.
5. Close **AL1-C3-PacTrek.accdb**.
6. Open **AL1-C3-Dearborn.accdb**.
7. Design a query by completing the following steps:
   a. Click the CREATE tab and then click the Query Design button.
   b. Double-click *Representatives* in the Show Table dialog box.

c. Double-click *Clients* in the Show Table dialog box.

d. Double-click *Sales* in the Show Table dialog box and then click the Close button.

e. At the query window, insert the *RepID* field from the *Representatives* field list box in the first *Field* row field.

f. Insert the *RepName* field from the *Representatives* field list box in the second *Field* row field.

g. Insert the *ClientID* field from the *Clients* field list box in the third *Field* row field.

h. Insert the *Sales* field from the *Sales* field list box in the fourth *Field* row field.

8. Move the *RepName* field by completing the following steps:

a. Position the mouse pointer at the top of the *RepName* column until the pointer turns into a small, black, down-pointing arrow and then click the left mouse button. (This selects the entire column.)

b. Position the mouse pointer toward the top of the selected column until the pointer turns into a white arrow.

c. Hold down the left mouse button; drag to the right until a thick, black horizontal line displays between the *ClientID* column and the *Sales* column; and then release the mouse button.

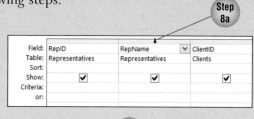

Step 8a

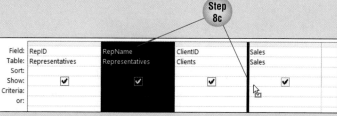

Step 8c

9. Delete the *RepID* field by clicking in a field in the column and then clicking the Delete Columns button in the Query Setup group.

10. Insert a new field column and insert a new field in the column by completing the following steps:

a. Click in the *Sales* field and then click the Insert Columns button in the Query Setup group.

b. Click the down-pointing arrow at the right side of the new field and then click *Clients.Client* at the drop-down list.

11. Hide the *ClientID* field so it does not display in the query results by clicking the *Show* check box in the *ClientID* column to remove the check mark.

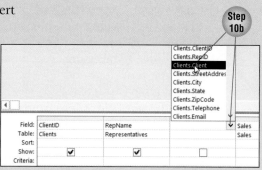

Step 10b

12. Insert the query criterion that extracts information on sales over $100,000 by completing the following steps:

a. Click in the *Criteria* row field in the *Sales* column.

b. Type >100000 and then press Enter. (Make sure you type zeros and not capital *O*s.)

13. Sort the *Sales* field values from highest to lowest by completing the following steps:

a. Click in the *Sort* row field in the *Sales* column.

b. Click the down-pointing arrow at the right side of the *Sort* row field and then click *Descending*.

14. Return the results of the query by clicking the Run button in the Results group.

15. Save the query and name it *SalesMoreThan$100000Query*. (See Project 1c query results on page 79.)

16. Print and then close the query.

Modifying a Query

You can modify a saved query and use it for a new purpose. For example, suppose that after designing the query that displays sales of more than $100,000, you decide that you want to find sales that are less than $100,000. Rather than design a new query, open the existing query, make any needed changes, and then run the query.

To modify an existing query, double-click the query in the Navigation pane. (This displays the query in Datasheet view.) Click the View button to display the query in Design view. You can also open a query in Design view by right-clicking the query in the Navigation pane and then clicking *Design View* at the shortcut menu. Make the desired changes and then click the Run button in the Results group. Click the Save button on the Quick Access toolbar to save the query with the same name. If you want to save the query with a new name, click the FILE tab, click the *Save As* option, click the *Save Object As* option, and then click the Save As button. At the Save As dialog box, type a name for the query and then press Enter.

If your database contains a number of queries, you can group and display them in the Navigation pane. To do this, click the down-pointing arrow in the Navigation pane menu bar and then click *Object Type* at the drop-down list. This displays objects grouped in categories, such as *Tables* and *Queries*.

▼ Quick Steps

Modify a Query
1. Double-click query in Navigation pane.
2. Click View button.
3. Make desired changes to query.
4. Click Run button.
5. Click Save button.

Save time designing a new query by modifying an existing query.

Renaming and Deleting a Query

If you modify a query, you may want to rename it. To do this, right-click the query name in the Navigation pane, click *Rename* at the shortcut menu, type the new name, and then press Enter. If you no longer need the query in the database, delete it by clicking the query name in the Navigation pane, clicking the Delete button in the Records group on the HOME tab, and then clicking the Yes button at the message asking if you want to permanently delete the query. Another method is to right-click the query in the Navigation pane, click *Delete* at the shortcut menu, and then click the Yes at the message. If you are deleting a query from your computer's hard drive, the message asking if you want to permanently delete the query will not display. This is because Access automatically sends the deleted query to the Recycle Bin, where it can be retrieved if necessary.

Project 1d   **Modifying Queries**   **Part 4 of 8**

1. With **AL1-C3-Dearborn.accdb** open, find sales less than $100,000 by completing the following steps:
   a. Double-click *SalesMoreThan$100000Query* in the Queries group in the Navigation pane.
   b. Click the View button in the Views group to switch to Design view.
   c. Click in the *Criteria* row field containing the text *>100000* and then edit the text so it displays as *<100000*.

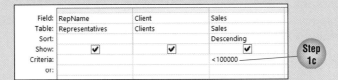

   d. Click the Run button in the Results group.

2. Save the query with a new name by completing the following steps:
   a. Click the FILE tab, click the *Save As* option, click the *Save Object As* option, and then click the Save As button.
   b. At the Save As dialog box, type **SalesLessThan$100000Query** and then press Enter. (See Project 1d query results on page 79.)
   c. Print and then close the query.

3. Modify an existing query and find employees with three weeks of vacation by completing the following steps:
   a. Right-click *MarToNov2011HiresQuery* in the Queries group in the Navigation pane and then click *Design View* at the shortcut menu.
   b. Click in the *Field* row field containing the text *HireDate*.
   c. Click the down-pointing arrow that displays at the right side of the field and then click *Vacation* at the drop-down list.
   d. Select the current text in the *Criteria* row field in the *Vacation* column, type **3 weeks**, and then press Enter.
   e. Click the Run button in the Results group.
   f. Save and then close the query.

4. Rename the query by completing the following steps:
   a. Right-click *MarToNov2011HiresQuery* in the Navigation pane and then click *Rename* at the shortcut menu.
   b. Type **RepsWith3WeekVacationsQuery** and then press Enter. (See Project 1d query results on page 79.)
   c. Open, print and then close the query.

5. Delete the *SalesOver$99999Query* by right-clicking the query name in the Navigation pane and then clicking *Delete* at the shortcut menu. If a message displays asking if you want to permanently delete the query, click Yes.

Step 2b

Save As   ?   ✕

Save 'SalesMoreThan$100000Query' to:

SalesLessThan$100000Query

As

Query   ⌄

OK   Cancel

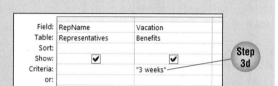

Step 3d

Field:	RepName	Vacation
Table:	Representatives	Benefits
Sort:		
Show:	✔	✔
Criteria:		"3 weeks"
or:		

Designing Queries with *Or* and *And* Criteria

The query design grid contains an *or* row that you can use to design a query that instructs Access to display records matching any of the criteria. Multiple criterion statements on different rows in a query become an Or statement, which means that any of the criterion can be met for a record to be displayed in the query results datasheet. For example, to display a list of employees with three weeks of vacation *or* four weeks of vacation, type *3 weeks* in the *Criteria* row field for the *Vacation* column and then type *4 weeks* in the field immediately below *3 weeks* in the *or* row. Other examples include finding clients that live in *Muncie* or *Lafayette* and finding representatives with quotas of *1* or *2*.

H I N T

You can design a query that combines *And* and *Or* statements.

You can also select records by entering criteria statements into more than one *Criteria* field. Multiple criteria all entered in the same row become an *And* statement, for which each criterion must be met for Access to select the record. For example, you can search for clients in the Indianapolis area with sales greater than $100,000.

1. With **AL1-C3-Dearborn.accdb** open, modify an existing query and find employees with three weeks or four weeks of vacation by completing the following steps:
   a. Double-click the *RepsWith3WeekVacationsQuery*.
   b. Click the View button in the Views group to switch to Design view.
   c. Click in the empty field below "*3 weeks*" in the *or* row, type **4 weeks**, and then press Enter.
   d. Click the Run button in the Results group.

2. Save the query with a new name by completing the following steps:
   a. Click the FILE tab, click the *Save As* option, click the *Save Object As* option, and then click the Save As button.
   b. At the Save As dialog box, type **RepsWith3Or4WeekVacationsQuery** and then press Enter. (See Project 1e query results on page 79.)
   c. Print and then close the query.
3. Design a query that finds records of clients in the Indianapolis area with sales over $100,000 by completing the following steps:
   a. Click the CREATE tab and then click the Query Design button.
   b. Double-click *Clients* in the Show Table dialog box.
   c. Double-click *Sales* in the Show Table dialog box and then click the Close button.
   d. At the query window, insert the *Client* field from the *Clients* field list box in the first *Field* row field.
   e. Insert the *City* field from the *Clients* field list box in the second *Field* row field.
   f. Insert the *Sales* field from the *Sales* field list box in the third *Field* row field.
   g. Insert the query criteria by completing the following steps:
      1) Click in the *Criteria* row field in the *City* column.
      2) Type **Indianapolis** and then press Enter.
      3) With the insertion point positioned in the *Criteria* row field in the *Sales* column, type **>100000** and then press Enter.

Field:	Client	City	Sales
Table:	Clients	Clients	Sales
Sort:			
Show:	✔	✔	✔
Criteria:		"Indianapolis"	>100000
or:			

Step 3g2   Step 3g3

   h. Click the Run button in the Results group.
   i. Save the query and name it *SalesOver$100000IndianapolisQuery*. (See Project 1e query results on page 79.)
   j. Print and then close the query.
4. Close **AL1-C3-Dearborn.accdb**.
5. Open **AL1-C3-PacTrek.accdb**.
6. Design a query that finds products available from supplier numbers 25, 31, and 42 by completing the following steps:
   a. Click the CREATE tab and then click the Query Design button.
   b. Double-click *Suppliers* in the Show Table dialog box.
   c. Double-click *Products* in the Show Table dialog box and then click the Close button.
   d. At the query window, insert the *SupplierID* field from the *Suppliers* field list box in the first *Field* row field.

e. Insert the *SupplierName* field from the *Suppliers* field list box in the second *Field* row field.

f. Insert the *Product* field from the *Products* field list box in the third *Field* row field.

g. Insert the query criteria by completing the following steps:

1) Click in the *Criteria* row field in the *SupplierID* column.

2) Type **25** and then press the Down Arrow key on your keyboard. (This makes active the field below *25*.)

3) Type **31** and then press the Down Arrow key on your keyboard. (This makes active the field below *31*.)

4) Type **42** and then press Enter.

Step 6g2
Step 6g3
Step 6g4

Field:	SupplierID	SupplierName	Product
Table:	Suppliers	Suppliers	Products
Sort:			
Show:	☑	☑	☑
Criteria:	"25"		
or:	"31"		
	"42"		

h. Click the Run button in the Results group.

i. Save the query and name it *Suppliers25-31-42Query*. (See Project 1e query results on page 79.)

j. Print and then close the query.

7. Design a query that finds ski hats or gloves on order and the numbers ordered by completing the following steps:

a. Click the CREATE tab and then click the Query Design button.

b. Double-click *Orders* in the Show Table dialog box.

c. Double-click *Suppliers* in the Show Table dialog box.

d. Double-click *Products* in the Show Table dialog box and then click the Close button.

e. At the query window, insert the *OrderID* field from the *Orders* field list box in the first *Field* row field.

f. Insert the *SupplierName* field from the *Suppliers* field list box in the second *Field* row field.

g. Insert the *Product* field from the *Products* field list box in the third *Field* row field.

h. Insert the *UnitsOrdered* field from the *Orders* field list box in the fourth *Field* row field.

i. Insert the query criteria by completing the following steps:

1) Click in the *Criteria* row field in the *Product* column.

2) Type ***ski hat*** and then press the Down Arrow key on your keyboard. (You need to type the asterisk before and after *ski hat* so the query will find any product that includes the words *ski hat* in the description, no matter what text comes before or after the words.)

3) Type ***gloves*** and then press Enter.

Step 7i2
Step 7i3

Field:	OrderID	SupplierName	Product	UnitsOrdered
Table:	Orders	Suppliers	Products	Orders
Sort:				
Show:	☑	☑	☑	☑
Criteria:			Like "*ski hat*"	
or:			Like "*gloves*"	

j. Click the Run button in the Results group.

k. Save the query and name it *SkiHatsGlovesOnOrderQuery*. (See Project 1e query results on page 79.)

l. Print and then close the query.

8. Design a query that finds boots, sleeping bags, or backpacks and the suppliers that produce them by completing the following steps:
   a. Click the CREATE tab and then click the Query Design button.
   b. Double-click *Products* in the Show Table dialog box.
   c. Double-click *Suppliers* in the Show Table dialog box and then click the Close button.
   d. At the query window, insert the *ProductID* field from the *Products* field list box in the first *Field* row field.
   e. Insert the *Product* field from the *Products* field list box in the second *Field* row field.
   f. Insert the *SupplierName* field from the *Suppliers* field list box in the third *Field* row field.
   g. Insert the query criteria by completing the following steps:
      1) Click in the *Criteria* row field in the *Product* column.
      2) Type *boots* and then press the Down Arrow key on your keyboard.
      3) Type *sleeping bag* and then press the Down Arrow key on your keyboard.
      4) Type *backpack* and then press Enter.

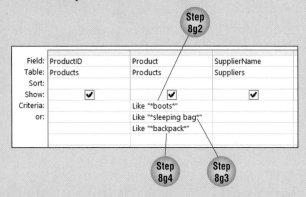

   h. Click the Run button in the Results group.
   i. Save the query and name it *BootsSleepingBagsBackpacksQuery*. (See Project 1e query results on page 79.)
   j. Print and then close the query.
9. Close **AL1-C3-PacTrek.accdb**.
10. Open **AL1-C3-CopperState.accdb**.
11. Design a query that finds clients that have only liability auto coverage by completing the following steps:
    a. Click the CREATE tab and then click the Query Design button.
    b. Double-click *Clients* in the Show Table dialog box.
    c. Double-click *Coverage* in the Show Table dialog box and then click the Close button.
    d. At the query window, insert the *ClientID* field from the *Clients* field list box in the first *Field* row field.
    e. Insert the *FirstName* field from the *Clients* field list box in the second *Field* row field.
    f. Insert the *LastName* field from the *Clients* field list box in the third *Field* row field.
    g. Insert the *Medical* field from the *Coverage* field list box in the fourth *Field* row field.
    h. Insert the *Liability* field from the *Coverage* field list box in the fifth *Field* row field.
    i. Insert the *Comprehensive* field from the *Coverage* field list box in the sixth *Field* row field.
    j. Insert the *UninsMotorist* field from the *Coverage* field list box in the seventh *Field* row field. (You may need to scroll down the *Coverage* field list box to display the *UninsMotorist* field.)
    k. Insert the *Collision* field from the *Coverage* field list box in the eighth *Field* row field. (You may need to scroll down the *Coverage* field list box to display the *Collision* field.)

1. Insert the query criteria by completing the following steps:
    1) Click in the *Criteria* row field in the *Medical* column, type 0, and then press Enter. (Access changes the *0* to *False.*)
    2) With the insertion point in the *Liability* column, type 1 and then press Enter. (Access changes the *1* to *True.*)
    3) With the insertion point in the *Comprehensive* column, type 0 and then press Enter.
    4) With the insertion point in the *UninsMotorist* column, type 0 and then press Enter.
    5) With the insertion point in the *Collision* column, type 0 and then press Enter.

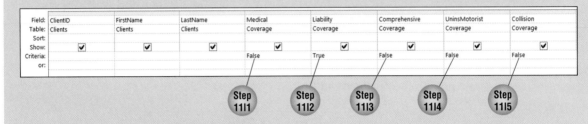

Field:	ClientID	FirstName	LastName	Medical	Liability	Comprehensive	UninsMotorist	Collision
Table:	Clients	Clients	Clients	Coverage	Coverage	Coverage	Coverage	Coverage
Sort:								
Show:	✔	✔	✔	✔	✔	✔	✔	✔
Criteria:				False	True	False	False	False
or:								

Step 11l1 Step 11l2 Step 11l3 Step 11l4 Step 11l5

  m. Click the Run button in the Results group.
  n. Save the query and name it *ClientsWithOnlyLiabilityQuery*. (See Project 1e query results on page 79.)
  o. Print the query in landscape orientation.
  p. Close the query.
12. Close **AL1-C3-CopperState.accdb**.

Performing Queries with the Simple Query Wizard ■■■■

Query Wizard

The Simple Query Wizard provided by Access guides you through the steps for preparing a query. To use this wizard, open the database, click the CREATE tab, and then click the Query Wizard button in the Queries group. At the New Query dialog box, make sure *Simple Query Wizard* is selected in the list box and then click the OK button. At the first Simple Query Wizard dialog box, shown in Figure 3.3, specify the table(s) in the *Tables/Queries* option box. After specifying the table(s), insert the fields you want included in the query in the *Selected Fields* list box and then click the Next button.

Figure 3.3 First Simple Query Wizard Dialog Box

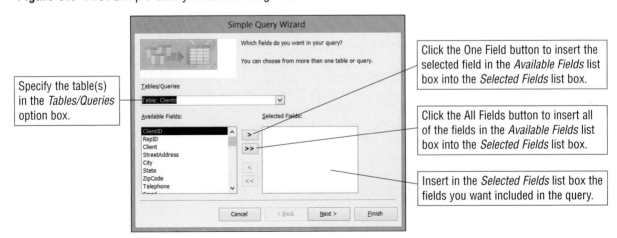

Specify the table(s) in the *Tables/Queries* option box.

Click the One Field button to insert the selected field in the *Available Fields* list box into the *Selected Fields* list box.

Click the All Fields button to insert all of the fields in the *Available Fields* list box into the *Selected Fields* list box.

Insert in the *Selected Fields* list box the fields you want included in the query.

At the second Simple Query Wizard dialog box, specify whether you want a detail or summary query and then click the Next button. At the third (and last) Simple Query Wizard dialog box, shown in Figure 3.4, type a name for the completed query or accept the name provided by the wizard. At this dialog box, you can also specify that you want to open the query to view the information or modify the query design. If you want to extract specific information, be sure to choose the *Modify the query design* option. After making any necessary changes, click the Finish button.

If you do not modify the query design in the last Simple Query Wizard dialog box, the query displays all records for the fields identified in the first Simple Query Wizard dialog box. In Project 1f, you will perform a query without modifying the design, and in Project 1g, you will modify the query design.

▼ Quick Steps

Create a Query with the Simple Query Wizard
1. Click CREATE tab.
2. Click Query Wizard button.
3. Make sure *Simple Query Wizard* is selected in list box and then click OK.
4. Follow query steps.

Figure 3.4 Last Simple Query Wizard Dialog Box

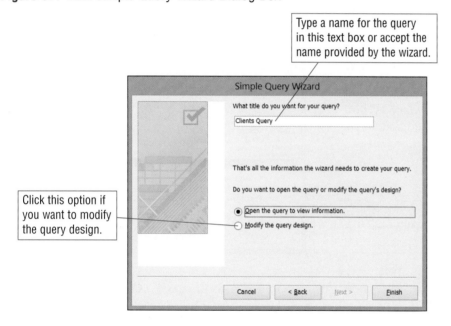

Type a name for the query in this text box or accept the name provided by the wizard.

Click this option if you want to modify the query design.

Project 1f **Performing Queries with the Simple Query Wizard** Part 6 of 8

1. Open **AL1-C3-Dearborn.accdb** and then use the Simple Query Wizard to create a query that displays client names along with sales by completing the following steps:
   a. Click the CREATE tab and then click the Query Wizard button in the Queries group.
   b. At the New Query dialog box, make sure *Simple Query Wizard* is selected in the list box and then click OK.
   c. At the first Simple Query Wizard dialog box, click the down-pointing arrow at the right of the *Tables/Queries* option box and then click *Table: Clients*.

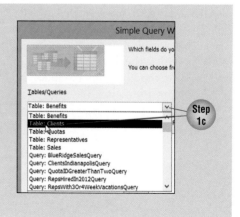

d. With *ClientID* selected in the *Available Fields* list box, click the One Field button (the button containing the greater-than symbol, >). This inserts the *ClientID* field in the *Selected Fields* list box.

e. Click *Client* in the *Available Fields* list box and then click the One Field button.

f. Click the down-pointing arrow at the right of the *Tables/Queries* option box and then click *Table: Sales*.

g. Click *Sales* in the *Available Fields* list box and then click the One Field button.

h. Click the Next button.

i. At the second Simple Query Wizard dialog box, click the Next button.

j. At the last Simple Query Wizard dialog box, select the name in the *What title do you want for your query?* text box, type **ClientSalesQuery**, and then press Enter.

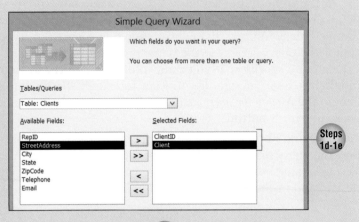

Steps 1d-1e

Step 1f

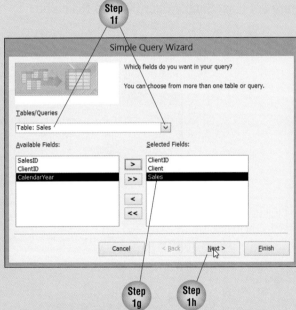

Step 1g

Step 1h

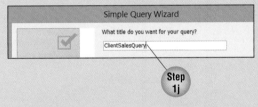

Step 1j

k. When the results of the query display, print the results. (See Project 1f query results on page 80.)

2. Close the query.
3. Close **AL1-C3-Dearborn.accdb**.
4. Open **AL1-C3-PacTrek.accdb**.
5. Create a query that displays the products on order, order amounts, and supplier names by completing the following steps:
   a. Click the CREATE tab and then click the Query Wizard button.
   b. At the New Query dialog box, make sure *Simple Query Wizard* is selected in the list box and then click OK.

c. At the first Simple Query Wizard dialog box, click the down-pointing arrow at the right side of the *Tables/Queries* option box and then click *Table: Suppliers*.

d. With *SupplierID* selected in the *Available Fields* list box, click the One Field button. (This inserts the *SupplierID* field in the *Selected Fields* list box.)

e. With *SupplierName* selected in the *Available Fields* list box, click the One Field button.

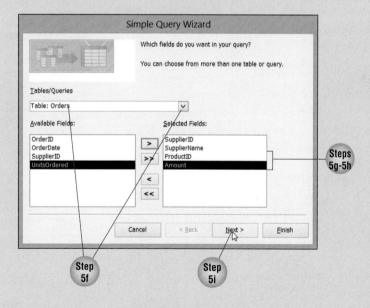

f. Click the down-pointing arrow at the right of the *Tables/Queries* option box and then click *Table: Orders*.

g. Click *ProductID* in the *Available Fields* list box and then click the One Field button.

h. Click *Amount* in the *Available Fields* list box and then click the One Field button.

i. Click the Next button.

j. At the second Simple Query Wizard dialog box, click the Next button.

k. At the last Simple Query Wizard dialog box, select the text in the *What title do you want for your query?* text box, type **ProductOrderAmountsQuery**, and then press Enter.

l. When the results of the query display, print the results. (See Project 1f query results on page 80.)

m. Close the query.

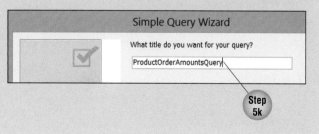

To extract specific information when using the Simple Query Wizard, tell the wizard that you want to modify the query design. This displays the query window with the query design grid, where you can insert query criteria.

1. With **AL1-C3-PacTrek.accdb** open, use the Simple Query Wizard to create a query that displays suppliers outside British Columbia by completing the following steps:
   a. Click the CREATE tab and then click the Query Wizard button.
   b. At the New Query dialog box, make sure *Simple Query Wizard* is selected and then click OK.
   c. At the first Simple Query Wizard dialog box, click the down-pointing arrow at the right side of the *Tables/Queries* option box and then click *Table: Suppliers*.
   d. Insert the following fields in the *Selected Fields* list box:
      SupplierName
      StreetAddress
      City
      Prov/State
      PostalCode
   e. Click the Next button.
   f. At the last Simple Query Wizard dialog box, select the current text in the *What title do you want for your query?* text box and then type **SuppliersNotBCQuery**.
   g. Click the *Modify the query design* option and then click the Finish button.
   h. At the query window, complete the following steps:
      1) Click in the *Criteria* row field in the *Prov/State* column in the query design grid.
      2) Type **Not BC** and then press Enter.

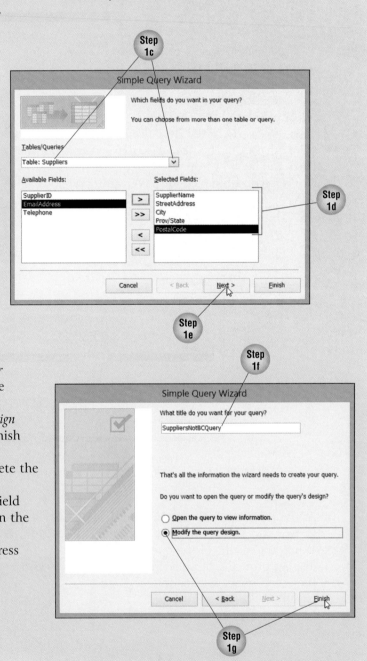

i. Specify that the fields are to be sorted in descending order by postal code by completing the following steps:
   1) Click in the *Sort* row field in the *PostalCode* column.
   2) Click the down-pointing arrow that displays at the right side of the field and then click *Descending*.

Field:	[SupplierName]	[StreetAddress]	[City]	[Prov/State]	[PostalCode]
Table:	Suppliers	Suppliers	Suppliers	Suppliers	Suppliers
Sort:					Descending
Show:	✔	✔	✔	✔	Ascending
Criteria:				Not "BC"	Descending
or:					(not sorted)

Step 1i2

j. Click the Run button in the Results group. (This displays suppliers that are not located in British Columbia and displays the records sorted by postal code in descending order. See Project 1g query results on page 80.)

k. Save, print, and then close the query.

2. Close **AL1-C3-PacTrek.accdb**.

3. Open **AL1-C3-Dearborn.accdb**.

4. Use the Simple Query Wizard to create a query that displays clients in Muncie by completing the following steps:

   a. Click the CREATE tab and then click the Query Wizard button.

   b. At the New Query dialog box, make sure *Simple Query Wizard* is selected and then click OK.

   c. At the first Simple Query Wizard dialog box, click the down-pointing arrow at the right of the *Tables/Queries* option box and then click *Table: Clients*. (You may need to scroll up the list to display this table.)

   d. Insert the following fields in the *Selected Fields* list box:
      Client
      StreetAddress
      City
      State
      ZipCode

   e. Click the Next button.

   f. At the last Simple Query Wizard dialog box, select the current text in the *What title do you want for your query?* text box and then type **ClientsMuncieQuery**.

   g. Click the *Modify the query design* option and then click the Finish button.

   h. At the query window, complete the following steps:
      1) Click in the *Criteria* row field in the *City* column in the query design grid.
      2) Type **Muncie** and then press Enter.

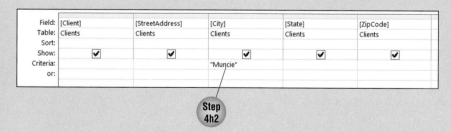

Field:	[Client]	[StreetAddress]	[City]	[State]	[ZipCode]
Table:	Clients	Clients	Clients	Clients	Clients
Sort:					
Show:	✔	✔	✔	✔	✔
Criteria:			"Muncie"		
or:					

Step 4h2

   i. Click the Run button in the Results group. (This displays clients located in Muncie. See Project 1g query results on page 80.)

   j. Save, print, and then close the query.

5. Close **AL1-C3-Dearborn.accdb**.
6. Open **AL1-C3-CopperState.accdb**.
7. Use the Simple Query Wizard to display clients that live in Phoenix with claims over $500 by completing the following steps:
   a. Click the CREATE tab and then click the Query Wizard button in the Queries group.
   b. At the New Query dialog box, make sure *Simple Query Wizard* is selected in the list box and then click OK.
   c. At the first Simple Query Wizard dialog box, click the down-pointing arrow at the right of the *Tables/Queries* option box and then click *Table: Clients*.
   d. Insert the following fields in the *Selected Fields* list box:
      ClientID
      FirstName
      LastName
      StreetAddress
      City
      State
      ZIP
   e. Click the down-pointing arrow at the right of the *Tables/Queries* option box and then click *Table: Claims*.
   f. With *ClaimID* selected in the *Available Fields* list box, click the One Field button.
   g. Click *AmountOfClaim* in the *Available Fields* list box and then click the One Field button.
   h. Click the Next button.
   i. At the second Simple Query Wizard dialog box, click the Next button.
   j. At the last Simple Query Wizard dialog box, select the current text in the *What title do you want for your query?* text box and then type PhoenixClientClaimsOver$500Query.
   k. Click the *Modify the query design* option and then click the Finish button.
   l. At the query window, complete the following steps:
      1) Click in the *Criteria* row field in the *City* column in the query design grid.
      2) Type "Phoenix" and then press Enter. (Type the quotation marks to tell Access that this is a criterion, otherwise Access will insert the query name *PhoenixClientClaimsOver$500Query* in the *Criteria* field.)
      3) Click in the *Criteria* row field in the *AmountOfClaim* column. (You may need to scroll to the right to display this field.)
      4) Type >500 and then press Enter.

City	State	ZIP	ClaimID	AmountOfClaim
Clients	Clients	Clients	Claims	Claims
✔	✔	✔	✔	✔
"Phoenix"				>500

Step 7l2

Step 7l4

   m. Click the Run button in the Results group. (This displays clients located in Phoenix with claims greater than $500. See Project 1g query results on page 80.)
   n. Save the query, print the query in landscape orientation, and then close the query.
8. Close **AL1-C3-CopperState.accdb**.

Creating Calculated Fields ■■■■■■■■■■■■■■■■■■■

In a query, you can calculate values from a field by inserting a *calculated field* in a *Field* row field in the query design grid. To insert a calculated field, click in the *Field* row field, type the desired field name followed by a colon, and then type the equation. For example, to determine pension contributions as 3% of an employee's annual salary, type *PensionContribution:[AnnualSalary]*0.03* in the *Field* row field. Use brackets to specify field names and use mathematical operators to perform the equation. Some basic operators include the plus (+) for addition, the hyphen (-) for subtraction, the asterisk (*) for multiplication, and the forward slash (/) for division.

Type a calculated field in the field or in the Expression Builder dialog box. To display the Expression Builder dialog box, display the query in Design view, click in the field where you want the calculated field expression inserted, and then click the Builder button in the Query Setup group on the QUERY TOOLS DESIGN tab. You can type field names in the Expression Builder and when you click OK, the equation is inserted in the field with the correct symbols. For example, you can type *AnnualSalary*0.03* in the Expression Builder and when you click OK, *Expr1: [AnnualSalary]*0.03* is inserted in the *Criteria* row field. If you do not type a name for the field, Access creates the alias *Expr1* for the field name. If you want a specific name for the field, such as *PensionContribution*, first type that in the Expression Builder, followed by a colon, and then type the expression.

Builder

Project 1h | **Creating a Calculated Field in a Query** | **Part 8 of 8**

1. Open **AL1-C3-MRInvestments.accdb** and enable the contents.
2. Create a query that displays employer pension contributions at 3% of employees' annual salary by completing the following steps:
   a. Click the CREATE tab and then click the Query Design button.
   b. Double-click *Employees* in the Show Table dialog box and then click the Close button.
   c. At the query window, insert the *EmpID* field from the *Employees* field list box in the first *Field* row field.
   d. Insert the *FirstName* field in the second *Field* row field.
   e. Insert the *LastName* field in the third *Field* row field.
   f. Insert the *AnnualSalary* field in the fourth *Field* row field.
   g. Click in the fifth *Field* row field.
   h. Type **PensionContribution:[AnnualSalary]*0.03** and then press Enter.
   i. Click the Run button in the Results group.
   j. Save the query and name it *PensionContributionsQuery*. (See Project 1h query results on page 80.)
   k. Print and then close the query.

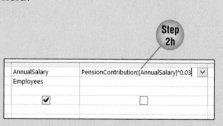

3. Modify *PensionContributionsQuery* and use the Expression Builder to write an equation finding the total amount of annual salary plus a 3% employer pension contribution by completing the following steps:
   a. Right-click *PensionContributionsQuery* in the Queries group in the Navigation pane and then click *Design View* at the shortcut menu.
   b. Click in the field containing *PensionContribution:[AnnualSalary]*0.03*.
   c. Click the Builder button in the Query Setup group on the QUERY TOOLS DESIGN tab.

d. In the Expression Builder, select the existing expression *PensionContribution: [AnnualSalary]*0.03*.

e. Type **Salary&Pension: [AnnualSalary]*1.03** and then click OK.

4. Click the Run button in the Results group.

5. Save the query by completing the following steps:

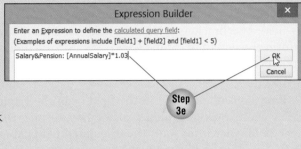

a. Click the FILE tab, click the *Save As* option, click the *Save Object As* option, and then click the Save As button.

b. At the Save As dialog box, type **Salary&PensionQuery** and then click OK. (See Project 1h query results on page 80.)

6. Print and then close the query.

7. Close **AL1-C3-MRInvestments.accdb**.

8. Open **AL1-C3-PacTrek.accdb**.

9. Create a query that displays orders and total order amounts by completing the following steps:

a. Click the CREATE tab and then click the Query Design button.

b. Double-click *Products* in the Show Table dialog box.

c. Double-click *Orders* in the Show Table dialog box and then click the Close button.

d. At the query window, insert the *Product* field from the *Products* field list box in the first *Field* row field.

e. Insert the *OrderID* field from the *Orders* field list box in the second *Field* row field.

f. Insert the *UnitsOrdered* field from the *Orders* field list box in the third *Field* row field.

g. Insert the *Amount* field from the *Orders* field list box in the fourth *Field* row field.

h. Click in the fifth *Field* row field.

i. Click the Builder button in the Query Setup group on the QUERY TOOLS DESIGN tab.

j. Type **Total:Amount*UnitsOrdered** in the Expression Builder and then click OK.

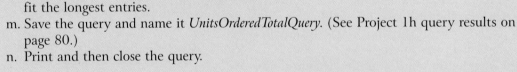

k. Click the Run button in the Results group.

l. Adjust the width of the columns to fit the longest entries.

m. Save the query and name it *UnitsOrderedTotalQuery*. (See Project 1h query results on page 80.)

n. Print and then close the query.

Project 2 **Create Aggregate Functions, Crosstab, Find Duplicates, and Find Unmatched Queries**   **6 Parts**

You will create an aggregate functions query that determines the total, average, minimum, and maximum order amounts and then calculate total and average order amounts grouped by supplier. You will also use the Crosstab, Find Duplicates, and Find Unmatched query wizards to design queries.

Designing Queries with Aggregate Functions ■■■■■■■■

You can include an *aggregate function*—such as Sum, Avg, Min, Max, or Count—in a query to calculate statistics from numeric field values of all the records in the table. When an aggregate function is used, Access displays one row in the query results datasheet with the formula result for the function used. For example, in a table with a numeric field containing annual salary amounts, you can use the Sum function to calculate the total of all salary amount values.

To display the aggregate function list, click the Totals button in the Show/Hide group on the QUERY TOOLS DESIGN tab. Access adds a *Total* row to the design grid with a drop-down list from which you select the desired function. Access also inserts the words *Group By* in the *Total* row field. Click the down-pointing arrow and then click the desired aggregate function from the drop-down list. In Project 2a, Step 1, you will create a query in Design view and use aggregate functions to find the total of all sales, average sales amount, maximum and minimum sales, and total number of sales. The completed query will display as shown in Figure 3.5. Access automatically determines the column heading names.

▼ **Quick Steps**

Design a Query with an Aggregate Function
1. At query window, click Totals button.
2. Click down-pointing arrow in *Total* row field.
3. Click desired aggregate function.
▼ **Quick Steps**

Design a Query with an Aggregate Function
1. At query window, click Totals button.
2. Click down-pointing arrow in *Total* row field.
3. Click desired aggregate function.

Totals

Figure 3.5 Query Results for Project 2a, Step 1

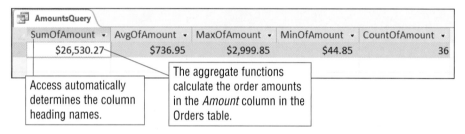

Access automatically determines the column heading names.

The aggregate functions calculate the order amounts in the *Amount* column in the Orders table.

Project 2a   Using Aggregate Functions in Queries   Part 1 of 6

1. With **AL1-C3-PacTrek.accdb** open, create a query with aggregate functions that determines total, average, maximum, and minimum order amounts, as well as the total number of orders, by completing the following steps:
   a. Click the CREATE tab and then click the Query Design button.
   b. At the Show Table dialog box, make sure *Orders* is selected in the list box, click the Add button, and then click the Close button.

   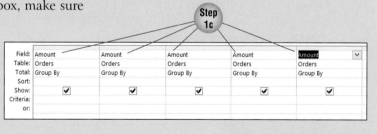

   Step 1c

   c. Insert the *Amount* field in the first, second, third, fourth, and fifth *Field* row fields. (You may need to scroll down the *Orders* field list box to display the *Amount* field.)
   d. Click the Totals button in the Show/Hide group on the QUERY TOOLS DESIGN tab. (This adds a *Total* row to the design grid between *Table* and *Sort* with the default option of *Group By*.)

   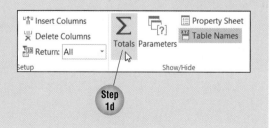

   Step 1d

Chapter 3 ■ Performing Queries   109

e. Specify a Sum function for the first *Total* row field by completing the following steps:
   1) Click in the first *Total* row field.
   2) Click the down-pointing arrow that displays at the right side of the field.
   3) Click *Sum* at the drop-down list.
f. Complete steps similar to those in Step 1e to insert *Avg* in the second *Total* row field.
g. Complete steps similar to those in Step 1e to insert *Max* in the third *Total* row field.
h. Complete steps similar to those in Step 1e to insert *Min* in the fourth *Total* row field.
i. Complete steps similar to those in Step 1e to insert *Count* in the fifth *Total* row field.

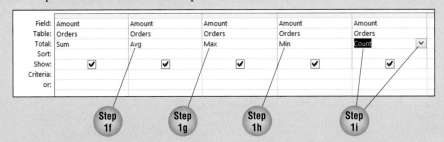

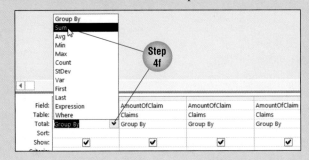

j. Click the Run button in the Results group. (Notice the headings that Access assigns to the columns.)
k. Automatically adjust the widths of the columns.
l. Save the query and name it *AmountsQuery*. (See Project 2a query results on page 81.)
m. Print and then close the query.
2. Close **AL1-C3-PacTrek.accdb**.
3. Open **AL1-C3-CopperState.accdb**.
4. Create a query with aggregate functions that determines total, average, maximum, and minimum claim amounts by completing the following steps:
   a. Click the CREATE tab and then click the Query Design button.
   b. At the Show Table dialog box, double-click *Claims*.
   c. Click the Close button to close the Show Table dialog box.
   d. Insert the *AmountOfClaim* field in the first, second, third, and fourth *Field* row fields.
   e. Click the Totals button in the Show/Hide group.
   f. Click in the first *Total* row field, click the down-pointing arrow that displays at the right side of the field, and then click *Sum* at the drop-down list.

g. Click in the second *Total* row field, click the down-pointing arrow, and then click *Avg* at the drop-down list.

h. Click in the third *Total* row field, click the down-pointing arrow, and then click *Max* at the drop-down list.

i. Click in the fourth *Total* row field, click the down-pointing arrow, and then click *Min* at the drop-down list.

j. Click the Run button in the Results group. (Notice the headings that Access chooses for the columns.)

k. Automatically adjust the widths of the columns.

l. Save the query and name it *ClaimAmountsQuery*. (See Project 2a query results on page 81.)

m. Print the query in landscape orientation and then close the query.

Using the *Group By* option in the *Total* field, you can add a field to the query on which you want Access to group records for statistical calculations. For example, to calculate the total of all orders for a specific supplier, add the *SupplierID* field to the design grid with the *Total* field set to *Group By*. In Project 2b, Step 1, you will create a query in Design view and use aggregate functions to find the total of all order amounts and the average order amounts grouped by supplier number.

<table>
<tr><td>**Project 2b**</td><td>**Using Aggregate Functions and Grouping Records**</td><td>**Part 2 of 6**</td></tr>
</table>

1. With **AL1-C3-CopperState.accdb** open, determine the sum and average of client claims by completing the following steps:

   a. Click the CREATE tab and then click the Query Design button.

   b. At the Show Table dialog box, double-click *Clients* in the list box.

   c. Double-click *Claims* in the list box and then click the Close button.

   d. Insert the *ClientID* field from the *Clients* field list box to the first *Field* row field.

   e. Insert the *AmountOfClaim* field from the *Claims* field list box to the second *Field* row field.

   f. Insert the *AmountOfClaim* field from the *Claims* field list box to the third *Field* row field.

   g. Click the Totals button in the Show/Hide group.

   h. Click in the second *Total* row field, click the down-pointing arrow, and then click *Sum* at the drop-down list.

   i. Click in the third *Total* row field, click the down-pointing arrow, and then click *Avg* at the drop-down list.

   j. Make sure *Group By* displays in the first *Total* row field.

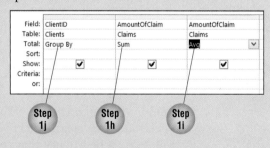

   k. Click the Run button in the Results group.

   l. Automatically adjust column widths.

   m. Save the query and name it *SumAvgClaimAmountsQuery*. (See Project 2b query results on page 81.)

   n. Print and then close the query.

2. Close **AL1-C3-CopperState.accdb**.

3. Open **AL1-C3-PacTrek.accdb**.
4. Determine the total and average order amounts for each supplier by completing the following steps:
   a. Click the CREATE tab and then click the Query Design button.
   b. At the Show Table dialog box, make sure *Orders* is selected in the list box and then click the Add button.
   c. Click *Suppliers* in the list box, click the Add button, and then click the Close button.
   d. Insert the *Amount* field from the *Orders* field list box to the first *Field* row field. (You may need to scroll down the *Orders* field list box to display the *Amount* field.)
   e. Insert the *Amount* field from the *Orders* field list box to the second *Field* row field.
   f. Insert the *SupplierID* field from the *Suppliers* field list box to the third *Field* row field.
   g. Insert the *SupplierName* field from the *Suppliers* field list box to the fourth *Field* row field.
   h. Click the Totals button in the Show/Hide group.
   i. Click in the first *Total* row field, click the down-pointing arrow, and then click *Sum* at the drop-down list.
   j. Click in the second *Total* row field, click the down-pointing arrow, and then click *Avg* at the drop-down list.

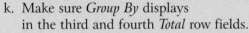

   k. Make sure *Group By* displays in the third and fourth *Total* row fields.
   l. Click the Run button in the Results group.
   m. Automatically adjust column widths.
   n. Save the query and name it *SupplierAmountsQuery*. (See Project 2b query results on page 81.)
   o. Print and then close the query.

Creating Crosstab Queries ■■■■■■■■■■■■■■■■■■

Quick Steps

Create a Crosstab Query
1. Click CREATE tab.
2. Click Query Wizard button.
3. Double-click *Crosstab Query Wizard*.
4. Complete wizard steps.

A *crosstab query* calculates aggregate functions, such as Sum and Avg, in which field values are grouped by two fields. A wizard is included that guides you through the steps to create the query. The first field selected causes one row to display in the query results datasheet for each group. The second field selected displays one column in the query results datasheet for each group. A third field is specified that is the numeric field to be summarized. The intersection of each row and column holds a value that is the result of the specified aggregate function for the designated row and column group.

Create a crosstab query from fields in one table. If you want to include fields from more than one table, you must first create a query containing the desired fields, and then create the crosstab query. For example, in Project 2c, Step 2, you will create a new query that contains fields from each of the three tables in AL1-C3-PacTrek.accdb. Using this query, you will use the Crosstab Query Wizard to create a query that summarizes the order amounts by supplier name and product ordered. Figure 3.6 displays the results of that crosstab query. The first column displays the supplier names, the second column displays the total amount for each supplier, and the remaining columns display the amounts by suppliers for specific items.

Figure 3.6 Crosstab Query Results for Project 2c, Step 2

Order amounts are grouped by supplier name and individual product.

OrdersBySupplierByProductQuery

SupplierName	Total Of Amc	Binoculars, 8	Cascade R4 jɛ	Cascade R4 jɛ	Cascade R4 jɛ	Cascade R4 jɛ	Deluxe map c	Eight-piece st
Bayside Supplies	$224.00							$99.75
Cascade Gear	$3,769.00		$1,285.00	$1,285.00	$599.50	$599.50		
Emerald City Products	$2,145.00	$2,145.00						
Fraser Valley Products	$3,892.75							
Freedom Corporation	$1,286.65							
Hopewell, Inc.	$348.60							
KL Distributions	$4,288.35							
Langley Corporation	$593.25							
Macadam, Inc.	$175.70						$129.75	
Manning, Inc.	$4,282.25							
Sound Supplies	$5,524.72							

Project 2c — Creating Crosstab Queries

Part 3 of 6

1. With **AL1-C3-PacTrek.accdb** open, create a query containing fields from the three tables by completing the following steps:
   a. Click the CREATE tab and then click the Query Design button.
   b. At the Show Table dialog box with *Orders* selected in the list box, click the Add button.
   c. Double-click *Products* in the list box.
   d. Double-click *Suppliers* in the list box and then click the Close button.
   e. Insert the following fields to the specified *Field* row fields:
      1) From the *Orders* field list box, insert the *ProductID* field in the first *Field* row field.
      2) From the *Products* field list box, insert the *Product* field in the second *Field* row field.
      3) From the *Orders* field list box, insert the *UnitsOrdered* field in the third *Field* row field.
      4) From the *Orders* field list box, insert the *Amount* field in the fourth *Field* row field.
      5) From the *Suppliers* field list box, insert the *SupplierName* field in the fifth *Field* row field.
      6) From the *Orders* field list box, insert the *OrderDate* field in the sixth *Field* row field.

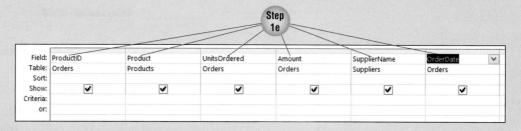

Step 1e

Field:	ProductID	Product	UnitsOrdered	Amount	SupplierName	OrderDate	v
Table:	Orders	Products	Orders	Orders	Suppliers	Orders	
Sort:							
Show:	✔	✔	✔	✔	✔	✔	
Criteria:							
or:							

   f. Click the Run button to run the query.
   g. Save the query and name it *ItemsOrderedQuery*.
   h. Close the query.

2. Create a crosstab query that
   summarizes the orders by supplier
   name and by product ordered by
   completing the following steps:
   a. Click the CREATE tab
      and then click the Query
      Wizard button.
   b. At the New Query dialog
      box, double-click *Crosstab
      Query Wizard* in the list
      box.
   c. At the first Crosstab
      Query Wizard dialog box,
      click the *Queries* option in
      the *View* section and then
      click *Query: ItemsOrderedQuery*
      in the list box.
   d. Click the Next button.
   e. At the second Crosstab Query
      Wizard dialog box, click
      SupplierName in the *Available
      Fields* list box and then
      click the One Field button.
      (This inserts *SupplierName*
      in the *Selected Fields* list box
      and specifies that you want
      SupplierName for the row
      headings.)
   f. Click the Next button.
   g. At the third Crosstab Query
      Wizard dialog box, click
      Product in the list box. (This
      specifies that you want *Product* for
      the column headings.)
   h. Click the Next button.
   i. At the fourth Crosstab Query
      Wizard dialog box, click *Amount*
      in the *Fields* list box and then click
      Sum in the *Functions* list box.
   j. Click the Next button.
   k. At the fifth Crosstab Query Wizard
      dialog box, select the current text
      in the *What do you want to name
      your query?* text box and then type
      OrdersBySupplierByProductQuery.
   l. Click the Finish button. (See Project
      2c query results on page 81.)

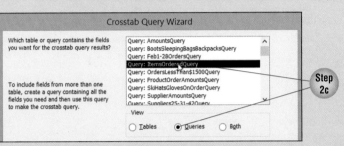
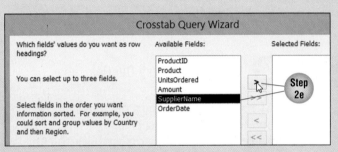
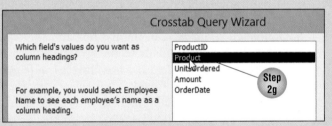
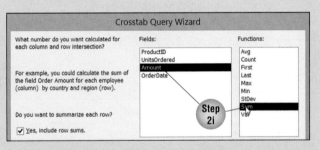
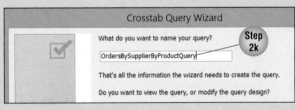

3. Display the query in Print Preview, change the orientation to landscape, change the
   left and right margins to 0.5 inch, and then print the query. (The query will print on
   four pages.)

4. Close the query.
5. Close **AL1-C3-PacTrek.accdb**.
6. Open **AL1-C3-CopperState.accdb**.
7. Create a crosstab query from fields in one table that summarizes clients' claims by completing the following steps:
   a. Click the CREATE tab and then click the Query Wizard button.
   b. At the New Query dialog box, double-click *Crosstab Query Wizard* in the list box.
   c. At the first Crosstab Query Wizard dialog box, click *Table: Claims* in the list box.
   d. Click the Next button.
   e. At the second Crosstab Query Wizard dialog box, click the One Field button. (This inserts the *ClaimID* field in the *Selected Fields* list box.)
   f. Click the Next button.
   g. At the third Crosstab Query Wizard dialog, make sure *ClientID* is selected in the list box and then click the Next button.
   h. At the fourth Crosstab Query Wizard dialog box, click *AmountOfClaim* in the *Fields* list box and click *Sum* in the *Functions* list box.
   i. Click the Next button.
   j. At the fifth Crosstab Query Wizard dialog box, select the current text in the *What do you want to name your query?* text box and then type **ClaimsByClaimIDByClientIDQuery**.
   k. Click the Finish button. (See Project 2c query results on page 81.)
8. Change the orientation to landscape and then print the query. The query will print on two pages.
9. Close the query.
10. Close **AL1-C3-CopperState.accdb**.

Creating Find Duplicates Queries ■■■■■■■■■■■■■■■■

Use a *find duplicates query* to search a specified table or query for duplicate field values within a designated field or fields. Create this type of query, for example, if you suspect a record (such as a product record) has inadvertently been entered twice (perhaps under two different product numbers). A find duplicates query has many applications. Here are a few other examples of how you can use a find duplicates query:

▼ **Quick Steps**
Create a Find Duplicates Query
1. Click CREATE tab.
2. Click Query Wizard button.
3. Double-click *Find Duplicates Query Wizard*.
4. Complete wizard steps.

- In an orders table, find records with the same customer number so you can identify loyal customers.
- In a customers table, find records with the same last name and mailing address so you can send only one mailing to a household and save on printing and postage costs.
- In an employee expenses table, find records with the same employee number so you can see which employee is submitting the most claims.

Access provides the Find Duplicates Query Wizard to build the query based on the selections made in a series of dialog boxes. To use this wizard, open the desired database, click the CREATE tab, and then click the Query Wizard button. At the New Query dialog box, double-click *Find Duplicates Query Wizard* in the list box and then complete the steps provided by the wizard.

In Project 2d, you will assume that you have been asked to update the address for a supplier in AL1-C3-PacTrek.accdb. Instead of updating the address, you create a new record. You will then use the Find Duplicates Query Wizard to find duplicate field values in the Suppliers table.

1. Open **AL1-C3-PacTrek.accdb** and then open the Suppliers table.
2. Add the following record to the table:

   SupplierID#   29
   SupplierName   Langley Corporation
   StreetAddress   1248 Larson Avenue
   City   Burnaby
   Prov/State   BC
   PostalCode   V5V 9K2
   EmailAddress   lc@emcp.net
   Telephone   (604) 555-1200

3. Close the Suppliers table.
4. Use the Find Duplicates Query Wizard to find any duplicate supplier names by completing the following steps:

   a. Click the CREATE tab and then click the Query Wizard button.
   b. At the New Query dialog box, double-click *Find Duplicates Query Wizard*.
   c. At the first wizard dialog box, click *Table: Suppliers* in the list box.

   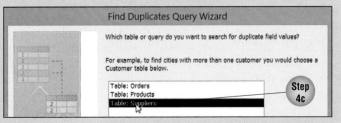

   d. Click the Next button.
   e. At the second wizard dialog box, click *SupplierName* in the *Available fields* list box and then click the One Field button. (This moves the *SupplierName* field to the *Duplicate-value fields* list box.)
   f. Click the Next button.
   g. At the third wizard dialog box, click the All Fields button (the button containing the two greater-than symbols, >>). This moves all the fields to the *Additional query fields* list box. You are doing this because if you find a duplicate supplier name, you want to view all the fields to determine which record is accurate.

   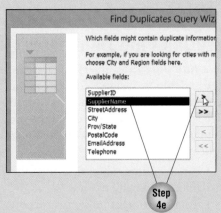

   h. Click the Next button.
   i. At the fourth (and last) wizard dialog box, type **DuplicateSuppliersQuery** in the *What do you want to name your query?* text box.
   j. Click the Finish button. (See Project 2d query results on page 81.)
   k. Change the orientation to landscape and then print the query.

   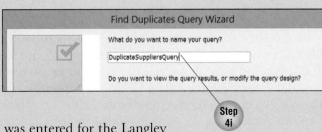

5. As you look at the query results, you realize that an inaccurate record was entered for the Langley Corporation, so you decide to delete one of the records. To do this, complete the following steps:

a. With the query open, click in the record selector bar next to the record with a supplier ID of *29*. (This selects the entire row.)

b. Click the HOME tab and then click the Delete button in the Records group.

c. At the message asking you to confirm, click the Yes button.

d. Close the query.

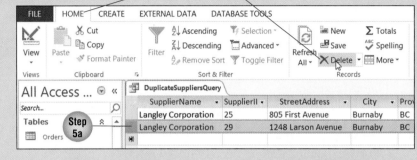

6. Change the street address for Langley Corporation by completing the following steps:

a. Open the Suppliers table in Datasheet view.

b. Change the address for Langley Corporation from *805 First Avenue* to *1248 Larson Avenue*. Leave the other fields as displayed.

c. Close the Suppliers table.

In Project 2d, you used the Find Duplicates Query Wizard to find records containing the same field.In Project 2e, you will use the Find Duplicates Query Wizard to find information on the suppliers you order from the most. You could use this information to negotiate for better prices or to ask for discounts.

Project 2e | **Finding Duplicate Orders** | **Part 5 of 6**

1. With **AL1-C3-PacTrek.accdb** open, create a query with the following fields (in the order shown) from the specified tables:

SupplierID	Suppliers table
SupplierName	Suppliers table
ProductID	Orders table
Product	Products table

2. Run the query.

3. Save the query with the name *SupplierOrdersQuery* and then close the query.

4. Use the Find Duplicates Query Wizard to find the suppliers you order from the most by completing the following steps:

a. Click the CREATE tab and then click the Query Wizard button.

b. At the New Query dialog box, double-click *Find Duplicates Query Wizard*.

c. At the first wizard dialog box, click the *Queries* option in the *View* section and then click *Query: SupplierOrdersQuery*. (You may need to scroll down the list to display this query.)

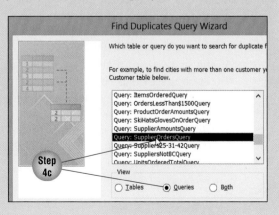

d. Click the Next button.
e. At the second wizard dialog box, click *SupplierName* in the *Available fields* list box and then click the One Field button.
f. Click the Next button.
g. At the third wizard dialog box, click the Next button.
h. At the fourth (and last) wizard dialog box, type **SupplierOrdersCountQuery** in the *What do you want to name your query?* text box.

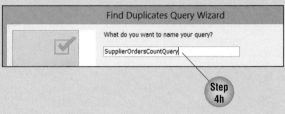

Find Duplicates Query Wizard

What do you want to name your query?

SupplierOrdersCountQuery

Step 4h

i. Click the Finish button.
j. Adjust the widths of the columns to fit the longest entries.
k. Print the query. (See Project 2e query results on page 82.)
5. Close the query.

Creating Find Unmatched Queries ■■■■■■■■■■■■■■■

▼ Quick Steps

Create a Find Unmatched Query
1. Click CREATE tab.
2. Click Query Wizard button.
3. Double-click *Find Unmatched Query Wizard*.
4. Complete wizard steps.

Create a *find unmatched query* to compare two tables and produce a list of the records in one table that have no matching record in the other table. This type of query is useful to produce lists such as customers who have never placed orders and invoices that have no records of payment. Access provides the Find Unmatched Query Wizard to build the select query by guiding you through a series of dialog boxes.

In Project 2f, you will use the Find Unmatched Query Wizard to find all of the products that have no units on order. This information is helpful in identifying which products are not selling and might need to be discontinued or returned. To use the Find Unmatched Query Wizard, click the CREATE tab and then click the Query Wizard button in the Queries group. At the New Query dialog box, double-click *Find Unmatched Query Wizard* in the list box and then follow the wizard steps.

Project 2f | Creating a Find Unmatched Query | Part 6 of 6

1. With **AL1-C3-PacTrek.accdb** open, use the Find Unmatched Query Wizard to find all products that do not have units on order by completing the following steps:
   a. Click the CREATE tab and then click the Query Wizard button.
   b. At the New Query dialog box, double-click *Find Unmatched Query Wizard*.
   c. At the first wizard dialog box, click *Table: Products* in the list box. (This is the table containing the fields you want to see in the query results.)
   d. Click the Next button.
   e. At the second wizard dialog box, make sure *Table: Orders* is selected in the list box. (This is the table containing the related records.)
   f. Click the Next button.

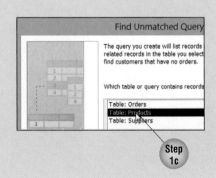

Find Unmatched Query

The query you create will list records related records in the table you select find customers that have no orders.

Which table or query contains records

Table: Orders
Table: Products
Table: Suppliers

Step 1c

g. At the third wizard dialog box, make sure *ProductID* is selected in both the *Fields in 'Products'* list box and in the *Fields in 'Orders'* list box.

h. Click the Next button.

i. At the fourth wizard dialog box, click the All Fields button to move all of the fields from the *Available fields* list box to the *Selected fields* list box.

j. Click the Next button.

k. At the fifth wizard dialog box, click the Finish button. (Let the wizard determine the query name: *Products Without Matching Orders*. See Project 2f query results on page 82.)

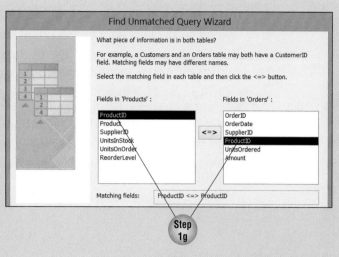

2. Print the query in landscape orientation and then close the query.

3. Close **AL1-C3-PacTrek.accdb**.

Chapter Summary

- One of the most important uses of a database is to select the information needed to answer questions and make decisions. Data can be extracted from an Access database by performing a query, which can be accomplished by designing a query or using a query wizard.

- Designing a query consists of identifying the table, the field or fields from which the data will be drawn, and the criteria for selecting the data.

- In designing a query, type the criterion (or criteria) for extracting the specific data. Access inserts any necessary symbols in the criterion when the Enter key is pressed.

- In a criterion, quotation marks surround field values and pound symbols (#) surround dates. Use the asterisk (*) as a wildcard character.

- You can perform a query on fields within one table or on fields from related tables.

- When designing a query, you can specify the sort order of a field or fields.

- You can modify an existing query and use it for a new purpose.

- Enter a criterion in the *or* row in the query design grid to instruct Access to display records that match any of the criteria.

- Multiple criteria entered in the *Criteria* row in the query design grid become an *And* statement, where each criterion must be met for Access to select the record.

- The Simple Query Wizard guides you through the steps for preparing a query. You can modify a query you create with the wizard.

- You can insert a calculated field in a *Field* row field when designing a query.

- Include an aggregate function (such as Sum, Avg, Min, Max, or Count) to calculate statistics from numeric field values. Click the Totals button in the Show/Hide group on the QUERY TOOLS DESIGN tab to display the aggregate function list.
- Use the *Group By* option in the *Total* row field to add a field to a query on which you want Access to group records for statistical calculations.
- Create a crosstab query to calculate aggregate functions (such as Sum and Avg), in which fields are grouped by two. Create a crosstab query from fields in one table. If you want to include fields from more than one table, create a query first and then create the crosstab query.
- Use a find duplicates query to search a specified table for duplicate field values within a designated field or fields.
- Create a find unmatched query to compare two tables and produce a list of the

Commands Review

FEATURE	RIBBON TAB, GROUP	BUTTON, OPTION
add *Total* row to query design	QUERY TOOLS DESIGN, Show/Hide	Σ
Crosstab Query Wizard	CREATE, Queries	, Crosstab Query Wizard
Find Duplicates Query Wizard	CREATE, Queries	, Find Duplicates Query Wizard
Find Unmatched Query Wizard	CREATE, Queries	, Find Unmatched Query Wizard
New Query dialog box	CREATE, Queries	
query results	QUERY TOOLS DESIGN, Results	!
query window	CREATE, Queries	
Simple Query Wizard	CREATE, Queries	, Simple Query Wizard

records in one table that have no matching records in the other related table.

Completion: In the space provided at the right, indicate the correct term, symbol, or command.

1. The Query Design button is located in the Queries group on this tab. _____

2. Click the Query Design button and the query window displays with this dialog box open. _____

3. To establish a criterion for a query, click in this row in the column containing the desired field name and then type the criterion. _____

4. This is the term used for the results of the query. _____

5. This is the symbol Access automatically inserts before and after a date when writing a criterion for the query. _____

6. Use this symbol to indicate a wildcard character when writing a query criterion. _____

7. This is the criterion you would type to return field values greater than $500. _____

8. This is the criterion you would type to return field values that begin with the letter *L*. _____

9. This is the criterion you would type to return field values that are not in Oregon. _____

10. You can sort a field in a query in ascending order or in this order. _____

11. Multiple criteria entered in the *Criteria* row in the query design grid become this type of statement. _____

12. This wizard guides you through the steps for preparing a query. _____

13. This type of query calculates aggregate functions, in which field values are grouped by two fields. _____

14. Use this type of query to compare two tables and produce a list of the records in one table that have no matching records in the other table. _____

Skills Check   Assess Your Performance

Assessment

1 DESIGN QUERIES IN A LEGAL SERVICES DATABASE

1. Display the Open dialog box with the AL1C3 folder on your storage medium the active folder.
2. Open **AL1-C3-WarrenLegal.accdb** and enable the contents.
3. Design a query that extracts information from the Billing table with the following specifications:
   a. Include the fields *BillingID*, *ClientID*, and *CategoryID* in the query.
   b. Extract those records with the *SE* category. (Type "**SE**" in the *Criteria* row field in the *CategoryID* column. You need to type the quotation marks to tell Access that SE is a criterion and not a built-in Access function.)
   c. Save the query and name it *SECategoryBillingQuery*.
   d. Print and then close the query.
4. Design a query that extracts information from the Billing table with the following specifications:
   a. Include the fields *BillingID*, *ClientID*, and *Date*.
   b. Extract those records in the *Date* field with dates between 6/8/2015 and 6/15/2015.
   c. Save the query and name it *June8-15BillingQuery*.
   d. Print and then close the query.
5. Design a query that extracts information from the Clients table with the following specifications:
   a. Include the fields *FirstName*, *LastName*, and *City*.
   b. Extract those records with cities other than Kent in the *City* field.
   c. Save the query and name it *ClientsNotInKentQuery*.
   d. Print and then close the query.
6. Design a query that extracts information from two tables with the following specifications:
   a. Include the fields *BillingID*, *ClientID*, *Date*, and *RateID* from the Billing table.
   b. Include the field *Rate* from the Rates table.
   c. Extract those records with rate IDs greater than *2*.
   d. Save the query and name it *RateIDGreaterThan2Query*.
   e. Print and then close the query.
7. Design a query that extracts information from three tables with the following specifications:
   a. Include the fields *AttorneyID*, *FName,* and *LName* from the Attorneys table.
   b. Include the fields *FirstName* and *LastName* from the Clients table.
   c. Include the fields *Date* and *Hours* from the Billing table.
   d. Extract those records with an attorney ID of *12*.
   e. Save the query and name it *Attorney12Query*.
   f. Print and then close the query.
8. Design a query that extracts information from four tables with the following specifications:
   a. Include the fields *AttorneyID*, *FName*, and *LName* from the Attorneys table.
   b. Include the field *Category* from the Categories table.
   c. Include the fields *RateID* and *Rate* from the Rates table.

d. Include the fields *Date* and *Hours* from the Billing table.

e. Extract those records with an attorney ID of *17* and a rate ID of *4*.

f. Save the query and name it *Attorney17RateID4Query*.

g. Print the query in landscape orientation and then close the query.

9. Open the Attorney17RateID4Query query, click the View button on the HOME tab to display the query in Design view, and then modify the query so it displays records with a rate ID of *4* and attorney IDs of *17* and *19* by making the following changes:

a. Click below the field value "*17*" in the *AttorneyID* column and then type 19.

b. Click below the field value "*4*" in the *RateID* column, type 4, and then press Enter.

c. Run the query.

d. Save the query with the new name *Attorney17&19RateID4Query*. **Hint: Do this at the Save As dialog box. Display this dialog box by clicking the FILE tab, clicking the Save As option, clicking the Save Object As option, and then clicking the Save As button.**

e. Print the query in landscape orientation and then close the query.

Assessment

2 USE THE SIMPLE QUERY WIZARD AND DESIGN QUERIES

1. With **AL1-C3-WarrenLegal.accdb** open, use the Simple Query Wizard to extract specific information from three tables with the following specifications:

a. At the first Simple Query Wizard dialog box, include the following fields:

From Attorneys table: *AttorneyID*, *FName*, and *LName*

From Categories table: *Category*

From Billing table: *Hours*

b. At the second Simple Query Wizard dialog box, click Next.

c. At the third Simple Query Wizard dialog box, click the *Modify the query design* option and then click the Finish button.

d. At the query window, insert *14* in the *Criteria* row field in the *AttorneyID* column.

e. Run the query.

f. Save the query with the default name.

g. Print and then close the query.

2. Create a query in Design view with the Billing table with the following specifications:

a. Insert the *Hours* field from the *Billing* field list box to the first, second, third, and fourth *Field* row fields.

b. Click the Totals button in the Show/Hide group.

c. Insert *Sum* in the first *Total* row field.

d. Insert *Min* in the second *Total* row field.

e. Insert *Max* in the third *Total* row field.

f. Insert *Count* in the fourth *Total* row field.

g. Run the query.

h. Automatically adjust the widths of the columns.

i. Save the query and name it *HoursAmountQuery*.

j. Print and then close the query.

3. Create a query in Design view with the following specifications:

a. Add the Attorneys table and Billing table to the query window.

b. Insert the *FName* field from the *Attorneys* field list box to the first *Field* row field.

c. Insert the *LName* field from the *Attorneys* field list box to the second *Field* row field.

d. Insert the *AttorneyID* field from the *Billing* field list box to the third *Field* row field. (You will need to scroll down the *Billing* field list box to display the *AttorneyID* field.)

e. Insert the *Hours* field from the *Billing* field list box to the fourth *Field* row field.

f. Click the Totals button in the Show/Hide group.

g. Insert *Sum* in the fourth *Total* row field in the *Hours* column.

h. Run the query.

i. Save the query and name it *AttorneyHoursQuery*.

j. Print and then close the query.

4. Create a query in Design view with the following specifications:

a. Add the Attorneys, Clients, Categories, and Billing tables to the query window.

b. Insert the *AttorneyID* field from the *Attorneys* field list box to the first *Field* row field.

c. Insert the *ClientID* field from the *Clients* field list box to the second *Field* row field.

d. Insert the *Category* field from the *Categories* field list box to the third *Field* row field.

e. Insert the *Hours* field from the *Billing* field list box to the fourth *Field* row field.

f. Run the query.

g. Save the query and name it *AttorneyClientHours*.

h. Print and then close the query.

Assessment

3 CREATE A CROSSTAB QUERY AND USE THE FIND DUPLICATES AND FIND UNMATCHED QUERY WIZARDS

1. With **AL1-C3-WarrenLegal.accdb** open, create a crosstab query that summarizes the hours by attorney by category with the following specifications:

a. At the first Crosstab Query Wizard dialog box, click the *Queries* option in the *View* section and then click *Query: AttorneyClientHours* in the list box.

b. At the second Crosstab Query Wizard dialog box with *AttorneyID* selected in the *Available Fields* list box, click the One Field button.

c. At the third Crosstab Query Wizard dialog box, click *Category* in the list box.

d. At the fourth Crosstab Query Wizard dialog box, click *Hours* in the *Fields* list box and click *Sum* in the *Functions* list box.

e. At the fifth Crosstab Query Wizard dialog box, select the current name in the *What do you want to name your query?* text box and then type **HoursByAttorneyByCategory**.

f. Display the query in Print Preview, change to landscape orientation, change the left and right margins to 0.5 inch, and then print the query.

g. Close the query.

2. Use the Find Duplicates Query Wizard to find those clients with the same last name with the following specifications:

a. At the first wizard dialog box, click *Table: Clients* in the list box.

b. At the second wizard dialog box, click *LastName* in the *Available fields* list box and then click the One Field button.

c. At the third wizard dialog box, click the All Fields button.

d. At the fourth wizard dialog box, name the query *DuplicateLastNamesQuery*.

e. Print the query in landscape orientation and then close the query.

3. Use the Find Unmatched Query Wizard to find all clients who do not have any billing hours with the following specifications:

   a. At the first wizard dialog box, click *Table: Clients* in the list box.

   b. At the second wizard dialog box, click *Table: Billing* in the list box.

   c. At the third wizard dialog box, make sure *ClientID* is selected in both the *Fields in 'Clients'* list box and in the *Fields in 'Billing'* list box.

   d. At the fourth wizard dialog box, click the All Fields button to move all fields from the *Available fields* list box to the *Selected fields* list box.

   e. At the fifth wizard dialog box, click the Finish button. (Let the wizard determine the query name: *Clients Without Matching Billing*.)

4. Print the query in landscape orientation and then close the query.

Assessment

4 DESIGN AND HIDE FIELDS IN A QUERY

1. You can use the check boxes in the query design grid *Show* row to show or hide fields in the query. Experiment with these check boxes and then with **AL1-C3-WarrenLegal.accdb** open design the following query:

   a. At the Show Table dialog box, add the Clients table, the Billing table, and the Rates table.

   b. At the query window, insert the following fields in *Field* row fields:

   > Clients table: *FirstName*
   >   *LastName*
   > Billing table: *Hours*
   > Rates table: *Rate*

   c. Insert in the fifth *Field* row field the calculated field *Total:[Hours]*[Rate]*.

   d. Hide the *Hours* and *Rate* fields.

   e. Run the query.

   f. Save the query and name it *ClientBillingQuery*.

   g. Print and then close the query. (The query will print on two pages.)

2. Close **AL1-C3-WarrenLegal.accdb**.

Visual Benchmark   Demonstrate Your Proficiency

CREATING RELATIONSHIPS AND DESIGNING A QUERY

1. Open **AL1-C3-MRInvestments.accdb** from the AL1C3 folder on your storage medium and, if necessary, enable the contents.

2. Display the Relationships window and then create the relationships shown in Figure 3.7. Enforce referential integrity and cascade fields and records. (The tables in Figure 3.7 have been rearranged in the Relationships window so you have a better view of the relationships.)

3. Save and then print the relationships.

4. Close the relationship report without saving it and then close the Relationships window.

5. Design the query shown in Figure 3.8.

6. Run the query.
7. Save the query with an appropriate name and then print the query.
8. Close **AL1-C3-MRInvestments.accdb**.

Figure 3.7 Visual Benchmark Relationships Window

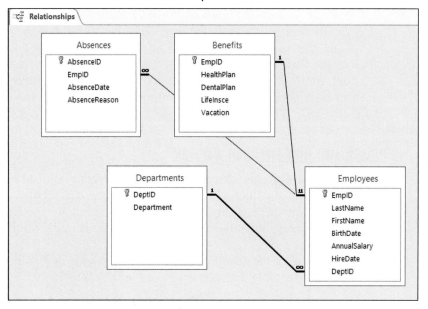

Figure 3.8 Visual Benchmark Query

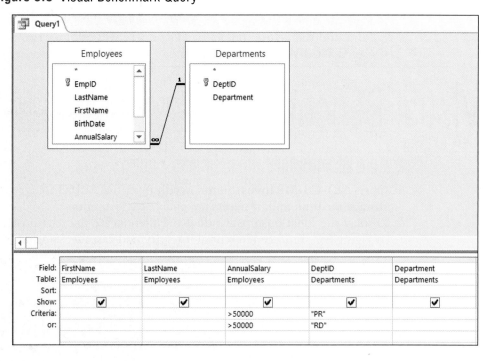

Case Study   Apply Your Skills

Part 1

You work for the Skyline Restaurant in Fort Myers, Florida. Your supervisor is reviewing the restaurant's operations and has asked for a number of query reports. Before running the queries, you realize that the tables in the restaurant database, **AL1-C3-Skyline.accdb**, are not related. Open **AL1-C3-Skyline. accdb**, enable the contents, and then create the following relationships (enforce referential integrity and cascade fields and records):

Field Name	"One" Table	"Many" Table
EmployeeID	Employees	Banquets
ItemID	Inventory	Orders
SupplierID	Suppliers	Orders
SupplierID	Suppliers	Inventory
EventID	Events	Banquets

Save and then print the relationships. Close the relationship report without saving it and then close the Relationships window.

Part 2

As part of the review of the restaurant's records, your supervisor has asked you for the following information. Create a separate query for each bulleted item listed below and save, name, and print the queries. (You determine the query names.)

- Suppliers in Fort Myers: From the Suppliers table, include the supplier identification number, supplier name, city, and telephone number.
- Suppliers not located in Fort Myers: From the Suppliers table, include the supplier identification number and supplier name, city, and telephone number.
- Employees hired in 2012: From the Employees table, include the employee identification number, first and last names, and hire date.
- Employees signed up for health insurance: From the Employees table, include employee first and last names and the health insurance field.
- Wedding receptions (event identification "WR") booked in the banquet room: From the Banquets table, include the reservation identification number; reservation date; event identification; and first name, last name, and telephone number of the person making the reservation.
- Banquet reservations between 6/14/2015 and 6/30/2015 and the employees making the reservations: From the Banquets table, include the reservation identification number; reservation date; and first name, last name, and telephone number of the person making the reservation; from the Employees table include the employee first and last names.
- Banquet reservations that have not been confirmed and the employees making the reservations: From the Banquets table, include the reservation identification number; reservation date; confirmed field; and first and last names of person making the reservation; from the Employees table, include employee first and last names.
- Banquet room reserved by someone whose last name begins with the letters *Wie:* From the Employees table, include the first and last names of the employee who booked the reservation; from the Banquets table, include the first and last names and telephone number of the person making the reservation.

Chapter 3 ■ Performing Queries   **127**

- A query that inserts a calculated field that multiplies the number of units ordered by the unit price for all orders for supplier number *2:* From the Orders table, include the order identification number, the supplier identification number, the units ordered, and the unit price; from the Inventory table, include the item field.

Part

3

Use the Find Duplicates Query Wizard to find duplicate items in the Orders table with the following specifications:
- At the first wizard dialog box, specify the Orders table.
- At the second wizard dialog box, specify *ItemID* as the duplicate value field.
- At the third wizard dialog, specify that you want all of the fields in the query.
- At the fourth wizard dialog box, determine the query name.
- Print and then close the query.

Use the Find Unmatched Query Wizard to find all of the employees who have not made banquet reservations with the following specifications:
- At the first wizard dialog box, specify the Employees table.
- At the second wizard dialog box, specify the Banquets table.
- At the third wizard dialog box, specify the *EmployeeID* field in both list boxes.
- At the fourth wizard dialog box, specify that you want all of the fields in the query.
- At the fifth wizard dialog box, determine the query name.
- Print the query in landscape orientation with 0.5-inch left and right margins and then close the query.

Use the Crosstab Query Wizard to create a query that summarizes order amounts by supplier with the following specifications:
- At the first wizard dialog box, specify the Orders table.
- At the second wizard dialog box, specify the *SupplierID* field for row headings.
- At the third wizard dialog box, specify the *ItemID* field for column headings.
- At the fourth wizard dialog box, click *UnitPrice* in the *Fields* list box and click *Sum* in the *Functions* list box.
- At the fifth wizard dialog box, determine the query name.
- Automatically adjust the columns in the query. (You will need to scroll to the right to view and adjust all of the columns containing data.)
- Print the query in landscape orientation and then close the query.

Part

4

Design three additional queries that require fields from at least two tables. Run the queries and then save and print the queries. In Microsoft Word, write the query information (including specific information about each query) and format the document to enhance the visual appearance. Save the document and name it **AL1-C3-CS-Queries**. Print and then close **AL1-C3-CS-Queries.docx**. Close **AL1-C3-Skyline.accdb**.

MICROSOFT®
ACCESS®

Creating and Modifying Tables in Design View

PERFORMANCE OBJECTIVES

Upon successful completion of Chapter 4, you will be able to:

- Create a table in Design view
- Assign a default value
- Use the Input Mask Wizard and the Lookup Wizard
- Validate field entries
- Insert, move, and delete fields in Design view
- Insert a *Total* row
- Sort records in a table
- Print selected records in a table
- Complete a spelling check
- Find and replace data in records in a table
- Apply text formatting
- Use the Help feature

Tutorials

In Chapter 1, you learned how to create a table in Datasheet view. You can also create a table in Design view, where you can establish the table's structure and properties before entering data. In this chapter, you will learn how to create a table in Design view and use the Input Mask Wizard and Lookup Wizards; insert, move, and delete fields in Design view; sort records; check spelling in a table; find and replace data; apply text formatting to a table; and use the Access Help feature. Model answers for this chapter's projects appear on the following pages.

Note: Before beginning the projects, copy the AL1C4 subfolder from the AL1 folder on the CD that accompanies this textbook to your storage medium and make AL1C4 the active folder.

Project 1 Create and Modify Tables in a Property Management Database

Project 1c

EmpID	EmpCategory	FName	LName	Address	City	State	ZIP	Telephone	HealthIns	DentalIns	LifeIns
02-59	Hourly	Christina	Solomon	12241 East 51st	Citrus Heights	CA	95611	(916) 555-8844	✔	✔	$100,000.00
03-23	Salaried	Douglas	Ricci	903 Mission Road	Roseville	CA	95678	(916) 555-4125	✔	☐	$25,000.00
03-55	Hourly	Tatiana	Kasadev	6558 Orchard Drive	Citrus Heights	CA	95610	(916) 555-8534	✔	☐	$0.00
04-14	Salaried	Brian	West	12232 142nd Avenue East	Citrus Heights	CA	95611	(916) 555-0967	✔	✔	$50,000.00
04-32	Temporary	Kathleen	Addison	21229 19th Street	Citrus Heights	CA	95621	(916) 555-3408	✔	✔	$50,000.00
05-20	Hourly	Teresa	Villanueva	19453 North 42nd Street	Citrus Heights	CA	95611	(916) 555-2302	✔	✔	$0.00
05-31	Salaried	Marcia	Griswold	211 Haven Road	North Highlands	CA	95660	(916) 555-1449	☐	☐	$100,000.00
06-24	Temporary	Tiffany	Gentry	12312 North 20th	Roseville	CA	95661	(916) 555-0043	✔	✔	$50,000.00
06-33	Hourly	Joanna	Gallegos	6850 York Street	Roseville	CA	95747	(956) 555-7446	☐	☐	$25,000.00
07-20	Salaried	Jesse	Scholtz	3412 South 21st Street	Fair Oaks	CA	95628	(916) 555-4204	✔	☐	$0.00
07-23	Salaried	Eugene	Bond	530 Laurel Road	Orangevale	CA	95662	(916) 555-9412	✔	☐	$100,000.00

Step 11, Employees Table

EmpID	FName	LName	Address	City	State	ZIP	Telephone	EmpCategory	HealthIns	LifeIns
02-59	Christina	Solomon	12241 East 51st	Citrus Heights	CA	95611	(916) 555-8844	Hourly	✔	$100,000.00
03-23	Douglas	Ricci	903 Mission Road	Roseville	CA	95678	(916) 555-4125	Salaried	✔	$25,000.00
03-55	Tatiana	Kasadev	6558 Orchard Drive	Citrus Heights	CA	95610	(916) 555-8534	Hourly	✔	$0.00
04-14	Brian	West	12232 142nd Avenue East	Citrus Heights	CA	95611	(916) 555-0967	Salaried	✔	$50,000.00
04-32	Kathleen	Addison	21229 19th Street	Citrus Heights	CA	95621	(916) 555-3408	Temporary	✔	$50,000.00
05-20	Teresa	Villanueva	19453 North 42nd Street	Citrus Heights	CA	95611	(916) 555-2302	Hourly	✔	$0.00
05-31	Marcia	Griswold	211 Haven Road	North Highlands	CA	95660	(916) 555-1449	Salaried	☐	$100,000.00
06-24	Tiffany	Gentry	12312 North 20th	Roseville	CA	95661	(916) 555-0043	Temporary	✔	$50,000.00
06-33	Joanna	Gallegos	6850 York Street	Roseville	CA	95747	(956) 555-7446	Hourly	☐	$25,000.00
07-20	Jesse	Scholtz	3412 South 21st Street	Fair Oaks	CA	95628	(916) 555-4204	Salaried	✔	$0.00
07-23	Eugene	Bond	530 Laurel Road	Orangevale	CA	95662	(916) 555-9412	Salaried	✔	$100,000.00

Step 16, Employees Table

PymntID	RenterID	PymntDate	PymntAmount	LateFee
1	130	3/1/2015	$1,800.00	
2	111	3/1/2015	$1,900.00	
3	136	3/1/2015	$1,250.00	
4	110	3/1/2015	$1,300.00	
5	135	3/2/2015	$1,900.00	
6	123	3/2/2015	$1,000.00	
7	117	3/2/2015	$1,100.00	
8	134	3/3/2015	$1,400.00	
9	131	3/3/2015	$1,200.00	
10	118	3/3/2015	$900.00	
11	125	3/5/2015	$1,650.00	
12	119	3/5/2015	$1,500.00	
13	133	3/8/2015	$1,650.00	
14	129	3/9/2015	$1,650.00	
15	115	3/12/2015	$1,375.00	$25.00
16	121	3/12/2015	$950.00	$25.00
17	127	3/19/2015	$1,300.00	$50.00
Total			**$23,825.00**	**$100.00**

Payments Table

Project 1d

RenterID	FirstName	LastName	PropID	EmpID	CreditScore	LeaseBegDate	LeaseEndDate
118	Mason	Ahn	1004	07-23	538	3/1/2015	2/28/2016
119	Michelle	Bertram	1001	03-23	621	3/1/2015	2/28/2016
110	Greg	Hamilton	1029	04-14	624	1/1/2015	12/31/2015
121	Travis	Jorgenson	1010	04-14	590	3/1/2015	2/28/2016
135	Marty	Lobdell	1006	04-14	510	6/1/2015	5/31/2016
129	Susan	Lowrey	1002	04-14	634	4/1/2015	3/31/2016
130	Ross	Molaski	1027	03-23	688	5/1/2015	4/30/2016
136	Nadine	Paschal	1022	05-31	702	6/1/2015	5/31/2016
111	Julia	Perez	1013	07-20	711	1/1/2015	12/31/2015
115	Dana	Rozinski	1026	02-59	538	2/1/2015	1/31/2016
131	Danielle	Rubio	1020	07-20	722	5/1/2015	4/30/2016
133	Katie	Smith	1018	07-23	596	5/1/2015	4/30/2016
123	Richard	Terrell	1014	07-20	687	3/1/2015	2/28/2016
117	Miguel	Villegas	1007	07-20	695	2/1/2015	1/31/2016
125	Rose	Wagoner	1015	07-23	734	4/1/2015	3/31/2016
134	Carl	Weston	1009	03-23	655	6/1/2015	5/31/2016
127	William	Young	1023	05-31	478	4/1/2015	3/31/2016

Step 2c, Renters Table

RenterID	FirstName	LastName	PropID	EmpID	CreditScore	LeaseBegDate	LeaseEndDate
125	Rose	Wagoner	1015	07-23	734	4/1/2015	3/31/2016
131	Danielle	Rubio	1020	07-20	722	5/1/2015	4/30/2016
111	Julia	Perez	1013	07-20	711	1/1/2015	12/31/2015
136	Nadine	Paschal	1022	05-31	702	6/1/2015	5/31/2016
117	Miguel	Villegas	1007	07-20	695	2/1/2015	1/31/2016
130	Ross	Molaski	1027	03-23	688	5/1/2015	4/30/2016
123	Richard	Terrell	1014	07-20	687	3/1/2015	2/28/2016
134	Carl	Weston	1009	03-23	655	6/1/2015	5/31/2016
129	Susan	Lowrey	1002	04-14	634	4/1/2015	3/31/2016
110	Greg	Hamilton	1029	04-14	624	1/1/2015	12/31/2015
119	Michelle	Bertram	1001	03-23	621	3/1/2015	2/28/2016
133	Katie	Smith	1018	07-23	596	5/1/2015	4/30/2016
121	Travis	Jorgenson	1010	04-14	590	3/1/2015	2/28/2016
118	Mason	Ahn	1004	07-23	538	3/1/2015	2/28/2016
115	Dana	Rozinski	1026	02-59	538	2/1/2015	1/31/2016
135	Marty	Lobdell	1006	04-14	510	6/1/2015	5/31/2016
127	William	Young	1023	05-31	478	4/1/2015	3/31/2016

Step 3c, Renters Table

PropID	CatID	MoRent	Address	City	State	ZIP
1007	A	$1,100.00	904 Everson Road	Fair Oaks	CA	95628
1004	A	$900.00	1932 Oakville Drive	North Highlands	CA	95660
1010	A	$950.00	19334 140th East	Citrus Heights	CA	95621
1014	A	$1,000.00	9045 Valley Avenue	Citrus Heights	CA	95611

Step 6f, Properties Table

PropID	CatID	MoRent	Address	City	State	ZIP
1007	A	$1,100.00	904 Everson Road	Fair Oaks	CA	95628
1004	A	$900.00	1932 Oakville Drive	North Highlands	CA	95660
1010	A	$950.00	19334 140th East	Citrus Heights	CA	95621
1014	A	$1,000.00	9045 Valley Avenue	Citrus Heights	CA	95611
1029	C	$1,300.00	155 Aldrich Road	Roseville	CA	95678
1002	C	$1,650.00	2650 Crestline Drive	Citrus Heights	CA	95611
1001	C	$1,500.00	4102 Tenth Street	Citrus Heights	CA	95611
1026	C	$1,375.00	10057 128th Avenue	Citrus Heights	CA	95611
1023	C	$1,300.00	750 Birch Drive	Orangevale	CA	95662
1009	C	$1,400.00	159 Meridian Street	Orangevale	CA	95662
1019	C	$1,700.00	765 Chellis Street	Fair Oaks	CA	95628
1018	C	$1,650.00	9945 North 20th Road	North Highlands	CA	95660
1017	D	$1,300.00	4500 Maple Lane	Orangevale	CA	95662
1011	D	$1,350.00	348 Hampton Avenue	Citrus Heights	CA	95611
1008	D	$1,575.00	5009 North Garden	Roseville	CA	95661
1020	D	$1,200.00	23390 South 22nd Street	Citrus Heights	CA	95610
1006	S	$1,900.00	3412 Mango Street	Orangevale	CA	95662
1003	S	$1,800.00	10234 122nd Avenue	North Highlands	CA	95660
1012	S	$1,775.00	1212 Fairhaven Road	North Highlands	CA	95660
1013	S	$1,900.00	2606 30th Street	Citrus Heights	CA	95610
1016	S	$1,825.00	21388 South 42nd Street	Citrus Heights	CA	95621
1030	S	$1,950.00	5430 112th Southeast	Citrus Heights	CA	95611
1021	S	$1,875.00	652 Seventh Street	Fair Oaks	CA	95628
1024	S	$1,650.00	1195 24th Street	North Highlands	CA	95660
1027	S	$1,800.00	2203 Center Road	Orangevale	CA	95662
1028	S	$1,750.00	488 Franklin Drive	Fair Oaks	CA	95628
1022	T	$1,250.00	4572 152nd Avenue	Citrus Heights	CA	95621
1005	T	$1,350.00	12110 55th Southeast	Citrus Heights	CA	95611
1025	T	$1,200.00	3354 North 62nd Street	Citrus Heights	CA	95610
1015	T	$1,650.00	560 Tenth Street East	North Highlands	CA	95660

Step 7f, Properties Table

Model Answers

Project 1d–continued

PymntID	RenterID	PymntDate	PymntAmount	LateFee
1	130	3/1/2015	$1,800.00	
2	111	3/1/2015	$1,900.00	
3	136	3/1/2015	$1,250.00	
4	110	3/1/2015	$1,300.00	
5	135	3/2/2015	$1,900.00	
6	123	3/2/2015	$1,000.00	
7	117	3/2/2015	$1,100.00	
8	134	3/3/2015	$1,400.00	
9	131	3/3/2015	$1,200.00	
10	118	3/3/2015	$900.00	
11	125	3/5/2015	$1,650.00	
12	119	3/5/2015	$1,500.00	
13	133	3/8/2015	$1,650.00	
14	129	3/9/2015	$1,650.00	
15	115	3/12/2015	$1,375.00	$25.00
16	121	3/12/2015	$950.00	$25.00
17	127	3/19/2015	$1,300.00	$50.00
Total			**$23,825.00**	**$100.00**

Step 8g, Payments Table

RenterID	FirstName	LastName	PropID	EmpID	CreditScore	LeaseBegDate	LeaseEndDate
110	Greg	Hamilton	1029	04-14	624	1/1/2015	12/31/2015
111	Julia	Perez	1013	07-20	711	1/1/2015	12/31/2015
115	Dana	Rozinski	1026	02-59	538	2/1/2015	1/31/2016
117	Miguel	Villegas	1007	07-20	695	2/1/2015	1/31/2016
118	Mason	Ahn	1004	07-23	538	3/1/2015	2/28/2016
119	Michelle	Bertram	1001	03-23	621	3/1/2015	2/28/2016
121	Travis	Jorgenson	1010	04-14	590	3/1/2015	2/28/2016
123	Richard	Terrell	1014	07-20	687	3/1/2015	2/28/2016
125	Rose	Wagoner	1015	07-23	734	4/1/2015	3/31/2016
127	William	Young	1023	05-31	478	4/1/2015	3/31/2016
129	Susan	Lowrey	1002	04-14	634	4/1/2015	3/31/2016
130	Ross	Molaski	1027	03-23	688	5/1/2015	4/30/2016
131	Danielle	Rubio	1020	07-20	722	5/1/2015	4/30/2016
133	Katie	Smith	1018	07-23	596	5/1/2015	4/30/2016
134	Carl	Weston	1009	03-23	655	6/1/2015	5/31/2016
135	Marty	Lobdell	1006	04-14	510	6/1/2015	5/31/2016
136	Nadine	Paschal	1022	05-31	702	6/1/2015	5/31/2016

Step 10j, Renters Table

Project 1e

EmpID	FName	LName	Address	City	State	ZIP	Telephone	EmpCategory	HealthIns
02-59	Christina	Solomon	12241 East 51st	Citrus Heights	CA	95611	(916) 555-8844	Hourly	✔
03-23	Douglas	Ricci	903 Mission Road	Roseville	CA	95678	(916) 555-4125	Salaried	✔
03-55	Tatiana	Kasadev	6558 Orchard Drive	Citrus Heights	CA	95610	(916) 555-8534	Hourly	✔
04-14	Brian	West	12232 142nd Avenue East	Citrus Heights	CA	95611	(916) 555-0967	Salaried	✔
04-32	Kathleen	Addison	21229 19th Street	Citrus Heights	CA	95621	(916) 555-3408	Temporary	✔
05-20	Teresa	Villanueva	19453 North 42nd Street	Citrus Heights	CA	95611	(916) 555-2302	Hourly	✔
05-31	Marcia	Griswold	211 Haven Road	North Highlands	CA	95660	(916) 555-1449	Salaried	☐
06-24	Tiffany	Gentry	12312 North 20th	Roseville	CA	95661	(916) 555-0043	Temporary	✔
06-33	Joanna	Gallegos	6850 York Street	Roseville	CA	95747	(956) 555-7446	Hourly	☐
07-20	Jesse	Scholtz	3412 South 21st Street	Fair Oaks	CA	95628	(916) 555-4204	Salaried	✔
07-23	Eugene	Bond	530 Laurel Road	Orangevale	CA	95662	(916) 555-9412	Salaried	✔
02-72	Robin	Wilder	9945 Valley Avenue	Citrus Heights	CA	95610	(916) 555-6522	Salaried	☐

Employees Table

Project 1f

PropID	CatID	MoRent	Address	City	State	ZIP
1007	A	$1,100.00	904 Everson Road	Fair Oaks	CA	95628
1004	A	$900.00	1932 Oakville Drive	North Highlands	CA	95668
1010	A	$950.00	19334 140th East	Citrus Heights	CA	95621
1014	A	$1,000.00	9045 Valley Avenue	Citrus Heights	CA	95611
1029	C	$1,300.00	155 Aldrich Road	Roseville	CA	95678
1002	C	$1,650.00	2650 Crestline Drive	Citrus Heights	CA	95611
1001	C	$1,500.00	4102 Tenth Street	Citrus Heights	CA	95611
1026	C	$1,375.00	10057 128th Avenue	Citrus Heights	CA	95611
1023	C	$1,300.00	750 Birch Drive	Orangevale	CA	95662
1009	C	$1,400.00	159 Meridian Street	Orangevale	CA	95662
1019	C	$1,700.00	765 Chellis Street	Fair Oaks	CA	95628
1018	C	$1,650.00	9945 North 20th Road	North Highlands	CA	95660
1017	D	$1,300.00	4500 Maple Lane	Orangevale	CA	95662
1011	D	$1,350.00	348 Hampton Avenue	Citrus Heights	CA	95611
1008	D	$1,575.00	5009 North Garden	Roseville	CA	95661
1020	D	$1,200.00	23390 South 22nd Street	Citrus Heights	CA	95610
1006	S	$1,900.00	3412 Mango Street	Orangevale	CA	95662
1003	S	$1,800.00	10234 122nd Avenue	North Highlands	CA	95668
1012	S	$1,775.00	1212 Fairhaven Road	North Highlands	CA	95660
1013	S	$1,900.00	2606 30th Street	Citrus Heights	CA	95610
1016	S	$1,825.00	21388 South 42nd Street	Citrus Heights	CA	95621
1030	S	$1,950.00	5430 112th Southeast	Citrus Heights	CA	95611
1021	S	$1,875.00	652 Seventh Street	Fair Oaks	CA	95628
1024	S	$1,650.00	1195 24th Street	North Highlands	CA	95660
1027	S	$1,800.00	2203 Center Road	Orangevale	CA	95662
1028	S	$1,750.00	488 Franklin Drive	Fair Oaks	CA	95628
1022	T	$1,250.00	4572 152nd Avenue	Citrus Heights	CA	95621
1005	T	$1,350.00	12110 55th Southeast	Citrus Heights	CA	95611
1025	T	$1,200.00	3354 North 62nd Street	Citrus Heights	CA	95610
1015	T	$1,650.00	560 Tenth Street East	North Highlands	CA	95668

PropertiesTable

Relationships Report

FName	LName	HealthIns
Christina	Solomon	✔
Douglas	Ricci	✔
Tatiana	Kasadev	✔
Brian	West	✔
Kathleen	Addison	✔
Teresa	Villanueva	✔
Tiffany	Gentry	✔
Jesse	Scholtz	✔
Eugene	Bond	✔

EmpsWithHealthInsQuery

PropID	Category	Address	City	State	ZIP
1010	Apartment	19334 140th East	Citrus Heights	CA	95621
1014	Apartment	9045 Valley Avenue	Citrus Heights	CA	95611
1001	Condominium	4102 Tenth Street	Citrus Heights	CA	95611
1002	Condominium	2650 Crestline Drive	Citrus Heights	CA	95611
1026	Condominium	10057 128th Avenue	Citrus Heights	CA	95611
1013	Single-family house	2606 30th Street	Citrus Heights	CA	95610
1016	Single-family house	21388 South 42nd Street	Citrus Heights	CA	95621
1030	Single-family house	5430 112th Southeast	Citrus Heights	CA	95611
1011	Duplex	348 Hampton Avenue	Citrus Heights	CA	95611
1020	Duplex	23390 South 22nd Street	Citrus Heights	CA	95610
1005	Townhouse	12110 55th Southeast	Citrus Heights	CA	95611
1022	Townhouse	4572 152nd Avenue	Citrus Heights	CA	95621
1025	Townhouse	3354 North 62nd Street	Citrus Heights	CA	95610

CitrusHeightsPropsQuery

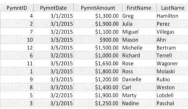

PymntID	PymntDate	PymntAmount	FirstName	LastName
4	3/1/2015	$1,300.00	Greg	Hamilton
2	3/1/2015	$1,900.00	Julia	Perez
7	3/2/2015	$1,100.00	Miguel	Villegas
10	3/3/2015	$900.00	Mason	Ahn
12	3/5/2015	$1,500.00	Michelle	Bertram
6	3/2/2015	$1,000.00	Richard	Terrell
11	3/5/2015	$1,650.00	Rose	Wagoner
1	3/1/2015	$1,800.00	Ross	Molaski
9	3/3/2015	$1,200.00	Danielle	Rubio
8	3/3/2015	$1,400.00	Carl	Weston
5	3/2/2015	$1,900.00	Marty	Lobdell
3	3/1/2015	$1,250.00	Nadine	Paschal

Pymnts3/1To3/5Query

Category	PropID	MoRent	Address	City	State	ZIP
Apartment	1010	$950.00	19334 140th East	Citrus Heights	CA	95621
Apartment	1014	$1,000.00	9045 Valley Avenue	Citrus Heights	CA	95611
Condominium	1001	$1,500.00	4102 Tenth Street	Citrus Heights	CA	95611
Condominium	1009	$1,400.00	159 Meridian Street	Orangevale	CA	95662
Condominium	1023	$1,300.00	750 Birch Drive	Orangevale	CA	95662
Condominium	1026	$1,375.00	10057 128th Avenue	Citrus Heights	CA	95611
Duplex	1011	$1,350.00	348 Hampton Avenue	Citrus Heights	CA	95611
Duplex	1017	$1,300.00	4500 Maple Lane	Orangevale	CA	95662
Duplex	1020	$1,200.00	23390 South 22nd Street	Citrus Heights	CA	95610
Townhouse	1005	$1,350.00	12110 55th Southeast	Citrus Heights	CA	95611
Townhouse	1022	$1,250.00	4572 152nd Avenue	Citrus Heights	CA	95621
Townhouse	1025	$1,200.00	3354 North 62nd Street	Citrus Heights	CA	95610

RentLessThan$1501InCHAndOVQuery

EmpID	FName	LName	Address	City	State	ZIP
07-20	Jesse	Scholtz	4102 Tenth Street	Citrus Heights	CA	95611
07-20	Jesse	Scholtz	2650 Crestline Drive	Citrus Heights	CA	95611
07-20	Jesse	Scholtz	12110 55th Southeast	Citrus Heights	CA	95611
07-20	Jesse	Scholtz	19334 140th East	Citrus Heights	CA	95621
07-20	Jesse	Scholtz	348 Hampton Avenue	Citrus Heights	CA	95611
07-20	Jesse	Scholtz	2606 30th Street	Citrus Heights	CA	95610
07-20	Jesse	Scholtz	9045 Valley Avenue	Citrus Heights	CA	95611
07-20	Jesse	Scholtz	21388 South 42nd Street	Citrus Heights	CA	95621
07-20	Jesse	Scholtz	23390 South 22nd Street	Citrus Heights	CA	95610
07-20	Jesse	Scholtz	4572 152nd Avenue	Citrus Heights	CA	95621
07-20	Jesse	Scholtz	3354 North 62nd Street	Citrus Heights	CA	95610
07-20	Jesse	Scholtz	10057 128th Avenue	Citrus Heights	CA	95611
07-20	Jesse	Scholtz	5430 112th Southeast	Citrus Heights	CA	95611

Emp07-20CHPropsQuery

Project 1 — Create and Modify Tables in a Property Management Database   8 Parts

You will open the Sun Properties database, create two new tables in Design view, modify existing tables, and sort data in tables. You will also complete a spelling check on data in tables, find data in a table and replace it with other data, create relationships and perform queries, and get help using the Access Help feature.

Creating Tables in Design View ■■■■■■■■■■■■■■■■■

Quick Steps

Create a Table in Design View
1. Open database.
2. Click CREATE tab.
3. Click Table button.
4. Click View button.
5. Type name for table.
6. Press Enter or click OK.
7. Type field names, specify data types, and include descriptions.
8. Click Save button.

Table

View

In Datasheet view, you can create a table by assigning each column a data type and typing the field name. Once the columns are defined, you enter the data into records. You can also create a table in Design view, where you can set field properties before you begin entering data. To display a table in Design view, open the desired database, click the CREATE tab, and then click the Table button. This opens a new blank table in Datasheet view. Display the table in Design view by clicking the View button that displays at the left side of the TABLE TOOLS FIELDS tab in the Views group. When you click the View button in a new table, Access displays the Save As dialog box, where you type the table name and then press Enter or click OK. Figure 4.1 displays the Properties table in Design view in AL1-C4-SunProperties.accdb.

In Design view, each row in the top section of the work area represents one field in the table and is used to define the field name, the field data type, and a description. The *Field Properties* section in the lower half of the work area displays the properties for the active field. The properties vary depending on the active field. In the lower right corner of Design view, Help information displays about an option as you make an option active in the Design window. In Figure 4.1, the *PropID* field name is active in Design view, so Access displays information on field names in the Help area.

Model Answers

Figure 4.1 Properties Table in Design View

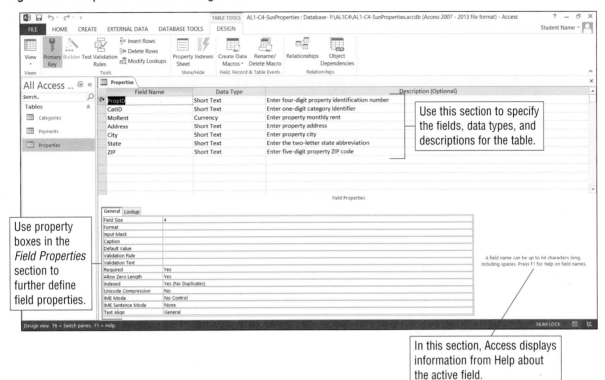

Use this section to specify the fields, data types, and descriptions for the table.

Use property boxes in the *Field Properties* section to further define field properties.

In this section, Access displays information from Help about the active field.

Define each field in the table in the rows in the top section of Design view. When you create a new table in Design view, Access automatically assigns the first field the name *ID* and assigns the AutoNumber data type. You can leave this field name or type a new name and you can also change the data type. To create a new field in the table, click in the field in the *Field Name* column, type the field name, and then press the Tab key or Enter key. This makes active the *Data Type* field. Click the down-pointing arrow in the *Data Type* field and then click the desired data type at the drop-down list. In Chapter 1, you created tables in Datasheet view and assigned data types of Short Text, Date/Time, Currency, and Yes/No. The *Data Type* field drop-down list includes these data types plus additional types, as described in Table 4.1.

When you click the desired data type at the drop-down list and then press the Tab key, the *Description* field becomes active. Type a description in the field that provides useful information to someone entering data in the table. When typing a description, consider identifying the field's purpose or contents or providing instructional information for data entry. The description you type displays in the Status bar when the field is active in the table in Datasheet view.

When creating the table, continue typing field names, assigning data types to fields, and typing field descriptions. When you have completed the table design, save the table by clicking the Save button on the Quick Access toolbar. Return to Datasheet view by clicking the View button in the Views group on the TABLE TOOLS DESIGN tab. In Datasheet view, type the records for the table.

Save

Table 4.1 Data Types

Data Type	Description
Short Text	Used for alphanumeric data up to 255 characters in length—for example, a name, address, or value (such as a telephone number or social security number) that is used as an identifier and not for calculating.
Long Text	Used for alphanumeric data up to 64,000 characters in length.
Number	Used for positive and negative values that can be used in calculations. Do not use for values that will calculate monetary amounts (see Currency).
Date/Time	Used to ensure dates and times are entered and sorted properly.
Currency	Used for values that involve money. Access will not round off during calculations.
AutoNumber	Used to automatically number records sequentially (incrementing by 1); each new record is numbered as it is typed.
Yes/No	Used for values of *Yes* or *No*, *True* or *False*, or *On* or *Off*.
OLE Object	Used to embed or link objects created in other Office applications.
Hyperlink	Used to store a hyperlink, such as a URL.
Attachment	Used to add file attachments to a record such as a Word document or Excel workbook.
Calculated	Used to display the Expression Builder dialog box, where an expression is entered to calculate the value of the calculated column.
Lookup Wizard	Used to enter data in the field from another existing table or to display a list of values in a drop-down list from which the user chooses.

Project 1a Creating a Table in Design View   Part 1 of 8

1. Open Access and then open **AL1-C4-SunProperties.accdb** located in the AL1C4 folder on your storage medium.
2. Click the Enable Content button in the message bar. (The message bar will display immediately below the ribbon.)
3. View the Properties table in Design view by completing the following steps:
   a. Open the Properties table.
   b. Click the View button in the Views group on the HOME tab.
   c. Click each field name and then look at the information that displays in the *Field Properties* section.
   d. Click in various options in the work area and then read the information that displays in the Help area located in the lower right corner of Design view.
   e. Click the View button to return the table to Datasheet view.
   f. Close the Properties table.

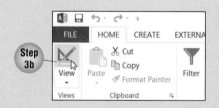

Step 3b

4. Create a new table in Design view, as shown in Figure 4.2, by completing the following steps:

   a. Click the CREATE tab and then click the Table button in the Tables group.

   b. Click the View button in the Views group on the TABLE TOOLS FIELDS tab.

   c. At the Save As dialog box, type **Renters** and then press Enter.

   d. Type **RenterID** in the *Field Name* column in the first row and then press the Tab key.

   e. Change the data type to Short Text by clicking the down-pointing arrow located in the *Data Type* column and then clicking *Short Text* at the drop-down list.

   f. Change the field size from the default of 255 characters to 3 characters by selecting *255* in the *Field Size* property box in the *Field Properties* section and then typing 3.

   g. Click in the *Description* column for the *RenterID* row, type **Enter three-digit renter identification number**, and then press the Tab key.

Step 4c

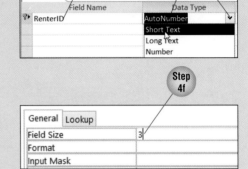

Step 4d   Step 4e

Step 4f

Step 4g

h. Type **FirstName** in the *Field Name* column and then press the Tab key.

i. Select *255* in the *Field Size* property box in the *Field Properties* section and then type 20.

j. Click in the *Description* column for the *FirstName* row, type **Enter renter's first name**, and then press the Tab key.

k. Type **LastName** in the *Field Name* column and then press the Tab key.

l. Change the field size to 30 characters (at the *Field Size* property box).

m. Click in the *Description* column for the *LastName* row, type **Enter renter's last name**, and then press the Tab key.

n. Enter the remaining field names, data types, and descriptions as shown in Figure 4.2. (Change the field sizes to 4 characters for the *PropID* field, 5 characters for the *EmpID* field, and 3 characters for the *CreditScore* field.)

o. After all of the fields are entered, click the Save button on the Quick Access toolbar.

p. Make sure the *RenterID* field is identified as the primary key. (A key icon displays in the *RenterID* field selector bar.)

q. Click the View button to return the table to Datasheet view.

5. Enter the records in the Renters table as shown in Figure 4.3.

6. After all of the records are entered, automatically adjust the column widths.

7. Save and then close the Renters table.

Figure 4.2 Project 1a Renters Table in Design View

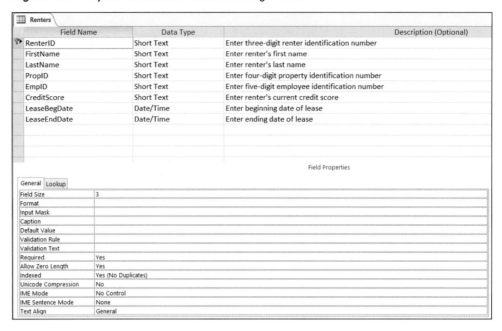

Figure 4.3 Project 1a Renters Table in Datasheet View

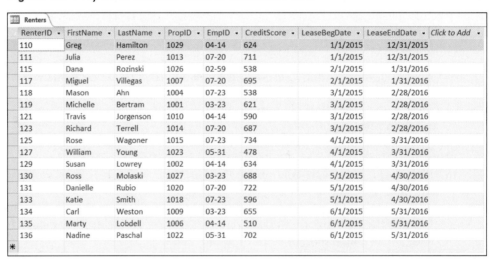

Assigning a Default Value

In Chapter 1, you learned how to specify a default value for a field in a table in Datasheet view using the Default Value button in the Properties group on the TABLE TOOLS FIELDS tab. In addition to this method, you can create a default value for a field in Design view with the *Default Value* property box in the *Field Properties* section. Click in the *Default Value* property box and then type the desired field value.

In Project 1b, you will create a health insurance field with a Yes/No data type. Since most of the agents of Sun Properties have signed up for health insurance benefits, you set the default value for the field to *Yes*. If you add a new field that contains a default value to an existing table, the existing records do not reflect the default value. Only new records entered in the table reflect the default value.

Using the Input Mask

For some fields, you may want to control the data entered in the field. For example, in a zip code field, you may want the nine-digit zip code entered (rather than the five-digit zip code) or you may want the three-digit area code included in a telephone number. Use the *Input Mask* field property to set a pattern for how data is entered in a field. An input mask ensures that data in records conforms to a standard format. Access includes an Input Mask Wizard that guides you through creating an input mask. The Input Mask is available for fields with a data type of Short Text or Date/Time.

Use the Input Mask Wizard when assigning a data type to a field. In Design view, click in the Input Mask property box in the *Field Properties* section and then run the Input Mask Wizard by clicking the Build button (contains three black dots) that appears at the right side of the Input Mask property box. This displays the first Input Mask Wizard dialog box, as shown in Figure 4.4. In the *Input Mask* list box, choose which input mask you want your data to look like and then click the Next button. At the second Input Mask Wizard dialog box, as shown in Figure 4.5, specify the appearance of the input mask and the desired placeholder character and then click the Next button. At the third Input Mask Wizard dialog box, specify whether you want the data stored with or without the symbol in the mask and then click the Next button. At the fourth dialog box, click the Finish button.

▼ Quick Steps

Use the Input Mask Wizard
1. Open table in Design view.
2. Type text in *Field Name* column.
3. Press Tab key.
4. Change data type to *Short Text* or *Date/Time*.
5. Click Save button.
6. Click in *Input Mask* property box.
7. Click Build button.
8. Complete wizard steps.

Build

An input mask is a set of characters that control what you can and cannot enter in a field.

Figure 4.4 First Input Mask Wizard Dialog Box

Choose the desired input mask from this list box.

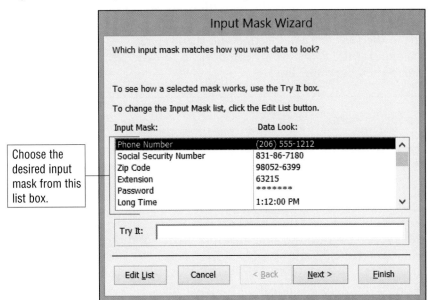

Figure 4.5 Second Input Mask Wizard Dialog Box

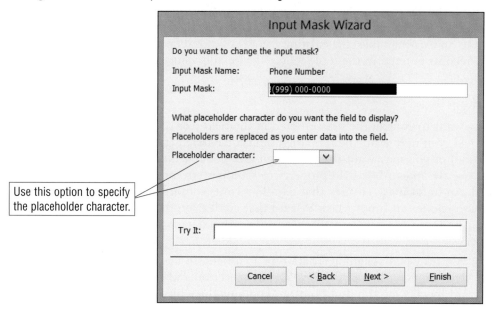

Use this option to specify the placeholder character.

Project 1b Creating an Employees Table

1. With **AL1-C4-SunProperties.accdb** open, create the Employees table in Design view as shown in Figure 4.6 on page 140. Begin by clicking the CREATE tab and then clicking the Table button.
2. Click the View button to switch to Design view.
3. At the Save As dialog box, type **Employees** and then press Enter.
4. Type EmpID in the *Field Name* column in the first row and then press the Tab key.
5. Change the data type to Short Text by clicking the down-pointing arrow located in the *Data Type* column and then clicking *Short Text* at the drop-down list.
6. Change the field size from the default of 255 characters to 5 characters by selecting *255* in the *Field Size* property box in the *Field Properties* section and then typing 5.
7. Click in the *Description* column for the *EmpID* row, type **Enter five-digit employee identification number**, and then press the Tab key.

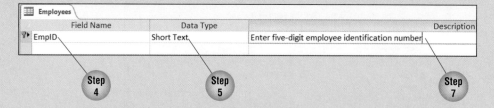

8. Type FName in the *Field Name* column and then press the Tab key.
9. Select *255* in the *Field Size* property box in the *Field Properties* section and then type 20.
10. Click in the *Description* column for the *FName* row, type **Enter employee's first name**, and then press the Tab key.
11. Complete steps similar to those in Steps 8 through 10 to create the *LName*, *Address*, and *City* fields as shown in Figure 4.6. Change the field size for the *LName* field and *Address* field to 30 characters and change the *City* field to 20 characters.

12. Create the *State* field with a default value of *CA,* since all employees live in California, by completing the following steps:

    a. Type **State** in the *Field Name* column in the row below the *City* row and then press the Tab key.

    b. Click in the *Default Value* property box in the *Field Properties* section and then type **CA.**

    c. Click in the *Description* column for the *State* row, type **CA automatically entered as state,** and then press the Tab key.

13. Type **ZIP** and then press the Tab key.

14. Select *255* that displays in the *Field Size* property box in the *Field Properties* section and then type **5.**

15. Click in the *Description* column for the *ZIP* row, type **Enter five-digit ZIP code,** and then press the Tab key.

16. Type **Telephone** and then press the Tab key.

17. Create an input mask for the telephone number by completing the following steps:

    a. Click the Save button on the Quick Access toolbar to save the table. (You must save the table before using the Input Mask Wizard.)

    b. Click in the *Input Mask* property box in the *Field Properties* section.

    c. Click the Build button (contains three black dots) that displays at the right side of the *Input Mask* property box.

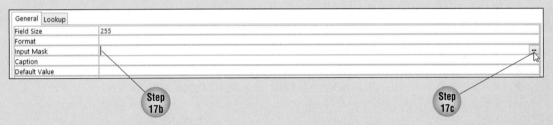

    d. At the first Input Mask Wizard dialog box, make sure *Phone Number* is selected in the *Input Mask* list box and then click the Next button.

    e. At the second Input Mask Wizard dialog box, click the down-pointing arrow at the right side of the *Placeholder character* option box and then click # at the drop-down list.

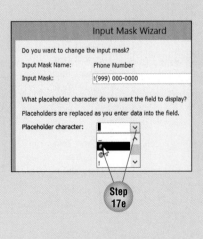

f. Click the Next button.
g. At the third Input Mask Wizard dialog box, click the *With the symbols in the mask, like this* option.

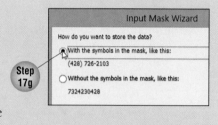

Step 17g

h. Click the Next button.
i. At the fourth Input Mask Wizard dialog box, click the Finish button.
18. Click in the *Description* column in the *Telephone* row, type **Enter employee's telephone number**, and then press the Tab key.
19. Type **HealthIns** and then press the Tab key.
20. Click the down-pointing arrow in the *Data Type* column and then click *Yes/No* at the drop-down list.
21. Click in the *Default Value* property box in the *Field Properties* section, delete the text *No*, and then type **Yes**.
22. Click in the *Description* column for the *HealthIns* row, type **Leave check mark if employee is signed up for health insurance**, and then press the Tab key.

General	Lookup
Format	Yes/No
Caption	
Default Value	Yes
Validation Rule	
Validation Text	
Indexed	No
Text Align	General

Step 21

23. Type **DentalIns** and then press the Tab key.
24. Click the down-pointing arrow in the *Data Type* column and then click *Yes/No* at the drop-down list. (The text in the *Default Value* property box will remain as *No*.)
25. Click in the *Description* column for the *DentalIns* row, type **Insert check mark if employee is signed up for dental insurance**, and then press the Tab key.
26. After all of the fields are entered, click the Save button on the Quick Access toolbar.
27. Click the View button to return the table to Datasheet view.
28. Enter the records in the Employees table as shown in Figure 4.7.
29. After all of the records are entered, automatically adjust the widths of the columns in the table.
30. Save and then close the Employees table.

Figure 4.6 Project 1b Employees Table in Design View

Field Name	Data Type	Description (Optional)
EmpID	Short Text	Enter five-digit employee identification number
FName	Short Text	Enter employee's first name
LName	Short Text	Enter employee's last name
Address	Short Text	Enter employee's address
City	Short Text	Enter employee's city
State	Short Text	CA automatically entered as state
ZIP	Short Text	Enter five-digit ZIP code
Telephone	Short Text	Enter employee's telephone number
HealthIns	Yes/No	Leave check mark if employee is signed up for health insurance
DentalIns	Yes/No	Insert check mark if employee is signed up for dental insurance

Employees

Field Properties

Figure 4.7 Project 1b Employees Table in Datasheet View

EmpID	FName	LName	Address	City	State	ZIP	Telephone	HealthIns	DentalIns
02-59	Christina	Solomon	12241 East 51st	Citrus Heights	CA	95611	(916) 555-8844	✔	✔
03-23	Douglas	Ricci	903 Mission Road	Roseville	CA	95678	(916) 555-4125	✔	
03-55	Tatiana	Kasadev	6558 Orchard Drive	Citrus Heights	CA	95610	(916) 555-8534	✔	
04-14	Brian	West	12232 142nd Avenue East	Citrus Heights	CA	95611	(916) 555-0967	✔	✔
04-32	Kathleen	Addison	21229 19th Street	Citrus Heights	CA	95621	(916) 555-3408	✔	✔
05-20	Teresa	Villanueva	19453 North 42nd Street	Citrus Heights	CA	95611	(916) 555-2302	✔	✔
05-31	Marcia	Griswold	211 Haven Road	North Highlands	CA	95660	(916) 555-1449		
06-24	Tiffany	Gentry	12312 North 20th	Roseville	CA	95661	(916) 555-0043	✔	✔
06-33	Joanna	Gallegos	6850 York Street	Roseville	CA	95747	(956) 555-7446		
07-20	Jesse	Scholtz	3412 South 21st Street	Fair Oaks	CA	95628	(916) 555-4204	✔	
07-23	Eugene	Bond	530 Laurel Road	Orangevale	CA	95662	(916) 555-9412	✔	
*					CA			✔	

Validating Field Entries

Use the *Validation Rule* property box in the *Field Properties* section in Design view to enter a statement containing a conditional test that is checked each time data is entered into a field. If data is entered that fails to satisfy the conditional test, Access does not accept the entry and displays an error message. By entering a conditional statement in the *Validation Rule* property box that checks each entry against the acceptable range, you can reduce errors. Enter in the *Validation Text* property box the content of the error message that you want to display.

Enter a validation rule in a field to control what is entered in the field and to reduce errors. Create validation text that displays when someone enters invalid data in the field.

Using the Lookup Wizard

Like the Input Mask Wizard, the Lookup Wizard can be used to control the data entered in a field. Use the Lookup Wizard to confine the data entered into a field to a specific list of items. For example, in Project 1c, you will use the Lookup Wizard to restrict the new *EmpCategory* field to one of three choices: *Salaried*, *Hourly*, and *Temporary*. When the user clicks in the field in the datasheet, a down-pointing arrow displays. The user clicks this down-pointing arrow to display a drop-down list of available entries and then clicks the desired item.

Use the Lookup Wizard when assigning a data type to a field. Click in the desired field in the *Data Type* column and then click the down-pointing arrow that displays at the right side of the field. At the drop-down list that displays, click *Lookup Wizard*. This displays the first Lookup Wizard dialog box, as shown in Figure 4.8. At this dialog box, indicate that you want to enter the field choices by clicking the *I will type in the values that I want* option and then click the Next button. At the second Lookup Wizard dialog box, shown in Figure 4.9, click in the blank text box below *Col1* and then type the first choice. Press the Tab key and then type the second choice. Continue in this manner until you have entered all the desired choices and then click the Next button. At the third Lookup Wizard dialog box, make sure the proper name displays in the *What label would you like for your lookup column?* text box and then click the Finish button.

▼ Quick Steps

Use the Lookup Wizard
1. Open table in Design view.
2. Type text in *Field Name* column.
3. Press Tab key.
4. Click down-pointing arrow.
5. Click *Lookup Wizard*.
6. Complete wizard steps.

Figure 4.8 First Lookup Wizard Dialog Box

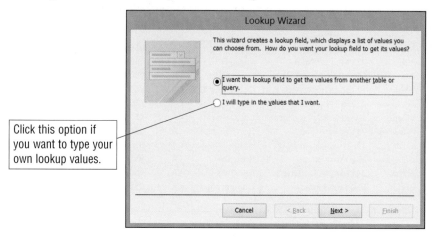

Click this option if you want to type your own lookup values.

Figure 4.9 Second Lookup Wizard Dialog Box

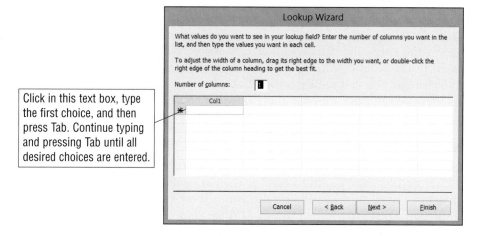

Click in this text box, type the first choice, and then press Tab. Continue typing and pressing Tab until all desired choices are entered.

Inserting, Moving, and Deleting Fields in Design View

▼ **Quick Steps**

Insert a Field in Design View
1. Open table in Design view.
2. Click in row that will follow new field.
3. Click Insert Rows button.

Insert Rows

In Chapter 1, you learned how to insert, move, and delete fields in a table in Datasheet view. You can also perform these tasks in Design view. To insert a new field in a table in Design view, position the insertion point in a field in the row that will be located immediately *below* the new field and then click the Insert Rows button in the Tools group on the TABLE TOOLS DESIGN tab. Another option is to position the insertion point on any text in the row that will display immediately *below* the new field, click the right mouse button, and then click *Insert Rows* at the shortcut menu. If you insert a row for a new field and then change your mind, immediately click the Undo button on the Quick Access toolbar. Remember that a *row* in the Design view creates a *field* in the table.

You can move a field in a table to a different location in Datasheet view or Design view. To move a field in Design view, click in the field selector bar at the left side of the row you want to move. With the row selected, position the arrow pointer in the field selector bar at the left side of the selected row, hold down the left mouse button, drag the arrow pointer with a gray square attached until a thick black line displays in the desired position, and then release the mouse button.

Delete a field in a table and all data entered in that field is also deleted. When you delete a field, it cannot be undone with the Undo button. Delete a field only if you are sure you really want it and the data associated with it completely removed from the table. To delete a field in Design view, click in the field selector bar at the left side of the row you want to delete and then click the Delete Rows button in the Tools group. At the message asking if you want to permanently delete the field and all of the data in the field, click Yes. You can also delete a row by positioning the mouse pointer in the row you want to delete, clicking the right mouse button, and then clicking *Delete Rows* at the shortcut menu.

▼ **Quick Steps**

Delete a Field in Design View
1. Open table in Design view.
2. Click in row to be deleted.
3. Click Delete Rows button.
4. Click Yes.

Delete Rows

Inserting a Total Row

You can add a *Total* row in a table in Datasheet view and then choose from a list of functions to find the sum, average, maximum, minimum, count, standard deviation, or variance result in a numeric column. To insert a *Total* row, click the Totals button in the Records group on the HOME tab. Access adds a row to the bottom of the table with the label *Total* at the left. Click in the *Total* row, click the down-pointing arrow that appears, and then click the desired function at the drop-down list.

▼ **Quick Steps**

Insert a Total Row
1. Open table in Datasheet view.
2. Click Totals button.
3. Click in *Total* row.
4. Click down-pointing arrow.
5. Click desired function.

Totals

Project 1c Validating Field Entries; Using the Lookup Wizard; and Inserting, Moving, and Deleting a Field   **Part 3 of 8**

1. With **AL1-C4-SunProperties.accdb** open, open the Employees table.
2. Insert in the Employees table a new field and apply a validation rule by completing the following steps:
   a. Click the View button to switch to Design view.
   b. Click in the empty field immediately below the *DentalIns* field in the *Field Name* column and then type **LifeIns**.
   c. Press the Tab key.
   d. Click the down-pointing arrow at the right side of the *Data Type* field and then click *Currency* at the drop-down list.
   e. Click in the *Validation Rule* property box, type **<=100000**, and then press Enter.
   f. With the insertion point positioned in the *Validation Text* property box, type **Enter a value that is equal to or less than $100,000.**
   g. Click in the field in the *Description* column for the *LifeIns* row and then type **Enter optional life insurance amount.**
   h. Click the Save button on the Quick Access toolbar. Since the validation rule was created *after* data was entered into the table, Access displays a warning message indicating that some data may not be valid. At this message, click No.
   i. Click the View button to switch to Datasheet view.

Step 2e

General	Lookup
Format	Currency
Decimal Places	Auto
Input Mask	
Caption	
Default Value	0
Validation Rule	<=100000
Validation Text	Enter a value that is equal to or less than $100,000
Required	No

Step 2f

3. Click in the first empty field in the *LifeIns* column, type **200000**, and then press the Down Arrow key.

4. Access displays the error message telling you to enter an amount that is equal to or less than $100,000. At this error message, click OK.
5. Edit the amount in the field so it displays as *100000* and then press the Down Arrow key.
6. Type the following entries in the remaining fields in the *LifeIns* column:

>Record 2: **25000**
>Record 3: **0**
>Record 4: **50000**
>Record 5: **50000**
>Record 6: **0**
>Record 7: **100000**
>Record 8: **50000**
>Record 9: **25000**
>Record 10: **0**
>Record 11: **100000**

7. Insert the field *EmpCategory* in the Employees table and use the Lookup Wizard to specify field choices by completing the following steps:

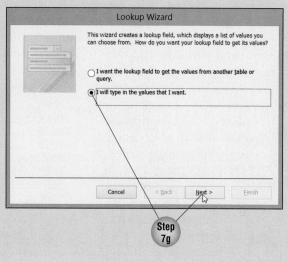

Step 7c

Step 7b

a. Click the View button to change to Design view.
b. Click on any character in the *FName* field entry in the *Field Name* column.
c. Click the Insert Rows button in the Tools group.
d. With the insertion point positioned in the new blank field in the *Field Name* column, type **EmpCategory**.
e. Press the Tab key. (This moves the insertion point to the *Data Type* column.)
f. Click the down-pointing arrow at the right side of the *Data Type* field and then click *Lookup Wizard* at the drop-down list.
g. At the first Lookup Wizard dialog box, click the *I will type in the values that I want* option and then click the Next button.

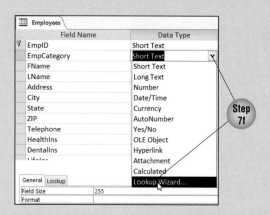

Step 7f

Step 7g

h. At the second Lookup Wizard dialog box, click in the blank text box below *Col1*, type **Salaried**, and then press the Tab key.

i. Type **Hourly** and then press the Tab key.

j. Type **Temporary**.

k. Click the Next button.

l. At the third Lookup Wizard dialog box, click the Finish button.

m. Press the Tab key and then type **Click down-pointing arrow and then click employee category** in the *Description* column.

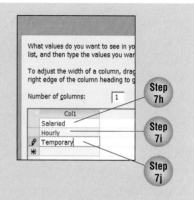

8. Click the Save button on the Quick Access toolbar.

9. Click the View button to switch to Datasheet view.

10. Insert information in the *EmpCategory* column by completing the following steps:

a. Click in the first blank field in the new *EmpCategory* field.

b. Click the down-pointing arrow at the right side of the field and then click *Hourly* at the drop-down list.

c. Click in the next blank field in the *EmpCategory* column, click the down-pointing arrow, and then click *Salaried* at the drop-down list.

d. Continue entering information in the *EmpCategory* column by completing similar steps. Choose the following in the specified record:

Third record: *Hourly*
Fourth record: *Salaried*
Fifth record: *Temporary*
Sixth record: *Hourly*
Seventh record: *Salaried*
Eighth record: *Temporary*
Ninth record: *Hourly*
Tenth record: *Salaried*
Eleventh record: *Salaried*

11. Print the Employees table. (The table will print on two pages.)

12. After looking at the printed table, you decide to move the *EmpCategory* field. You also need to delete the *DentalIns* field, since Sun Properties no longer offers dental insurance benefits to employees. Move the *EmpCatgory* field and delete the *DentalIns* field in Design view by completing the following steps:

a. With the Employees table open, click the View button to switch to Design view.

b. Click in the field selector bar at the left side of the *EmpCategory* field to select the row.

c. Position the arrow pointer in the *EmpCategory* field selector bar, hold down the left mouse button, drag down until a thick black line displays below the *Telephone* field, and then release the mouse button.

	Field Name	Data Type
ⓦ	EmpID	Short Text
	EmpCategory	Short Text
	FName	Short Text
	LName	Short Text
	Address	Short Text
	City	Short Text
	State	Short Text
	ZIP	Short Text
	Telephone	Short Text
	HealthIns	Yes/No
	DentalIns	Yes/No

Step 12c

13. Delete the *DentalIns* field by completing the following steps:
   a. Click in the field selector bar at the left side of the *DentalIns* row. (This selects the row.)
   b. Click the Delete Rows button in the Tools group.
   c. At the message asking if you want to permanently delete the field and all of the data in the field, click Yes.
14. Click the Save button on the Quick Access toolbar.
15. Click the View button to switch to Datasheet view.
16. Print the Employees table. (The table will print on two pages.)
17. Close the Employees table.
18. Open the Payments table and then insert a new field and apply a validation rule by completing the following steps:

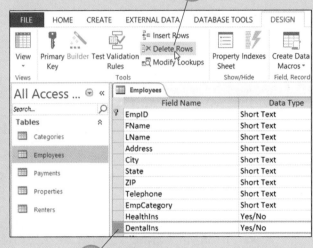

Step 13b

Step 13a

   a. Click the View button to switch to Design view.
   b. Click in the empty field immediately below the *PymntAmount* field in the *Field Name* column and then type LateFee.
   c. Press the Tab key.
   d. Click the down-pointing arrow at the right side of the *Data Type* field and then click *Currency* at the drop-down list.
   e. Click in the *Validation Rule* property box, type <=50, and then press Enter.
   f. With the insertion point positioned in the *Validation Text* property box, type Late fee must be $50 or less.
   g. Click in the box in the *Description* column for the *LateFee* field and then type Enter a late fee amount if applicable.

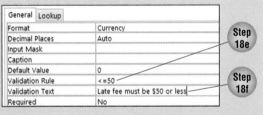

Step 18e

Step 18f

   h. Click the Save button on the Quick Access toolbar. Since the validation rule was created *after* data was entered into the table, Access displays a warning message indicating that some data may not be valid. At this message, click No.
   i. Click the View button to switch to Datasheet view.
19. Insert late fees for the last three records by completing the following steps:
   a. Click in the *LateFee* field for record 15, type 25, and then press the Down Arrow key.
   b. With the *LateFee* field for record 16 active, type 25 and then press the Down Arrow key.
   c. With the *LateFee* field for record 17 active, type 50 and then press the Up Arrow key.

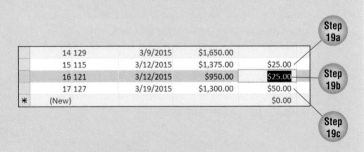

Step 19a

Step 19b

Step 19c

20. Insert a *Total* row by completing the following steps:

   a. In Datasheet view, click the Totals button in the Records group on the HOME tab.

   b. Click in the blank field in the *PymntAmount* column in the *Total* row.

   c. Click the down-pointing arrow at the left side of the field and then click *Sum* at the drop-down list.

   d. Click in the blank field in the *LateFee* column in the *Total* row.

   e. Click the down-pointing arrow at the left side of the field and then click *Sum* at the drop-down list.

   f. Click in any other field.

21. Save, print, and then close the Payments table.

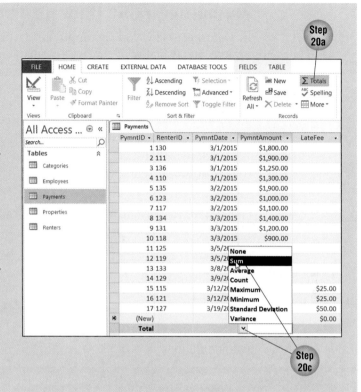

Step 20a

Step 20c

Sorting Records ■■■■■■■■■■■■■■■■■■■■■■■■■

The Sort & Filter group on the HOME tab contains two buttons for sorting data in records. When you click the Ascending button to sort data in the active field, text is sorted in alphabetical order from A to Z and numbers are sorted from lowest to highest. When you click the Descending button to sort data in the active field, text is sorted in alphabetical order from Z to A and numbers are sorted from highest to lowest.

▼ **Quick Steps**

Sort Records
1. Open table in Datasheet view.
2. Click in field in desired column.
3. Click Ascending button or Descending button.

Ascending

Descending

Printing Specific Records ■■■■■■■■■■■■■■■■■■■■■

If you want to print specific records in a table, select the records and then display the Print dialog box by clicking the FILE tab, clicking the *Print* option, and then clicking the Print button. At the Print dialog box, click the *Selected Record(s)* option in the *Print Range* section and then click OK. To select specific records, display the table in Datasheet view, click the record selector of the first record, and then drag to select the desired records. The record selector is the light gray square that displays at the left side of the record. When you position the mouse pointer on the record selector, the pointer turns into a right-pointing black arrow.

▼ **Quick Steps**

Print Selected Records
1. Open table and select records.
2. Click FILE tab.
3. Click *Print* option.
4. Click Print button.
5. Click *Selected Record(s)*.
6. Click OK.

Formatting Table Data ■■■■■■■■■■■■■■■■■■■■■■

In Datasheet view, you can apply formatting to data in a table. Formatting options are available in the Text Formatting group on the HOME tab, as shown in Figure 4.10. To apply formatting, open a table in Datasheet view and then click the desired button in the Text Formatting group. The button formatting is applied to all of the data in the table. (Some of the buttons in the Text Formatting group are dimmed and unavailable. These buttons are available for fields formatted as rich text.) The buttons available for formatting a table are shown in Table 4.2.

Click the Align Left, Center, or Align Right button and formatting is applied to text in the currently active column. Click one of the other buttons shown in

Figure 4.10 HOME Tab Text Formatting Group

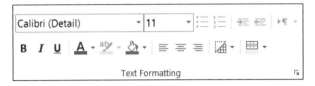

Table 4.2 Text Formatting Buttons

Button	Name	Description
Calibri (Detail)	Font	Change the text font.
11	Font Size	Change the text size.
B	Bold	Bold the text.
I	Italic	Italicize the text.
U	Underline	Underline the text.
A ▾	Font Color	Change the text color.
◇ ▾	Background Color	Apply a background color to all fields.
▤	Align Left	Align all text in the currently active column at the left side of the fields.
▤	Center	Center all text in the currently active column in the center of the fields.
▤	Align Right	Align all text in the currently active column at the right side of the fields.
▨ ▾	Gridlines	Specify whether to display vertical and/or horizontal gridlines.
▦ ▾	Alternate Row Color	Apply a specified color to alternating rows in the table.

Table 4.2 and formatting is applied to all columns and rows of data in the table. The exception is the Background Color button, which applies formatting to all fields in the table.

When creating a table, you specify a data type for a field, such as the Short Text, Date/Time, or Currency data type. If you want to format text in a field rather than all of the fields in a column or the entire table, choose the Long Text data type and then specify rich text formatting. For example, in Project 1d, you will format specific credit scores in the *CreditScore* field column. To be able to format specific scores, you change the data type to Long Text and then specify rich text formatting. Use the Long Text data type only for fields containing text—not for fields containing currency amounts, numbers, and dates.

By default, the Long Text data type uses plain text formatting. To change to rich text, click in the *Text Format* property box in the *Field Properties* section (displays with the text *Plain Text*), click the down-pointing arrow that displays at the right side of the property box, and then click *Rich Text* at the drop-down list.

Project 1d   **Sorting, Printing, and Formatting Records and Fields in Tables**   **Part 4 of 8**

1. With **AL1-C4-SunProperties.accdb** open, open the Renters table.
2. With the table in Datasheet view, sort records in ascending alphabetical order by last name by completing the following steps:
   a. Click any last name in the *LastName* field in the table.
   b. Click the Ascending button in the Sort & Filter group on the HOME tab.
   c. Print the Renters table in landscape orientation.

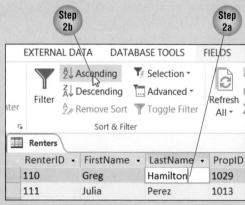

3. Sort records in descending order (highest to lowest) by credit score number by completing the following steps:
   a. Click any number in the *CreditScore* field.
   b. Click the Descending button in the Sort & Filter group.
   c. Print the Renters table in landscape orientation.
4. Close the Renters table without saving the changes.
5. Open the Properties table.
6. Sort and then print selected records with the apartment property type by completing the following steps:
   a. Click any entry in the *CatID* field.
   b. Click the Ascending button in the Sort & Filter group.
   c. Position the mouse pointer on the record selector of the first record with *A* for a category ID, hold down the mouse button, and then drag to select the four records with a category ID of *A*.

d. Click the FILE tab and then click the *Print* option.
e. Click the Print button.
f. At the Print dialog box, click the *Selected Record(s)* option in the *Print Range* section.
g. Click OK.

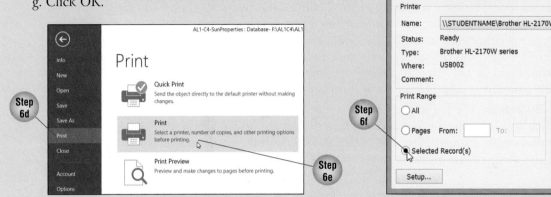

7. With the Properties table open, apply the following text formatting:
   a. Click in any field in the *CatID* column and then click the Center button in the Text Formatting group on the HOME tab.

b. Click in any field in the *PropID* column and then click the Center button in the Text Formatting group.
c. Click the Bold button in the Text Formatting group. (This applies bold to all text in the table.)
d. Click the Font Color button arrow and then click *Dark Blue* (fourth column, first row in the *Standard Colors* section).
e. Adjust the column widths.
f. Save, print, and then close the Properties table.
8. Open the Payments table and apply the following text formatting:
   a. With the first field active in the *PymntID* column, click the Center button in the Text Formatting group on the HOME tab.

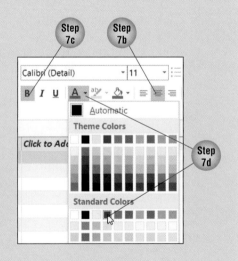

b. Click in any field in the *RenterID* column and then click the Center button in the Text Formatting group.

c. Click the Font button arrow, scroll down the drop-down list that displays, and then click *Candara*. (Fonts are listed in alphabetical order in the drop-down list.)

d. Click the Font Size button arrow and then click *12* at the drop-down list.

e. Click the Alternate Row Color button arrow and then click *Green 2* (seventh column, third row in the *Standard Colors* section).

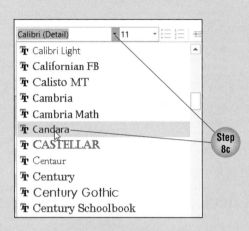

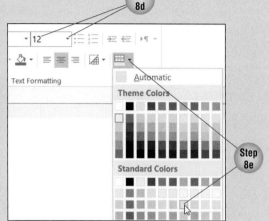

f. Adjust the column widths.

g. Save, print, and then close the Payments table.

9. Open the Renters table and then apply the following formatting to columns in the table:

a. With the first field active in the *RenterID* column, click the Center button in the Text Formatting group on the HOME tab.

b. Click in any field in the *PropID* column and then click the Center button.

c. Click in any field in the *EmpID* column and then click the Center button

d. Click in any field in the *CreditScore* column and then click the Center button.

10. Change the data type for the *CreditScore* field to Long Text with rich text formatting and apply formatting by completing the following steps:

a. Click the View button to switch to Design view.

b. Click in the *Data Type* column in the *CreditScore* row, click the down-pointing arrow that displays in the field, and then click *Long Text* at the drop-down list.

c. Click in the *Text Format* property box in the *Field Properties* section (displays with the words *Plain Text*), click the down-pointing arrow that displays at the right side of the property box, and then click *Rich Text* at the drop-down list.

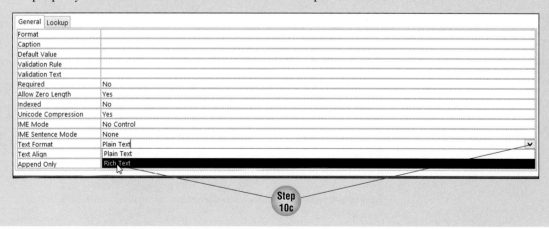

d. At the message that displays telling you that the field will be converted to rich text, click the Yes button.

e. Click the Save button on the Quick Access toolbar.

f. Click the View button to switch to Datasheet view.

g. Double-click the field value *538* that displays in the *CreditScore* column in the row for Dana Rozinski. (Double-clicking in the field selects the field value *538*.)

h. With *538* selected, click the Font Color button in the Text Formatting group. (This changes the number to red. If the font color does not change to red, click the Font Color button arrow and then click *Red* in the second column, bottom row of the *Standard Colors* section.)

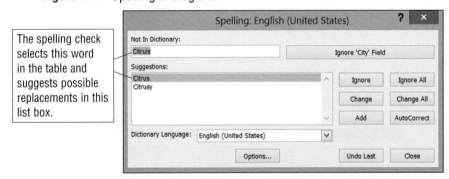

i. Change the font to red for any credit scores below 600.

j. Print the Renters table in landscape orientation and then close the table.

Completing a Spelling Check ■■■■■■■■■■■■■■■■■■■■■

▼ **Quick Steps**

Complete a Spelling Check
1. Open table in Datasheet view.
2. Click Spelling button.
3. Change or ignore spelling as needed.
4. Click OK.

Spelling

H I N T

You can also begin a spelling check with the keyboard shortcut F7.

The spelling check feature in Access finds misspelled words and suggests replacement words. It also finds duplicate words and irregular capitalizations. When you spell check an object in a database, such as a table, the spelling check compares the words in your table with the words in its dictionary. If a match is found, the word is passed over. If no match is found, the spelling check selects the word and suggests possible replacements.

To complete a spelling check, open the desired table in Datasheet view and then click the Spelling button in the Records group on the HOME tab. If the spelling check does not find a match for a word in your table, the Spelling dialog box displays with replacement options. Figure 4.11 displays the Spelling dialog box with the word *Citruis* selected and possible replacements displayed in the *Suggestions* list box. At the Spelling dialog box, you can choose to ignore the word (for example, if the spelling check has selected a proper name), change to one of the replacement options, or add the word to the dictionary or AutoCorrect feature. You can also complete a spelling check on other objects in a database, such as a query, form, and report. (You will learn about forms and reports in future chapters.)

Figure 4.11 Spelling Dialog Box

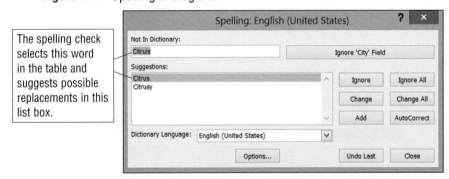

The spelling check selects this word in the table and suggests possible replacements in this list box.

1. With **AL1-C4-SunProperties.accdb** open, open the Employees table.
2. Delete the *LifeIns* field by completing the following steps:
   a. Click the View button to switch to the Design view.
   b. Click in the field selector bar at the left side of the *LifeIns* row. (This selects the row.)
   c. Click the Delete Rows button in the Tools group.
   d. At the message asking if you want to permanently delete the field and all of the data in the field, click Yes.
   e. Click the Save button on the Quick Access toolbar.
   f. Click the View button to switch to Datasheet view.
3. Add the following record to the Employees table. (Type the misspelled words as shown below. You will correct the spelling in a later step.)

EmpID	02-72
FName	Roben
LName	Wildre
Address	9945 Valley Avenue
City	Citruis Heights
State	(CA automatically inserted)
ZIP	95610
Telephone	9165556522
EmpCategory	(choose *Salaried*)
HealthIns	No (Remove check mark)

4. Save the Employees table.
5. Click in the first entry in the *EmpID* column.
6. Click the Spelling button in the Records group on the HOME tab.
7. The spelling check selects the name *Kasadev*. This is a proper name, so click the Ignore button to tell the spelling check to leave the name as written.
8. The spelling check selects the name *Scholtz*. This is a proper name, so click the Ignore button to tell the spelling check to leave the name as written.
9. The spelling check selects *Roben*. The proper spelling *(Robin)* is selected in the *Suggestions* list box, so click the Change button.
10. The spelling check selects *Wildre*. The proper spelling *(Wilder)* is selected in the *Suggestions* list box, so click the Change button.

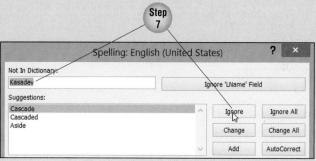

11. The spelling check selects *Citruis*. The proper spelling *(Citrus)* is selected in the *Suggestions* list box, so click the Change button.
12. At the message telling you that the spelling check is complete, click the OK button.
13. Print the Employees table in landscape orientation and then close the table.

Finding and Replacing Data ■■■■■■■■■■■■■■■■■■

▼ Quick Steps

Find Data
1. Open table in Datasheet view.
2. Click Find button.
3. Type data in *Find What* text box.
4. Click Find Next button.

Find and Replace Data
1. Open table in Datasheet view.
2. Click Replace button.
3. Type find data in *Find What* text box.
4. Type replace data in *Replace With* text box.
5. Click Find Next button.
6. Click Replace button or Find Next button.

Find

Replace

Press Ctrl + F to display the Find and Replace dialog box with the Find tab selected.

Press Ctrl + H to display the Find and Replace dialog box with the Replace tab selected.

If you need to find a specific entry in a field in a table, consider using options at the Find and Replace dialog box with the Find tab selected, as shown in Figure 4.12. Display this dialog box by clicking the Find button in the Find group on the HOME tab. At the Find and Replace dialog box, enter the data you want to locate in the *Find What* text box. By default, Access looks only in the specific column where the insertion point is positioned. Click the Find Next button to find the next occurrence of the data or click the Cancel button to close the Find and Replace dialog box.

The *Look In* option defaults to the column where the insertion point is positioned. You can choose to look in the entire table by clicking the down-pointing arrow at the right side of the *Look In* option and then clicking the table name at the drop-down list. The *Match* option has a default setting of *Whole Field*. You can change this to *Any Part of Field* or *Start of Field*. The *Search* option has a default setting of *All*, which means that Access will search all of the data in a specific column. This can be changed to *Up* or *Down*. If you want to find data that contains specific uppercase and lowercase letters, insert a check mark in the *Match Case* check box and Access will return results that match the case formatting of the search text you entered.

Use the Find and Replace dialog box with the Replace tab selected to search for specific data and replace it with other data. Display this dialog box by clicking the Replace button in the Find group on the HOME tab.

Figure 4.12 Find and Replace Dialog Box with Find Tab Selected

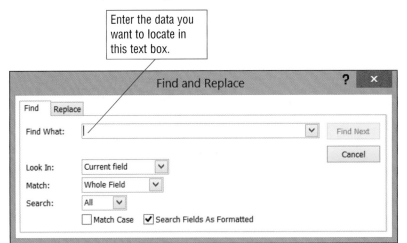

1. With **AL1-C4-SunProperties.accdb** open, open the Properties table.
2. Find records containing the zip code *95610* by completing the following steps:
   a. Click in the first field in the *ZIP* column.
   b. Click the Find button in the Find group on the HOME tab.
   c. At the Find and Replace dialog box with the Find tab selected, type *95610* in the *Find What* text box.
   d. Click the Find Next button. (Access finds and selects the first occurrence of *95610*. If the Find and Replace dialog box covers the data, drag the dialog box to a different location on the screen.)

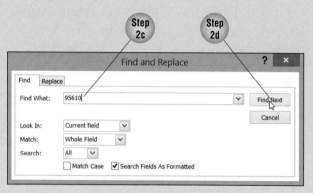

   e. Continue clicking the Find Next button until a message displays telling you that Access has finished searching the records. At this message, click OK.
   f. Click the Cancel button to close the Find and Replace dialog box.
3. Suppose a new zip code has been added to the city of North Highlands and you need to change to this new zip for some of the North Highlands properties. Complete the following steps to find *95660* and replace it with *95668*:
   a. Click in the first field in the *ZIP* column.
   b. Click the Replace button in the Find group.
   c. At the Find and Replace dialog box with the Replace tab selected, type *95660* in the *Find What* text box.
   d. Press the Tab key. (This moves the insertion point to the *Replace With* text box.)
   e. Type *95668* in the *Replace With* text box.
   f. Click the Find Next button.
   g. When Access selects the first occurrence of *95660*, click the Replace button.
   h. When Access selects the second occurrence of *95660*, click the Find Next button.

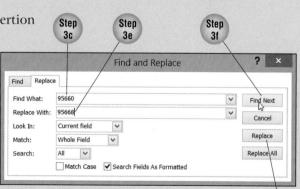

   i. When Access selects the third occurrence of *95660*, click the Replace button.
   j. When Access selects the fourth occurrence of *95660*, click the Find Next button.
   k. When Access selects the fifth occurrence of *95660*, click the Find Next button.
   l. When Access selects the sixth occurrence of *95660*, click the Replace button.
   m. Access selects the first occurrence of *95660* (record 1018) in the table. Click the Cancel button to close the Find and Replace dialog box.
4. Print and then close the Properties table.

5. Display the Relationships window and then create the following relationships (enforce referential integrity and cascade fields and records):

   a. Create a one-to-many relationship with the *CatID* field in the Categories table the "one" and the *CatID* field in the Properties table the "many."

   b. Create a one-to-many relationship with the *EmpID* field in the Employees table the "one" and the *EmpID* field in the Renters table the "many."

   c. Create a one-to-many relationship with the *PropID* field in the Properties table the "one" and the *PropID* field in the Renters table the "many."

   d. Create a one-to-many relationship with the *RenterID* field in the Renters table the "one" and the *RenterID* field in the Payments table the "many."

   e. Save the relationships and then print the relationships in landscape orientation.

   f. Close the relationships report without saving it and then close the Relationships window.

6. Design a query that displays employees with health insurance benefits with the following specifications:

   a. Insert the Employees table in the query window.

   b. Insert the *EmpID* field in the first *Field* row field.

   c. Insert the *FName* field in the second *Field* row field.

   d. Insert the *LName* field in the third *Field* row field.

   e. Insert the *HealthIns* field in the fourth *Field* row field.

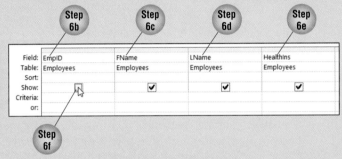

   f. Click in the check box in the *Show* row field in the *EmpID* column to remove the check mark. (This hides the EmpID numbers in the query results.)

   g. Extract those employees with health benefits. (Type a *1* for the criteria.)

   h. Run the query.

   i. Save the query and name it *EmpsWithHealthInsQuery*.

   j. Print and then close the query.

7. Design a query that displays all properties in the city of Citrus Heights with the following specifications:

   a. Insert the Properties table and the Categories table in the query window.

   b. Insert the *PropID* field from the Properties table in the first *Field* row field.

   c. Insert the *Category* field from the Categories table in the second *Field* row field.

   d. Insert the *Address*, *City*, *State*, and *ZIP* fields from the Properties table to the third, fourth, fifth, and sixth *Field* row fields, respectively.

   e. Extract those properties in the city of Citrus Heights.

   f. Run the query.

   g. Save the query and name it *CitrusHeightsPropsQuery*.

   h. Print and then close the query.

8. Design a query that displays rent payments made between 3/1/2015 and 3/5/2015 with the following specifications:

   a. Insert the Payments table and the Renters table in the query window.

   b. Insert the *PymntID*, *PymntDate*, and *PymntAmount* fields from the Payments table in the first, second, and third *Field* row fields, respectively.

   c. Insert the *FirstName* and *LastName* fields from the Renters table in the fourth and fifth *Field* row fields, respectively.

d. Extract those payments made between 3/1/2015 and 3/5/2015.

e. Run the query.

f. Save the query and name it *Pymnts3/1To3/5Query*.

g. Print and then close the query.

9. Design a query that displays properties in Citrus Heights or Orangevale that rent for less than $1,501 a month as well as the type of property with the following specifications:

a. Insert the Categories table and the Properties table in the query window.

b. Insert the *Category* field from the Categories table.

c. Insert the *PropID, MoRent, Address, City, State*, and *ZIP* fields from the Properties table.

d. Extract those properties in Citrus Heights and Orangevale that rent for less than $1,501.

e. Run the query.

f. Save the query and name it *RentLessThan$1501InCHAndOVQuery*.

g. Print the query in landscape orientation and then close the query.

10. Design a query that displays properties in Citrus Heights assigned to employee identification number *07-20* with the following specifications:

a. Insert the Employees table and Properties table in the query window.

b. Insert the *EmpID, FName*, and *LName* fields from the Employees table.

c. Insert the *Address, City, State*, and *ZIP* fields from the Properties table.

d. Extract those properties in Citrus Heights assigned to EmpID 07-20.

e. Run the query.

f. Save the query and name it *Emp07-20CHPropsQuery*.

g. Print and then close the query.

Using Help ■■■■■■■■■■■■■■■■■■■■■■■■■■■■■■■

Microsoft Access includes a Help feature that contains information about Access features and commands. This on-screen reference manual is similar to Windows Help and the Help features in Word, PowerPoint, and Excel. Click the Microsoft Access Help button (the question mark) located in the upper right corner of the screen or press the keyboard shortcut F1 to display the Access Help window, as shown in Figure 4.13. In this window, type a topic, feature, or question in the search text box and then press the Enter key. Topics related to the search text display in the Access Help window. Click a topic that interests you. If the topic window contains a <u>Show All</u> hyperlink in the upper right corner, click this hyperlink to expand the topic options to show additional help information related to the topic. When you click the <u>Show All</u> hyperlink, it becomes the <u>Hide All</u> hyperlink.

Getting Help on a Button

When you position the mouse pointer on a button, a ScreenTip displays with information about the button. Some button ScreenTips display with a Help icon and the text *Tell me more*. Click this hyperlinked text or press F1 and the Access Help window opens with information about the button feature.

▼ **Quick Steps**

Use the Help Feature
1. Click Microsoft Access Help button.
2. Type topic or feature.
3. Press Enter.
4. Click desired topic.

Help

Press F1 to display the Access Help window.

Figure 4.13 Access Help Window

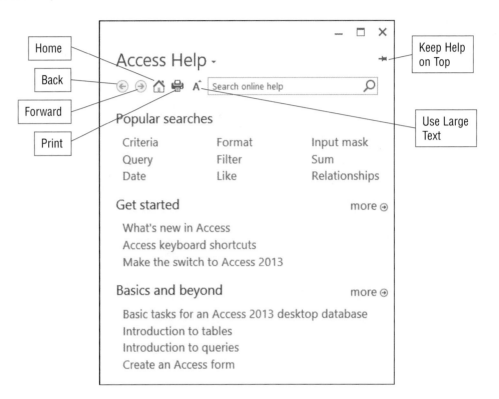

Project 1g Using the Help Feature   **Part 7 of 8**

1. With **AL1-C4-SunProperties.accdb** open, click the Microsoft Access Help button located in the upper right corner of the screen.
2. At the Access Help window, type **input mask** in the search text box and then press Enter.
3. When the list of topics displays, click the <u>Guide data entry by using input masks</u> hyperlink. (If this article is not available, choose a similar article.)
4. Read the information on creating an input mask. (If you want a printout of the information, click the Print button located toward the top of the Access Help window and then click the Print button at the Print dialog box.)
5. Close the Access Help window by clicking the Close button located in the upper right corner of the window.

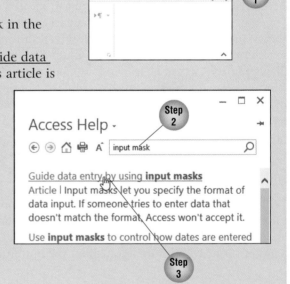

6. Click the CREATE tab.
7. Hover the mouse over the Table button and then click the <u>Tell me more</u> hyperlink that displays toward the bottom of the ScreenTip.
8. At the Access Help window, read the information on tables and then click the Close button located in the upper right corner of the Access Help window.

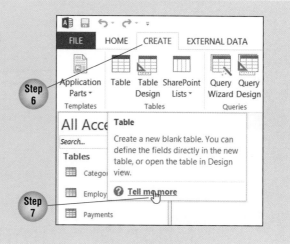

Getting Help in a Dialog Box or Backstage Area

Some dialog boxes and backstage areas provide a Help button you can click to display the Access Help window with specific information about the dialog box or backstage area. After reading and/or printing the information, close the dialog box by clicking the Close button located in the upper right corner of the dialog box or close the backstage area by clicking the Back button or pressing the Esc key.

Project 1h Getting Help in a Dialog Box and Backstage View   Part 8 of 8

1. With **AL1-C4-SunProperties.accdb** open, click the DATABASE TOOLS tab.
2. Click the Relationships button. (Make sure the Show Table dialog box displays. If it does not, click the Show Table button in the Relationships group.)
3. Click the Help button that displays in the upper right corner of the Show Table dialog box.

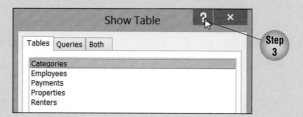

4. Click the <u>Guide to table relationships</u> hyperlink. (If this article is not available, choose a similar article.)
5. Read the information that displays about table relationships and then close the Access Help window.
6. Close the Show Table dialog box and then close the Relationships window.
7. Click the FILE tab and then click the *Open* option.

8. At the Open backstage area, click the Microsoft Access Help button that displays in the upper right corner.
9. Read the information that displays in the Access Help window.
10. Close the Access Help window and then press the Esc key to return to the database.
11. Close **AL1-C4-SunProperties.accdb**.

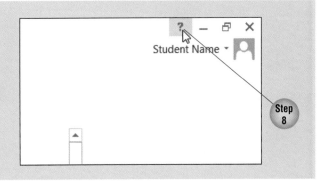

Student Name

Step 8

Chapter Summary

- You can create a table in Datasheet view or Design view. Click the View button on the TABLE TOOLS FIELDS tab or the HOME tab to switch between Datasheet view and Design view.

- Define each field in a table in the rows in the top section of Design view. Access automatically assigns the first field the name *ID* and assigns the AutoNumber data type.

- In Design view, specify a field name, data type, and description for each field.

- Assign a data type in Design view by clicking in the *Data Type* field in the desired row, clicking the down-pointing arrow at the right side of the field, and then clicking the desired data type at the drop-down list.

- Create a default value for a field in Design view with the *Default Value* property box in the *Field Properties* section.

- Use the Input Mask Wizard to set a pattern for how data is entered in a field.

- Use the *Validation Rule* property box in the *Field Properties* section in Design view to enter a statement containing a conditional test. Enter in the *Validation Text* property box the error message you want to display if the data entered violates the validation rule.

- Use the Lookup Wizard to confine data entered in a field to a specific list of items.

- Insert a field in Design view by clicking in the row immediately below where you want the new field inserted and then clicking the Insert Rows button.

- Move a field in Design view by clicking in the field selector bar of the field you want to move and then dragging with the mouse to the desired position.

- Delete a field in Design view by clicking in the field selector bar at the left side of the row you want deleted and then clicking the Delete Rows button.

- Insert a *Total* row in a table in Datasheet view by clicking the Totals button in the Records group on the HOME tab, clicking the down-pointing arrow in the *Total* row field, and then clicking the desired function at the drop-down list.

- Click the Ascending button in the Sort & Filter group on the HOME tab to sort records in ascending order and click the Descending button to sort records in descending order.

- To print specific records in a table, select the records, display the Print dialog box, make sure *Selected Record(s)* is selected, and then click OK.

- Apply formatting to a table in Datasheet view with buttons in the Text Formatting group on the HOME tab. Depending on the button you click in the Text Formatting group, formatting is applied to all of the data in a table or data in a specific column in the table.

- If you want to format text in a specific field, change the data type to Long Text and then specify rich text formatting. Do this in Design view with the *Text Format* property box in the *Field Properties* section.

- Use the spelling check to find misspelled words in a table and consider possible replacement words.

- Use options at the Find and Replace dialog box with the Find tab selected to search for specific field entries in a table. Use options at the Find and Replace dialog box with the Replace tab selected to search for specific data and replace it with other data.

- Click the Microsoft Access Help button or press F1 to display the Access Help window. At this window, type a topic in the search text box and then press Enter.

- The ScreenTip for some buttons displays with a Help icon and the text *Tell me more*. Click this hyperlinked text or press F1 and the Access Help window opens with information about the button.

- Some dialog boxes and backstage areas contain a Help button you can click to display information specific to the dialog box or backstage area.

Commands Review

FEATURE	RIBBON TAB, GROUP	BUTTON, OPTION	KEYBOARD SHORTCUT
Access Help window		?	F1
align text left	HOME, Text Formatting	≡	
align text right	HOME, Text Formatting	≡	
alternate row color	HOME, Text Formatting	▦ ▾	
background color	HOME, Text Formatting	🖌 ▾	
bold formatting	HOME, Text Formatting	B	
center text	HOME, Text Formatting	≡	
delete field	TABLE TOOLS DESIGN, Tools	⇥X	
Design view	HOME, Views OR TABLE TOOLS FIELDS, Views	⊾	

FEATURE	RIBBON TAB, GROUP	BUTTON, OPTION	KEYBOARD SHORTCUT
Find and Replace dialog box with Find tab selected	HOME, Find	🔍	Ctrl + F
Find and Replace dialog box with Replace tab selected	HOME, Find	ab→ac	Ctrl + H
font	HOME, Text Formatting	Calibri (Detail)	
font color	HOME, Text Formatting	A ▾	
font size	HOME, Text Formatting	11 ▾	
gridlines	HOME, Text Formatting	▦ ▾	
insert field	TABLE TOOLS DESIGN, Tools	▤	
italic formatting	HOME, Text Formatting	*I*	
sort records ascending	HOME, Sort & Filter	A↓Z	
sort records descending	HOME, Sort & Filter	Z↓A	
spelling check	HOME, Records	ABC ✓	F7
Total row	HOME, Records	Σ	
underline formatting	HOME, Text Formatting	U	

Concepts Check   Test Your Knowledge

Completion: In the space provided at the right, indicate the correct term, symbol, or command.

1. The lower half of the work area in Design view that displays the properties for the active field is referred to as this. _____

2. When you create a new table in Design view, Access automatically assigns the first field the name *ID* and assigns this data type. _____

3. The description you type in the *Description* field displays in this location when the field is active in the table in Datasheet view. _____

4. Use this field property to set a pattern for how data is entered in a field. _____

5. Use this property box in Design view to enter a statement containing a conditional test that is checked each time data is entered into a field. _____

6. Use this wizard to confine the data entered in a field to a
   specific list of items.   _____

7. To insert a new field in a table in Design view, click this button.   _____

8. To insert a *Total* row in a table, click the Totals button in this
   group on the HOME tab.   _____

9. The Ascending and Descending sort buttons are located in
   this group on the HOME tab.   _____

10. Click this button to change the text size of data in a table.   _____

11. Click this button to align all text in the active column in the
    center of the fields.   _____

12. Click this button to specify a color for alternating rows in a table.   _____

13. Use options at the Find and Replace dialog box with this tab
    selected to search for specific data and replace it with other data.   _____

14. This is the keyboard shortcut to display the Access Help window.   _____

Skills Check   Assess Your Performance

Assessment

1   **CREATE AN EMPLOYEES TABLE WITH THE INPUT MASK
        AND LOOKUP WIZARDS**

1. Open Access and then create a new database by completing the following
   steps:
   a. At the Access 2013 opening screen, click the Blank desktop database
      template.
   b. Type **AL1-C4-Hudson** in the *File Name* text box.
   c. Click the Browse button.
   d. At the File New Database dialog box, navigate to the AL1C4 folder on your
      storage medium and then click OK.
   e. Click the Create button.
2. Create the Employees table in Design view as shown in Figure 4.14 with the
   following specifications:
   a. Limit the *EmpID* field size to 4 characters, the *FirstName* and *LastName*
      fields to 20 characters, and the *Address* field to 30 characters.
   b. Create a default value of *Pueblo* for the *City* field since most of the
      employees live in Pueblo.

Figure 4.14 Employees Table in Design View

Field Name	Data Type	Description
▶ EmpID	Short Text	Enter four-digit employee identification number
FirstName	Short Text	Enter employee first name
LastName	Short Text	Enter employee last name
Address	Short Text	Enter employee street address
City	Short Text	Pueblo automatically inserted
State	Short Text	CO automatically inserted
ZIP	Short Text	Enter employee ZIP code
Telephone	Short Text	Enter employee telephone number
Status	Short Text	Click down-pointing arrow and then click employee status
HireDate	Date/Time	Enter employee hire date

    c. Create a default value of *CO* for the *State* field, since all of the employees live in Colorado.

    d. Create an input mask for the telephone number.

    e. Use the Lookup Wizard to specify field choices for the *Status* field and include the following choices: *Full-time, Part-time, Temporary,* and *Contract.*

3. Save the table, switch to Datasheet view, and then enter the records as shown in Figure 4.15.

4. Adjust the column widths.

5. Save the table and then print it in landscape orientation.

6. Switch to Design view and then add a row immediately above the *FirstName* row. Type **Title** in the *Field Name* field, limit the field size to 20 characters, and type the description **Enter employee job title.**

7. Delete the *HireDate* field.

8. Move the *Status* field so it is positioned between the *EmpID* row and the *Title* row.

9. Save the table and then switch to Datasheet view.

10. Enter the following information in the *Title* field:

EmpID	Title	EmpID	Title
1466	Design Director	2301	Assistant
1790	Assistant	2440	Assistant
1947	Resources Director	3035	Clerk
1955	Accountant	3129	Clerk
1994	Assistant	3239	Assistant
2019	Production Director	4002	Contractor
2120	Assistant	4884	Contractor

11. Apply the following text formatting to the table:

    a. Change the font to Arial and the font size to 10 points.

    b. Center the data in the *EmpID* field column and the *State* field column.

    c. Apply the Aqua Blue 2 alternating row color (ninth column, third row in the *Standard Colors* section) to the table.

12. Adjust the column widths.

13. Save the table and then print it in landscape orientation with left and right margins of 0.5 inch.

Figure 4.15 Employees Table in Datasheet View

EmpID	FirstName	LastName	Address	City	State	ZIP	Telephone	Status	HireDate	Click
1466	Samantha	O'Connell	9105 Pike Avenue	Pueblo	CO	81011	(719) 555-7658	Full-time	8/15/2013	
1790	Edward	Sorrell	9958 Franklin Avenue	Pueblo	CO	81006	(719) 555-3724	Full-time	11/15/2009	
1947	Brandon	Byrne	102 Hudson Avenue	Pueblo	CO	81012	(719) 555-1202	Full-time	8/1/2011	
1955	Leland	Hughes	4883 Caledonia Road	Pueblo	CO	81005	(719) 555-1211	Full-time	3/1/2013	
1994	Rosa	Martinez	310 Graham Avenue	Pueblo	CO	81004	(719) 555-8394	Part-time	8/15/2010	
2019	Jean	Perrault	123 Chinook Lake	Pueblo	CO	81012	(719) 555-4027	Full-time	11/15/2009	
2120	Michael	Turek	5503 East 27th Street	Boone	CO	81025	(719) 555-5423	Full-time	3/15/2011	
2301	Gregory	Nitsche	12055 East 18th Street	Pueblo	CO	81007	(719) 555-6657	Part-time	3/15/2010	
2440	Bethany	Rosario	858 West 27th Street	Pueblo	CO	81012	(719) 555-9481	Part-time	2/15/2014	
3035	Alia	Shandra	7740 West Second Street	Avondale	CO	81022	(719) 555-0059	Temporary	2/1/2013	
3129	Gloria	Cushman	6590 East 14th Street	Pueblo	CO	81006	(719) 555-0332	Temporary	5/1/2015	
3239	Rudolph	Powell	8874 Hood Avenue	Pueblo	CO	81008	(719) 555-2223	Temporary	4/1/2015	
4002	Alice	Murray	4300 East 14th Street	Pueblo	CO	81003	(719) 555-4230	Contract	9/12/2009	
4884	Simon	Banister	1022 Division Avenue	Boone	CO	81025	(719) 555-2378	Contract	5/15/2015	
*				Pueblo	CO					

14. Find all occurrences of *Director* and replace them with *Manager*. **Hint: Position the insertion point in the first entry in the** Title **column and then display the Find and Replace dialog box. At the dialog box, change the** Match **option to Any Part of Field.**

15. Find all occurrences of *Assistant* and replace them with *Associate*.

16. Save the table, print it in landscape orientation with left and right margins of 0.5 inch, and then close it.

Assessment

2 CREATE A PROJECTS TABLE

Grade It

1. With **AL1-C4-Hudson.accdb** open, create a Projects table in Design view. Include the following fields (making sure the *ProjID* field is identified as the primary key) and create an appropriate description for each field:

Field Name	Data Type
ProjID	Short Text (field size = 4 characters)
EmpID	Short Text (field size = 4 characters)
BegDate	Date/Time
EndDate	Date/Time
EstCosts	Currency

2. Save the table, switch to Datasheet view, and then type the following data in the specified field:

ProjID	08-A	*ProjID*	08-B	
EmpID	2019	*EmpID*	1466	
BegDate	8/1/2015	*BegDate*	8/15/2015	
EndDate	10/31/2015	*EndDate*	12/15/2015	
EstCosts	$5,250.00	*EstCosts*	$2,000.00	
ProjID	10-A	*ProjID*	10-B	
EmpID	1947	*EmpID*	2019	
BegDate	10/1/2015	*BegDate*	10/1/2015	
EndDate	1/15/2016	*EndDate*	12/15/2015	
EstCosts	$10,000.00	*EstCosts*	$3,500.00	

ProjID	11-A	ProjID	11-B
EmpID	1466	EmpID	1947
BegDate	11/1/2015	BegDate	11/1/2015
EndDate	2/1/2016	EndDate	3/31/2016
EstCosts	$8,000.00	EstCosts	$12,000.00

3. Adjust the column widths.
4. Save, print, and then close the Projects table.

Assessment

3 CREATE AN EXPENSES TABLE WITH A VALIDATION RULE AND INPUT MASK

1. With **AL1-C4-Hudson.accdb** open, create an Expenses table in Design view. Include the following fields (making sure the *ItemID* field is identified as the primary key) and include an appropriate description for each field:

Field Name	Data Type
ItemID	AutoNumber
EmpID	Short Text (field size = 4 characters)
ProjID	Short Text (field size = 4 characters)
Amount	Currency (Type a condition in the *Validation Rule* property box that states the entry must be $500 or less. Type an appropriate error message in the *Validation Text* property box.)
DateSubmitted	Date/Time (Use the Input Mask to control the date so it is entered as a short date.)

2. Save the table, switch to Datasheet view, and then type the following data in the fields (recall that Access automatically fills in the *ItemID* field):

EmpID	1466	EmpID	2019
ProjID	08-B	ProjID	08-A
Amount	$245.79	Amount	$500.00
DateSubmitted	09/04/2015	DateSubmitted	09/10/2015
EmpID	4002	EmpID	1947
ProjID	08-B	ProjID	10-A
Amount	$150.00	Amount	$500.00
DateSubmitted	09/18/2015	DateSubmitted	10/03/2015
EmpID	2019	EmpID	1947
ProjID	10-B	ProjID	10-A
Amount	$487.25	Amount	$85.75
DateSubmitted	10/22/2015	DateSubmitted	10/24/2015
EmpID	1466	EmpID	1790
ProjID	08-B	ProjID	08-A
Amount	$175.00	Amount	$110.50
DateSubmitted	10/29/2015	DateSubmitted	10/30/2015
EmpID	2120	EmpID	1466
ProjID	10-A	ProjID	08-B
Amount	$75.00	Amount	$300.00
DateSubmitted	11/05/2015	DateSubmitted	11/07/2015
EmpID	1466	EmpID	2019
ProjID	11-A	ProjID	10-B
Amount	$75.00	Amount	$300.00
DateSubmitted	11/14/2015	DateSubmitted	11/19/2015

3. Adjust the column widths.
4. Insert a *Total* row with the following specifications:
    a. Click the Totals button in the Records group on the HOME tab.
    b. Click in the blank field in the *Amount* column in the *Total* row.
    c. Click the down-pointing arrow at the left side of the field and then click *Sum* at the drop-down list.
    d. Click in any other field.
5. Save, print, and then close the Expenses table.
6. Create a one-to-many relationship where *EmpID* in the Employees table is the "one" and *EmpID* in the Expenses table is the "many." (Enforce referential integrity and cascade fields and records.)
7. Create a one-to-many relationship where *EmpID* in the Employees table is the "one" and *EmpID* in the Projects table is the "many." (Enforce referential integrity and cascade fields and records.)
8. Create a one-to-many relationship where *ProjID* in the Projects table is the "one" and *ProjID* in the Expenses table is the "many." (Enforce referential integrity and cascade fields and records.)
9. Save the relationships, print the relationships, and then close the relationship report and the Relationships window.
10. Design and run a query that displays all full-time employees with the following specifications:
    a. Insert the Employees table in the query window.
    b. Insert the *EmpID*, *FirstName*, *LastName*, and *Status* fields.
    c. Click in the check box in the *Show* row field in the *EmpID* column to remove the check mark. (This hides the EmpID numbers in the query results.)
    d. Extract full-time employees.
    e. Save the query and name it *FTEmpsQuery*.
    f. Print and then close the query.
11. Design and run a query that displays projects managed by employee number 1947 with the following specifications:
    a. Insert the Employees table and Projects table in the query window.
    b. Insert the *EmpID*, *FirstName*, and *LastName* fields from the Employees table.
    c. Insert the *ProjID* field from the Projects table.
    d. Extract those projects managed by employee number 1947.
    e. Save the query and name it *ProjsManagedByEmp1947Query*.
    f. Print and then close the query.
12. Design and run a query that displays expense amounts over $250 and the employees submitting the expenses with the following specifications:
    a. Insert the Expenses table and Employees table in the query window.
    b. Insert the *ItemID*, *Amount*, and *DateSubmitted* fields from the Expenses table.
    c. Insert the *FirstName* and *LastName* fields from the Employees table.
    d. Hide the *ItemID* field in the query results by clicking in the check box in the *Show* row field in the *ItemID* column to remove the check mark.
    e. Extract those expense amounts over $250.
    f. Save the query and name it *ExpensesOver$250Query*.
    g. Print and then close the query.
13. Design and run a query that displays expenses submitted by employee number 1947 with the following specifications:
    a. Insert the Employees table and Expenses table in the query window.
    b. Insert the *EmpID*, *FirstName*, and *LastName* fields from the Employees table.
    c. Insert the *ProjID*, *Amount*, and *DateSubmitted* from the Expenses table.

d. Click in the check box in the *Show* row field in the *EmpID* column to remove the check mark. (This hides the EmpID numbers in the query results.)

e. Extract those expenses submitted by employee number 1947.

f. Save the query and name it *ExpSubmittedBy1947Query*.

g. Print and then close the query.

Assessment

4 EDIT THE EMPLOYEES TABLE

1. With **AL1-C4-Hudson.accdb** open, open the Employees table.
2. Display the table in Design view, click in the *ZIP* field row in the *Data Type* column, and then click in the *Input Mask* property box in the *Field Properties* section.
3. Use the Input Mask Wizard to create a nine-digit zip code input mask.
4. Save the table and then switch to Datasheet view.
5. Delete the records for employee number 3035 (Alia Shandra), employee number 3129 (Gloria Cushman), and employee number 4884 (Simon Banister).
6. Insert the following new records:

EmpID	2286	EmpID	2970
Status	Full-time	Status	Full-time
Title	Associate	Title	Associate
FirstName	Erica	FirstName	Daniel
LastName	Bonari	LastName	Ortiz
Address	4850 55th Street	Address	12021 Cedar Lane
City	(Pueblo automatically inserted)	City	(Pueblo automatically inserted)
State	(CO automatically inserted)	State	(CO automatically inserted)
ZIP	81005-5002	ZIP	81011-1255
Telephone	(719) 555-1293	Telephone	(719) 555-0790

7. Adjust the width of the *ZIP* column. (Only the two new records will contain the nine-digit zip code.)
8. Save the Employees table.
9. Display the table in Print Preview, change to landscape orientation, and then change the left and right margins to 0.5 inch. Print and then close the table.
10. Close **AL1-C4-Hudson.accdb**.

Visual Benchmark Demonstrate Your Proficiency

DESIGN AND FORMAT A QUERY

1. Open **AL1-C4-AlpineServices.accdb** from the AL1C4 folder on your storage medium and enable the contents.
2. Design and run the query that displays in Figure 4.16. (Make sure you include the calculated field to determine the order totals and the *Total* row.)
3. Change the font for the data in the query to 12-point Candara, add an alternating row color, and adjust column widths so your query displays in a manner similar to the query in Figure 4.16.
4. Save, print the query in landscape orientation, and then close the query.
5. Close **AL1-C4-AlpineServices.accdb**.

Figure 4.16 Visual Benchmark

OrderDate ▾	SupplierName ▾	ProductID ▾	UnitsOrdered ▾	UnitPrice ▾	Total ▾
5/4/2015	Manning, Inc.	101-S2R	15	$129.95	1949.25
5/4/2015	Manning, Inc.	101-S3B	15	$119.95	1799.25
5/4/2015	Freedom Corporation	209-L	25	$6.95	173.75
5/4/2015	Freedom Corporation	209-XL	25	$7.20	180
5/4/2015	Freedom Corporation	209-XXL	20	$7.29	145.8
5/4/2015	Freedom Corporation	210-M	15	$6.49	97.35
5/4/2015	Freedom Corporation	210-L	25	$6.49	162.25
5/18/2015	Sound Supplies	299-M2	10	$88.79	887.9
5/18/2015	Sound Supplies	299-M3	10	$88.79	887.9
5/18/2015	Sound Supplies	299-M5	10	$88.79	887.9
5/18/2015	Sound Supplies	299-W1	8	$75.29	602.32
5/18/2015	Sound Supplies	299-W3	10	$75.29	752.9
5/18/2015	Sound Supplies	299-W4	10	$75.29	752.9
5/18/2015	Sound Supplies	299-W5	10	$75.29	752.9
5/18/2015	Emerald City Products	602-XR	5	$429.00	2145
Total				**$1,280.85**	**12177.37**

Case Study   Apply Your Skills

Part 1

You work for Blue Ridge Enterprises and your supervisor has asked you to create a database with information about representatives and clients. Create a new database named **AL1-C4-BlueRidge.accdb** and then create a Representatives table with the following fields:

- Create a field for the representative identification number, change the data type to Short Text, and limit the field size to 3 characters. (This is the primary key field.)
- Create a field for the representative's first name and limit the field size to 20 characters.
- Create a field for the representative's last name and limit the field size to 20 characters.
- Create a field for the representative's telephone number and use the Input Mask Wizard.
- Create a field for the insurance plan and use the Lookup Wizard and include four options: *Platinum*, *Premium*, *Standard*, and *None*.
- Create a field for the yearly bonus amount, type a validation rule that states the bonus must be less than $10,001, and include an error message. (You determine the message.)

In Datasheet view, enter six records in the table. (You determine the data to enter.) When entering the data, make sure that at least two representatives will receive a yearly bonus over $5,000 and that at least two representatives are signed up for the *Platinum* insurance plan. Insert a *Total* row that sums the yearly bonus amounts. Change the font for the data in the table to Cambria, change the font size to 10 points, and apply a light green alternating row color. Center the data in the representative identification column. Adjust the column widths and then save the Representatives table. Print the table in landscape orientation and then close the table.

Part 2

With **AL1-C4-BlueRidge.accdb** open, create a second table named Clients (containing information on companies doing business with Blue Ridge Enterprises) with the following fields:

- Create a field for the client identification number and limit the field size to 2 characters. (This is the primary key field.)
- Create a field for the representative identification number (using the same field name you used in Part 1 in the Representatives table) and limit the field size to 3 characters.
- Create fields for the company name, address, city, state (or province), and zip (or postal code). Insert the city you live in as the default value for the city field and insert the two-letter state or province abbreviation where you live as the default value for the state or province field.
- Create a field for the client's telephone number and use the Input Mask.
- Create a field for the client's type of business and insert the word *Wholesaler* as the default value.

In Datasheet view, enter at least eight companies. (You determine the data to enter.) Make sure you use the representative identification numbers in the Clients table that match numbers in the Representatives table. Identify at least one company as a *Retailer*, rather than a *Wholesaler*, and make at least one representative represent two or more companies. Change the font for the data in the table to Cambria, change the font size to 10 points, and apply a light green alternating row color (the same color you chose in Part 1). Center the data in the client identification column, the representative identification column, and the state (or province) column. Adjust the column widths and then save the Clients table. Print the table in landscape orientation and then close the table.

Part 3

Create a one-to-many relationship with the representative identification number in the Representatives table as the "one" and the representative identification number in the Clients table as the "many." Save the relationship, print the relationships report, and then close the report without saving it.

Part 4

Your supervisor has asked you for specific information about representatives and clients. To provide answers to your supervisor, create and print the following queries:

- Create a query that extracts records of representatives earning a yearly bonus over $5,000. (You determine the fields to insert in the query window.) Save, print, and then close the query.
- Create a query that extracts records of representatives signed up for the Platinum insurance plan. (You determine the fields to insert in the query window.) Save, print, and then close the query.
- Create a query that extracts records of wholesale clients. (You determine the fields to insert in the query window.) Save, print, and then close the query.
- Create a query that extracts records of companies represented by a specific representative. (Use a representative identification number you entered in Part 2 that represents two or more companies.) Save, print, and then close the query.

ACCESS MICROSOFT® Performance Assessment

Access
AL1U1

Note: The Student Resources CD does not include an Access Level 1, Unit 1 subfolder of files because no data files are required for the Unit 1 assessments. You will create all of the files yourself. Before beginning the assessments, create a folder for the new files and name it AL1U1.

Assessing Proficiency ▪▪▪▪▪▪▪▪▪▪▪▪▪▪▪

In this unit, you have learned to design, create, and modify tables and to create one-to-many relationships and one-to-one relationships between tables. You have also learned how to perform queries on data in tables.

Assessment 1 Create Tables in a Cornerstone Catering Database

1. Use Access to create tables for Cornerstone Catering. Name the database **AL1-U1-Cornerstone**. Create a table named *Employees* that includes the following fields. If no data type is specified for a field, use the Short Text data type. You determine the field size and specify the same field size for a field that is contained in different tables. For example, if you specify a field size of 2 characters for the *EmployeeID* field in the Employees table, specify a field size of 2 characters for the *EmployeeID* field in the Events table. Provide a description for each field.

   EmployeeID (primary key)
   FirstName
   LastName
   CellPhone (Use the Input Mask Wizard for this field.)

2. After creating the table, switch to Datasheet view and then enter the following data in the appropriate fields:

EmployeeID	10		*EmployeeID*	14
FirstName	Erin		*FirstName*	Mikio
LastName	Jergens		*LastName*	Ogami
CellPhone	(505) 555-3193		*CellPhone*	(505) 555-1087
EmployeeID	19		*EmployeeID*	21
FirstName	Martin		*FirstName*	Isabelle
LastName	Vaughn		*LastName*	Baptista
CellPhone	(505) 555-4461		*CellPhone*	(505) 555-4425

EmployeeID	24		EmployeeID	26
FirstName	Shawn		FirstName	Madison
LastName	Kettering		LastName	Harris
CellPhone	(505) 555-3885		CellPhone	(505) 555-2256

EmployeeID	28		EmployeeID	30
FirstName	Victoria		FirstName	Isaac
LastName	Lamesa		LastName	Hobart
CellPhone	(505) 555-6650		CellPhone	(505) 555-7430

EmployeeID	32		EmployeeID	35
FirstName	Lester		FirstName	Manuela
LastName	Franklin		LastName	Harte
CellPhone	(505) 555-0440		CellPhone	(505) 555-1221

3. Change the font for data in the table to Cambria, change the font size to 10 points, and apply a light blue alternating row color. Center-align the data in the *EmployeeID* column.
4. Adjust the column widths.
5. Save, print, and then close the Employees table.
6. Create a table named *Plans* that includes the following fields:

   PlanCode (primary key)
   Plan

7. After creating the table, switch to Datasheet view and then enter the following data in the appropriate fields:

PlanCode	A		PlanCode	B
Plan	Sandwich Buffet		Plan	Cold Luncheon Buffet

PlanCode	C		PlanCode	D
Plan:	Hot Luncheon Buffet		Plan	Combination Dinner

PlanCode	E		PlanCode	F
Plan:	Vegetarian Luncheon Buffet		Plan:	Vegetarian Dinner Buffet

PlanCode	G		PlanCode	H
Plan:	Seafood Luncheon Buffet		Plan	Seafood Dinner Buffet

8. Change the font for data in the table to Cambria, change the font size to 10 points, and apply a light blue alternating row color. Center-align the data in the *PlanCode* column.
9. Adjust the column widths.
10. Save, print, and then close the Plans table.
11. Create a table named *Prices* that includes the following fields:

    PriceCode (primary key)
    PricePerPerson (Identify as the Currency data type.)

12. After creating the table, switch to Datasheet view and then enter the following data in the appropriate fields:

PriceCode	1	PriceCode	2
PricePerPerson	$11.50	PricePerPerson	$12.75

PriceCode	3	PriceCode	4
PricePerPerson	$14.50	PricePerPerson	$16.00

PriceCode	5	PriceCode	6
PricePerPerson	$18.50	PricePerPerson	$21.95

13. Change the font for data in the table to Cambria, change the font size to 10 points, and apply a light blue alternating row color. Center-align the data in both columns.
14. Adjust the column widths.
15. Save, print, and then close the Prices table.
16. Create a table named *Clients* that includes the following fields:

    ClientID (primary key)
    ClientName
    StreetAddress
    City
    State (Insert *NM* as the default value.)
    ZIP
    Telephone (Use the Input Mask Wizard for this field.)

17. After creating the table, switch to Datasheet view and then enter the following data in the appropriate fields:

ClientID	104	ClientID	155
ClientName	Sarco Corporation	ClientName	Creative Concepts
StreetAddress	340 Cordova Road	StreetAddress	1026 Market Street
City	Santa Fe	City	Los Alamos
State	NM	State	NM
ZIP	87510	ZIP	87547
Telephone	(505) 555-3880	Telephone	(505) 555-1200

ClientID	218	ClientID	286
ClientName	Allenmore Systems	ClientName	Sol Enterprises
StreetAddress	7866 Second Street	StreetAddress	120 Cerrillos Road
City	Espanola	City	Santa Fe
State	NM	State	NM
ZIP	87535	ZIP	87560
Telephone	(505) 555-3455	Telephone	(505) 555-7700

ClientID	295	ClientID	300
ClientName	Benson Productions	ClientName	Old Town Corporation
StreetAddress	555 Junction Road	StreetAddress	1035 East Adams Way
City	Santa Fe	City	Santa Fe
State	NM	State	NM
ZIP	87558	ZIP	87561
Telephone	(505) 555-8866	Telephone	(505) 555-2125

ClientID	305	ClientID	350
ClientName	Cromwell Company	ClientName	GH Manufacturing
StreetAddress	752 Rialto Way	StreetAddress	9550 Stone Road
City	Santa Fe	City	Los Alamos
State	NM	State	NM
ZIP	87512	ZIP	87547
Telephone	(505) 555-7500	Telephone	(505) 555-3388

18. Change the font for data in the table to Cambria, change the font size to 10 points, and apply a light blue alternating row color. Center-align the data in the *ClientID* column.
19. Adjust the column widths.
20. Save the table and then print it in landscape orientation.
21. Close the Clients table.
22. Create a table named *Events* that includes the following fields:

> *EventID* (primary key) (Identify as the AutoNumber data type.)
> *ClientID*
> *EmployeeID*
> *DateOfEvent* (Identify as the Date/Time data type.)
> *PlanCode*
> *PriceCode*
> *NumberOfPeople* (Identify as the Number data type.)

23. After creating the table, switch to Datasheet view and then enter the following data in the appropriate fields:

EventID	(AutoNumber)	EventID	(AutoNumber)
ClientID	218	ClientID	104
EmployeeID	14	EmployeeID	19
DateOfEvent	7/11/2015	DateOfEvent	7/12/2015
PlanCode	B	PlanCode	D
PriceCode	3	PriceCode	5
NumberOfPeople	250	NumberOfPeople	120

EventID	(AutoNumber)	EventID	(AutoNumber)
ClientID	155	ClientID	286
EmployeeID	24	EmployeeID	10
DateOfEvent	7/17/2015	DateOfEvent	7/18/2015
PlanCode	A	PlanCode	C
PriceCode	1	PriceCode	4
NumberOfPeople	300	NumberOfPeople	75

EventID	(AutoNumber)	EventID	(AutoNumber)
ClientID	218	ClientID	104
EmployeeID	14	EmployeeID	10
DateOfEvent	7/19/2015	DateOfEvent	7/22/2015
PlanCode	C	PlanCode	B
PriceCode	4	PriceCode	3
NumberOfPeople	50	NumberOfPeople	30

EventID	(AutoNumber)	EventID	(AutoNumber)
ClientID	305	ClientID	295
EmployeeID	30	EmployeeID	35
DateOfEvent	7/24/2015	DateOfEvent	7/25/2015
PlanCode	H	PlanCode	E
PriceCode	6	PriceCode	4
NumberOfPeople	150	NumberOfPeople	75
EventID	(AutoNumber)	EventID	(AutoNumber)
ClientID	300	ClientID	350
EmployeeID	32	EmployeeID	28
DateOfEvent	7/26/2015	DateOfEvent	7/30/2015
PlanCode	B	PlanCode	D
PriceCode	3	PriceCode	6
NumberOfPeople	200	NumberOfPeople	100

24. Change the font for data in the table to Cambria, change the font size to 10 points, and apply a light blue alternating row color. Center-align the data in all of the columns except the *DateOfEvent* column.
25. Adjust the column widths.
26. Save the table and then print it in landscape orientation.
27. Close the Events table.

Assessment 2 Create Relationships between Tables

1. With **AL1-U1-Cornerstone.accdb** open, create the following one-to-many relationships and enforce referential integrity:
   a. *ClientID* in the Clients table is the "one" and *ClientID* in the Events table is the "many."
   b. *EmployeeID* in the Employees table is the "one" and *EmployeeID* in the Events table is the "many."
   c. *PlanCode* in the Plans table is the "one" and *PlanCode* in the Events table is the "many."
   d. *PriceCode* in the Prices table is the "one" and *PriceCode* in the Events table is the "many."
2. Save and then print the relationships in landscape orientation.
3. Close the relationship report without saving it and then close the Relationships window.

Assessment 3 Modify Tables

1. With **AL1-U1-Cornerstone.accdb** open, open the Plans table in Datasheet view and then add the following record at the end of the table:

   PlanCode I
   Plan   Hawaiian Luau Dinner Buffet

2. Adjust the column widths.
3. Save, print, and then close the Plans table.
4. Open the Events table in Datasheet view and then add the following record at the end of the table:

   EventID   (AutoNumber)   PlanCode   I
   ClientID   104   PriceCode   5
   EmployeeID 21   NumberOfPeople 125
   Date   7/31/2015

5. Save, print (in landscape orientation), and then close the Events table.

Assessment 4 Design Queries

1. With **AL1-U1-Cornerstone.accdb** open, create a query to extract records from the Events table with the following specifications:
   a. Include the fields *ClientID*, *DateOfEvent*, and *PlanCode*.
   b. Extract those records with a PlanCode of C. (You will need to type "C" in the *Criteria* row.)
   c. Run the query.
   d. Save the query and name it *PlanCodeCQuery*.
   e. Print and then close the query.
2. Extract records from the Clients table with the following specifications:
   a. Include the fields *ClientName*, *City*, and *Telephone*.
   b. Extract those records with a city of Santa Fe.
   c. Run the query.
   d. Save the query and name it *SantaFeClientsQuery*.
   e. Print and then close the query.
3. Extract information from two tables with the following specifications:
   a. From the Clients table, include the fields *ClientName* and *Telephone*.
   b. From the Events table, include the fields *DateOfEvent*, *PlanCode*, and *NumberOfPeople*.
   c. Extract those records with dates between July 1, 2015, and July 15, 2015.
   d. Run the query.
   e. Save the query and name it *July1-15EventsQuery*.
   f. Print and then close the query.

Assessment 5 Design a Query with a Calculated Field Entry

1. With **AL1-U1-Cornerstone.accdb** open, create a query in Design view with the Events table and Prices table and insert the following fields in the specified locations:
   a. Insert *EventID* from the Events table to the first *Field* row field.
   b. Insert *DateOfEvent* from the Events table to the second *Field* row field.
   c. Insert *NumberOfPeople* from the Events table to the third *Field* row field.
   d. Insert *PricePerPerson* from the Prices table to the fourth *Field* row field.
2. Insert the following calculated field entry in the fifth *Field* row field: *Amount: [NumberOfPeople]*[PricePerPerson]*.

3. Run the query.
4. Save the query and name it *EventAmountsQuery*.
5. Print and then close the query.

Assessment 6 Design a Query with Aggregate Functions

1. With **AL1-U1-Cornerstone.accdb** open, create a query in Design view using EventAmountsQuery with the following specifications:
   a. Click the CREATE tab and then click the Query Design button.
   b. At the Show Tables dialog box, click the Queries tab.
   c. Double-click *EventAmountsQuery* in the list box and then click the Close button.
   d. Insert the *Amount* field in the first, second, third, and fourth *Field* row field.
   e. Click the Totals button in the Show/Hide group.
   f. Insert *Sum* in the first *Total* row field.
   g. Insert *Avg* in the second *Total* row field.
   h. Insert *Min* in the third *Total* row field.
   i. Insert *Max* in the fourth *Total* row field.
2. Run the query.
3. Automatically adjust the column widths.
4. Save the query and name it *AmountTotalsQuery*.
5. Print and then close the query.

Assessment 7 Design a Query Using Fields from Tables and a Query

1. With **AL1-U1-Cornerstone.accdb** open, create a query in Design view using the Employees table, Clients table, Events table, and EventAmountsQuery with the following specifications:
   a. Click the CREATE tab and then click the Query Design button.
   b. At the Show Tables dialog box, double-click *Employees*.
   c. Double-click *Clients*.
   d. Double-click *Events*.
   e. Click the Queries tab, double-click *EventAmountsQuery* in the list box, and then click the Close button.
   f. Insert the *LastName* field from the *Employees* field list box to the first *Field* row field.
   g. Insert the *ClientName* field from the *Clients* field list box to the second *Field* row field.
   h. Insert the *Amount* field from *EventAmountsQuery* field list box to the third *Field* row field.
   i. Insert the *DateOfEvent* field from the *Events* field list box to the fourth *Field* row field.
2. Run the query.
3. Save the query and name it *EmployeeEventsQuery*.
4. Close the query.
5. Using the Crosstab Query Wizard, create a query that summarizes the total event amounts by employee by client using the following specifications:
   a. At the first Crosstab Query Wizard dialog box, click the *Queries* option in the *View* section and then click *Query: EmployeeEventsQuery* in the list box.
   b. At the second Crosstab Query Wizard dialog box, click *LastName* in the *Available Fields* list box and then click the One Field button.

c. At the third Crosstab Query Wizard dialog box, make sure *ClientName* is selected in the list box.

d. At the fourth Crosstab Query Wizard dialog box, make sure *Amount* is selected in the *Fields* list box and then click *Sum* in the *Functions* list box.

e. At the fifth Crosstab Query Wizard dialog box, type **AmountsByEmployeeByClientQuery** in the *What do you want to name your query?* text box.

6. Automatically adjust the column widths.

7. Print the query in landscape orientation and then close the query.

Assessment 8 Use the Find Duplicates Query Wizard

1. With **AL1-U1-Cornerstone.accdb** open, use the Find Duplicates Query Wizard to find employees who are responsible for at least two events with the following specifications:

a. At the first wizard dialog box, double-click *Table: Events* in the list box.

b. At the second wizard dialog box, click *EmployeeID* in the *Available fields* list box and then click the One Field button.

c. At the third wizard dialog box, move the *DateOfEvent* field and the *NumberOfPeople* field from the *Available fields* list box to the *Additional query fields* list box.

d. At the fourth wizard dialog box, name the query *DuplicateEventsQuery*.

2. Print and then close the query.

Assessment 9 Use the Find Unmatched Query Wizard

1. With **AL1-U1-Cornerstone.accdb** open, use the Find Unmatched Query Wizard to find employees who do not have upcoming events scheduled with the following specifications:

a. At the first wizard dialog box, click *Table: Employees* in the list box.

b. At the second wizard dialog box, click *Table: Events* in the list box.

c. At the third wizard dialog box, make sure *EmployeeID* is selected in the *Fields in 'Employees'* list box and in the *Fields in 'Events'* list box.

d. At the fourth wizard dialog box, click the All Fields button to move all fields from the *Available fields* list box to the *Selected fields* list box.

e. At the fifth wizard dialog box, click the Finish button. (Let the wizard determine the query name: *Employees Without Matching Events*.)

2. Print and then close the *Employees Without Matching Events* query.

Writing Activities ▪■■■■■■■ ■■■■■■

The following activity gives you the opportunity to practice your writing skills along with demonstrating an understanding of some of the important Access features you have mastered in this unit. Use correct grammar, appropriate word choices, and clear sentence constructions.

Create a Payroll Table and Word Report

The manager of Cornerstone Catering has asked you to add information to the **AL1-U1-Cornerstone.accdb** database on employee payroll. You need to create another table that will contain information on payroll. The manager wants the table to include the following information (you determine the appropriate field name, data type, field size, and description):

Employee Number	10	*Employee Number*	14
Status	Full-time	*Status*	Part-time
Monthly Salary	$2,850	*Monthly Salary*	$1,500
Employee Number	19	*Employee Number*	21
Status	Part-time	*Status*	Full-time
Monthly Salary	$1,400	*Monthly Salary*	$2,500
Employee Number	24	*Employee Number*	26
Status	Part-time	*Status*	Part-time
Monthly Salary	$1,250	*Monthly Salary*	$1,000
Employee number	28	*Employee number*	30
Status	Full-time	*Status*	Part-time
Monthly salary	$2,500	*Monthly salary*	$3,000
Employee number	32	*Employee number*	35
Status	Full-time	*Status*	Full-time
Monthly salary	$2,300	*Monthly salary*	$2,750

Print and then close the payroll table. Open Word and then write a report to the manager detailing how you created the table. Include a title for the report, steps on how the table was created, and any other pertinent information. Save the completed report and name it **AL1-U1-Act01-TableRpt**. Print and then close **AL1-U1-Act01-TableRpt.docx** and then close Word.

Internet Research ■■■■■■■■■■■■■■■■■■■■■■■■

Vehicle Search

In this activity, you will search the Internet for information on different vehicles before doing actual test drives. Learning about a major product, such as a vehicle, can increase your chances of finding a good buy, potentially guide you away from making a poor purchase, and help speed up the process of narrowing the search to the type of vehicle that will meet your needs. Before you begin, list the top five criteria you would look for in a vehicle. For example, it must be a four-door vehicle, needs to be four-wheel drive, and so on.

Using key search words, find at least two websites that provide vehicle reviews. Use the search engines provided within the different review sites to find vehicles that fulfill the criteria you listed. Create a database in Access and create a table in that database that will contain the results from your vehicle search. Design the table to accommodate the types of data you need to record for each vehicle that meets your requirements. Include at least the make, model, year, price, description, and special problems in the table. Also include the ability to rate the vehicle as poor, fair, good, or excellent. You will decide on the rating of each vehicle depending on your findings. Print the table you created and then close the database.

MICROSOFT
ACCESS

Level 1

Unit 2 ■ Creating Forms and Reports

MICROSOFT®
ACCESS®

Creating Forms

CHAPTER
5

PERFORMANCE OBJECTIVES

Upon successful completion of Chapter 5, you will be able to:

- Create a form using the Form button
- Change views in a form
- Print and navigate in a form
- Add records to and delete records from a form
- Create a form with a related table
- Customize a form
- Create a split form and multiple items form
- Create a form using the Form Wizard

In this chapter, you will learn how to create forms from database tables, improving the data display and making data entry easier. Access offers several methods for presenting data on the screen for easier data entry. You will create a form using the Form button, create a split form and multiple items form, and use the Form Wizard to create a form. You will also learn how to customize control objects in a form and insert control objects and fields in a form. Model answers for this chapter's projects appear on the following pages.

Access
AL1C5

Note: Before beginning the projects, copy to your storage medium the AL1C5 subfolder from the AL1 folder on the CD that accompanies this textbook and make AL1C5 the active folder.

183

Project 1 Create Forms with the Form Button

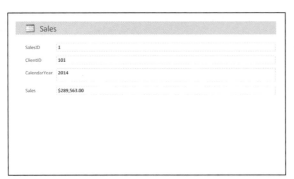

Project 1a, Dearborn Clients Form

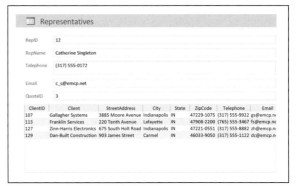

Project 1c, Dearborn Representatives Form

Project 1g, Dearborn Sales Form

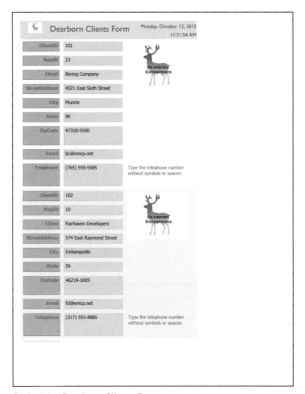

Project 1g, Dearborn Clients Form

Project 2 Add Fields, Create a Split Form and Multiple Items Form, and Use the Form Wizard

Project 2a, Skyline Inventory Form

Project 2b, Skyline Suppliers Form

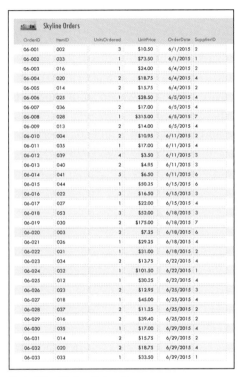

Project 2c, Skyline Orders Form

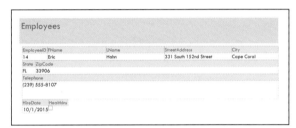

Project 2d, Skyline Employees Form, Carol Thompson

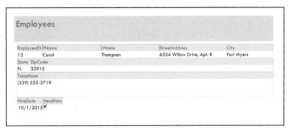

Project 2d, Skyline Employees Form, Eric Hahn

Project 2e, Skyline Upcoming Banquets Form

Project Create Forms with the Form Button   7 Parts

You will use the Form button to create forms with fields in the Clients, Representatives, and Sales tables. You will also add, delete, and print records and use buttons in the FORM LAYOUT TOOLS FORMAT tab to apply formatting to control objects in the forms.

Creating Forms ■■■■■■■■■■■ ■■■■■■■■■■■■■■■■■■

A form allows you to focus on a single record at a time.

Save a form before making changes or applying formatting to it.

Access offers a variety of options for presenting data in a clear and attractive format. For instance, you can view, add, or edit data in a table in Datasheet view. When you enter data in a table in Datasheet view, you will see multiple records at the same time. If a record contains several fields, you may not be able to view all of the fields within the record at the same time. If you create a form, however, all of the fields for a record are generally visible on the screen.

A *form* is an object you can use to enter and edit data in a table or query. It is a user-friendly interface for viewing, adding, editing, and deleting records. A form is also useful in helping to prevent incorrect data from being entered and it can be used to control access to specific data.

Several methods are available for creating forms. In this chapter, you will learn how to create forms using the Form, Split Form, and Multiple Items buttons as well as the Form Wizard.

Creating a Form with the Form Button

▼ Quick Steps

Create a Form with the Form Button
1. Click desired table.
2. Click CREATE tab.
3. Click Form button.

The simplest method for creating a form is to click a table in the Navigation pane, click the CREATE tab, and then click the Form button in the Forms groups. Figure 5.1 shows the form you will create in Project 1a with the Sales table in AL1-C5-Dearborn.accdb. Access creates the form using all fields in the table in a vertical layout and displays the form in Layout view with the FORM LAYOUT TOOLS DESIGN tab active.

Changing Views

Form

Form View

Layout View

When you click the Form button to create a form, the form displays in Layout view. This is one of three views for working with forms. Use the Form view to enter and manage records. Use the Layout view to view the data and modify the appearance and contents of the form. Use the Design view to view the structure of the form and modify the form. Change views with the View button in the Views group on the FORM LAYOUT TOOLS DESIGN tab or with buttons in the view area located at the right side of the Status bar.

You can open an existing form in Layout view. To do this, right-click the form name in the Navigation pane and then click *Layout View* at the shortcut menu.

Printing a Form

Print all of the records in a form by clicking the FILE tab, clicking the *Print* option, and then clicking the Quick Print button. If you want to print a specific record in a form, click the FILE tab, click the *Print* option, and then click the Print button.

Figure 5.1 Form Created from Data in the Sales Table

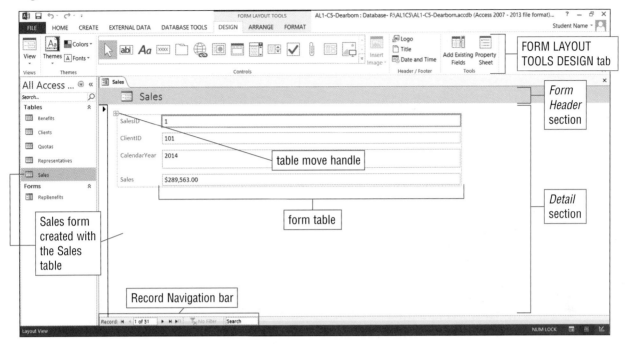

At the Print dialog box that displays, click the *Selected Record(s)* option and then click OK. You can also print a range of records by clicking the *Pages* option in the *Print Range* section of the Print dialog box and then entering the beginning record number in the *From* text box and the ending record number in the *To* text box.

Deleting a Form

If you no longer need a form in a database, delete the form. Delete a form by clicking the form name in the Navigation pane, clicking the Delete button in the Records group on the HOME tab, and then clicking the Yes button at the message asking if you want to permanently delete the form. Another method is to right-click the form name in the Navigation pane, click *Delete* at the shortcut menu, and then click Yes at the message. If you are deleting a form from your computer's hard drive, the message asking if you want to permanently delete the form will not display. This is because Access automatically sends the deleted form to the Recycle Bin, where it can be retrieved if necessary.

Navigating in a Form

When a form displays in Form view or Layout view, navigation buttons display along the bottom of the form in the Record Navigation bar, as identified in Figure 5.1. Use these navigation buttons to display the first, previous, next, or last record in the form or add a new record. Navigate to a specific record by clicking in the *Current Record* box, selecting the current number, typing the number of the record you want to view, and then pressing Enter. You can also navigate using the keyboard. Press the Page Down key to move forward or press the Page Up key to move back a single record. Press Ctrl + Home to display the first record or Press Ctrl + End to display the last record.

▼ **Quick Steps**

Print a Specific Record
1. Display form.
2. Click FILE tab.
3. Click *Print* option.
4. Click Print button.
5. Click *Selected Record(s)*.
6. Click OK.

◄◄	◄
First record	Previous record

►	►►
Next record	Last record

1. Display the Open dialog box with the AL1C5 folder on your storage medium the active folder.
2. Open **AL1-C5-Dearborn.accdb** and enable the contents.
3. Create a form with the Sales table by completing the following steps:
   a. Click the Sales table in the Tables group in the Navigation pane.
   b. Click the CREATE tab.
   c. Click the Form button in the Forms group.

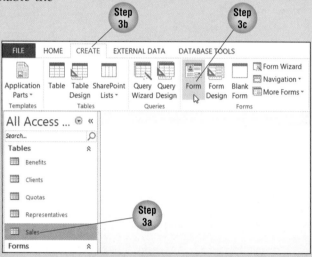

4. Switch to Form view by clicking the View button in the Views group on the FORM LAYOUT TOOLS DESIGN tab.
5. Navigate in the form by completing the following steps:
   a. Click the Next record button in the Record Navigation bar to display the next record.
   b. Click in the *Current Record* box, select any numbers that display, type 15, and then press Enter.
   c. Click the First record button in the Record Navigation bar to display the first record.

6. Save the form by completing the following steps:
   a. Click the Save button on the Quick Access toolbar.
   b. At the Save As dialog box, with *Sales* inserted in the *Form Name* text box, click OK.
7. Print the current record in the form by completing the following steps:
   a. Click the FILE tab and then click the *Print* option.
   b. Click the Print button.
   c. At the Print dialog box, click the *Selected Record(s)* option in the *Print Range* section and then click OK.

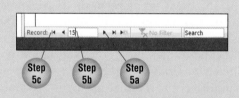

8. Close the Sales form.
9. Delete the RepBenefits form by right-clicking *RepBenefits* in the Navigation pane, clicking *Delete* at the shortcut menu, and then clicking Yes at the message asking if you want to permanently delete the form.

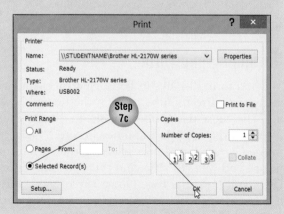

Adding and Deleting Records

Add a new record to the form by clicking the New (blank) record button (contains a right-pointing arrow and a yellow asterisk) that displays on the Record Navigation bar along the bottom of the form. You can also add a new record to a form by clicking the HOME tab and then clicking the New button in the Records group. To delete a record, display the record, click the HOME tab, click the Delete button arrow in the Records group, and then click *Delete Record* at the drop-down list. At the message telling you that the record will be deleted permanently, click Yes. Add records to or delete records from the table from which the form was created and the form will reflect the additions or deletions. Also, if you make additions or deletions to the form, the changes are reflected in the table on which the form was created.

Sorting Records

Sort data in a form by clicking in the field containing data on which you want to sort and then clicking the Ascending button or Descending button in the Sort & Filter group on the HOME tab. Click the Ascending button to sort text in alphabetic order from A to Z or numbers from lowest to highest or click the Descending button to sort text in alphabetic order from Z to A or numbers from highest to lowest.

▼ Quick Steps

Add a Record
Click New (blank)
record button on Record
Navigation bar.
OR
1. Click HOME tab.
2. Click New button.

Delete a Record
1. Click HOME tab.
2. Click Delete button
   arrow.
3. Click *Delete Record.*
4. Click Yes.

New   Delete
(blank)
record

Project 1b | **Adding and Deleting Records in a Form** | **Part 2 of 7**

1. Open the Sales table (not the form) and add a new record by completing the following steps:
   a. Click the New (blank) record button located in the Record Navigation bar.

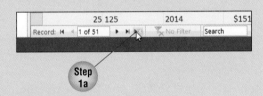

Step
1a

   b. At the new blank record, type the following information in the specified fields. (Move to the next field by pressing Tab or Enter; move to the previous field by pressing Shift + Tab.)

SalesID	(This is an AutoNumber field, so press Tab.)
ClientID	127
CalendarYear	2015
Sales	176420

2. Close the Sales table.
3. Open the Sales form.
4. Click the Last record button on the Record Navigation bar and notice that the new record you added to the table has been added to the form.

5. Delete the second record (sales ID 3) in the form by completing the following steps:
   a. Click the First record button in the Record Navigation bar.
   b. Click the Next record button in the Record Navigation bar.
   c. With Record 2 active, click the Delete button arrow in the Records group on the HOME tab and then click *Delete Record* at the drop-down list.

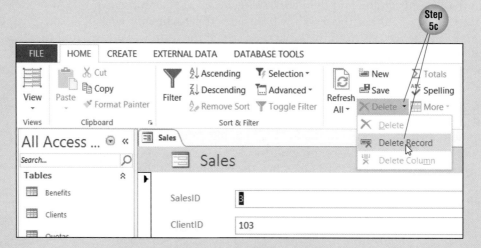

   d. At the message that displays telling you that you will not be able to undo the deletion, click the Yes button.
6. Click the New (blank) record button in the Record Navigation bar and then type the following information in the specified fields:
SalesID	(Press Tab.)
ClientID	103
CalendarYear	2014
Sales	110775
7. Sort the records in the form by completing the following steps:
   a. Click in the field containing the data *103* and then click the Ascending button in the Sort & Filter group on the HOME tab.
   b. Click in the field containing the data *$289,563.00* and then click the Descending button in the Sort & Filter group.
   c. Click in the field containing the data *36* and then click the Ascending button in the Sort & Filter group.
8. Close the Sales form.

Creating a Form with a Related Table

When you created the form with the Sales table, only the Sales table fields displayed in the form. If you create a form with a table that has a one-to-many relationship established, Access adds a datasheet to the form that is based on the related table.

For example, in Project 1c, you will create a form with the Representatives table, and since it is related to the Clients table by a one-to-many relationship, Access inserts a datasheet at the bottom of the form containing all of the records in the Clients table. Figure 5.2 displays the form you will create in Project 1c. Notice the datasheet that displays at the bottom of the form.

If you have created only a single one-to-many relationship, the datasheet for the related table displays in the form. If you have created multiple one-to-many relationships in a table, Access will not display any datasheets when you create a form with the table.

Figure 5.2 Representatives Form with Clients Datasheet

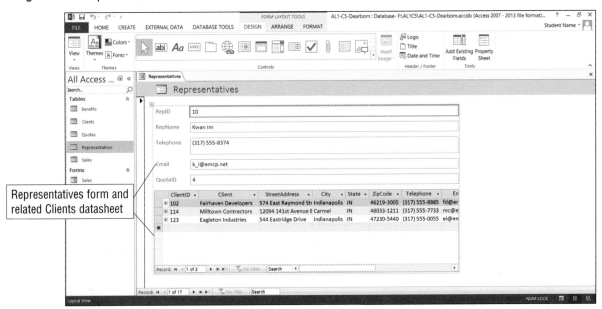

Representatives form and related Clients datasheet

1. With **AL1-C5-Dearborn.accdb** open, create a form with the Representatives table by completing the following steps:
   a. Click the Representatives table in the Navigation pane.
   b. Click the CREATE tab.
   c. Click the Form button in the Forms group.
2. Insert a new record in the Clients table for representative 12 (Catherine Singleton) by completing the following steps:
   a. Click twice on the Next record button in the Record Navigation bar at the bottom of the form window (not the Record Navigation bar in the Clients datasheet) to display the record for Catherine Singleton.
   b. Click in the cell immediately below *127* in the *ClientID* field in the Clients datasheet.

c. Type the following information in the specified fields:

ClientID	129
Client	**Dan-Built Construction**
StreetAddress	**903 James Street**
City	**Carmel**
State	**IN**
ZipCode	460339050
Telephone	3175551122
Email	dc@emcp.net

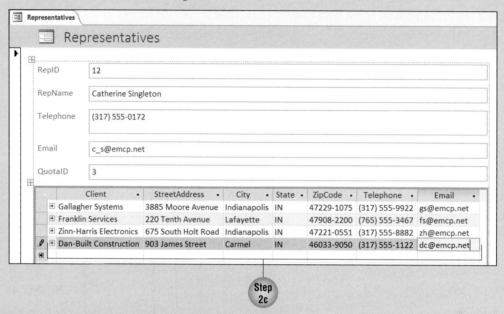

Step 2c

3. Click the Save button on the Quick Access toolbar and at the Save As dialog box with *Representatives* in the *Form Name* text box, click OK.
4. Print the current record in the form by completing the following steps:
   a. Click the FILE tab and then click the *Print* option.
   b. Click the Print button.
   c. At the Print dialog box, click the *Select Record(s)* option in the *Print Range* section and then click OK.
5. Close the Representatives form.

Customizing Forms ■■■■■■■■■■■■■■■■■■■■■■■■■■■■

A form is comprised of a series of ***control objects***, which are objects that display titles or descriptions, accept data, or perform actions. Control objects are contained in the *Form Header* section and *Detail* section of the form. (Refer to Figure 5.1 on page 187.) The control objects in the *Detail* section are contained within a form table.

You can customize control objects in the *Detail* section and data in the *Form Header* section with buttons on the FORM LAYOUT TOOLS ribbon with the DESIGN tab, ARRANGE tab, or FORMAT tab selected. When you open a form in Layout view, the FORM LAYOUT TOOLS DESIGN tab is active. This tab contains options for applying a theme, inserting controls, inserting header or footer data, and adding existing fields.

Applying Themes

Access provides a number of themes for formatting objects in a database. A **theme** is a set of formatting choices that include a color theme (a set of colors) and a font theme (a set of heading and body text fonts). To apply a theme, click the Themes button in the Themes group on the FORM LAYOUT TOOLS DESIGN tab. At the drop-down gallery that displays, click the desired theme. Position the mouse pointer over a theme and the **live preview feature** will display the form with the theme formatting applied. With the live preview feature, you can see how the theme formatting affects your form before you make your final choice. When you apply a theme, any new objects you create in the database will be formatted with the theme.

You can further customize the formatting of a form with the Colors button and the Fonts button in the Themes group on the FORM LAYOUT TOOLS DESIGN tab. If you want to customize the theme colors, click the Colors button in the Themes group and then click the desired option at the drop-down list. Change the theme fonts by clicking the Themes button and then clicking the desired option at the drop-down list.

Themes

Themes available in Access are the same as the themes available in Word, Excel, and PowerPoint.

Colors   Font

Inserting Data in the Form Header

Use buttons in the Header/Footer group on the FORM LAYOUT TOOLS DESIGN tab to insert a logo, form title, or date and time. Click the Logo button and the Insert Picture dialog box displays. Browse to the folder containing the desired image and then double-click the image file. Click the Title button and the current title is selected. Type the new title and then press the Enter key. Click the Date and Time button in the Header/Footer group and the Date and Time dialog box displays. At this dialog box, choose the desired date and time format and then click OK. The date and time are inserted at the right side of the *Form Header* section.

You can resize and move control objects in the *Form Header* section. To resize an object, click the object to select it and then drag a left or right border to increase or decrease the width. To increase or decrease the height of the object, as well as the *Form Header* section, drag a top or bottom border. To move a selected object in the *Form Header* section, position the mouse pointer over the selected object until the pointer displays with a four-headed arrow attached. Hold down the left mouse button, drag the object to the desired position, and then release the mouse button.

Logo

Title

Date and Time

Modifying a Control Object

When Access creates a form from a table, the first column in the form contains the label control objects and displays the field names from the table. The second column contains the text box control objects that display the field values you entered in the table. The width of either column can be resized. To do this, click in any control object in the desired column, position the mouse pointer on the right or left border of the selected control object until the pointer displays as a black left-and-right-pointing arrow. Hold down the left mouse button, drag left or right to change the width of the column, and then release the mouse button. Complete similar steps to change the height of the row containing the selected control object. As you drag a border, a line and character count displays at the left side of the Status bar. Use the line and character count numbers to move the border to a precise location.

To delete a control object from the form, click the desired object and then press the Delete key. You can also right-click the object and then click *Delete* at the shortcut menu. If you want to delete a form row, right-click an object in the row you want to delete and then click *Delete Row* at the shortcut menu. To delete a column, right-click in one of the objects in the column you want to delete and then click *Delete Column* at the shortcut menu. In addition to the label and text box control objects, the sizes and positions of objects in the *Form Header* section, such as the logo and title, can be modified.

Inserting a Control

Select

Text Box

Each cell can contain only one control object.

The Controls group on the FORM LAYOUT TOOLS DESIGN tab contains a number of control objects you can insert in a form. By default, the Select button is active. With this button active, use the mouse pointer to select control objects. You can insert a new label control and text box control object in your form by clicking the Text Box button in the Controls group and then clicking in the desired position in the form. Click in the label control object, select the default text, and then type the label text. You can enter text in a label control object in Layout view but you cannot enter data in a text box control object. In Form view, you can enter data in a text box control object but you cannot edit text in a label control object. The Controls group contains a number of additional buttons for inserting control objects in a form, such as a hyperlink, combo box, or image.

Project 1d   Creating a Form and Customizing the Design of a Form   Part 4 of 7

1. With **AL1-C5-Dearborn.accdb** open, create a form with the Clients table and delete the datasheet by completing the following steps:
   a. Click the Clients table in the Navigation pane.
   b. Click the CREATE tab.
   c. Click the Form button in the Forms group.
   d. Click in the SalesID field in the datasheet that displays below the form.
   e. Click the table move handle that displays in the upper left corner of the datasheet (see image at right).
   f. Press the Delete key.

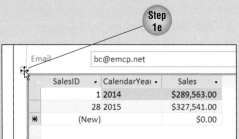

2. Apply a theme to the form by clicking the Themes button in the Themes group on the FORM LAYOUT TOOLS DESIGN tab and then clicking *Facet* at the drop-down gallery (first row, second column).

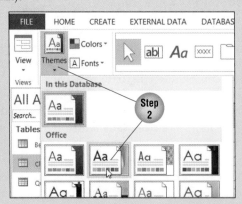

3. Change the theme fonts by clicking the Fonts button in the Themes group and then clicking *Gill Sans MT* at the drop-down gallery. (You will need to scroll down the list to display *Gill Sans MT*.)

4. Change the theme colors by clicking the Colors button in the Themes group and then clicking *Orange* at the drop-down gallery.

5. Insert a logo image in the *Form Header* section by completing the following steps:

   a. Right-click the logo object that displays in the *Form Header* section (located to the left of the title *Clients*) and then click *Delete* at the shortcut menu.

   b. Click the Logo button in the Header/Footer group.

   c. At the Insert Picture dialog box, navigate to the AL1C5 folder on your storage medium and then double-click the file named ***DearbornLogo.jpg***.

6. Change the title by completing the following steps:

   a. Click the Title button in the Header/Footer group. (This selects *Clients* in the *Form Header* section.)

   b. Type **Dearborn Clients Form** and then press Enter.

7. Insert the date and time in the *Form Header* section by completing the following steps:

   a. Click the Date and Time button in the Header/Footer group.

   b. At the Date and Time dialog box, click OK.

8. Size the control object containing the title by completing the following steps:

   a. Click in any field outside the title and then click the title to select the header control object.

   b. Position the mouse pointer on the right border of the selected object until the pointer displays as a black left-and-right-pointing arrow.

   c. Hold down the left mouse button, drag to the left until the right border is immediately right of the title, and then release the mouse button.

Step 3

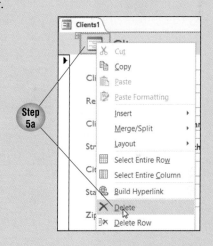

Step 5a

Step 6b

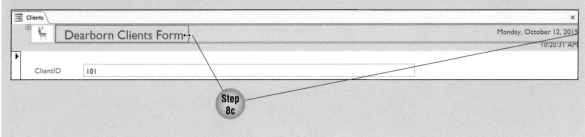

Step 8c

9. Size and move the control objects containing the date and time by completing the following steps:
   a. Click the date to select the control object.
   b. Hold down the Shift key, click the time, and then release the Shift key. (Both control objects should be selected.)
   c. Position the mouse pointer on the left border of the selected objects until the pointer displays as a black left-and-right-pointing arrow.
   d. Hold down the left mouse button, drag to the right until the border displays immediately left of the date, and then release the mouse button.
   e. Position the mouse pointer in the selected objects until the pointer displays with a four-headed arrow attached.
   f. Hold down the left mouse button and then drag the outline of the date and time objects to the left until the outline displays near the title.

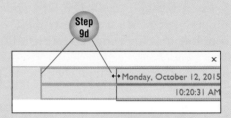

10. Decrease the size of the second column of control objects in the *Detail* section by completing the following steps:
    a. Click in the text box control object containing the client number *101*. (This selects and inserts an orange border around the object.)
    b. Position the mouse pointer on the right border of the selected object until the pointer displays as a black left-and-right-pointing arrow.
    c. Hold down the left mouse button, drag to the left until *Lines: 1 Characters: 30* displays at the left side of the Status bar, and then release the mouse button.

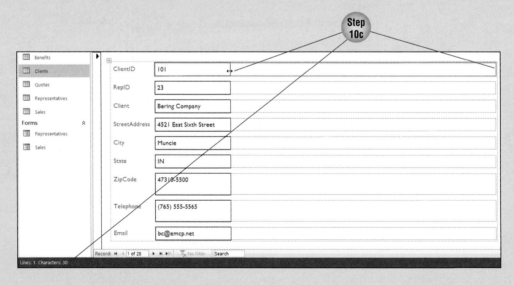

11. Insert a label control object by completing the following steps:
    a. Click the Label button in the Controls group.

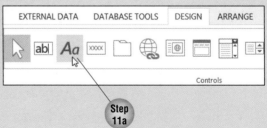

b. Click immediately right of the text box containing the telephone number *(765) 555-5565.* (This inserts the label to the right of the *Telephone* text box.)

c. With the insertion point positioned inside the label, type **Type the telephone number without symbols or spaces** and then press the Enter key.

12. Change the size of the new label control object by completing the following steps:

a. Position the arrow pointer on the right border of the new label control object until the pointer displays as a black left-and-right-pointing arrow.

b. Hold down the left mouse button, drag the border to the right until *Lines: 6 Characters: 32* displays at the left side of the Status bar, and then release the mouse button. The text line in the label should break after the word *number*.

c. Decrease the height of the new label control object by dragging the bottom border up so it is positioned just below the second line of text.

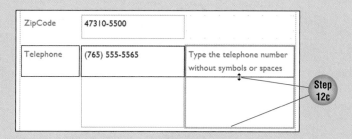

13. Click the Save button on the Quick Access toolbar. At the Save As dialog box with *Clients* in the *Form Name* text box, click OK.

Moving a Form Table

The control objects in the *Detail* section in a form in Layout view are contained within the form table. Click in a control object and the table is selected and the table move handle is visible. The table move handle is a small square with a four-headed arrow inside that displays in the upper left corner of the table. (Refer to Figure 5.1 on page 187.) Move the table and all of the control objects within the table by dragging the table move handle using the mouse. When you position the mouse pointer on the table move handle and then hold down the left mouse button, all of the control objects are selected. You can also click the table move handle to select the control objects.

You can move a control object by dragging it to the desired location.

Arranging Objects

With options on the FORM LAYOUT TOOLS ARRANGE tab, you can select, insert, delete, arrange, merge, and split cells. When you inserted a label control object to the right of the *Telephone* text box control in Project 1d, empty cells were inserted in the form above and below the new label control object. Select a control object or cell by clicking in the desired object or cell. Select adjacent objects or cells by holding down the Shift key while clicking in the desired objects or cells. To select nonadjacent objects or cells, hold down the Ctrl key while clicking in the desired objects or cells.

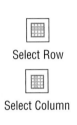

Select Row

Select Column

Select a row of control objects and cells by clicking the Select Row button in the Rows & Columns group or by right-clicking in an object or cell and then clicking *Select Entire Row* at the shortcut menu. To select a column of control objects and cells, click the Select Column button in the Rows & Columns group or right-click an object or cell and then click *Select Entire Column* at the shortcut menu. You can also select a column by positioning the mouse pointer at the top of the column until the pointer displays as a small, black, down-pointing arrow and then clicking the left mouse button.

Insert
Above

Insert
Below

The Rows & Columns group contains buttons for inserting a row or column of blank cells. To insert a new row, select a cell or object in a row and then click the Insert Above button to insert a row of blank cells above the current row or click the Insert Below button to insert a row of blank cells below the current row. Complete similar steps to insert a new column of blank cells to the left or right of the current column.

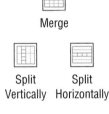

Merge

Split
Vertically

Split
Horizontally

Merge adjacent selected cells by clicking the Merge button in the Merge/Split group on the FORM LAYOUT TOOLS ARRANGE tab. Split a control object or cell by clicking the object or cell to make it active and then clicking the Split Vertically button or Split Horizontally button in the Merge/Split group. When you split a control object, an empty cell is created to the right of the control object or below the control object.

Control
Margins

Control
Padding

You can also move up or down a row of control objects. To do this, select the desired row and then click the Move Up button in the Move group to move the row above the current row or click the Move Down button to move the row below the current row. Use the Control Margins button in the Position group to increase or decrease margins within control objects. The Position group also contains a Control Padding button you can use to increase or decrease spacing between control objects.

The Table group is located at the left side of the FORM LAYOUT TOOLS ARRANGE tab. It contains buttons for applying gridlines to control objects and changing the layout of the objects to a stacked layout or columnar layout.

1. With the Clients form in **AL1-C5-Dearborn.accdb** open in Design view, select and merge cells by completing the following steps:
   a. Click to the right of the text box control object containing the text *101*. (This selects the empty cell.)
   b. Hold down the Shift key and then click to the right of the text box control containing the text *Muncie*. (This selects five adjacent cells.)
   c. Click the FORM LAYOUT TOOLS ARRANGE tab.
   d. Click the Merge button in the Merge/Split group.
2. With the cells merged, insert an image control object and then insert an image by completing the following steps:
   a. Click the FORM LAYOUT TOOLS DESIGN tab.
   b. Click the Image button in the Controls group.

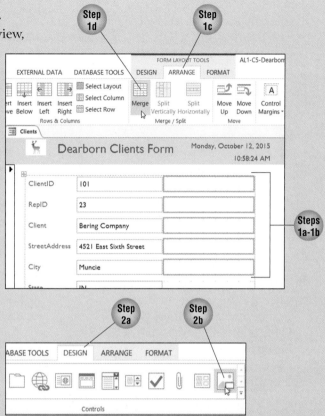

   c. Move the mouse pointer (which displays as a plus symbol next to an image icon) to the location of the merged cell until the cell displays with pink fill color and then click the left mouse button.

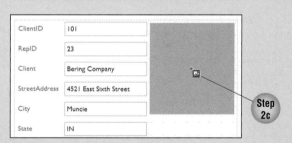

   d. At the Insert Picture dialog box, navigate to the AL1C5 folder on your storage medium and then double-click *Dearborn.jpg*.

3. Move down the telephone row by completing the following steps:
   a. Click the FORM LAYOUT TOOLS ARRANGE tab.
   b. Click in the control object containing the text *Telephone*.
   c. Click the Select Row button in the Rows & Columns group.
   d. Click the Move Down button in the Move group.
4. Decrease the margins within objects and cells, increase the spacing (padding) between objects and cells in the form, and apply gridlines by completing the following steps:
   a. If necessary, click the FORM LAYOUT TOOLS ARRANGE tab.
   b. Click the Select Layout button in the Rows & Columns group. (This selects all objects and cells in the form.)

   c. Click the Control Margins button in the Position group and then click *Narrow* at the drop-down list.

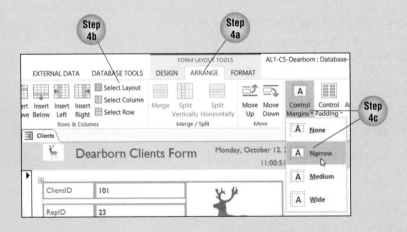

   d. Click the Control Padding button in the Position group and then click *Medium* at the drop-down list.

e. Click the Gridlines button in the Table group and then click *Top* at the drop-down list.

f. Click the Gridlines button in the Table group, point to *Color*, and then click the *Orange, Accent 2, Darker 50%* option (sixth column, bottom row in the *Theme Colors* section).

5. Move the form table by completing the following steps:

a. Position the mouse pointer on the table move handle (which displays as a small square with a four-headed arrow inside and is located in the upper left corner of the table).

b. Hold down the left mouse button, drag the form table up and to the left so it is positioned close to the top left border of the *Detail* section, and then release the mouse button.

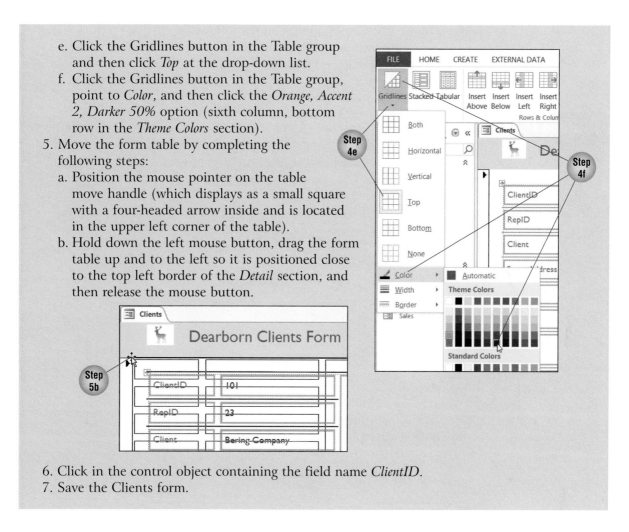

6. Click in the control object containing the field name *ClientID*.

7. Save the Clients form.

Formatting a Form

Click the FORM LAYOUT TOOLS FORMAT tab and buttons and options display for applying formatting to a form or specific objects in a form. If you want to apply formatting to a specific object, click the object in the form or click the Object button arrow in the Selection group and then click the desired object at the drop-down list. To format all objects in the form, click the Select All button in the Selection group. This selects all objects in the form, including objects in the *Form Header* section. If you want to select all of the objects in the *Detail* section (and not the *Form Header* section), click an object in the *Detail* section and then click the table move handle.

Object

Select All

With buttons in the Font, Number, Background, and Control Formatting groups, you can apply formatting to a control object or cell and to selected objects and cells in a form. Use buttons in the Font group to change the font, apply a different font size, apply text effects (such as bold and underline), and change the alignment of data in objects. If the form contains data with a Number or Currency data type, use buttons in the Number group to apply specific formatting

Background Image

to numbers. Insert a background image in the form using the Background Image button and apply formatting to objects or cells with buttons in the Control Formatting group. Depending on what is selected in the form, some of the buttons may not be active.

1. With the Clients form in **AL1-C5-Dearborn.accdb** open and in Layout view, change the font and font size of text in the form by completing the following steps:
   a. Click in any control object in the form.
   b. Select all control objects and cells in the form by clicking the table move handle that displays in the upper left corner of the *Detail* section.

Step 1b

   c. Click the FORM LAYOUT TOOLS FORMAT tab.
   d. Click the Font button arrow, scroll down the drop-down list, and then click *Tahoma*. (Fonts are alphabetized in the drop-down list.)
   e. Click the Font Size button arrow and then click *10* at the drop-down list.

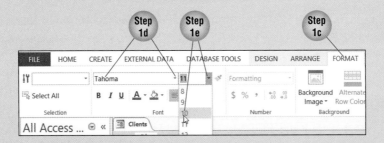

Step 1d   Step 1e   Step 1c

2. Apply formatting and change the alignment of the first column by completing the following steps:
   a. Click the control object containing the field name *ClientID*, hold down the Shift key, click the bottom control object containing the field name *Telephone*, and then release the Shift key.
   b. Click the Bold button in the Font group.
   c. Click the Shape Fill button in the Control Formatting group and then click the *Brown, Accent 3, Lighter 60%* color option (seventh column, third row in the *Theme Colors* section).
   d. Click the Shape Outline button in the Control Formatting group and then click the *Brown, Accent 3, Darker 50%* option (seventh column, bottom row in the *Theme Colors* section).
   e. Click the Align Right button in the Font group.

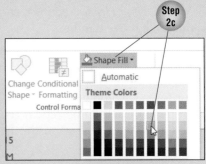

Step 2c

3. Apply shape fill to the second column by completing the following steps:
   a. Click the text box control object containing the text *101*.
   b. Position the mouse pointer at the top border of the selected object until the pointer displays as a small, black, down-pointing arrow and then click the left mouse button. (Make sure all of the objects in the second column are selected.)

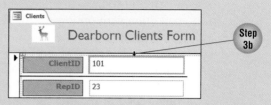

   c. Click the Shape Fill button in the Control Formatting group and then click the *Brown, Accent 3, Lighter 80%* color option (seventh column, second row in the *Theme Colors* section).
4. Remove the gridlines by completing the following steps:
   a. Click the FORM LAYOUT TOOLS ARRANGE tab.
   b. Click the Select Layout button in the Rows & Columns group.
   c. Click the Gridlines button in the Table group and then click *None* at the drop-down list.
5. Click the Save button on the Quick Access toolbar to save the Clients form.
6. Insert a background image by completing the following steps:
   a. Click the FORM LAYOUT TOOLS FORMAT tab.
   b. Click the Background Image button in the Background group and then click *Browse* at the drop-down list.
   c. Navigate to the AL1C5 folder on your storage medium and then double-click **Mountain.jpg**.
   d. View the form and background image in Print Preview. (To display Print Preview, click the FILE tab, click the *Print* option, and then click the Print Preview button.)
   e. After viewing the form in Print Preview, return to the form by clicking the Close Print Preview button.
7. Click the Undo button on the Quick Access toolbar to remove the background image. (If this does not remove the image, close the form without saving it and then reopen the form.)
8. Save the Clients form.

Applying Conditional Formatting

With the Conditional Formatting button in the Control Formatting group on the FORM LAYOUT TOOLS FORMAT tab, you can apply formatting to data that meets a specific criterion or apply conditional formatting to data in all records in a form. For example, you can apply conditional formatting to sales amounts in a form that displays amounts higher than a specified number in a different color or you can apply conditional formatting to states' names and specify a color for companies in a particular state. You can also include conditional formatting that inserts data bars that visually compare data among records. The data bars provide a visual representation of the comparison of data in records. For example, in Project 1g, you will insert data bars in the *Sales* field that provide a visual representation of how the sales amount in one record compares to the sales amounts in other records.

Conditional
Formatting

To apply conditional formatting, click the Conditional Formatting button in the Control Formatting group and the Conditional Formatting Rules Manager dialog box displays. At this dialog box, click the New Rule button and the New Formatting Rule dialog box displays, as shown in Figure 5.3. In the *Select a rule type* list box, choose the *Check values in the current record or use an expression* option if the conditional formatting is applied to a field in the record that matches a specific condition. Click the *Compare to other records* option if you want to insert data bars in a field in all records that compare the data among the records.

If you want to apply conditional formatting to a field, specify the field and field condition with options in the *Edit the rule description* section of the dialog box. Specify the type of formatting you want applied to data in a field that meets the specific criterion. For example, in Project 1g, you will specify that you want to change the shape fill to a light green for all *City* fields containing *Indianapolis*. When you have made all the desired changes to the dialog box, click OK to close the dialog box and then click OK to close the Conditional Formatting Rules Manager dialog box.

To insert data bars in a field, click the Conditional Formatting button, click the New Rule button at the Conditional Formatting Rules Manager dialog box, and then click the *Compare to other records* option in the *Select a rule type* list box. This changes the options in the dialog box, as shown in Figure 5.4. Make the desired changes in the *Edit the rule description* section.

Figure 5.3 New Formatting Rule Dialog Box with the *Check values in the current record or use an expression* Option Selected

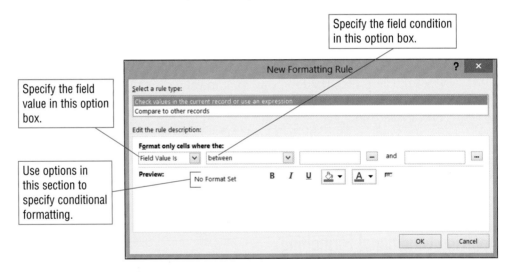

Figure 5.4 New Formatting Rule Dialog Box with the *Compare to other records* Option Selected

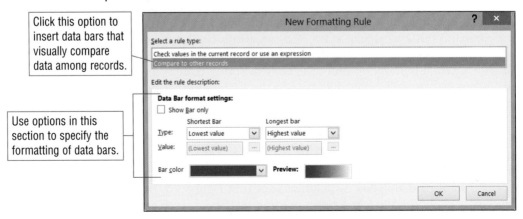

1. With the Clients form in **AL1-C5-Dearborn.accdb** open and in Layout view, apply conditional formatting so that the *City* field displays all Indianapolis entries with a light green shape fill by completing the following steps:
   a. Click in the text box control object containing the text *Muncie*.
   b. Click the FORM LAYOUT TOOLS FORMAT tab.
   c. Click the Conditional Formatting button in the Control Formatting group.
   d. At the Conditional Formatting Rules Manager dialog box, click the New Rule button.

   e. At the New Formatting Rule dialog box, click the down-pointing arrow at the right side of the option box containing the word *between* and then click *equal to* at the drop-down list.
   f. Click in the text box to the right of the *equal to* option box and then type Indianapolis.
   g. Click the Background color button arrow and then click the *Green 3* color option (seventh column, fourth row).
   h. Click OK to close the New Formatting Rule dialog box.
   i. Click OK to close the Conditional Formatting Rules Manager dialog box.

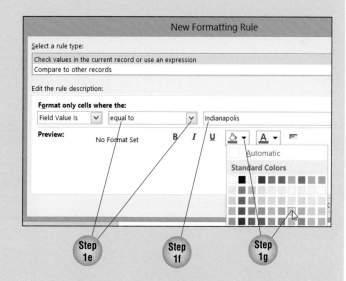

2. Click the HOME tab and then click the View button to switch to Form view.
3. Click the Next record button to display the next record in the form. Continue clicking the Next record button to view records and notice that *Indianapolis* entries display with a light green shape fill.
4. Click the First record button in the Record Navigation bar.
5. Click the Save button on the Quick Access toolbar.
6. Print page 1 of the form by completing the following steps:
   a. Click the FILE tab and then click the *Print* option.
   b. Click the Print button.
   c. At the Print dialog box, click the *Pages* option in the *Print Range* section, type 1 in the *From* text box, press the Tab key, and then type 1 in the *To* text box.
   d. Click OK.
7. Close the Clients form.
8. Open the Sales form and switch to Layout View by clicking the View button in the Views group on the HOME tab.

9. With the text box control object containing the sales ID number *1* selected, drag the right border to the left until *Lines: 1 Characters: 21* displays at the left side of the Status bar.

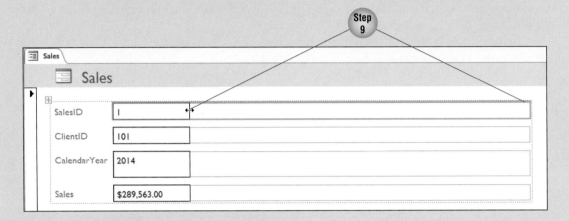

10. Change the alignment of text by completing the following steps:
    a. Right-click the selected text box control object (the object containing *1*) and then click *Select Entire Column* at the shortcut menu.
    b. Click the FORM LAYOUT TOOLS FORMAT tab.
    c. Click the Align Right button in the Font group.
11. Apply data bars to the *Sales* field by completing the following steps:
    a. Click in the text box control object containing the text *$289,563.00*.
    b. Make sure the FORM LAYOUT TOOLS FORMAT tab is active.
    c. Click the Conditional Formatting button.
    d. At the Conditional Formatting Rules Manager dialog box, click the New Rule button.
    e. At the New Formatting Rule dialog box, click the *Compare to other records* option in the *Select a rule type* list box.
    f. Click the down-pointing arrow at the right side of the *Bar color* option box and then click the *Green 4* color option (seventh column, fifth row).

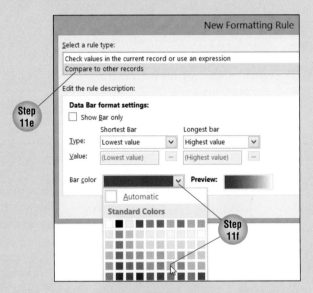

    g. Click OK to close the New Formatting Rule dialog box and then click OK to close the Conditional Formatting Rules Manager dialog box.
12. Click the Next record button in the Record Navigation bar to display the next record. Continue clicking the Next record button and notice the data bars that display in the *Sales* field.
13. Click the First record button in the Record Navigation bar.
14. Click the Save button on the Quick Access toolbar.

15. Print page 1 of the form by completing the following steps:
    a. Click the FILE tab and then click the *Print* option.
    b. Click the Print button.
    c. At the Print dialog box, click the *Pages* option in the *Print Range* section, type 1 in the *From* text box, press the Tab key, type 1 in the *To* text box, and then click OK.
16. Close the Sales form.
17. Close **AL1-C5-Dearborn.accdb**.

Project 2 **Add Fields, Create a Split Form and Multiple Items Form, and Use the Form Wizard**   **5 Parts**

You will open the Skyline database, create a form and add related fields to the form, create a split and multiple items form, and create a form using the Form Wizard.

Adding Existing Fields

If you create a form and then realize that you forgot a field or want to insert an existing field in the form, display the form in Layout view and then click the Add Existing Fields button located in the Tools group on the FORM LAYOUT TOOLS DESIGN tab. When you click the Add Existing Fields button, the Field List task pane opens and displays at the right side of the screen. This task pane displays the fields available in the current view, fields available in related tables, and fields available in other tables. Figure 5.5 displays the Field List task pane that you will open in Project 2a.

Add Existing Fields

In the *Fields available for this view* section, Access displays all fields in any tables used to create the form. So far, you have been creating a form with all fields in one table. In the *Fields available in related tables* section, Access displays tables that are related to the table(s) used to create the form. To display the fields in the related table, click the plus symbol that displays before the table name in the Field List task pane and the list expands to display all of the field names.

Alt + F8 is the keyboard shortcut to display the Field List task pane.

To add a field to the form, double-click the desired field in the Field List task pane. This inserts the field below the existing fields in the form. You can also drag a field from the Field List task pane into the form. To do this, position the mouse pointer on the desired field in the Field List task pane, hold down the left mouse button, drag into the form window, and then release the mouse button. A pink insert indicator bar displays as you drag the field in the existing fields in the form. When you drag over a cell, the cell displays with pink fill. When the insert indicator bar is in the desired position or the desired cell is selected, release the mouse button.

Use the Field List task pane to add fields from a table or query to your form.

You can insert multiple fields in a form from the Field List task pane. To do this, hold down the Ctrl key while clicking the desired fields and then drag the fields into the form. If you try to drag a field from a table in the *Fields available in other tables* section, the Specify Relationship dialog box will display. To move a field from the Field List task pane to the form, the field must be located in a table that is related to the table(s) used to create the form.

Figure 5.5 Field List Task Pane

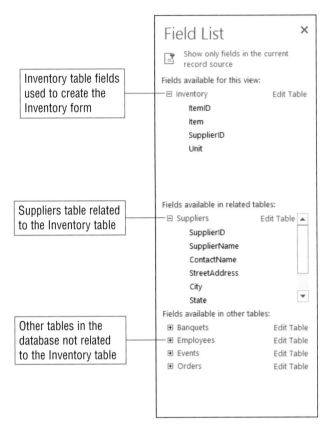

Inventory table fields used to create the Inventory form

Suppliers table related to the Inventory table

Other tables in the database not related to the Inventory table

Field List ✕

Show only fields in the current record source

Fields available for this view:
⊟ Inventory   Edit Table
   ItemID
   Item
   SupplierID
   Unit

Fields available in related tables:
⊟ Suppliers   Edit Table ▲
   SupplierID
   SupplierName
   ContactName
   StreetAddress
   City
   State   ▼

Fields available in other tables:
⊞ Banquets   Edit Table
⊞ Employees   Edit Table
⊞ Events   Edit Table
⊞ Orders   Edit Table

Project 2a   **Adding Existing Fields to a Form**   **Part 1 of 5**

1. Display the Open dialog box with the AL1C5 folder on your storage medium the active folder, open **AL1-C5-Skyline.accdb**, and enable the contents.
2. Create a form with the Inventory table by clicking the Inventory table in the Navigation pane, clicking the CREATE tab, and then clicking the Form button in the Forms group.
3. With the text box control object containing the text *001* selected, drag the right border to the left until the selected object is approximately one-half the original width.

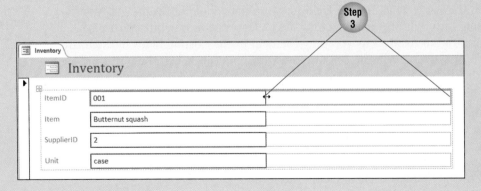

Step 3

Inventory

Inventory

ItemID	001
Item	Butternut squash
SupplierID	2
Unit	case

4. With the text box control object still selected, click the FORM LAYOUT TOOLS ARRANGE tab and then click the Split Horizontally button in the Merge/Split group. (This splits the text box control object into one object and one empty cell.)

5. You decide that you want to add the supplier name to the form so the name displays when the form is entered. Add the supplier name field by completing the following steps:

   a. Click the FORM LAYOUT TOOLS DESIGN tab.

   b. Click the Add Existing Fields button in the Tools group.

   c. Click the <u>Show all tables</u> hyperlink that displays toward the top of the Field List task pane.

   d. Click the plus symbol that displays immediately left of the Suppliers table name located in the *Fields available in related tables* section of the Field List task pane.

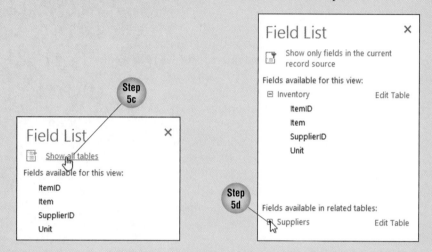

   e. Position the mouse pointer on the *SupplierName* field, hold down the left mouse button, drag into the form until the pink insert indicator bar displays immediately right of the text box control containing *2* (the text box control that displays at the right side of the *SupplierID* label control), and then release the mouse button. Access inserts the field as a Lookup field (a down-pointing arrow displays at the right side of the field).

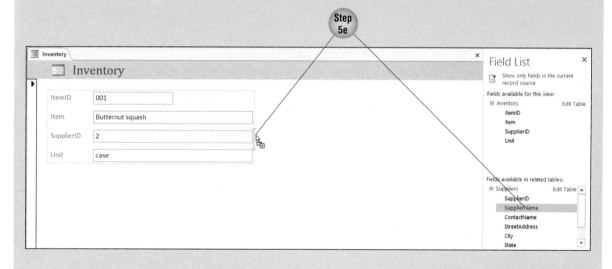

f. Change the *SupplierName* field from a Lookup field to a text box by clicking the Options button that displays below the field and then clicking *Change to Text Box* at the drop-down list. (This removes the down-pointing arrow at the right side of the field.)

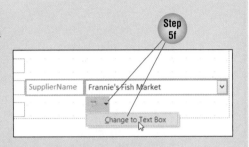

g. Close the Field List task pane by clicking the Close button located in the upper right corner of the task pane.

6. Insert a logo image in the *Form Header* section by completing the following steps:
   a. Right-click the logo object that displays in the *Form Header* section (located to the left of the title *Inventory*) and then click *Delete* at the shortcut menu.
   b. Click the Logo button in the Header/Footer group.
   c. At the Insert Picture dialog box, navigate to the AL1C5 folder on your storage medium and then double-click the file named ***Cityscape.jpg***.

7. Change the title by completing the following steps:
   a. Click the Title button in the Header/Footer group. (This selects *Inventory* in the *Form Header* section.)
   b. Type **Skyline Inventory Input Form** and then press Enter.

8. Insert the date and time in the *Form Header* section by clicking the Date and Time button in the Header/Footer group and then clicking OK at the Date and Time dialog box.

9. Click in any field outside the title, click the title to select the header control object, and then drag the right border of the title control object to the left until the border displays near the title.

10. Select the date and time control objects, drag in the left border until the border displays near the date and time, and then drag the objects so they are positioned near the title.

11. Scroll through the records in the form.

12. Click the First record button in the Record Navigation bar.

13. Click the Save button on the Quick Access toolbar and save the form with the name *Inventory*.

14. Print the current record.

15. Close the Inventory form.

Creating Split Forms ■■■■■■■■■■■■■■■■■■■■■■■■

▼ Quick Steps

Create a Split Form
1. Click desired table.
2. Click CREATE tab.
3. Click More Forms button.
4. Click *Split Form*.

More Forms

Another method for creating a form is to use the *Split Form* option at the More Forms button drop-down list in the Forms group on the CREATE tab. When you use this option to create a form, Access splits the screen in the work area and provides two views of the form. The top half of the work area displays the form in Layout view and the bottom half of the work area displays the form in Datasheet view. The two views are connected and are **synchronous**, which means that displaying or modifying a specific field in the Form view portion will cause the same action to occur in the field in the Datasheet view portion. Figure 5.6 displays the split form you will create for Project 2b.

Figure 5.6 Split Form

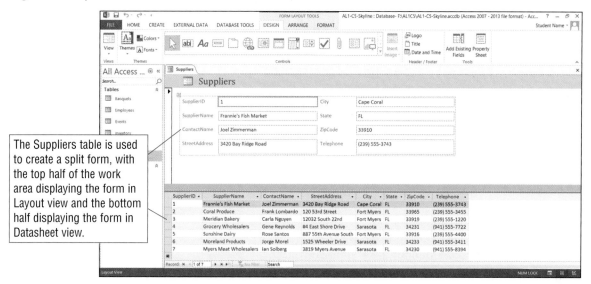

The Suppliers table is used to create a split form, with the top half of the work area displaying the form in Layout view and the bottom half displaying the form in Datasheet view.

Project 2b **Creating a Split Form** **Part 2 of 5**

1. With **AL1-C5-Skyline.accdb** open, create a split form with the Suppliers table by completing the following steps:
   a. Click the Suppliers table in the Navigation pane.
   b. Click the CREATE tab.
   c. Click the More Forms button in the Forms group and then click *Split Form* at the drop-down list.

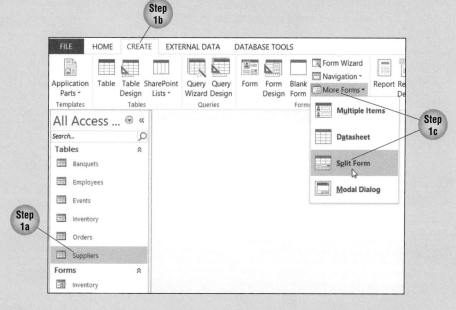

   d. Click several times on the Next record button in the Record Navigation bar. (As you display records, notice that the current record in the Form view in the top portion of the window is the same record selected in Datasheet view in the lower portion of the window.)
   e. Click the First record button.

2. Apply a theme by clicking the Themes button in the Themes group on the FORM LAYOUT TOOLS DESIGN tab and then clicking *Integral* at the drop-down gallery (third column, first row).

3. Insert a logo image in the *Form Header* section by completing the following steps:
   a. Right-click the logo object that displays in the *Form Header* section (located to the left of the title *Suppliers*) and then click *Delete* at the shortcut menu.
   b. Click the Logo button in the Header/Footer group.
   c. At the Insert Picture dialog box, navigate to the AL1C5 folder on your storage medium and then double-click ***Cityscape.jpg***.

4. Change the title by completing the following steps:
   a. Click the Title button in the Header/Footer group. (This selects *Suppliers* in the *Form Header* section.)
   b. Type **Skyline Suppliers Input Form** and then press Enter.
   c. Click in any field outside the title, click the title again to select the header control object, and then drag the right border to the left until the border displays near the title.

5. Click the text box control object containing the supplier identification number *1*, and then drag the right border of the text box control object to the left until *Lines: 1 Characters: 35* displays at the left side of the Status bar.

6. Click the text box control object containing the city *Cape Coral* and drag the right border of the text box control object to the left until *Lines: 1 Characters: 35* displays at the left side of the Status bar.

7. Insert a new record in the Suppliers form by completing the following steps:
   a. Click the View button to switch to Form view.
   b. Click the New (blank) record button in the Record Navigation bar.
   c. Click in the *SupplierID* field in the Form view portion of the window and then type the following information in the specified fields:

SupplierID	8
SupplierName	Jackson Produce
ContactName	Marshall Jackson
StreetAddress	5790 Cypress Avenue
City	Fort Myers
State	FL
ZipCode	33917
Telephone	2395555002

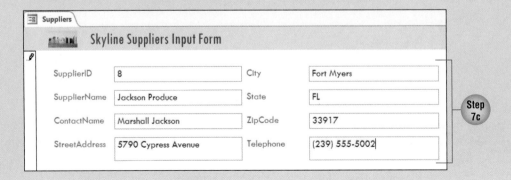

8. Click the Save button on the Quick Access toolbar and save the form with the name *Suppliers*.
9. Print the current form by completing the following steps:
    a. Click the FILE tab and then click the *Print* option.
    b. Click the Print button.
    c. At the Print dialog box, click the Setup button.
    d. At the Page Setup dialog box, click the *Print Form Only* option in the *Split Form* section of the dialog box and then click OK.
    e. At the Print dialog box, click the *Selected Record(s)* option and then click OK.
10. Close the Suppliers form.

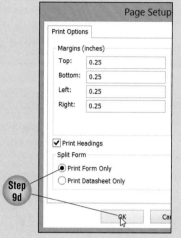

Creating Multiple Items Forms ■■■■■■■■■■■■■■■■

When you create a form with the Form button, a single record displays. You can use the *Multiple Items* option at the More Forms button drop-down list to create a form that displays multiple records. The advantage to creating a multiple items form over displaying the table in Datasheet view is that you can customize the form using buttons in the FORM LAYOUT TOOLS ribbon with the DESIGN, ARRANGE, or FORMAT tab selected.

▼ **Quick Steps**

Create a Multiple Items Form
1. Click desired table.
2. Click CREATE tab.
3. Click More Forms button.
4. Click *Multiple Items*.

Project 2c   Creating a Multiple Items Form   Part 3 of 5

1. With **AL1-C5-Skyline.accdb** open, create a multiple items form by completing the following steps:
    a. Click the Orders table in the Navigation pane.
    b. Click the CREATE tab.
    c. Click the More Forms button in the Forms group and then click *Multiple Items* at the drop-down list.
2. Insert the **Cityscape.jpg** image as the logo.
3. Insert the title *Skyline Orders*.
4. Click in any field outside the title, click the title again to select the header control object, and then drag the right border to the left until the border displays near the title.
5. Save the form with the name *Orders*.
6. Print the first page of the form by completing the following steps:
    a. Click the FILE tab and then click the *Print* option.
    b. Click the Print button.
    c. At the Print dialog box, click the *Pages* option in the *Print Range* section.
    d. Type 1 in the *From* text box, press the Tab key, and then type 1 in the *To* text box.
    e. Click OK.
7. Close the Orders form.

Creating Forms Using the Form Wizard ■■■■■■■■■■■

▼ **Quick Steps**

Create a Form Using the Form Wizard
1. Click CREATE tab.
2. Click Form Wizard button.
3. Choose desired options at each Form Wizard dialog box.

Form Wizard

With the Form Wizard, you can be more selective about what fields you insert in a form.

Access offers a Form Wizard that guides you through the creation of a form. To create a form using the Form Wizard, click the CREATE tab and then click the Form Wizard button in the Forms group. At the first Form Wizard dialog box, shown in Figure 5.7, specify the table and then the fields you want included in the form. To select the table, click the down-pointing arrow at the right side of the *Table/Queries* option box and then click the desired table. Select the desired field in the *Available Fields* list box and then click the button containing the One Field button (the button containing the greater-than [>] symbol). This inserts the field in the *Selected Fields* list box. Continue in this manner until you have inserted all of the desired fields in the *Selected Fields* list box. If you want to insert all of the fields into the *Selected Fields* list box at one time, click the All Fields button (the button containing two greater-than symbols). After specifying the fields, click the Next button.

At the second Form Wizard dialog box, specify the layout for the records. You can choose from these layout type options: *Columnar*, *Tabular*, *Datasheet*, and *Justified*. Click the Next button and the third and final Form Wizard dialog box displays. It offers a title for the form and also provides the option *Open the form to view or enter information*. Make any necessary changes in this dialog box and then click the Finish button.

Figure 5.7 First Form Wizard Dialog Box

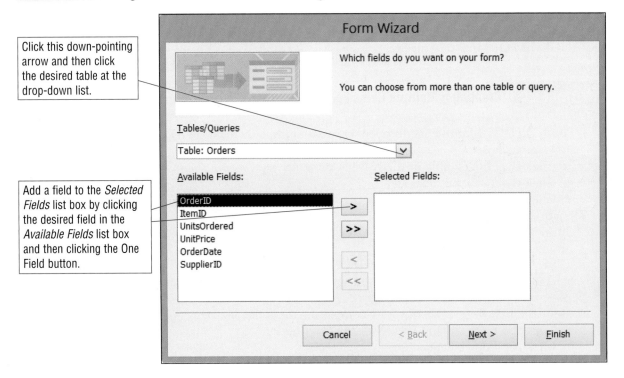

1. With **AL1-C5-Skyline.accdb** open, create a form with the Form Wizard by completing the following steps:
   a. Click the CREATE tab.
   b. Click the Form Wizard button in the Forms group.
   c. At the first Form Wizard dialog box, click the down-pointing arrow at the right side of the *Tables/Queries* option box and then click *Table: Employees* at the drop-down list.
   d. Specify that you want all of the fields included in the form by clicking the All Fields button (the button containing the two greater-than symbols).
   e. Click the Next button.
   f. At the second Form Wizard dialog box, click the *Justified* option and then click the Next button.

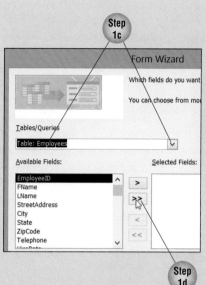

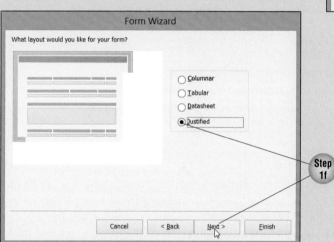

   g. At the third and final Form Wizard dialog box, click the Finish button.
2. Format the field headings by completing the following steps:
   a. Click the View button to switch to Layout view.
   b. Click the *EmployeeID* label control object. (This selects the object.)
   c. Hold down the Ctrl key and then click on each of the following label control objects: *FName, LName, StreetAddress, City, State, ZipCode, Telephone, HireDate,* and *HealthIns*.
   d. With all of the label control objects selected, release the Ctrl key.
   e. Click the FORM LAYOUT TOOLS FORMAT tab.
   f. Click the Shape Fill button and then click the *Aqua Blue 2* color option (ninth column, third row in the *Standard Colors* section).
   g. Click the FORM LAYOUT TOOLS DESIGN tab and then click the View button to switch to Form view.

3. In Form view, click the New (blank) record button and then add the following records:

EmployeeID	13
FName	Carol
LName	Thompson
StreetAddress	6554 Willow Drive, Apt. B
City	Fort Myers
State	FL
ZipCode	33915
Telephone	2395553719
HireDate	10/1/2015
HealthIns	(Click in the check box to insert a check mark.)
EmployeeID	14
FName	Eric
LName	Hahn
StreetAddress	331 South 152nd Street
City	Cape Coral
State	FL
ZipCode	33906
Telephone	2395558107
HireDate	10/1/2015
HealthIns	(Leave blank.)

4. Click the Save button on the Quick Access toolbar.
5. Print the record for Eric Hahn and then print the record for Carol Thompson.
6. Close the Employees form.

In Project 2d, you used the Form Wizard to create a form with all of the fields in one table. If tables are related, you can create a form using fields from related tables. At the first Form Wizard dialog box, choose fields from the selected table and then choose fields from a related table. To change to the related table, click the down-pointing arrow at the right of the *Tables/Queries* option box and then click the name of the desired table.

1. With **AL1-C5-Skyline.accdb** open, create a form with related tables by completing the following steps:
   a. Click the CREATE tab.
   b. Click the Form Wizard button in the Forms group.
   c. At the first Form Wizard dialog box, click the down-pointing arrow at the right of the *Tables/Queries* option box and then click *Table: Banquets*.
   d. Click *ResDate* in the *Available Fields* list box and then click the One Field button. (This inserts *ResDate* in the *Selected Fields* list box.)
   e. Click *AmountTotal* in the *Available Fields* list box, click the One Field button.
   f. With *AmountPaid* selected in the *Available Fields* list box, click the One Field button.
   g. Click the down-pointing arrow at the right side of the *Tables/Queries* option box and then click *Table: Events* at the drop-down list.
   h. Click *Event* in the *Available Fields* list box and then click the One Field button.
   i. Click the down-pointing arrow at the right side of the *Tables/Queries* option box and then click *Table: Employees* at the drop-down list.
   j. Click *LName* in the *Available Fields* list box and then click the One Field button.
   k. Click the Next button.
   l. At the second Form Wizard dialog box, click the Next button.
   m. At the third Form Wizard dialog box, click the Next button.
   n. At the fourth Form Wizard dialog box, select the text in the *What title do you want for your form?* text box, type **Upcoming Banquets**, and then click the Finish button.

2. When the first record displays, print the record.
3. Save and then close the form.
4. Close **AL1-C5-Skyline.accdb**.

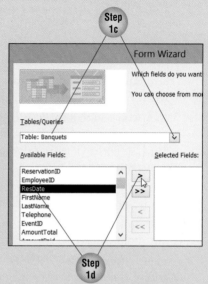

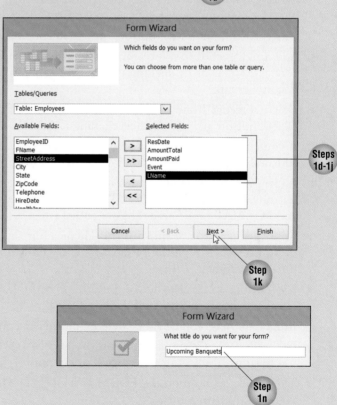

Chapter Summary

- Creating a form generally improves the ease of entering data into a table. Some methods for creating a form include using the Form, Split Form, and Multiple Items buttons or the Form Wizard.

- A form is an object you can use to enter and edit data in a table or query and to help prevent incorrect data from being entered in a database.

- The simplest method for creating a form is to click a table in the Navigation pane, click the CREATE button, and then click the Form button in the Forms group.

- When you create a form, it displays in Layout view. Use this view to display data and modify the appearance and contents of the form. Other form views include Form view and Design view. Use Form view to enter and manage records and use Design view to view and modify the structure of the form.

- Open an existing form in Layout view by right-clicking the form in the Navigation pane and then clicking *Layout View* at the shortcut menu.

- Print a form with options at the Print dialog box. To print an individual record, display the Print dialog box, click the *Selected Record(s)* option, and then click OK.

- Delete a form with the Delete button in the Records group on the HOME tab or by right-clicking the form in the Navigation pane and then clicking *Delete* at the shortcut menu. A message may display asking you to confirm the deletion.

- Navigate in a form with buttons in the Record Navigation bar.

- Add a new record to a form by clicking the New (blank) record button in the Record Navigation bar or by clicking the HOME tab and then clicking the New button in the Records group.

- Delete a record from a form by displaying the record, clicking the HOME tab, clicking the Delete button arrow, and then clicking *Delete Record* at the drop-down list.

- If you create a form with a table that has a one-to-many relationship established, Access adds a datasheet at the bottom of the form.

- A form is comprised of a series of control objects. Customize these control objects with buttons on the FORM LAYOUT TOOLS ribbon under the DESIGN tab, ARRANGE tab, and FORMAT tab. These tabs are active when a form displays in Layout view.

- Apply a theme to a form with the Themes button in the Themes group on the FORM LAYOUT TOOLS DESIGN tab. Use the Colors and Fonts buttons in the Themes group to further customize a theme.

- Use buttons in the Header/Footer group on the FORM LAYOUT TOOLS DESIGN tab to insert a logo, form title, and date and time.

- In Layout view, you can size, delete, and insert control objects.

- In the Rows & Columns group on the FORM LAYOUT TOOLS ARRANGE tab, you can use buttons to select or insert rows or columns.

- The Controls group on the FORM LAYOUT TOOLS DESIGN tab contains control objects you can insert in a form.

- Merge cells in a form by selecting cells and then clicking the Merge button in the Merge/Split group on the FORM LAYOUT TOOLS ARRANGE tab. Split selected cells by clicking the Split Vertically or Split Horizontally button.

- Format control objects and cells in a form with buttons on the FORM LAYOUT TOOLS FORMAT tab.
- Use the Conditional Formatting button in the Control Formatting group on the FORM LAYOUT TOOLS FORMAT tab to apply specific formatting to data that matches a specific criterion.
- Click the Add Existing Fields button in the Tools group on the FORM LAYOUT TOOLS DESIGN tab to display the Field List task pane. Add fields to the form by double-clicking a field or dragging the field from the task pane.
- Create a split form by clicking the More Forms button on the CREATE tab and then clicking *Split Form* in the drop-down list. Access displays the form in Form view in the top portion of the work area and in Datasheet view in the bottom portion of the work area. The two views are connected and synchronous.
- Create a Multiple Items form by clicking the More Forms button on the CREATE tab and then clicking *Multiple Items* in the drop-down list.
- The Form Wizard walks you through the steps for creating a form and lets you specify the fields you want included in the form, a layout for the records, and a name for the form.
- You can create a form with the Form Wizard that contains fields from tables connected by a one-to-many relationship.

Commands Review

FEATURE	RIBBON TAB, GROUP	BUTTON, OPTION
Conditional Formatting Rules Manager dialog box	FORM LAYOUT TOOLS FORMAT, Control Formatting	
Field List task pane	FORM LAYOUT TOOLS DESIGN, Tools	
form	CREATE, Forms	
Form Wizard	CREATE, Forms	
multiple items form	CREATE, Forms	, *Multiple Items*
split form	CREATE, Forms	, *Split Form*

Concepts Check   Test Your Knowledge

Completion: In the space provided at the right, indicate the correct term, symbol, or command.

1. The simplest method for creating a form is to click this tab and then click the Form button.   _____

2. When you click the Form button to create a form, the form displays in this view.   _____

3. To print the current record in a form, click this option at the Print dialog box and then click OK.   _____

4. Navigate in a form using buttons in this bar.   _____

5. Click this button to add a new record to a form.   _____

6. The FORM LAYOUT TOOLS DESIGN tab is active when a form displays in this view.   _____

7. The Themes group on the FORM LAYOUT TOOLS DESIGN tab contains three buttons: the Themes button, the Colors button, and this button.   _____

8. Click the Logo button on the FORM LAYOUT TOOLS DESIGN tab and this dialog box displays.   _____

9. To select nonadjacent objects or cells, hold down this key on the keyboard while clicking the desired objects or cells.   _____

10. This group on the FORM LAYOUT TOOLS ARRANGE tab contains buttons for selecting and inserting rows and columns in a form.   _____

11. With this button in the Control Formatting group on the FORM LAYOUT TOOLS FORMAT tab, you can apply formatting to data that meets a specific criterion.   _____

12. Click the Add Existing Fields button in the Tools group on the FORM LAYOUT TOOLS DESIGN tab and this task pane displays.   _____

13. Create a split form or multiple items form with options at this button's drop-down list.   _____

14. When you create a form with the *Split Form* option, the form displays in this view in the top half of the work area.   _____

Skills Check   Assess Your Performance

Assessment

1   **CREATE AND CUSTOMIZE A SUPPLIERS FORM**

1. Display the Open dialog box with the AL1C5 folder on your storage medium the active folder.
2. Open **AL1-C5-PacTrek.accdb** and enable the contents.
3. Use the Form button in the Forms group on the CREATE tab to create a form with the Suppliers table.
4. Switch to Form view and then add the following records to the Suppliers form:

SupplierID	12
SupplierName	Seaside Suppliers
StreetAddress	4120 Shoreline Drive
City	Vancouver
Prov/State	BC
PostalCode	V2V 8K4
EmailAddress	seaside@emcp.net
Telephone	6045557945

SupplierID	34
SupplierName	Carson Company
StreetAddress	120 Plaza Center
City	Vancouver
Prov/State	BC
PostalCode	V2V 1K6
EmailAddress	carson@emcp.net
Telephone	6045551955

5. Delete the record containing information on Manning, Inc.
6. Switch to Layout view and then apply the Organic theme to the form.
7. Select and delete the logo object in the *Form Header* section and then click the Logo button in the Header/Footer group. At the Insert Picture dialog box, navigate to the AL1C5 folder on your storage medium and then double-click **River.jpg**.
8. Create the title *Pacific Trek Suppliers* for the form. Click in any field outside the title and then click in the title (which selects the header control object). Drag the right border of the title control object to the left until the border displays near the title.
9. Insert the date and time in the *Form Header* section.
10. Select the date and time control objects, drag in the left border until the border displays near the date and time, and then drag the objects so they are positioned near the title.
11. Click the text box control object containing the supplier number and then drag the right border to the left until *Lines: 1 Characters: 30* displays at the left side of the Status bar.

12. Select the fields in the first column (*SupplierID* through *Telephone*) and then apply the following formatting:
    a. Apply bold formatting.
    b. Apply the Dark Blue font color (ninth column, bottom row in the *Standard Colors* section).
    c. Apply the Align Right alignment.
    d. Apply the Light Blue 2 shape fill (fifth column, third row in the *Standard Colors* section).
    e. Apply the Dark Blue shape outline color (ninth column, bottom row in the *Standard Colors* section).
13. Select the second column and then apply the following formatting:
    a. Apply the Light Blue 1 shape fill (fifth column, second row in the *Standard Colors* section).
    b. Apply the Dark Blue shape outline color (ninth column, bottom row in the *Standard Colors* section).
14. Switch to Form view.
15. Save the form with the name *Suppliers*.
16. Make active the record for supplier number 12 (one of the new records you entered) and then print the record. (Make sure you print only the record for supplier number 12.)
17. Make active the record for supplier number 34 and then print the record.
18. Close the Suppliers table.

Assessment

2 CREATE AND CUSTOMIZE AN ORDERS FORM

1. With **AL1-C5-PacTrek.accdb** open, create a form with the Orders table using the Form button on the CREATE tab.
2. Insert a field from a related table by completing the following steps:
    a. Display the Field List task pane and then, if necessary, click the <u>Show all tables</u> hyperlink.
    b. Expand the Suppliers table in the *Fields available in related tables* section.
    c. Drag the field named *SupplierName* into the form and position it between *SupplierID* and *ProductID*.
    d. Change the *SupplierName* field from a Lookup field to a text box by clicking the Options button that displays below the field and then clicking *Change to Text Box* at the drop-down list.
    e. Close the Field List task pane.
3. Click the text box control object containing the text *1010* and then drag the right border to the left until *Lines: 1 Characters: 30* displays at the left side of the Status bar.
4. Select all of the objects in the *Detail* section by clicking an object in the *Detail* section and then clicking the table move handle (the small, square button with a four-headed arrow inside). With the objects selected, apply the following formatting:
    a. Change the font to Cambria and the font size to 12 points.
    b. Apply the Align Right alignment.

5. Select the first column and then apply the following formatting:
   a. Apply the Green 2 shape fill (seventh column, third row in the *Standard Colors* section).
   b. Apply bold formatting.
6. Apply conditional formatting that changes the font color to blue for any *Amount* field entry that contains an amount greater than $999. **Hint: Click the text box control object containing the amount $199.50, click the Conditional Formatting button, click the New Rule button, change the second option in the** Edit the rule description *section to* greater than, *and then enter 999 in the third option box (without the dollar sign)*.
7. Save the form with the name *Orders*.
8. Print the fifteenth record in the form and then close the form.

Assessment

3 CREATE A SPLIT FORM WITH THE PRODUCTS TABLE

1. With **AL1-C5-PacTrek.accdb** open, create a form with the Products table using the *Split Form* option from the More Forms button drop-down list.
2. Decrease the width of the second column until *Lines: 1 Characters: 35* displays at the left side of the Status bar
3. Select the first column and then apply the following formatting:
   a. Apply bold formatting.
   b. Apply the Aqua Blue 1 shape fill (ninth column, second row in the *Standard Colors* section).
   c. Apply the Blue shape outline color (eighth column, bottom row in the *Standard Colors* section).
4. Click in the text box control object containing the number *0* (the *UnitsOnOrder* number) and then apply conditional formatting that displays the number in red in any field value equal to zero.
5. Change to Form view, create a new record, and then enter the following information in the specified fields:

ProductID	205-CS
Product	Timberline solo cook set
SupplierID	15
UnitsInStock	8
UnitsOnOrder	0
ReorderLevel	5

6. Save the form with the name *Products*.
7. Print the current record (the record you just typed). **Hint: At the Print dialog box, click the Setup button. At the Page Setup dialog box, click the** Print Form Only *option*.
8. Close the Products form.
9. Close **AL1-C5-PacTrek.accdb**.

4 CREATE AND CUSTOMIZE AN EMPLOYEES FORM

1. Open **AL1-C5-Griffin.accdb** from the AL1C5 folder on your storage medium and enable the contents.
2. Suppose you want to create a form for entering employee information but you do not want to include the employees' salaries, since that is confidential information and accessible only to the account manager. Use the Form Wizard to create an Employees form that includes all fields *except* the *AnnualSalary* field and name the form *Employees*.
3. Type a new record with the following information in the specified fields:

EmpID	1099
LastName	Williamson
FirstName	Carrie
BirthDate	6/24/1986
HireDate	8/1/2014
DeptID	RD

4. Switch to layout view, apply the Slice theme, change the theme colors to *Blue Warm*, and change the theme fonts to *Franklin Gothic*.
5. Print the new record you typed.
6. Close the Employees form.

Visual Benchmark   Demonstrate Your Proficiency

CREATE AND FORMAT A PROPERTIES FORM

1. Open **AL1-C5-SunProperties.accdb** located in the AL1C5 folder on your storage medium and enable the contents.
2. Create a form with the Properties table and format the form so it appears similar to the form in Figure 5.8 using the following specifications:
   a. Apply the Facet theme and apply the Paper theme colors.
   b. Insert the logo, title, date, and time in the *Form Header* section, as shown in the figure. (Insert the file **SunPropLogo.jpg** for the logo. Adjust the size of the title control object and then move the date and time, as shown in the figure.)
   c. Select all of the objects in the *Detail* section and then change the font color to Maroon 5 (sixth column, sixth row in the *Standard Colors* section).
   d. Select the first column; apply bold formatting; apply Light Yellow, Background 2, Darker 10% shape fill (third column, second row in the *Theme Colors* section); apply the Maroon 5 shape outline color (sixth column, sixth row in the *Standard Colors* section); and then change the alignment to Align Right.

e. Decrease the size of the second column as shown in the figure.
f. Insert a new column to the right of the second column, merge cells in the new column to accommodate the sun image, and then insert the image **SunProp.jpg** (as a control object). Adjust the width of the third column so the image displays as shown in Figure 5.8.
g. Apply conditional formatting to the *MoRent* field that displays in green any rent amount greater than $999.
h. Adjust the position of the control objects so that the form displays similar to what is shown in Figure 5.8.
3. Save the form with the name *Properties* and then print the current record.
4. Close the form and then close **AL1-C5-SunProperties.accdb**.

Figure 5.8 Visual Benchmark

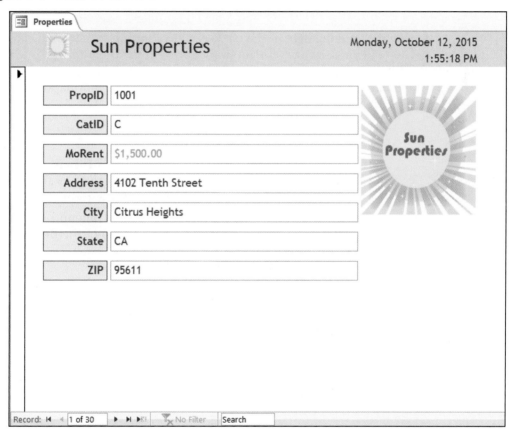

Case Study   Apply Your Skills

Part 1

You are the office manager at the Lewis Vision Care Center and your center is switching over to Access to manage files. You have already created four basic tables and now need to create relationships and enter data. Open **AL1-C5-LewisCenter.accdb** and then create the following relationships between tables (enforce referential integrity and cascade fields and records):

Field Name	"One" Table	"Many" Table
PatientID	Patients	Billing
ServiceID	Services	Billing
DoctorID	Doctors	Billing

Save and then print the relationships.

Part 2

Before entering data in the tables, create a form for each table and apply a theme of your choosing. Enter data in the forms in the order in which it appears in Figure 5.10 on the next page. Apply any additional formatting to enhance the visual appearance of each form. After entering the information in the forms, print the first record of each form.

Part 3

Apply the following conditions to fields in forms:

- In the Patients form, apply the condition that the city *Tulsa* displays in red and the city *Broken Arrow* displays in blue in the *City* field. Print the first record of the Patients form and then close the form.
- In the Billing form, apply the condition that amounts in the *Fee* field over $99 display in green. Print the second record of the Billing form and then close the form.

Close **AL1-C5-LewisCenter.accdb**.

Part 4

Your center has a procedures manual that describes workplace processes and procedures. Open Word and then create a document for the procedures manual that describes the formatting and conditions you applied to the forms in **AL1-C5-LewisCenter.accdb**. Save the completed document and name it **AL1-C5-CS-Manual**. Print and then close **AL1-C5-CS-Manual.docx**.

Figure 5.10 Case Study Part 2

Patients form

Patient number 030	Patient number 076	Patient number 092
Rhonda J. Mahler	Patrick S. Robbins	Oren L. Vargas
130 East 41st Street	3281 Aspen Avenue	21320 Tenth Street
Tulsa, OK 74155	Tulsa, OK 74108	Broken Arrow, OK 74012
(918) 555-3107	(918) 555-9672	(918) 555-1188
Patient number 085	Patient number 074	Patient number 023
Michael A. Dempsey	Wendy L. Holloway	Maggie M. Winters
506 Houston Street	23849 22nd Street	4422 South 121st
Tulsa, OK 74142	Broken Arrow, OK 74009	Tulsa, OK 74142
(918) 555-5541	(918) 555-8842	(918) 555-8833

Doctors form

Doctor number 1	Doctor number 2	Doctor number 3
Carolyn Joswick	Gerald Ingram	Kay Feather
(918) 555-4772	(918) 555-9890	(918) 555-7762
Doctor number 4	Doctor number 5	
Sean Granger	Jerome Deltoro	
(918) 555-1039	(918) 555-8021	

Services form

Co = Consultation	V = Vision Screening	G = Glaucoma Testing
C = Cataract Testing	S = Surgery	E = Emergency

Billing form

Patient number 076	Patient number 076	Patient number 085
Doctor number 2	Doctor number 3	Doctor number 1
Date of visit = 4/1/2015	Date of visit = 4/1/2015	Date of visit = 4/1/2015
Service ID = C	Service ID = V	Service ID = Co
Fee = $85	Fee = $150	Fee = $0
Patient number 074	Patient number 023	Patient number 092
Doctor number 3	Doctor number 5	Doctor number 1
Date of visit = 4/1/2015	Date of visit = 4/1/2015	Date of visit = 4/1/2015
Service ID = V	Service ID = S	Service ID = G
Fee = $150	Fee = $750	Fee = $85

MICROSOFT
ACCESS

Creating Reports and Mailing Labels

PERFORMANCE OBJECTIVES

Upon successful completion of Chapter 6, you will be able to:

- Create a report using the Report button
- Display a report in Print Preview
- Create a report with a query
- Format and customize a report
- Group and sort records in a report
- Create a report using the Report Wizard
- Create mailing labels using the Label Wizard

Tutorials

6.1 Creating and Editing a Report

6.2 Modifying a Report

6.3 Adding a Calculation to a Report

6.4 Applying Conditional Formatting to a Report

6.5 Grouping, Sorting, and Adding Totals to a Report

6.6 Creating a Report Using the Report Wizard

6.7 Creating Mailing Labels

In this chapter, you will learn how to prepare reports from data in a table using the Report button in the Reports group on the CREATE tab and using the Report Wizard. You will also learn how to format and customize a report and create mailing labels using the Label Wizard. Model answers for this chapter's projects appear on the following pages.

Access
AL1C6

Note: Before beginning the projects, copy to your storage medium the AL1C6 subfolder from the AL1 folder on the CD that accompanies this textbook and make AL1C6 the active folder.

Project 1 Create and Customize Reports Using Tables and Queries

Project 1b, Dearborn 2014Sales Report

Project 1b, Dearborn Representatives Report

Project 1c, Dearborn 2014Sales Report

Project 1d, Dearborn ClientsGroupedRpt Report

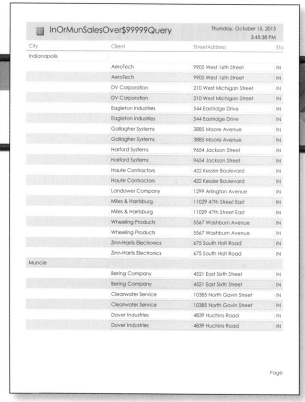

Project 1d, Dearborn InOrMunOver$99999 Report

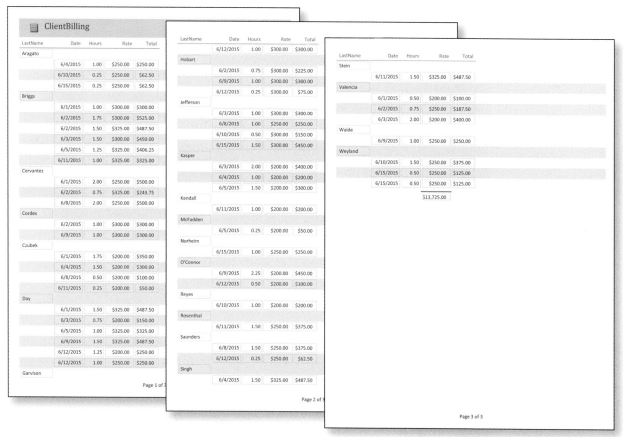

Project 1d, Warren Legal ClientBillingRpt Report

Project 2 Use Wizards to Create Reports and Labels

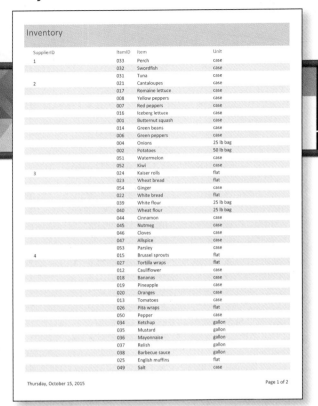

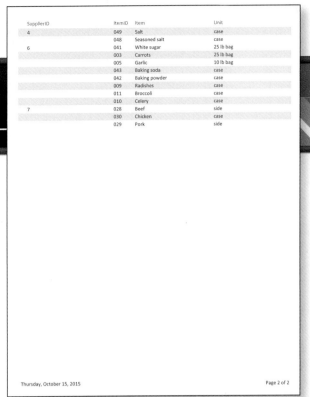

Project 2a, Skyline Inventory Report

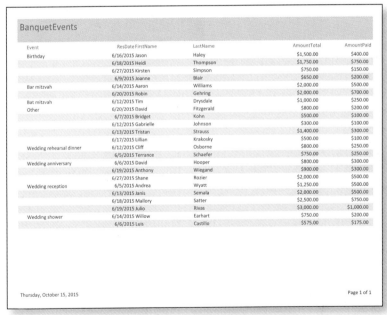

Project 2b, Skyline BanquetEvents Report

Haley Brown
3219 North 33rd Street
Auburn, WA 98001

Margaret Kasper
40210 42nd Avenue
Auburn, WA 98001

Abigail Jefferson
1204 Meridian Road
Auburn, WA 98001

Doris Sturtevant
3713 Nelton Road
Auburn, WA 98001

Carlina McFadden
7809 52nd Street East
Auburn, WA 98001

Ewan Aragato
904 Marine View Drive
Auburn, WA 98002

Tricia O'Connor
3824 Sanders Court
Auburn, WA 98002

Carol Kendall
24 Ferris Parkway
Kent, WA 98003

James Weyland
2533 145th Street East
Kent, WA 98031

Janice Saunders
2757 179th Avenue East
Kent, WA 98032

Jeffrey Day
317 Meridian Street
Kent, WA 98033

Mindy Garvison
68 Queens Avenue
Kent, WA 98033

Kevin Stein
12034 South 22nd Avenue
Kent, WA 98035

Jean Briggs
2110 West Valley Avenue
Kent, WA 98036

Arthur Norheim
10533 Ashton Boulevard
Kent, WA 98036

Consuelo Day
13321 North Lake Drive
Kent, WA 98036

Christina Miles
13043 South 25th Avenue
Kent, WA 98036

Matthew Waide
18391 North 45th Street
Renton, WA 98055

Karl Cordes
240 Mill Avenue
Renton, WA 98055

Mira Valencia
114 Springfield Avenue
Renton, WA 98056

Charles Hobart
11038 132nd Street
Renton, WA 98056

Taylor Reyes
201 Northwest Boulevard
Renton, WA 98056

Eric Rosenthal
1230 Maplewood Road
Auburn, WA 98071

Jennifer Czubek
8790 34th Avenue
Renton, WA 98228

Maddie Singh
450 Mill Avenue
Renton, WA 98228

Chris Cervantez
8722 Riverside Road
Renton, WA 98228

Arthur Jefferson
23110 North 33rd Street
Renton, WA 98230

Project 2c, WarrenLegal Mailing Labels

Project 1 — Create and Customize Reports Using Tables and Queries — 4 Parts

You will create reports with the Report button using tables and queries. You will change the report views; select, move, and resize control objects; sort records; customize reports; apply conditional formatting; and group and sort fields in a report.

Creating Reports

The primary purposes for inserting data in a form are to improve the display of the data and to make data entry easier. You can also insert data in a report. The purpose for doing this is to control what data appears on the page when printed. Reports generally answer specific questions (queries). For example, a report could answer the question *What customers have submitted claims?* or *What products do we currently have on order?* The record source for a report can be a table or query. Create a report with the Report button in the Reports group or use the Report Wizard, which walks you through the process of creating a report.

Creating a Report with the Report Button

To create a report with the Report button, click the desired table or query in the Navigation pane, click the CREATE tab, and then click the Report button in the Reports group. This displays the report in columnar style in Layout view with the REPORT LAYOUT TOOLS DESIGN tab active, as shown in Figure 6.1. Access creates the report using all of the fields in the table or query.

▼ **Quick Steps**

Create a Report
1. Click desired table or query in Navigation pane.
2. Click CREATE tab.
3. Click Report button.

Report

H I N T
Create a report to control what data appears on the page when printed.

Figure 6.1 Report Created with Sales Table

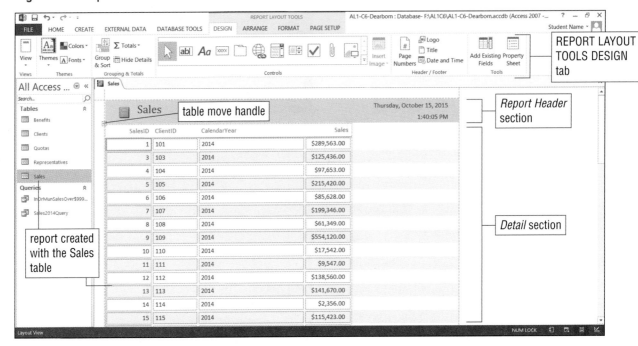

Modifying the Record Source

The record source for a report is the table or query used to create the report. If changes are made to the record source, such as adding or deleting records, those changes are reflected in the report. For example, in Project 1a, you will create a report based on the Sales table. You will then add a record to the Sales table (the record source for the report) and the added record will display in the Sales report.

Project 1a	Creating a Report with the Report Button	Part 1 of 4

1. Display the Open dialog box with the AL1C6 folder on your storage medium the active folder.
2. Open **AL1-C6-Dearborn.accdb** and enable the contents.
3. Create a report based on the Sales table by completing the following steps:
   a. Click the Sales table in the Navigation pane.
   b. Click the CREATE tab.
   c. Click the Report button in the Reports group.

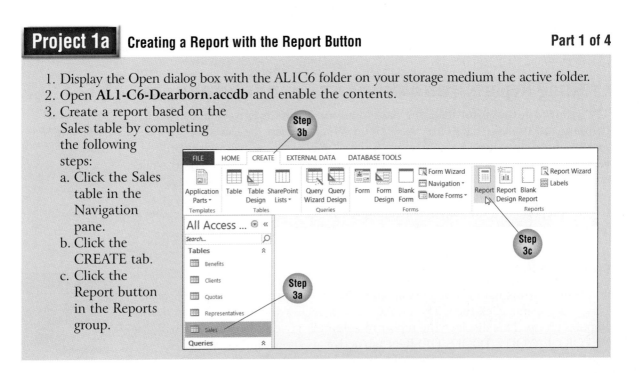

d. Save the report by clicking the Save button on the Quick Access toolbar and then clicking OK at the Save As dialog box. (This saves the report with the default name, *Sales*.)

e. Close the Sales report.

4. Add a record to the Sales table by completing the following steps:

a. Double-click the Sales table in the Navigation pane. (Make sure you open the Sales table and not the Sales report.)

b. Click the New button in the Records group on the HOME tab.

c. Press the Tab key to accept the default number in the *SalesID* field.

d. Type **127** in the *ClientID* field and then press the Tab key.

e. Type **2015** in the *CalendarYear* field and then press the Tab key.

f. Type **176420** in the *Sales* field.

g. Close the Sales table.

5. Open the Sales report and then scroll down to the bottom. Notice that the new record you added to the Sales table displays in the report.

6. Close the Sales report.

7. Use the query named *Sales2014Query* to create a report by completing the following steps:

a. Click *Sales2014Query* in the Queries group in the Navigation pane.

b. Click the CREATE tab.

c. Click the Report button in the Reports group.

8. Access automatically inserted a total amount for the *Sales* column of the report. Delete this amount by scrolling down to the bottom of the report, clicking the total amount at the bottom of the *Sales* column, and then pressing the Delete key. (This deletes the total amount but not the underline above the amount.)

9. Save the report by clicking the Save button on the Quick Access toolbar, typing **2014Sales** in the *Report Name* text box in the Save As dialog box, and then clicking OK.

Modifying Control Objects

A report, like a form, is comprised of control objects, such as logos, titles, labels, and text boxes. You can select an object in a report by clicking the object. A selected object displays with an orange border. If you click a data field in the report, Access selects all of the objects in the column except the column heading.

Like a form, a report contains a *Header* section and a *Detail* section. Select all of the control objects in the report in both the *Header* and *Detail* sections by pressing Ctrl + A. Control objects in the *Detail* section are contained in a report table. To select the control objects in the report table, click in any cell in the report and then click the table move handle. The table move handle is a small square with a four-headed arrow inside that displays in the upper left corner of the table (see Figure 6.1). Move the table and all of the control objects within the table by dragging the table move handle using the mouse.

Adjust column widths in a report by dragging the column border left or right. In addition to adjusting column width, you can change the position of a selected column. To do this, select the desired column, position the mouse pointer in the column heading until the pointer displays with a four-headed arrow attached, and then drag the column left or right to the desired position. As you drag the column, a vertical pink bar displays indicating where the column will be placed when you release the mouse button.

Some control objects in a report, such as a column heading or title, are label control objects. Edit a label control by double-clicking in the object and then making the desired change. For example, if you want to rename a label control, double-click in the label control and then edit or type the desired text.

Ascending

Descending

▼ **Quick Steps**

Sort Records
1. Click in field containing data.
2. Click Ascending button or click Descending button.

Sorting Records

Sort data in a report by clicking in the field containing the data you want to sort and then clicking the Ascending button or Descending button in the Sort & Filter group on the HOME tab. Click the Ascending button to sort text in alphabetical order from A to Z or sort numbers from lowest to highest or click the Descending button to sort text in alphabetical order from Z to A or sort numbers from highest to lowest.

Displaying and Customizing a Report in Print Preview

Print Preview

View

When you create a report, the report displays in the work area in Layout view. In addition to Layout view, three other views are available: Report, Print Preview, and Design. Use Print Preview to display the report as it will appear when printed. To change to Print Preview, click the Print Preview button in the view area located at the right side of the Status bar. You can also click the View button arrow in the Views group on the HOME tab or REPORT LAYOUT TOOLS DESIGN tab and then click *Print Preview* at the drop-down list.

In Print Preview, send the report to the printer by clicking the Print button on the PRINT PREVIEW tab. Use options in the Page Size group to change the page size and margins. If you want to print only the report data and not the column headings, report title, shading, and gridlines, insert a check mark in the *Print Data Only* check box. Use options in the Page Layout group to specify the page orientation, specify columns, and display the Page Setup dialog box. Click the Page Setup button and the Page Setup dialog box displays with options for customizing margins, orientation, size, and columns.

Deleting a Report

If you no longer need a report in a database, delete the report. Delete a report by clicking the report name in the Navigation pane, clicking the Delete button in the Records group on the HOME tab, and then clicking the Yes button at the message asking if you want to permanently delete the report. Another method is to right-click the report in the Navigation pane, click *Delete* at the shortcut menu, and then click the Yes at the message. If you are deleting a report from your computer's hard drive, the message asking if you want to permanently delete the report will not display. This is because Access automatically sends the deleted report to the Recycle Bin, where it can be retrieved if necessary.

Finding Data in a Report ■■■■■■■■■■■■■■■■■■■■■

You can find specific data in a report with options at the Find dialog box. Display this dialog box by clicking the Find button in the Find group on the HOME tab. At the Find dialog box, enter the data you want to search for in the *Find What* text box. The *Match* option at the Find dialog box is set at *Whole Field* by default. At this setting, the data you enter must match the entire entry in a field. If you want to search for partial data in a field, change the *Match* option to *Any Part of Field* or *Start of Field*. If you want the text you enter in the *Find What* text box to match the case in a field entry, click the *Match Case* option check box to insert a check mark. Access will search the entire report by default. You can change this to *Up* if you want to search from the currently active field to the beginning of the report or *Down* if you want to search from the currently active field to the end of the report. Click the Find Next button to find data that matches the data in the *Find What* text box.

Project 1b	Adjusting Control Objects, Renaming Labels, Finding and Sorting Data, Displaying a Report in Print Preview, and Deleting a Report	Part 2 of 4

1. With the 2014Sales report open, reverse the order of the *RepName* and *Client* columns by completing the following steps:
   a. Make sure the report displays in Layout view.
   b. Click the *RepName* column heading.
   c. Hold down the Shift key and then click in the last control object in the *RepName* column (the control object containing *Catherine Singleton*).
   d. Position the mouse pointer inside the *RepName* column heading until the pointer displays with a four-headed arrow attached.
   e. Hold down the left mouse button, drag to the left until the vertical pink bar displays to the left of the *Client* column, and then release the mouse button.

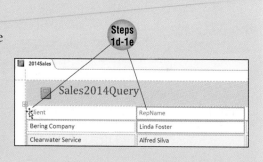

2. Sort the data in the *Sales* column in descending order by completing the following steps:
   a. Click the HOME tab.
   b. Click in any field in the *Sales* column.
   c. Click the Descending button in the Sort & Filter group.

3. Rename the *RepName* label control as *Representative* by double-clicking in the label control object containing the text *RepName*, selecting *RepName*, and then typing **Representative**.

4. Double-click in the *Sales* label control and then rename it *Sales 2014*.

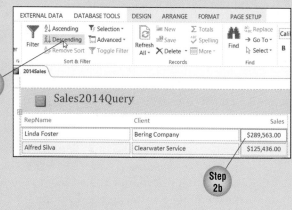

5. Move the report table by completing the following steps:
   a. Click in a cell in the report.
   b. Position the mouse pointer on the table move handle (which displays as a small square with a four-headed arrow inside and is located in the upper left corner of the table).
   c. Hold down the left mouse button, drag the report table to the right until it is centered between the left and right sides of the *Detail* section, and then release the mouse button. (When you drag with the mouse, you will see only outlines of some of the control objects.)

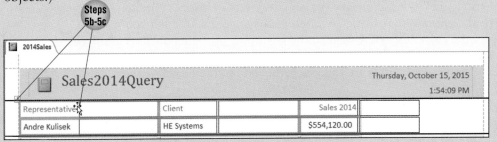

6. Display the report in Print Preview by clicking the Print Preview button in the view area at the right side of the Status bar.

7. Click the One Page button (already active) in the Zoom group to display the entire page.
8. Click the Zoom button arrow in the Zoom group and then click *50%* at the drop-down list.
9. Click the One Page button in the Zoom group.
10. Print the report by clicking the Print button on the PRINT PREVIEW tab and then clicking OK at the Print dialog box.
11. Close Print Preview by clicking the Close Print Preview button located at the right side of the PRINT PREVIEW tab.
12. Save and then close the 2014Sales report.
13. Create a report with the Representatives table by completing the following steps:
    a. Click *Representatives* in the Tables group in the Navigation pane.
    b. Click the CREATE tab.
    c. Click the Report button in the Reports group.
14. Adjust the width of the second column by completing the following steps:
    a. Click in the *RepName* column heading.
    b. Drag the right border of the selected column heading to the left until the border displays near the longest entry in the column.
15. Complete steps similar to those in Step 14 to decrease the width of the third column (*Telephone*) and the fourth column (*Email*).
16. Search for fields containing a quote of *2* by completing the following steps:
    a. Click in the *RepID* column heading.
    b. Click the HOME tab and then click the Find button in the Find group.

c. At the Find dialog box, type 2 in the *Find What* text box.

d. Make sure the *Match* option is set to *Whole Field*. (If not, click the down-pointing arrow at the right side of the *Match* option and then click *Whole Field* at the drop-down list.)

e. Click the Find Next button.

f. Continue clicking the Find Next button until a message displays telling you that Access has finished searching the records. At this message, click OK.

g. Click the Cancel button to close the Find dialog box.

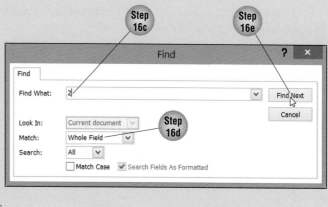

17. Suppose you want to find information on a representative and you remember the first name but not the last name. Search for a field containing the first name *Lydia* by completing the following steps:

a. Click in the *RepID* column heading.

b. Click the Find button in the Find group.

c. At the Find dialog box, type **Lydia** in the *Find What* text box.

d. Click the down-pointing arrow at the right side of the *Match* option and then click *Any Part of Field* at the drop-down list.

e. Click the Find Next button. (Access will find and select the representative name *Lydia Alvarado*.)

f. Click the Cancel button to close the Find dialog box.

18. Click the control object at the bottom of the *RepID* column containing the number *17* and then press the Delete key. (This does not delete the underline above the amount.)

19. Switch to Print Preview by clicking the View button arrow in the Views group on the REPORT LAYOUT TOOLS DESIGN tab and then clicking *Print Preview* at the drop-down list.

20. Click the Margins button in the Page Size group and then click *Normal* at the drop-down list.

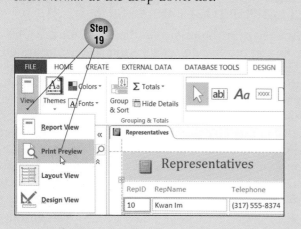

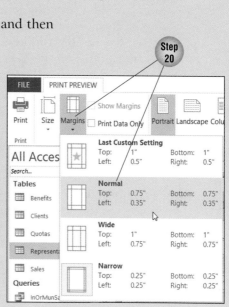

21. Print the first page of the report (the second page contains only shading) by completing the following steps:
    a. Click the Print button that displays at the left side of the PRINT PREVIEW tab.
    b. At the Print dialog box, click the *Pages* option in the *Print Range* section.
    c. Type 1 in the *From* text box, press the Tab key, and then type 1 in the *To* text box.
    d. Click OK.
22. Close Print Preview by clicking the Close Print Preview button.
23. Save the report with the name *Representatives*.
24. Close the Representatives report.
25. Delete the Sales report by right-clicking the Sales report in the Navigation pane, clicking *Delete* at the shortcut menu, and then clicking Yes at the message that displays.

Customizing Reports ■■■■■■■■■■■■■■■■■■■■■■■

Customize a report in much the same manner as you customize a form. When you first create a report, the report displays in Layout view and the REPORT LAYOUT TOOLS DESIGN tab is active. Customize control objects in the *Detail* section and the *Header* section with buttons on the REPORT LAYOUT TOOLS ribbon using the DESIGN tab, ARRANGE tab, FORMAT tab, or PAGE SETUP tab selected.

The themes available in Access are the same as the themes available in Word, Excel, and PowerPoint.

Totals

The REPORT LAYOUT TOOLS DESIGN tab contains many of the same options at the FORM LAYOUT TOOLS DESIGN tab. Use options on this tab to apply a theme, insert controls, insert header or footer data, and add existing fields. The tab also contains the Grouping & Totals group, which you will learn about in the next section. Use the Totals button in the Grouping & Totals group to perform functions such as finding the sum, average, maximum, or minimum of the numbers in a column. To use the Totals button, click the column heading of the column containing the data you want to total, click the Totals button, and then click the desired function at the drop-down list. Use the Page Number button on the REPORT LAYOUT TOOLS DESIGN tab to insert and format page numbers.

Click the REPORT LAYOUT TOOLS ARRANGE tab and options display for inserting and selecting rows, splitting cells horizontally and vertically, moving data up or down, controlling margins, and changing the padding between objects and cells. The options on the REPORT LAYOUT TOOLS ARRANGE tab are the same as the options on the FORM LAYOUT TOOLS ARRANGE tab.

Customize the formatting of control objects with options at the REPORT LAYOUT TOOLS FORMAT tab.

Select and format data in a report with options on the REPORT LAYOUT TOOLS FORMAT tab. The options on this tab are the same as the options on the FORM LAYOUT TOOLS FORMAT tab. You can apply formatting to a report or specific objects in a report. If you want to apply formatting to a specific object, click the object in the report or click the Object button arrow in the Selection group on the REPORT LAYOUT TOOLS FORMAT tab and then click the desired object at the drop-down list. To format all objects in the report, click the Select All button in the Selection group. This selects all objects in the report, including objects in the *Header* section. If you want to select all of the objects in the report, click the table move handle. You can also click the table move handle and then drag with the mouse to move the objects in the form.

With buttons in the Font, Number, Background, and Control Formatting groups, you can apply formatting to a control object or cell and to selected objects or cells in a report. Use buttons in the Font group to change the font, apply a different font size, apply text effects (such as bold and underline), and change the alignment of data in objects. Insert a background image in the report using the Background button and apply formatting to objects or cells with buttons in the Control Formatting group. Depending on what is selected in the report, some of the buttons may not be active.

Background

Click the REPORT LAYOUT TOOLS PAGE SETUP tab and the buttons that display are buttons that are also available in Print Preview. For example, you can change the page size and page layout of the report and display the Page Setup dialog box.

Project 1c | **Applying Formatting to a Report** | **Part 3 of 4**

1. With **AL1-C6-Dearborn.accdb** open, open the 2014Sales report.
2. Display the report in Layout view.
3. Click the Themes button in the Themes group on the REPORT LAYOUT TOOLS DESIGN tab and then click *Ion* at the drop-down gallery (fourth column, first row).
4. Click the Title button in the Header/Footer group (which selects the current title), type **2014 Sales**, and then press Enter.
5. Insert new control objects by completing the following steps:
   a. Click in the *Representative* cell.
   b. Click the REPORT LAYOUT TOOLS ARRANGE tab.
   c. Click the Insert Above button in the Rows & Columns group.

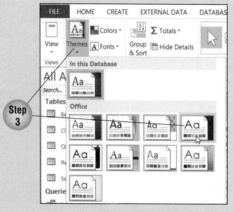

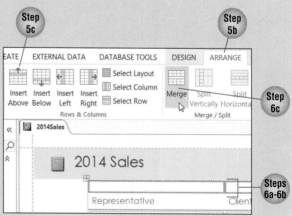

6. Merge the cells in the new row by completing the following steps:
   a. Click in the blank cell immediately above the *Representative* cell.
   b. Hold down the Shift key and then click immediately above the *Sales 2014* cell. (This selects three cells.)
   c. Click the Merge button in the Merge/Split group.
   d. Type **Dearborn 2014 Sales** in the new cell.
7. Split a cell by completing the following steps:
   a. Click in the *2014 Sales* title in the *Header* section.
   b. Split the cell containing the title by clicking the Split Horizontally button in the Merge/Split group.
   c. Click in the empty cell immediately right of the cell containing the title *Sales 2014* and then press the Delete key. (Deleting the empty cell causes the date and time to move to the left in the *Header* section.)
8. Change the report table margins and padding by completing the following steps:
   a. Click in any cell in the *Detail* section and then click the table move handle that displays in the upper left corner of the *Dearborn 2014 Sales* cell. (This selects the control objects in the report table in the *Detail* section.)

b. Click the Control Margins button in the Position group and then click *Narrow* at the drop-down list.

c. Click the Control Padding button in the Position group and then click *Medium* at the drop-down list.

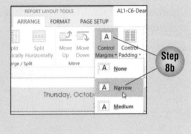

Step 8b

9. Click in the *Dearborn 2014 Sales* cell and then drag down the bottom border so all of the text in the cell is visible.

10. Change the font for all control objects in the report by completing the following steps:

a. Press Ctrl + A to select all control objects in the report. (An orange border displays around selected objects.)

b. Click the REPORT LAYOUT TOOLS FORMAT tab.

Step 10b

c. Click the Font button arrow in the Font group and then click *Cambria* at the drop-down list. (You may need to scroll down the list to display *Cambria*.)

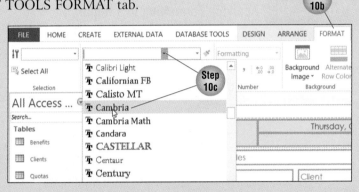

Step 10c

11. Apply bold formatting and change the alignment of the column headings by completing the following steps:

a. Click *Dearborn 2014 Sales* to select the control object.

b. Hold down the Shift key and then click *Sales 2014*. (This selects four cells.)

c. Click the Bold button in the Font group.

d. Click the Center button in the Font group.

Step 11c   Step 11d

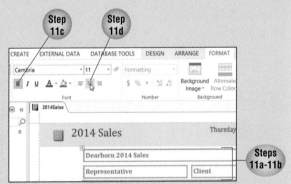

Steps 11a-11b

12. Format amounts and apply conditional formatting to the amounts by completing the following steps:

a. Click the first field value below the *Sales 2014* column heading. (This selects all of the amounts in the column.)

b. Click twice on the Decrease Decimals button in the Number group.

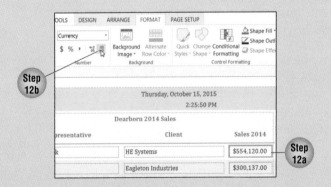

Step 12b

Step 12a

c. Click the Conditional Formatting button in the Control Formatting group.

d. At the Conditional Formatting Rules Manager dialog box, click the New Rule button.

e. At the New Formatting Rule dialog box, click the down-pointing arrow at the right side of the second option box in the *Edit the rule description* section and then click *greater than* at the drop-down list.

f. Click in the text box immediately right of the option box containing *greater than* and then type 199999.

g. Click the Background color button arrow and then click the *Green 2* color option (seventh column, third row).

h. Click the OK button.

i. At the Conditional Formatting Rules Manager dialog box, click the New Rule button.

j. At the New Formatting Rule dialog box, click the down-pointing arrow at the right side of the second option box in the *Edit the rule description* section and then click *less than* at the drop-down list.

k. Click in the text box immediately right of the option containing *less than* and then type 200000.

l. Click the Background color button arrow and then click the *Maroon 2* color option (sixth column, third row).

m. Click OK to close the New Formatting Rule dialog box.

n. Click OK to close the Conditional Formatting Rules Manager dialog box.

13. Sum the totals in the *Sales 2014* column by completing the following steps:
   a. Click in the *Sales 2014* column heading.
   b. Click the REPORT LAYOUT TOOLS DESIGN tab.
   c. Click the Totals button in the Grouping & Totals group and then click *Sum* at the drop-down list.

14. Click in the *Sales 2014* sum amount (located at the bottom of the *Sales 2014* column) and then drag down the bottom border so the entire amount is visible in the cell.

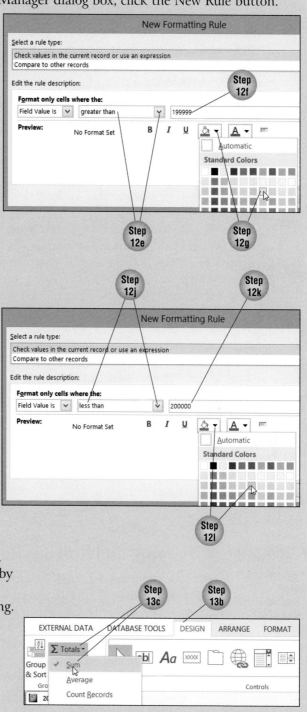

15. Change the top margin by completing the following steps:
    a. Click in the *Representative* column heading and then click the REPORT LAYOUT TOOLS PAGE SETUP tab.
    b. Click the Page Setup button in the Page Layout group.
    c. At the Page Setup dialog box with the Print Options tab selected, select the current measurement in the *Top* measurement box and then type 0.5.
    d. Click OK to close the Page Setup dialog box.

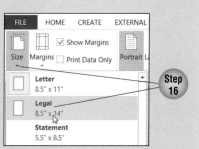

16. Change the page size by clicking the Size button in the Page Size group and and then clicking *Legal* at the drop-down list.
17. Display the report in Print Preview by clicking the FILE tab, clicking the *Print* option, and then clicking the Print Preview button.
18. Click the One Page button in the Zoom group and notice that the entire report will print on one legal-sized page.
19. Click the Close Print Preview button to return to the report.
20. Change the page size by clicking the PAGE LAYOUT TOOLS PAGE SETUP tab, clicking the Size button in the Page Size group, and then clicking *Letter* at the drop-down list.
21. Insert and then remove a background image by completing the following steps:
    a. Click the REPORT LAYOUT TOOLS FORMAT tab.
    b. Click the Background Image button in the Background group and then click *Browse* at the drop-down list.
    c. At the Insert Picture dialog box, navigate to the AL1C6 folder on your storage medium and then double-click *Mountain.jpg*.
    d. Scroll through the report and notice how the image displays in the report.
    e. Click the Undo button on the Quick Access toolbar to remove the background image. (You may need to click the Undo button more than once.)
22. Print the report by clicking the FILE tab, clicking the *Print* option, and then clicking the Quick Print button.
23. Save and then close the report.

▼ **Quick Steps**

Group and Sort Records
1. Open desired report in Layout view.
2. Click Group & Sort button.
3. Click Add a group button.
4. Click desired group field.

Group & Sort

Add a group

Grouping and Sorting Records ■■■■■■■■■■■■■■■■■■

A report presents database information in a printed form and generally displays data that answers a specific question. To make the data in a report easy to understand, divide the data into groups. For example, you can divide data in a report by regions, sales, dates, or any other division that helps clarify the data for the reader. Access contains a powerful group and sort feature that you can use in a report. In this section, you will complete basic group and sort functions. For more detailed information on grouping and sorting, refer to the Access help files.

Click the Group & Sort button in the Grouping & Totals group on the REPORT LAYOUT TOOLS DESIGN tab and the Group, Sort, and Total pane displays at the bottom of the work area, as shown in Figure 6.2. Click the Add a group button in the Group, Sort, and Total pane and Access adds a new grouping level row to the pane, along with a list of available fields. Click the field on which you want to group data in the report and Access adds the grouping level in the report. With options in the grouping level row, change the group, specify the sort order, and expand the row to display additional options.

Figure 6.2 Group, Sort, and Total Pane

ClientID	RepID	Client	StreetAddress	City	State	ZipCode	Telephone	Email
101	23	Bering Company	4521 East Sixth Street	Muncie	IN	47310-5500	(765) 555-5565	bc@emcp.net
102	10	Fairhaven Developers	574 East Raymond Street	Indianapolis	IN	46219-3005	(317) 555-8885	fd@emcp.net
103	13	Clearwater Service	10385 North Gavin Street	Muncie	IN	47308-1236	(765) 555-1166	cs@emcp.net
104	17	Landower Company	1299 Arlington Avenue	Indianapolis	IN	46236-1299	(317) 555-1255	lc@emcp.net
105	15	Harford Systems	9654 Jackson Street	Indianapolis	IN	46247-9654	(317) 555-7665	hs@emcp.net
106	19	Providence, Inc.	12490 141st Street	Muncie	IN	47306-3410	(765) 555-3210	pi@emcp.net
107	12	Gallagher Systems	3885 Moore Avenue	Indianapolis	IN	47229-1075	(317) 555-9922	gs@emcp.net
108	26	Karris Supplies	12003 East 16th Street	Fishers	IN	46038-1200	(317) 555-2005	ks@emcp.net
109	18	HE Systems	321 Midland Avenue	Greenwood	IN	46143-3120	(317) 555-3311	he@emcp.net
110	21	Blue Ridge, Inc.	29 South 25th Street	Indianapolis	IN	46227-1355	(317) 555-7742	br@emcp.net

Clients — Thursday, October 15, 2015 — 3:35:14 PM

Group, Sort, and Total

[≡ Add a group   ↓ Add a sort]

Group records by a specific field by clicking this button and then clicking the desired field.

Sort records by a specific field by clicking this button and then clicking the desired field.

When you specify a grouping level, Access automatically sorts that level in ascending order (from A to Z or lowest to highest). You can then sort additional data within the report by clicking the Add a sort button in the Group, Sort, and Total pane. This inserts a sorting row in the pane below the grouping level row, along with a list of available fields. At this list, click the field on which you want to sort. For example, in Project 1d, you will specify that a report is grouped by city (which will display in ascending order) and then specify that the client names display in alphabetical order within the city.

To delete a grouping or sorting level in the Group, Sort, and Total pane, click the Delete button that displays at the right side of the level row. After specifying the grouping and sorting levels, close the Group, Sort, and Total pane by clicking the Close button located in the upper right corner of the pane.

HINT

Grouping allows you to separate groups of records visually.

Add a sort

Project 1d Grouping and Sorting Data   **Part 4 of 4**

1. With **AL1-C6-Dearborn.accdb** open, create a report with the Clients table using the Report button on the CREATE tab.
2. Click each column heading individually and then decrease the size of each column so the right border is just right of the longest entry.
3. Change the orientation to landscape by completing the following steps:
   a. Click the REPORT LAYOUT TOOLS PAGE SETUP tab.
   b. Click the Landscape button in the Page Layout group.
4. Group the report by representative ID and then sort by clients by completing the following steps:
   a. Click the REPORT LAYOUT TOOLS DESIGN tab.
   b. Click the Group & Sort button in the Grouping & Totals group.

c. Click the Add a group button in the Group, Sort, and Total pane.

Step 4c

d. Click the *RepID* field in the list box.
e. Scroll through the report and notice that the records are grouped by the *RepID* field. Also, notice that the client names within each RepID field group are not in alphabetic order.
f. Click the Add a sort button in the Group, Sort, and Total pane.
g. Click the *Client* field in the list box.
h. Scroll through the report and notice that client names are now alphabetized within *RepID* field groups.
i. Close the Group, Sort, and Total pane by clicking the Close button located in the upper right corner of the pane.

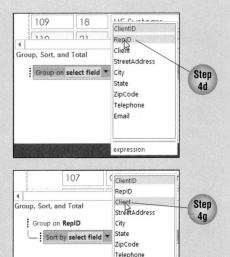

5. Save the report and name it *ClientsGroupedRpt*.
6. Print the first page of the report by completing the following steps:
   a. Click the FILE tab, click the *Print* option, and then click the Print button.
   b. At the Print dialog box, click the *Pages* option in the *Print Range* section.
   c. Type 1 in the *From* text box, press the Tab key, and then type 1 in the *To* text box.
   d. Click OK.
7. Close the ClientsGroupedRpt report.
8. Create a report with the InOrMunSalesOver$99999Query query using the Report button on the CREATE tab.
9. Make sure the report displays in Layout view.
10. Group the report by city and then sort by clients by completing the following steps:
    a. Click the Group & Sort button in the Grouping & Totals group on the REPORT LAYOUT TOOLS DESIGN tab.
    b. Click the Add a group button in the Group, Sort, and Total pane.
    c. Click the *City* field in the list box.
    d. Click the Add a sort button in the Group, Sort, and Total pane and then click the *Client* field in the list box.
    e. Close the Group, Sort, and Total pane by clicking the Close button located in the upper right corner of the pane.
11. Print the first page of the report. (Refer to Step 6.)
12. Save the report and name it *InMunSalesOver$99999*.
13. Close the report.
14. Close **AL1-C6-Dearborn.accdb**.
15. Display the Open dialog box with the AL1C6 folder on your storage medium the active folder, open **AL1-C6-WarrenLegal.accdb**, and enable the contents.

16. Design a query that extracts records from three tables with the following specifications:
    a. Add the Billing, Clients, and Rates tables to the query window.
    b. Insert the *LastName* field from the *Clients* field list box to the first *Field* row field.
    c. Insert the *Date* field from the *Billing* field list box to the second *Field* row field.
    d. Insert the *Hours* field from the *Billing* field list box to the third *Field* row field.
    e. Insert the *Rate* field from the *Rates* field list box to the fourth *Field* row field.
    f. Click in the fifth *Field* row field, type **Total: [Hours]*[Rate]**, and then press Enter.

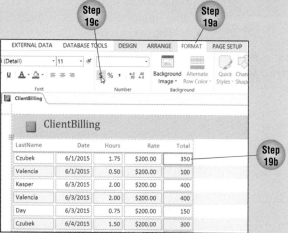

	Step 16b	Step 16c	Step 16d	Step 16e	Step 16f
Field:	LastName	Date	Hours	Rate	Total: [Hours]*[Rate]
Table:	Clients	Billing	Billing	Rates	
Sort:					
Show:	✔	✔	✔	✔	✔
Criteria:					
or:					

    g. Run the query.
    h. Save the query and name it *ClientBilling*.
    i. Close the query.
17. Create a report with the ClientBilling query using the Report button on the CREATE tab.
18. Click each column heading individually and then decrease the size of each column so the right border is near the longest entry.
19. Apply Currency formatting to the numbers in the *Total* column by completing the following steps:
    a. Click the REPORT LAYOUT TOOLS FORMAT tab.
    b. Click in the first field below the *Total* column (the field containing the number *350*).
    c. Click the Apply Currency Format button in the Number group.
    d. If necessary, increase the size of the *Total* column so the entire amounts (including the dollar signs) are visible.

Step 19c   Step 19a

Step 19b

LastName	Date	Hours	Rate	Total
Czubek	6/1/2015	1.75	$200.00	350
Valencia	6/1/2015	0.50	$200.00	100
Kasper	6/3/2015	2.00	$200.00	400
Valencia	6/3/2015	2.00	$200.00	400
Day	6/3/2015	0.75	$200.00	150
Czubek	6/4/2015	1.50	$200.00	300

20. Group the report by last name by completing the following steps:
    a. Click the REPORT LAYOUT TOOLS DESIGN tab.
    b. Click the Group & Sort button in the Grouping & Totals group.
    c. Click the Add a group button in the Group, Sort, and Total pane.
    d. Click the *LastName* field in the list box.
    e. Click the Add a sort button in the Group, Sort, and Total pane.
    f. Click the *Date* field in the list box.
    g. Close the Group, Sort, and Total pane by clicking the Close button located in the upper right corner of the pane.
21. Scroll to the bottom of the report and, if necessary, increase the size of the column and row so the total amount in the *Rate* column is visible.
22. Save the report and name it *ClientBillingRpt*.
23. Print and then close the report. (The report will print on three pages.)
24. Close **AL1-C6-WarrenLegal.accdb**.

You will create reports using the Report Wizard and prepare mailing labels using the Label Wizard.

Creating Reports Using the Report Wizard ■■■■■■■■

Access offers a Report Wizard that will guide you through the steps for creating a report. To create a report using the wizard, click the CREATE tab and then click the Report Wizard button in the Reports group. At the first wizard dialog box, shown in Figure 6.3, choose the desired table or query with options from the *Tables/Queries* option box. Specify the fields you want included in the report by inserting them in the *Selected Fields* list box and then clicking the Next button.

At the second Report Wizard dialog box, shown in Figure 6.4, specify the grouping level of data in the report. To group data by a specific field, click the field in the list box at the left side of the dialog box and then click the One Field button. Use the button containing the left-pointing arrow to remove an option as a grouping level. Use the up-pointing and down-pointing arrows to change the priority of the field.

Specify a sort order with options at the third Report Wizard dialog box, shown in Figure 6.5. To specify a sort order, click the down-pointing arrow at the right of the option box preceded by the number *1* and then click the field name. The default sort order is ascending. You can change this to descending by clicking the button that displays at the right side of the text box. After identifying the sort order, click the Next button.

Figure 6.3 First Report Wizard Dialog Box

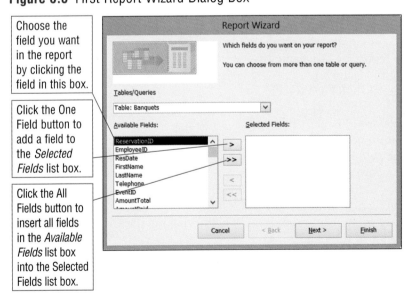

Figure 6.4 Second Report Wizard Dialog Box

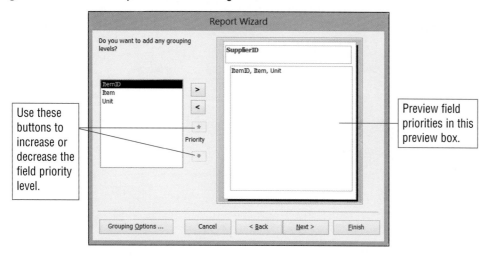

Use these buttons to increase or decrease the field priority level.

Preview field priorities in this preview box.

Figure 6.5 Third Report Wizard Dialog Box

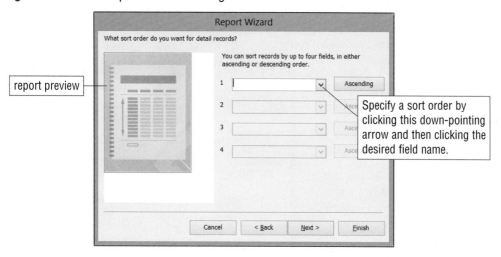

report preview

Specify a sort order by clicking this down-pointing arrow and then clicking the desired field name.

Use options at the fourth Report Wizard dialog box, shown in Figure 6.6, to specify the layout and orientation of the report. The *Layout* section has the default setting of *Stepped*. You can change this to *Block* or *Outline*. By default, the report will print in portrait orientation. You can change to landscape orientation in the *Orientation* section of the dialog box. Access will adjust field widths in the report so all of the fields fit on one page. If you do not want Access to make this adjustment, remove the check mark from the *Adjust the field width so all fields fit on a page* option.

At the fifth and final Report Wizard dialog box, type a name for the report and then click the Finish button.

Figure 6.6 Fourth Report Wizard Dialog Box

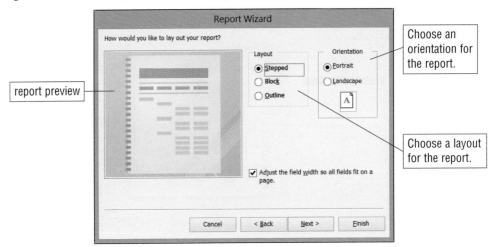

report preview

Choose an orientation for the report.

Choose a layout for the report.

Project 2a   **Using the Report Wizard to Prepare a Report**   **Part 1 of 3**

1. Display the Open dialog box with the AL1C6 folder on your storage medium the active folder.
2. Open **AL1-C6-Skyline.accdb** and enable the contents.
3. Create a report using the Report Wizard by completing the following steps:
   a. Click the CREATE tab.
   b. Click the Report Wizard button in the Reports group.
   c. At the first Report Wizard dialog box, click the down-pointing arrow at the right side of the *Tables/Queries* option box and then click *Table: Inventory* at the drop-down list.
   d. Click the All Fields button to insert all of the Inventory fields in the *Selected Fields* list box.
   e. Click the Next button.
   f. At the second Report Wizard dialog box, make sure *SupplierID* displays in blue at the top of the preview page at the right side of the dialog box and then click the Next button.
   g. At the third Report Wizard dialog box, click the Next button. (You want to use the sorting defaults.)
   h. At the fourth Report Wizard dialog box, click the *Block* option in the *Layout* section and then click the Next button.

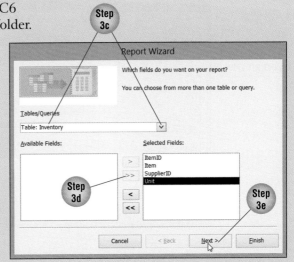

Step 3c

Step 3d

Step 3e

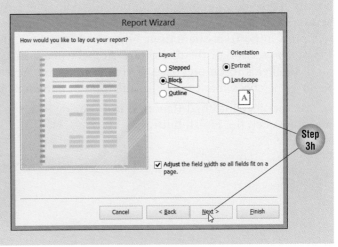

Step 3h

i. At the fifth Report Wizard dialog box, make sure *Inventory* displays in the *What title do you want for your report?* text box and then click the Finish button. (The report displays in Print Preview.)
4. With the report in Print Preview, click the Print button at the left side of the PRINT PREVIEW tab and then click OK at the Print dialog box. (The report will print on two pages.)
5. Close Print Preview.
6. Switch to Report view by clicking the View button on the REPORT DESIGN TOOLS DESIGN tab.
7. Close the Inventory report.

If you create a report with fields from only one table, you will choose options from five Report Wizard dialog boxes. If you create a report with fields from more than one table, you will choose options from six Report Wizard dialog boxes. After choosing the tables and fields at the first dialog box, the second dialog box that displays asks how you want to view the data. For example, if you specify fields from a Suppliers table and fields from an Orders table, the second Report Wizard dialog box will ask you if you want to view data "by Suppliers" or "by Orders."

Project 2b   Creating a Report with Fields from Multiple Tables   Part 2 of 3

1. With **AL1-C6-Skyline.accdb** open, create a report with the Report Wizard by completing the following steps:
   a. Click the CREATE tab.
   b. Click the Report Wizard button in the Reports group.
   c. At the first Report Wizard dialog box, click the down-pointing arrow at the right side of the *Tables/Queries* option box and then click *Table: Events* at the drop-down list.
   d. Click the *Event* field in the *Available Fields* list box and then click the One Field button.
   e. Click the down-pointing arrow at the right side of the *Tables/Queries* option box and then click *Table: Banquets* at the drop-down list.
   f. Insert the following fields in the *Selected Fields* list box:
        ResDate
        FirstName
        LastName
        AmountTotal
        AmountPaid
   g. After inserting the fields, click the Next button.
   h. At the second Report Wizard dialog box, make sure *by Events* is selected and then click the Next button.

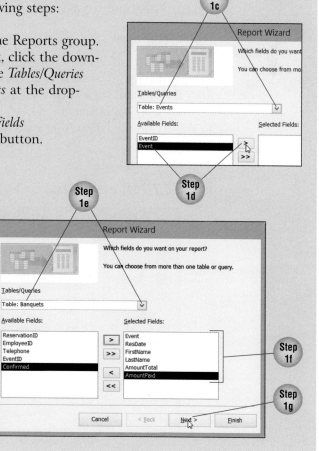

i. At the third Report Wizard dialog box, click the Next button. (The report preview shows that the report will be grouped by event.)

j. At the fourth Report Wizard dialog box, click the Next button. (You want to use the sorting defaults.)

k. At the fifth Report Wizard dialog box, click the *Block* option in the *Layout* section, click *Landscape* in the *Orientation* section, and then click the Next button.

Step 1l

l. At the sixth Report Wizard dialog box, select the current name in the *What title do you want for your report?* text box, type **BanquetEvents**, and then click the Finish button.

2. Close Print Preview and then change to Layout view.

3. Print and then close the BanquetEvents report.

4. Close **AL1-C6-Skyline.accdb**.

Preparing Mailing Labels

▼ Quick Steps

Create Mailing Labels Using the Label Wizard
1. Click desired table.
2. Click CREATE tab.
3. Click Labels button.
4. Choose desired options at each Label Wizard dialog box.

Labels

Access includes a mailing label wizard that walks you through the steps for creating mailing labels with fields in a table. To create mailing labels, click the desired table, click the CREATE tab, and then click the Labels button in the Reports group. At the first Label Wizard dialog box, shown in Figure 6.7, specify the label size, units of measure, and label type and then click the Next button. At the second Label Wizard dialog box, shown in Figure 6.8, specify the font name, size, weight, and color and then click the Next button.

Specify the fields you want included in the mailing labels at the third Label Wizard dialog box, shown in Figure 6.9. To do this, click the field in the *Available fields* list box and then click the One Field button. This moves the field to the *Prototype label* box. Insert the fields in the *Prototype label* box as you want the text to display on the label. After inserting the fields in the *Prototype label* box, click the Next button.

Figure 6.7 First Label Wizard Dialog Box

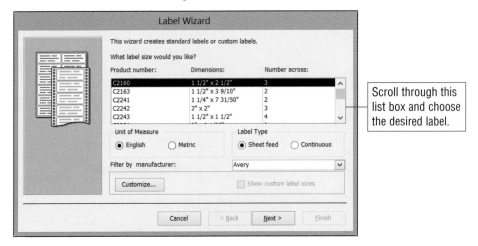

Scroll through this list box and choose the desired label.

Figure 6.8 Second Label Wizard Dialog Box

label preview

Choose the desired label font name, size, weight, and color in this section.

Figure 6.9 Third Label Wizard Dialog Box

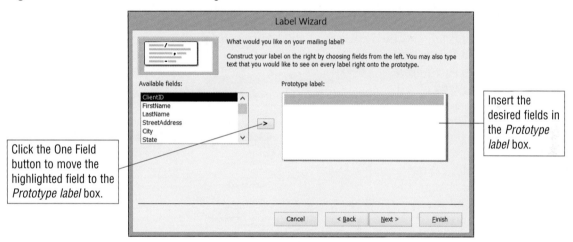

Click the One Field button to move the highlighted field to the *Prototype label* box.

Insert the desired fields in the *Prototype label* box.

At the fourth Label Wizard dialog box, shown in Figure 6.10, specify a field from the database by which the labels will be sorted. If you want the labels sorted (for example, by last name, postal code, etc.), insert the field in the *Sort by* list box and then click the Next button.

At the last Label Wizard dialog box, type a name for the label file and then click the Finish button. After a few moments, the labels display on the screen in Print Preview. Print the labels and/or close Print Preview.

Figure 6.10 Fourth Label Wizard Dialog Box

If you want the labels sorted by a particular field, insert that field in the *Sort by* box.

Project 2c   **Preparing Mailing Labels**   **Part 3 of 3**

1. Open **AL1-C6-WarrenLegal.accdb**.
2. Click *Clients* in the Tables group in the Navigation pane.
3. Click the CREATE tab and then click the Labels button in the Reports group.
4. At the first Label Wizard dialog box, make sure *English* is selected in the *Unit of Measure* section, *Avery* is selected in the *Filter by manufacturer* list box, *Sheet feed* is selected in the *Label Type* section, and *C2160* is selected in the *Product number* list box and then click the Next button.
5. At the second Label Wizard dialog box, if necessary, change the font size to 10 points and then click the Next button.
6. At the third Label Wizard dialog box, complete the following steps to insert the fields in the *Prototype label* box:
   a. Click *FirstName* in the *Available fields* list box and then click the One Field button.
   b. Press the spacebar, make sure *LastName* is selected in the *Available fields* list box, and then click the One Field button.
   c. Press the Enter key. (This moves the insertion point down to the next line in the *Prototype label* box.)
   d. With *StreetAddress* selected in the *Available fields* list box, click the One Field button.
   e. Press the Enter key.
   f. With *City* selected in the *Available fields* list box, click the One Field button.
   g. Type a comma (,) and then press the spacebar.

h. With *State* selected in the *Available fields* list box, click the One Field button.

i. Press the spacebar.

j. With *ZipCode* selected in the *Available fields* list box, click the One Field button.

k. Click the Next button.

7. At the fourth Label Wizard dialog box, sort by zip code. To do this, click *ZipCode* in the *Available fields* list box and then click the One Field button.

8. Click the Next button.

9. At the last Label Wizard dialog box, click the Finish button. (The Label Wizard automatically names the label report *Labels Clients*.)

10. Print the labels by clicking the Print button that displays at the left side of the PRINT PREVIEW tab and then click OK at the Print dialog box.

11. Close Print Preview.

12. Switch to Report view by clicking the View button on the REPORT DESIGN TOOLS DESIGN tab.

13. Close the labels report and then close **AL1-C6-WarrenLegal.accdb**.

Chapter Summary

- Create a report with data in a table or query to control how data appears on the page when printed.

- Create a report with the Report button in the Reports group on the CREATE tab.

- Four views are available for viewing a report: Report view, Print Preview, Layout view, and Design view.

- Use options on the PRINT PREVIEW tab to specify how a report prints.

- In Layout view, you can select a report control object and then size or move the object. You can also change the column width by clicking a column heading and then dragging the border to the desired width.

- Sort data in a record using the Ascending button or Descending button in the Sort & Filter group on the HOME tab.

- Customize a report with options on the REPORT LAYOUT TOOLS ribbon with the DESIGN tab, ARRANGE tab, FORMAT tab, or PAGE SETUP tab selected.

- To make data in a report easier to understand, divide the data into groups using the Group, Sort, and Total pane. Display this pane by clicking the Group & Sort button in the Grouping & Totals group on the REPORT LAYOUT TOOLS DESIGN tab.
- Use the Report Wizard to guide you through the steps for creating a report. Begin the wizard by clicking the CREATE tab and then clicking the Report Wizard button in the Reports group.
- Create mailing labels with data in a table using the Label Wizard. Begin the wizard by clicking the desired table, clicking the CREATE tab, and then clicking the Labels button in the Reports group.

Commands Review

FEATURE	RIBBON TAB, GROUP	BUTTON
Group, Sort, and Total pane	REPORT LAYOUT TOOLS DESIGN, Grouping & Totals	
Labels Wizard	CREATE, Reports	
report	CREATE, Reports	
Report Wizard	CREATE, Reports	

Concepts Check   Test Your Knowledge

Completion: In the space provided at the right, indicate the correct term, symbol, or command.

1. The Report button is located in the Reports group on this tab. _____

2. Press these keys on the keyboard to select all control objects in a report in Layout view. _____

3. The Ascending button is located in this group on the HOME tab. _____

4. Four views are available in a report, including Layout view, Report view, Design view, and this view. _____

5. With options on this tab, you can insert controls, insert header or footer data, and add existing fields. _____

6. Click this button in the Grouping & Totals group on the REPORT LAYOUT TOOLS DESIGN tab to perform functions such as finding the sum, average, maximum, and minimum of the numbers in a column. _____

7. The Group & Sort button is located in this group on the REPORT LAYOUT TOOLS DESIGN tab. _____

8. Click the Group & Sort button and this pane displays. _____

9. Use this to guide you through the steps for creating a report. _____

10. To create mailing labels, click the desired table, click the CREATE tab, and then click the Labels button in this group. _____

Skills Check   Assess Your Performance

Assessment

1 CREATE AND FORMAT REPORTS IN THE HILLTOP DATABASE

1. Open **AL1-C6-Hilltop.accdb** and enable the contents.
2. Create a report with the Inventory table using the Report button.
3. With the report in Layout view, apply the following formatting:
   a. Center the data below each of the following column headings: *EquipmentID, AvailableHours, ServiceHours,* and *RepairHours.*
   b. Select all of the control objects and then change the font to Constantia.
   c. Select the money amounts below the *PurchasePrice* column heading and then click the Decrease Decimals button (in the Number group) until the amounts display without any places past the decimal point.
   d. Click in the *$473,260.00* amount and then click the Decrease Decimals button until the amount displays with no places past the decimal point.
   e. If necessary, increase the height of the total amount row so the entire amount is visible.
   f. Change the title of the report to *Inventory Report.*
4. Save the report and name it *InventoryReport.*
5. Print and then close InventoryReport.
6. Create a query in Design view with the following specifications:
   a. Add the Customers, Equipment, Invoices, and Rates tables to the query window.
   b. Insert the *Customer* field from the *Customers* field list box in the first *Field* row field.
   c. Insert the *Equipment* field from the *Equipment* field list box in the second *Field* row field.
   d. Insert the *Hours* field from the *Invoices* field list box in the third *Field* row field.
   e. Insert the *Rate* field from the *Rates* field list box in the fourth *Field* row field.
   f. Click in the fifth *Field* row field, type **Total: [Hours]*[Rate]**, and then press Enter.

g. Run the query.

h. Save the query and name it *CustomerRentals* and then close the query.

7. Create a report with the CustomerRentals query using the Report button.

8. With the report in Layout view, apply the following formatting:

a. Decrease the widths of the columns so the right border of each column displays near the right side of the longest entry.

b. Select the money amounts and then click the Decrease Decimals button until the amounts display with no places past the decimal point.

c. Click in the *Total* column and then total the amounts by clicking the REPORT LAYOUT TOOLS DESIGN tab, clicking the Totals button in the Grouping & Totals group, and then clicking *Sum* at the drop-down list.

d. Click the total amount (located at the bottom of the *Total* column), click the REPORT LAYOUT TOOLS FORMAT tab, and then click the Apply Currency Format button in the Number group.

e. Increase the height of the total amount row so the entire amount is visible.

f. Select and then delete the amount that displays at the bottom of the *Rate* column.

g. Display the Group, Sort, and Total pane; group the records by *Customer*; sort by *Equipment*; and then close the pane.

h. Apply the Integral theme. (Do this with the Themes button in the Themes group on the REPORT LAYOUT TOOLS DESIGN tab.)

i. Select the five column headings and change the font color to black.

j. Change the title of the report to *Rentals*.

9. Save the report and name it *RentalReport*.

10. Print and then close RentalReport.

Assessment

2 CREATE REPORTS USING THE REPORT WIZARD

1. With **AL1-C6-Hilltop.accdb** open, create a report using the Report Wizard with the following specifications:

a. At the first Report Wizard dialog box, insert the following fields in the *Selected Fields* list box:

From the Equipment table:	*Equipment*
From the Inventory table:	*PurchaseDate*
	PurchasePrice
	AvailableHours

b. Do not make any changes at the second Report Wizard dialog box.

c. Do not make any changes at the third Report Wizard dialog box.

d. At the fourth Report Wizard dialog box, choose the *Columnar* option.

e. At the fifth and last Report Wizard dialog box, click the Finish button. (This accepts the default report name *Equipment*.)

2. Print and then close the report.

3. Create a report using the Report Wizard with the following specifications:
  a. At the first Report Wizard dialog box, insert the following fields in the *Selected Fields* list box:

      From the Customers table: *Customer*

      From the Invoices table: *BillingDate*
                                          Hours

      From the Equipment table: *Equipment*

      From the Rates table: *Rate*

  b. Do not make any changes at the second Report Wizard dialog box.
  c. Do not make any changes at the third Report Wizard dialog box.
  d. Do not make any changes at the fourth Report Wizard dialog box.
  e. At the fifth Report Wizard dialog box, choose the *Block* option.
  f. At the sixth and last Report Wizard dialog box, name the report *Rentals*.
4. Print and then close the report.

Assessment

3   CREATE MAILING LABELS

1. With **AL1-C6-Hilltop.accdb** open, click *Customers* in the Tables group in the Navigation pane.
2. Use the Label Wizard to create mailing labels (you determine the label type) with customer names and addresses and sort the labels by customer names. Name the mailing label report *CustomerMailingLabels*.
3. Print the mailing labels.
4. Close the mailing labels report.

Assessment

4   ADD A FIELD TO A REPORT

1. In Chapter 5, you added a field list to an existing form using the Field List task pane. Experiment with adding a field to an existing report and then complete the following:
  a. Open the RentalReport report (created in Assessment 1) in Layout view.
  b. Display the Field List task pane and display all of the tables.
  c. Drag the *BillingDate* field from the Invoices table so the field is positioned between the *Equipment* column and *Hours* column.
  d. At the message indicating that Access will modify the RecordSource property and asking if you want to continue, click Yes.
  e. Close the Field List task pane.
2. Save, print, and then close the report.
3. Close **AL1-C6-Hilltop.accdb**.

Visual Benchmark

Demonstrate Your Proficiency

DESIGN A QUERY AND CREATE A REPORT WITH THE QUERY

1. Open **AL1-C6-Skyline.accdb** and then create and run the query shown in Figure 6.11.
2. Save the query and name it *Suppliers2&4Orders* and then close the query.
3. Use the Report button to create the report shown in Figure 6.12 using the *Suppliers2&4Orders* query with the following specifications:
   a. Apply the Facet theme.
   b. Adjust the column widths and change the alignment of data as shown in Figure 6.12.
   c. Change the title as shown in Figure 6.12.
   d. Select the column headings and then apply the Black font color.
   e. Insert the total of the amounts in the *Total* column. Format the total amount as shown in Figure 6.12.
   f. Delete the sum amount at the bottom of the *UnitPrice* column.
4. Save the report and name it *Suppliers2&4OrdersRpt*.
5. Print the report, close the report, and then close **AL1-C6-Skyline.accdb**.

Figure 6.11 Visual Benchmark Query

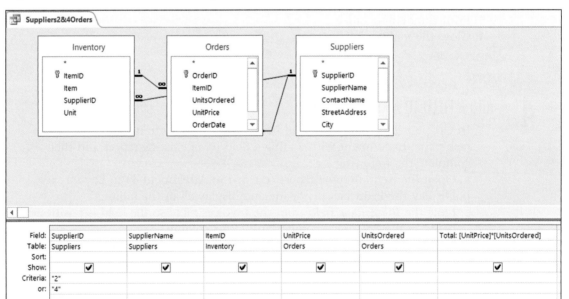

Figure 6.12 Visual Benchmark Report

SupplierID	SupplierName	ItemID	UnitPrice	UnitsOrdered	Total
	Suppliers 2 and 4 Orders			Thursday, October 15, 2015	
				4:45:53 PM	
2	Coral Produce	002	$10.50	3	$31.50
2	Coral Produce	016	$24.00	1	$24.00
4	Grocery Wholesalers	020	$18.75	2	$37.50
2	Coral Produce	014	$15.75	2	$31.50
4	Grocery Wholesalers	025	$28.50	1	$28.50
4	Grocery Wholesalers	036	$17.00	2	$34.00
4	Grocery Wholesalers	013	$14.00	2	$28.00
2	Coral Produce	004	$10.95	2	$21.90
4	Grocery Wholesalers	035	$17.00	1	$17.00
4	Grocery Wholesalers	027	$22.00	1	$22.00
4	Grocery Wholesalers	026	$29.25	1	$29.25
2	Coral Produce	021	$31.00	1	$31.00
4	Grocery Wholesalers	034	$13.75	2	$27.50
4	Grocery Wholesalers	012	$30.25	1	$30.25
4	Grocery Wholesalers	018	$45.00	1	$45.00
2	Coral Produce	016	$39.40	2	$78.80
4	Grocery Wholesalers	035	$17.00	1	$17.00
2	Coral Produce	014	$15.75	2	$31.50
4	Grocery Wholesalers	020	$18.75	2	$37.50
					$603.70

Case Study   Apply Your Skills

Part 1

As the office manager at Millstone Legal Services, you need to enter records for three new clients in **AL1-C6-Millstone.accdb**. Using the following information, enter the data in the appropriate tables:

Client number 42
Martin Costanzo
1002 Thomas Drive
Casper, WY 82602
(307) 555-5001
Mr. Costanzo saw Douglas Sheehan regarding divorce proceedings with a billing date of 3/15/2015 and a fee of $150.

Client number 43
Susan Nordyke
23193 Ridge Circle East
Mills, WY 82644
(307) 555-2719
Ms. Nordyke saw Loretta Ryder regarding support enforcement with a billing date of 3/15/2015 and a fee of $175.

Client number 44
Monica Sommers
1105 Riddell Avenue
Casper, WY 82609
(307) 555-1188
Ms. Sommers saw Anita Leland regarding a guardianship with a billing date of 3/15/2015 and a fee of $250.

Part 2

Create and print the following queries, reports, and labels:

- Create a report with the Clients table. Apply formatting to enhance the appearance of the report.
- Create a query that displays the client ID, first name, and last name; attorney last name; billing date; and fee. Name the query *ClientBilling*.
- Create a report with the ClientBilling query. Group the records in the report by attorney last name (the *LName* field in the drop-down list) and sort alphabetically in ascending order by client last name (the *LastName* field in the drop-down list). Apply formatting to enhance the appearance of the report.
- Produce a telephone directory by creating a report that includes client last names, first names, and telephone numbers. Sort the records in the report alphabetically by last name in ascending order.
- Edit the ClientBilling query so it includes a criterion that displays only billing dates between 3/10/2015 and 3/13/2015. Save the query with Save Object As and name it *ClientBilling10-13*.
- Create a report with the ClientBilling10-13 query. Apply formatting to enhance the appearance of the report.
- Create mailing labels for the clients.

Part 3

Apply the following conditions to fields in reports and then print the reports:

- In the Clients report, apply the condition that the city *Casper* displays in the Red font color and the city *Mills* displays the Blue font color in the *City* field.
- In the ClientBilling report, apply the condition that fees over $199 display in the Green font color and fees less than $200 display in the Blue font color.

Part 4

Your center has a manual that describes processes and procedures in the workplace. Open Word and create a document for the manual that describes how to create a report using the Report button and Report Wizard and how to create mailing labels using the Label Wizard. Save the completed document and name it **AL1-C6-CS-Manual**. Print and then close **AL1-C6-CS-Manual.docx**.

MICROSOFT® ACCESS®

Modifying, Filtering, and Viewing Data

PERFORMANCE OBJECTIVES

Upon successful completion of Chapter 7, you will be able to:

- Filter data by selection and form
- Remove a filter
- View object dependencies
- Compact and repair a database
- Encrypt a database with a password
- View and customize document properties
- Save a database in an earlier version of Access
- Save a database object in PDF file format

Tutorials

7.1 Filtering Records

7.2 Viewing Object Dependencies

7.3 Compacting, Repairing, and Backing Up a Database

7.4 Encrypting a Database with a Password and Modifying Document Properties

7.5 Saving Databases and Database Objects in Different Formats

You can filter data in a database object to view specific records without having to change the design of the object. In this chapter, you will learn how to filter data by selection and form. You will also learn how to view object dependencies, manage a database with options at the Info backstage area, save a database in an earlier version of Access, and save a database object in PDF file format. Model answers for this chapter's projects appear on the following pages.

Access
AL1C7

Note: Before beginning the projects, copy to your storage medium the AL1C7 subfolder from the AL1 folder on the CD that accompanies this textbook and make AL1C7 the active folder.

Project 1 Filter Records

Project 1a

Skyline Employees Filtered Records, Page 1

EmployeeID	FName	LName	StreetAddress	City	State	ZipCode
02	Wayne	Weber	17362 North Tenth	Fort Myers	FL	33994
03	Owen	Pasqual	4010 Shannon Drive	Fort Myers	FL	33910
04	Vadim	Sayenko	1328 St. Paul Avenue	Fort Myers	FL	33907
07	Donald	Sellars	23103 Summer Highway	Fort Myers	FL	33919
09	Elizabeth	Mohr	1818 Brookdale Road	Fort Myers	FL	33902
11	Nicole	Bateman	5001 150th Street	Fort Myers	FL	33908

Skyline Employees Filtered Records, Page 2

Telephone	HireDate	HealthIns
(239) 555-6041	4/1/2010	☐
(239) 555-3492	4/15/2009	☐
(239) 555-9487	6/15/2009	✔
(239) 555-4348	6/6/2012	✔
(239) 555-0430	5/1/2011	✔
(239) 555-2631	2/1/2013	☐

Project 1b

Skyline Banquet Reservations Query

ResDate	FirstName	LastName	Telephone	Event	EmployeeID
6/5/2015	Terrance	Schaefer	(239) 555-6239	Wedding rehearsal dinner	03
6/5/2015	Andrea	Wyatt	(239) 555-4282	Wedding reception	01
6/6/2015	Luis	Castillo	(239) 555-4001	Wedding shower	11
6/6/2015	David	Hooper	(941) 555-2338	Wedding anniversary	04
6/7/2015	Bridget	Kohn	(239) 555-1299	Other	02
6/9/2015	Joanne	Blair	(239) 555-7783	Birthday	03
6/12/2015	Tim	Drysdale	(941) 555-0098	Bat mitzvah	02
6/12/2015	Gabrielle	Johnson	(239) 555-1882	Other	05
6/12/2015	Cliff	Osborne	(239) 555-7823	Wedding rehearsal dinner	12
6/13/2015	Janis	Semala	(239) 555-0476	Wedding reception	06
6/13/2015	Tristan	Strauss	(941) 555-7746	Other	03
6/14/2015	Aaron	Williams	(239) 555-3821	Bar mitzvah	04
6/14/2015	Willow	Earhart	(239) 555-0034	Wedding shower	04

BanquetReservations — Friday, October 16, 2015 1:41:29 PM

ResDate	FirstName	LastName	Telephone	Event	EmployeeID
6/9/2015	Joanne	Blair	(239) 555-7783	Birthday	03
6/5/2015	Terrance	Schaefer	(239) 555-6239	Wedding rehearsal dinner	03

Skyline Banquet Report

Project 1c

ItemID	Item	SupplierID	Unit
003	Carrots	6	25 lb bag
005	Garlic	6	10 lb bag
009	Radishes	6	case
010	Celery	6	case
011	Broccoli	6	case
041	White sugar	6	25 lb bag
042	Baking powder	6	case
043	Baking soda	6	case

Skyline Filtered Inventory Records, Step 2c

ItemID	Item	SupplierID	Unit
006	Green peppers	2	case
007	Red peppers	2	case
008	Yellow peppers	2	case

Skyline Filtered Inventory Records, Step 3d

ResDate	FirstName	LastName	Telephone	Event	EmployeeID
6/6/2015	Luis	Castillo	(239) 555-4001	Wedding shower	11
6/14/2015	Willow	Earhart	(239) 555-0034	Wedding shower	04
6/9/2015	Joanne	Blair	(239) 555-7783	Birthday	03
6/16/2015	Jason	Haley	(239) 555-6641	Birthday	06
6/18/2015	Heidi	Thompson	(941) 555-3215	Birthday	01
6/27/2015	Kirsten	Simpson	(941) 555-4425	Birthday	02
6/14/2015	Aaron	Williams	(239) 555-3821	Bar mitzvah	04
6/20/2015	Robin	Gehring	(239) 555-0126	Bar mitzvah	06
6/12/2015	Tim	Drysdale	(941) 555-0098	Bat mitzvah	02
6/7/2015	Bridget	Kohn	(239) 555-1299	Other	02
6/12/2015	Gabrielle	Johnson	(239) 555-1882	Other	05
6/13/2015	Tristan	Strauss	(941) 555-7746	Other	03
6/17/2015	Lillian	Krakosky	(239) 555-8890	Other	03
6/20/2015	David	Fitzgerald	(941) 555-3792	Other	01
6/5/2015	Terrance	Schaefer	(239) 555-6239	Wedding rehearsal dinner	03
6/12/2015	Cliff	Osborne	(239) 555-7823	Wedding rehearsal dinner	12
6/6/2015	David	Hooper	(941) 555-2338	Wedding anniversary	04
6/19/2015	Anthony	Wiegand	(239) 555-7853	Wedding anniversary	11
6/27/2015	Shane	Rozier	(239) 555-1033	Wedding anniversary	12

Skyline Filtered Banquet Reservations Records, Step 6c

ResDate	FirstName	LastName	Telephone	Event	EmployeeID
6/14/2015	Aaron	Williams	(239) 555-3821	Bar mitzvah	04
6/20/2015	Robin	Gehring	(239) 555-0126	Bar mitzvah	06
6/12/2015	Tim	Drysdale	(941) 555-0098	Bat mitzvah	02

Skyline Filtered Banquet Reservations Records, Step 7d

Project 1d

Skyline Filtered Banquets Records, Step 3c

ReservationID	EmployeeID	ResDate	FirstName	LastName	Telephone	EventID	AmountTotal	AmountPaid	Confirmed
1	03	6/5/2015	Terrance	Schaefer	(239) 555-6239	RD	$750.00	$250.00	✔
6	03	6/9/2015	Joanne	Blair	(239) 555-7783	BD	$650.00	$200.00	✔
11	03	6/13/2015	Tristan	Strauss	(941) 555-7746	OT	$1,400.00	$300.00	☐
15	03	6/17/2015	Lillian	Krakosky	(239) 555-8890	OT	$500.00	$100.00	☐

ItemID	Item	SupplierID	Unit
001	Butternut squash	2	case
002	Potatoes	2	50 lb bag
004	Onions	2	25 lb bag
006	Green peppers	2	case
007	Red peppers	2	case
008	Yellow peppers	2	case
014	Green beans	2	case
016	Iceberg lettuce	2	case
017	Romaine lettuce	2	case
021	Cantaloupes	2	case
028	Beef	7	side
029	Pork	7	side
030	Chicken	7	case
051	Watermelon	2	case
052	Kiwi	2	case

Skyline Filtered Inventory Records, Step 6h

Model Answers

Project 2 View Object Dependencies, Manage a Database, and Save a Database in a Different File Format

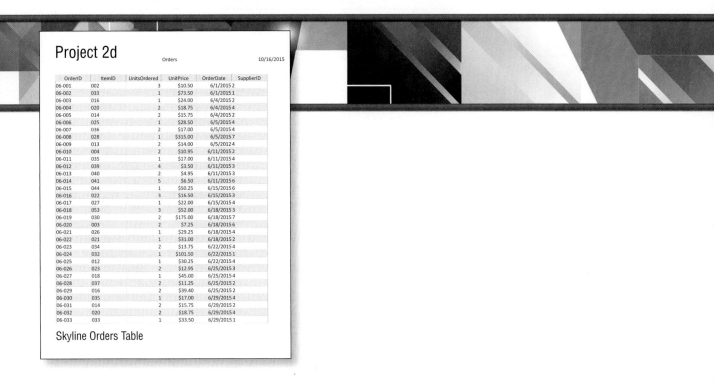

Project 2d

Orders   10/16/2015

OrderID	ItemID	UnitsOrdered	UnitPrice	OrderDate	SupplierID
06-001	002	3	$10.50	6/1/2015	2
06-002	033	1	$73.50	6/1/2015	1
06-003	016	1	$24.00	6/4/2015	2
06-004	020	2	$18.75	6/4/2015	4
06-005	014	2	$15.75	6/4/2015	2
06-006	025	1	$28.50	6/5/2015	4
06-007	036	2	$17.00	6/5/2015	4
06-008	028	1	$315.00	6/5/2015	7
06-009	013	2	$14.00	6/5/2012	4
06-010	004	2	$10.95	6/11/2015	2
06-011	035	1	$17.00	6/11/2015	4
06-012	039	4	$3.50	6/11/2015	3
06-013	040	2	$4.95	6/11/2015	3
06-014	041	5	$6.50	6/11/2015	6
06-015	044	1	$50.25	6/15/2015	6
06-016	022	3	$16.50	6/15/2015	3
06-017	027	1	$22.00	6/15/2015	4
06-018	053	3	$52.00	6/18/2015	3
06-019	030	2	$175.00	6/18/2015	7
06-020	003	2	$7.25	6/18/2015	6
06-021	026	1	$29.25	6/18/2015	4
06-022	021	1	$31.00	6/18/2015	2
06-023	034	2	$13.75	6/22/2015	4
06-024	032	1	$101.50	6/22/2015	1
06-025	012	1	$30.25	6/22/2015	4
06-026	023	2	$12.95	6/25/2015	3
06-027	018	1	$45.00	6/25/2015	4
06-028	037	2	$11.25	6/25/2015	2
06-029	016	2	$39.40	6/25/2015	2
06-030	035	1	$17.00	6/29/2015	4
06-031	014	2	$15.75	6/29/2015	2
06-032	020	2	$18.75	6/29/2015	4
06-033	033	1	$33.50	6/29/2015	1

Skyline Orders Table

Project 1 Filter Records   4 Parts

You will filter records in a table, query, and report in the Skyline database using the Filter button, Selection button, Toggle Filter button, and shortcut menu. You will also remove filters and filter by form.

Filtering Data ■■■■■■■■■■■■■■■■■■■■■■■■■■■■■■■

You can place a set of restrictions, called a *filter*, on records in a table, query, form, or report to isolate temporarily specific records. A filter, like a query, lets you view specific records without having to change the design of the table, query, form, or report. Access provides a number of buttons and options for filtering data. You can filter data using the Filter button in the Sort & Filter group on the HOME tab, right-click specific data in a record and then specify a filter, and use the Selection and Advanced buttons in the Sort & Filter group.

Filtering Using the Filter Button

Use the Filter button in the Sort & Filter group on the HOME tab to filter records in an object (a table, query, form, or report). To use this button, open the desired object, click in any entry in the field column on which you want to filter, and then click the Filter button. This displays a drop-down list with sorting options and a list of all of the field entries. In a table, display this drop-down list by clicking the

▼ Quick Steps

Filter Records
1. Open desired object.
2. Click in entry of desired field column to filter.
3. Click Filter button.
4. Select desired sorting option at drop-down list.

Filter

Figure 7.1 *City* Field Drop-down List

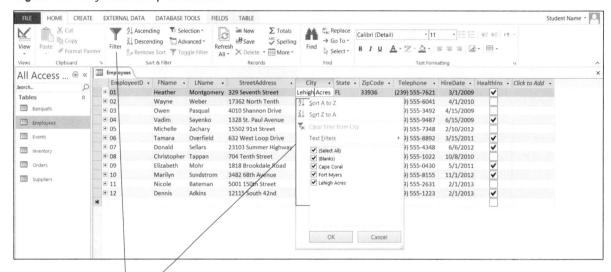

To filter on the *City* field, click in any entry in the field column and then click the Filter button. This displays a drop-down list with sorting options and a list of all field entries.

Filters available depend on the type of data selected in a column.

filter arrow that displays at the right side of a column heading. Figure 7.1 displays the drop-down list that displays when you click in the *City* field and then click the Filter button. To sort on a specific criterion, click the *(Select All)* check box to remove all check marks from the list of field entries. Click the item in the list box on which you want to sort and then click OK.

When you open a table, query, or form, the Record Navigation bar contains the dimmed words *No Filter* preceded by a filter icon with a delete symbol (X). If you filter records in one of these objects, *Filtered* displays in place of *No Filter*, the delete symbol is removed, and the text and filter icon display with an orange background. In a report, if you apply a filter to records, the word *Filtered* displays at the right side of the Status bar.

Removing a Filter

▼ **Quick Steps**

Remove a Filter
1. Click in field column containing filter.
2. Click Filter button.
3. Click *Clear filter from xxx.*
OR
1. Click Advanced button.
2. Click *Clear All Filters* at drop-down list.

Toggle Filter

When you filter data, the underlying data in the object is not deleted. You can switch back and forth between the data and filtered data by clicking the Toggle Filter button in the Sort & Filter group on the HOME tab. If you click the Toggle Filter button and turn off the filter, all of the data in the table, query, or form displays and the message *Filtered* in the Record Navigation bar changes to *Unfiltered*.

Clicking the Toggle Filter button may redisplay all of the data in an object, but it does not remove the filter. To remove the filter, click in the field column containing the filter and then click the Filter button in the Sort & Filter group on the HOME tab. At the drop-down list that displays, click *Clear filter from xxx* (where *xxx* is the name of the field). You can remove all of the filters from an object by clicking the Advanced button in the Sort & Filter group and then clicking the *Clear All Filters* option.

1. Display the Open dialog box with the AL1C7 folder on your storage medium the active folder.
2. Open **AL1-C7-Skyline.accdb** and enable the contents.
3. Filter records in the Employees table by completing the following steps:
   a. Open the Employees table.
   b. Click in any entry in the *City* field.
   c. Click the Filter button in the Sort & Filter group on the HOME tab. (This displays a drop-down list of options for the *City* field.)

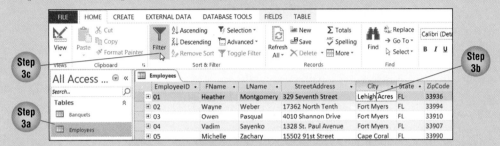

   d. Click the *(Select All)* check box in the filter drop-down list box. (This removes all check marks from the list options.)
   e. Click the *Fort Myers* check box in the list box. (This inserts a check mark in the check box.)
   f. Click OK. (Access displays only those records with a city field of *Fort Myers* and also displays *Filtered* and the filter icon with an orange background in the Record Navigation bar.)
   g. Print the filtered records by pressing Ctrl + P (the keyboard shortcut to display the print dialog box) and then clicking OK at the Print dialog box.
4. Toggle the display of filtered data by clicking the Toggle Filter button in the Sort & Filter group on the HOME tab. (This redisplays all of the data in the table.)
5. Remove the filter by completing the following steps:
   a. Click in any entry in the *City* field.
   b. Click the Filter button in the Sort & Filter group.
   c. Click the *Clear filter from City* option at the drop-down list. (Notice that the message on the Record Navigation bar changes to *No Filter* and dims the words.)

6. Save and then close the Employees table.
7. Create a form by completing the following steps:
    a. Click *Orders* in the Tables group in the Navigation pane.
    b. Click the CREATE tab and then click the Form button in the Forms group.
    c. Click the Form View button in the view area at the right side of the Status bar.
    d. Save the form with the name *Orders*.
8. Filter the records and display only those records with a supplier identification number of 2 by completing the following steps:
    a. Click in the *SupplierID* field containing the text *2*.
    b. Click the Filter button in the Sort & Filter group.
    c. At the filter drop-down list, click *(Select All)* to remove all of the check marks from the list options.
    d. Click the *2* option to insert a check mark.
    e. Click OK.
    f. Navigate through the records and notice that only the records with a supplier identification number of 2 display.
9. Close the Orders form.

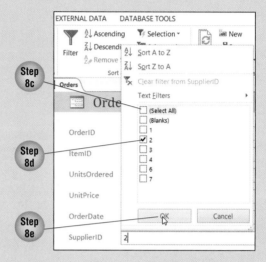

Step 8c

Step 8d

Step 8e

Filtering on Specific Values

When you filter on a specific field, you can display a list of unique values for that field. If you click the Filter button for a field containing text, the drop-down list for the specific field will contain a *Text Filters* option. Click this option and a values list displays next to the drop-down list. The options in the values list vary depending on the type of data in the field. If you click the Filter button for a field containing number values, the option in the drop-down list displays as *Number Filters* and if you are filtering dates, the option in the drop-down list displays as *Date Filters*. Use the options in the values list to refine a filter for a specific field. For example, you can use the values list to display money amounts within a specific range or order dates from a certain time period. You can also use the values list to find fields that are "equal to" or "not equal to" text in the current field.

Project 1b **Filtering Records in a Query and Report**   Part 2 of 4

1. With **AL1-C7-Skyline.accdb** open, create a query in Design view with the following specifications:
    a. Add the Banquets and Events tables to the query window.
    b. Insert the *ResDate* field from the *Banquets* field list box to the first *Field* row field.
    c. Insert the *FirstName* field from the *Banquets* field list box to the second *Field* row field.
    d. Insert the *LastName* field from the *Banquets* field list box to the third *Field* row field.
    e. Insert the *Telephone* field from the *Banquets* field list box to the fourth *Field* row field.
    f. Insert the *Event* field from the *Events* field list box to the fifth *Field* row field.
    g. Insert the *EmployeeID* field from the *Banquets* field list box to the sixth *Field* row field.
    h. Run the query.
    i. Save the query and name it *BanquetReservations*.

2. Filter records of reservations on or before June 15, 2015, in the query by completing the following steps:
   a. With the BanquetReservations query open, make sure the first entry is selected in the *ResDate* field.
   b. Click the Filter button in the Sort & Filter group on the HOME tab.
   c. Point to the *Date Filters* option in the drop-down list box.
   d. Click *Before* in the values list.
   e. At the Custom Filter dialog box, type 6/15/2015 and then click OK.

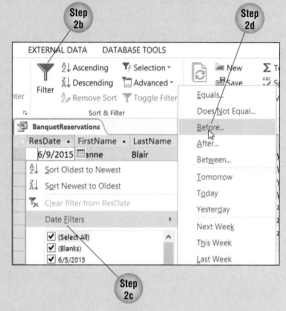

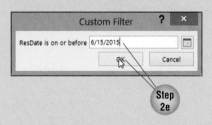

   f. Print the filtered query by pressing Ctrl + P and then clicking OK at the Print dialog box.

3. Remove the filter by clicking the filter icon that displays at the right side of the *ResDate* column heading and then clicking *Clear filter from ResDate* at the drop-down list.

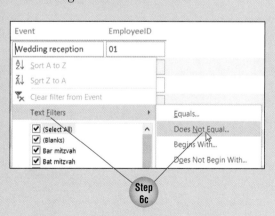

4. Save and then close the BanquetReservations query.
5. Create a report by completing the following steps:
   a. Click *BanquetReservations* in the Queries group in the Navigation pane.
   b. Click the CREATE tab and then click the Report button in the Reports group.
   c. Delete the total amount at the bottom of the *ResDate* column.
   d. With the report in Layout view, decrease the column widths so the right column border displays near the longest entry in each column.
   e. Click the Report View button in the view area at the right side of the Status bar.
   f. Save the report and name it *BanquetReport*.
6. Filter the records and display all records of events except *Other* events by completing the following steps:
   a. Click in the first entry in the *Event* field.
   b. Click the Filter button in the Sort & Filter group.
   c. Point to the *Text Filters* option in the drop-down list box and then click *Does Not Equal* at the values list.
   d. At the Custom Filter dialog box, type Other and then click OK.

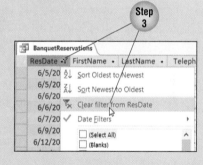

7. Further refine the filter by completing the following steps:
   a. Click in the first entry in the *EmployeeID* field.
   b. Click the Filter button.
   c. At the filter drop-down list, click the *(Select All)* check box to remove all of the check marks from the list options.
   d. Click the *03* check box to insert a check mark.
   e. Click OK.
8. Print only the first page of the report (the second page contains only shading) by completing the following steps:
   a. Press Ctrl + P to display the Print dialog box.
   b. Click the *Pages* option in the *Print Range* section.
   c. Type 1 in the *From* text box, press the Tab key, and then type 1 in the *To* text box.
   d. Click OK.
9. Save and then close the BanquetReport report.

Filtering by Selection

Selection

If you click in a field in an object and then click the Selection button in the Sort & Filter group on the HOME tab, a drop-down list displays below the button with options for filtering on the data in the field. For example, if you click in a field containing the city name *Fort Myers*, clicking the Selection button will cause a drop-down list to display as shown in Figure 7.2. Click one of the options at the drop-down list to filter records. You can select specific text in a field entry and then filter based on the specific text. For example, in Project 1c you will select the word *peppers* in the entry *Green peppers* and then filter records containing the word *peppers*.

Figure 7.2 Selection Button Drop-down List

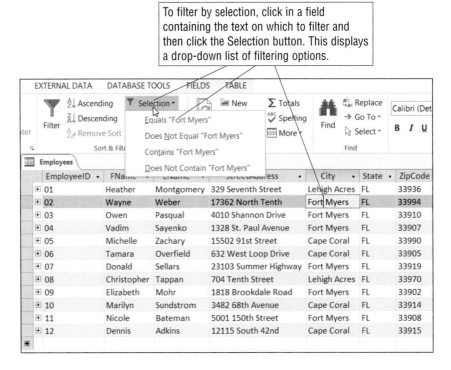

Filtering by Shortcut Menu

If you right-click a field entry, a shortcut menu displays with options to sort the text, display a values list, or filter on a specific value. For example, if you right-click the field entry *Birthday* in the *Event* field, a shortcut menu displays, as shown in Figure 7.3. Click a sort option to sort text in the field in ascending or descending order, point to the *Text Filters* option to display a values list, or click one of the values filters located toward the bottom of the menu. You can also select specific text within a field entry and then right-click the selection to display the shortcut menu.

Figure 7.3 Filtering Shortcut Menu

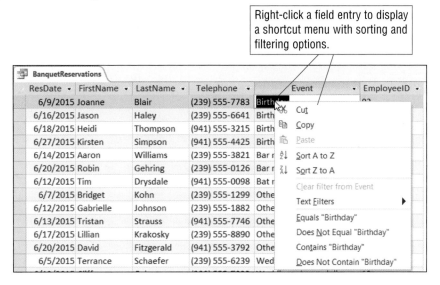

Right-click a field entry to display a shortcut menu with sorting and filtering options.

Project 1c Filtering Records by Selection   Part 3 of 4

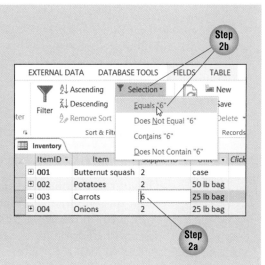

1. With **AL1-C7-Skyline.accdb** open, open the Inventory table.
2. Filter only those records with a supplier number of 6 by completing the following steps:
   a. Click in the first entry containing *6* in the *SupplierID* field.
   b. Click the Selection button in the Sort & Filter group on the HOME tab and then click *Equals "6"* at the drop-down list.
   c. Print the filtered table by pressing Ctrl + P and then clicking OK at the Print dialog box.
   d. Click the Toggle Filter button in the Sort & Filter group.

3. Filter any records in the *Item* field containing the word *peppers* by completing the following steps:
   a. Click in an entry in the *Item* field containing the text *Green peppers*.
   b. Using the mouse, select the word *peppers*.
   c. Click the Selection button and then click *Contains "peppers"* at the drop-down list.
   d. Print the filtered table by pressing Ctrl + P and then clicking OK at the Print dialog box.
4. Close the Inventory table without saving the changes.
5. Open the BanquetReservations query.
6. Filter records in the *Event* field except *Wedding reception* by completing the following steps:
   a. Right-click in the first *Wedding reception* entry in the *Event* field.
   b. Click *Does Not Equal "Wedding reception"* at the shortcut menu.
   c. Print the filtered query.
   d. Click the Toggle Filter button in the Sort & Filter group.
7. Filter any records in the *Event* field containing the word *mitzvah* by completing the following steps:
   a. Click in an entry in the *Event* field containing the entry *Bar mitzvah*.
   b. Using the mouse, select the word *mitzvah*.
   c. Right-click on the selected word and then click *Contains "mitzvah"* at the shortcut menu.
   d. Print the filtered query.
8. Close the BanquetReservations query without saving the changes.

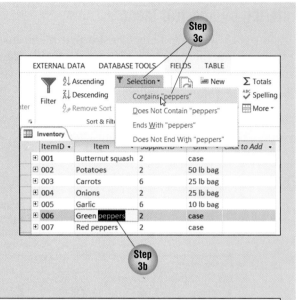

▼ **Quick Steps**

Use the *Filter By Form* Option
1. Click Advanced button.
2. Click *Filter By Form*.
3. Click in empty field below desired column to filter.
4. Click down-pointing arrow.
5. Click item to filter.

Advanced

Using the *Filter By Form* Option

One of the options from the Advanced button drop-down list is *Filter By Form*. Click this option and a blank record displays in a Filter by Form window in the work area. In the Filter by Form window, the Look for tab and the Or tab display toward the bottom of the form. The Look for tab is active by default and tells Access to look for whatever data you insert in a field. Click in the empty field below the desired column and a down-pointing arrow displays at the right side of the field. Click the down-pointing arrow and then click the item on which you want to filter. Click the Toggle Filter button to display the desired records. Add an additional value to a filter by clicking the Or tab at the bottom of the form.

1. With **AL1-C7-Skyline.accdb** open, open the Banquets table.
2. Filter records for a specific employee identification number by completing the following steps:
   a. Click the Advanced button in the Sort & Filter group on the HOME tab and then click *Filter By Form* at the drop-down list.

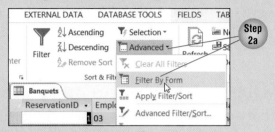

   b. At the Filter by Form window, click in the blank record below the *EmployeeID* field.
   c. Click the down-pointing arrow at the right side of the field and then click *03* at the drop-down list.
   d. Click the Toggle Filter button in the Sort & Filter group.
3. Print the filtered table by completing the following steps:
   a. Click the FILE tab, click the *Print* option, and then click the Print Preview button.
   b. Change the orientation to landscape and the left and right margins to 0.5 inch.
   c. Click the Print button and then click OK at the Print dialog box.
   d. Click the Close Print Preview button.
4. Close the Banquets table without saving the changes.
5. Open the Inventory table.
6. Filter records for the supplier number 2 or 7 by completing the following steps:
   a. Click the Advanced button in the Sort & Filter group on the HOME tab and then click *Filter By Form* at the drop-down list.
   b. At the Filter by Form window, click in the blank record below the *SupplierID* field.
   c. Click the down-pointing arrow at the right side of the field and then click *2* at the drop-down list.
   d. Click the Or tab located toward the bottom of the form.
   e. If necessary, click in the blank record below the *SupplierID* field.
   f. Click the down-pointing arrow at the right side of the field and then click *7* at the drop-down list.

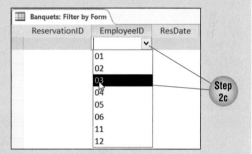

   g. Click the Toggle Filter button in the Sort & Filter group.
   h. Print the filtered table.
   i. Click the Toggle Filter button to redisplay all records in the table.
   j. Click the Advanced button and then click *Clear All Filters* from the drop-down list.
7. Close the Inventory table without saving the changes.

<table>
<tr>
<td>

Project 2   **View Object Dependencies, Manage a Database, and Save a Database in a Different File Format**   **4 Parts**

You will display object dependencies in the Skyline database, compact and repair the database, encrypt it with a password, view and customize document properties, save an object in the database in PDF file format, and save the database in a previous version of Access.

</td>
</tr>
</table>

Viewing Object Dependencies ■■■■■■■■■■■■■■■■■■■■■■■

Quick Steps

View Object Dependencies
1. Open desired database.
2. Click object in Navigation pane.
3. Click DATABASE TOOLS tab.
4. Click Object Dependencies button.

Object Dependencies

The structure of a database is comprised of table, query, form, and report objects. Tables are related to other tables by the relationships that have been created. Queries, forms, and reports draw the source data from the records in the tables to which they have been associated, and forms and reports can include subforms and subreports, which further expand the associations between objects. A database with a large number of interdependent objects is more complex to work with than a simpler database. Viewing a list of the objects within a database and viewing the dependencies between objects can be beneficial to ensure an object is not deleted or otherwise modified, causing an unforeseen effect on another object.

Display the structure of a database—including tables, queries, forms, and reports, as well as relationships—at the Object Dependencies task pane. Display this task pane by opening the database, clicking the desired object in the Navigation pane, clicking the DATABASE TOOLS tab, and then clicking the Object Dependencies button in the Relationships group. The Object Dependencies task pane, shown in Figure 7.4, displays the objects in AL1-C7-Skyline.accdb that depend on the Banquets table.

Figure 7.4   Object Dependencies Task Pane

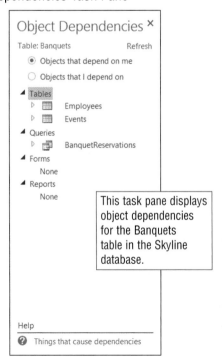

By default, *Objects that depend on me* is selected in the Object Dependencies task pane and the list box displays the names of the objects for which the selected object is the source. Next to each object in the task pane list is an expand button (a right-pointing, white triangle). Clicking the expand button next to an object shows the other objects that depend on it. For example, if a query is based on the Banquets and Events tables and the query is used to generate a report, clicking the expand button next to the query name will show the report name. Clicking an object name in the Object Dependencies task pane opens the object in Design view.

Project 2a **Viewing Object Dependencies** **Part 1 of 4**

1. With **AL1-C7-Skyline.accdb** open, display the structure of the database by completing the following steps:
   a. Click *Banquets* in the Tables group in the Navigation pane.
   b. Click the DATABASE TOOLS tab and then click the Object Dependencies button in the Relationships group. (This displays the Object Dependencies task pane. By default, *Objects that depend on me* is selected and the task pane lists the names of the objects for which the Banquets table is the source.)

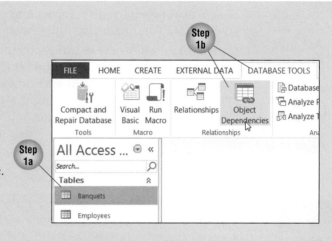

   c. Click the expand button (the right-pointing, white triangle that turns pink when you hover your mouse pointer over it) to the left of *Employees* in the *Tables* section. (This displays all of the objects that depend on the Employees table.)
   d. Click the *Objects that I depend on* option located toward the top of the Object Dependencies task pane.

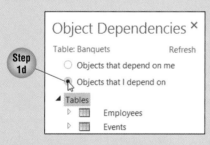

   e. Click *Events* in the Tables group in the Navigation pane. (Make sure to click *Events* in the Navigation pane and not the Object Dependencies task pane.)
   f. Click the <u>Refresh</u> hyperlink in the upper right corner of the Object Dependencies task pane.
   g. Click the *Objects that depend on me* option located toward the top of the Object Dependencies task pane.

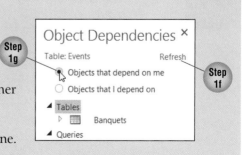

2. Close the Object Dependencies task pane.

Using Options at the Info Backstage Area ■■■■■■■■■■■

The Info backstage area contains options for compacting and repairing a database, encrypting a database with a password, and displaying and customizing database properties. Display the Info backstage area, shown in Figure 7.5, by opening a database and then clicking the FILE tab.

Compacting and Repairing a Database

▼ **Quick Steps**

Compact and Repair a Database
1. Open database.
2. Click FILE tab.
3. Click Compact & Repair Database button.

Compact & Repair Database

To optimize the performance of your database, compact and repair it on a regular basis. As you work with a database, data in it can become fragmented, causing the amount of space the database takes on the storage medium or in the folder to be larger than necessary. To compact and repair a database, open the database, click the FILE tab and then click the Compact & Repair Database button.

You can tell Access to compact and repair a database each time you close the database. To do this, click the FILE tab and then click *Options*. At the Access Options dialog box, click the *Current Database* option in the left panel. Click the *Compact on Close* option to insert a check mark and then click OK to close the dialog box. Before compacting and repairing a database in a multi-user environment, make sure that no other user has the database open.

Figure 7.5 Info Backstage Area

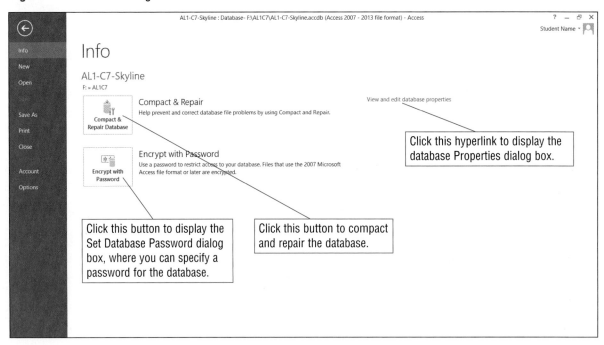

Encrypting a Database with a Password

If you want to prevent unauthorized access to a database, encrypt the database with a password to ensure that it can be opened only by someone who knows the password. Be careful when encrypting a database with a password because if you lose the password, you will be unable to use the database. You will not be able to remove the password from a database if you do not remember the password.

To encrypt a database with a password, you must open the database in Exclusive mode. To do this, display the Open dialog box, navigate to the desired folder, and then click the database to select it. Click the down-pointing arrow at the right side of the Open button located in the lower right corner of the dialog box and then click *Open Exclusive* at the drop-down list. When the database opens, click the FILE tab and then click the Encrypt with Password button in the Info backstage area. This displays the Set Database Password dialog box, as shown in Figure 7.6. At this dialog box, type a password in the *Password* text box, press the Tab key, and then type the password again. The text you type will display as asterisks. Click OK to close the Set Database Password dialog box. To remove a password from a database, open the database in Exclusive mode, click the FILE tab, and then click the Decrypt Database button. At the Unset Database Password dialog box, type the password and then click OK.

▼ Quick Steps

Open a Database in Exclusive Mode
1. Display Open dialog box.
2. Click desired database.
3. Click down-pointing arrow at right of Open button.
4. Click *Open Exclusive.*

Encrypt a Database with a Password
1. Open database in Exclusive mode.
2. Click FILE tab.
3. Click Encrypt with Password button.
4. Type password, press Tab, and type password again.
5. Click OK.

Figure 7.6 Set Database Password Dialog Box

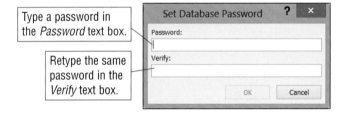

Type a password in the *Password* text box.

Retype the same password in the *Verify* text box.

Encrypt with Password   Decrypt Database

H I N T

When encrypting a database with a password, use a password that combines uppercase and lowercase letters, numbers, and symbols.

Project 2b **Compact and Repair and Encrypt a Database** **Part 2 of 4**

1. With **AL1-C7-Skyline.accdb** open, compact and repair the database by completing the following steps:
   a. Click the FILE tab. (This displays the Info backstage area.)
   b. Click the Compact & Repair Database button.
2. Close **AL1-C7-Skyline.accdb**.
3. Open the database in Exclusive mode by completing the following steps:
   a. Display the Open dialog box and make AL1C7 the active folder.
   b. Click **AL1-C7-Skyline.accdb** in the Content pane to select it.

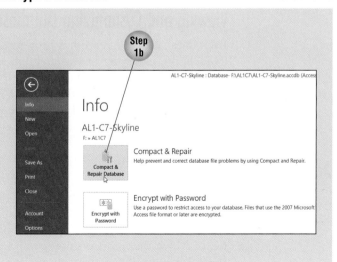

c. Click the down-pointing arrow at the right side of the Open button that displays in the lower right corner of the dialog box and then click *Open Exclusive* at the drop-down list.

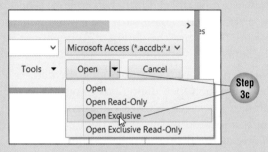

Step 3c

4. Encrypt the database with a password by completing the following steps:
   a. Click the FILE tab.
   b. At the Info backstage area, click the Encrypt with Password button.
   c. At the Set Database Password dialog box, type your first and last names in all lowercase letters with no space, press the Tab key, and then type your first and last names again in lowercase letters.
   d. Click OK to close the dialog box.
   e. If a message displays with information about encrypting with a block cipher, click OK.

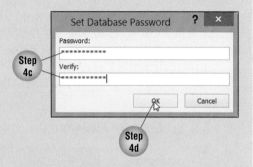

Step 4c

Step 4d

5. Close **AL1-C7-Skyline.accdb**.
6. Display the Open dialog box with AL1C7 the active folder and then open **AL1-C7-Skyline.accdb** in Exclusive mode.
7. At the Password Required dialog box, type your password and then click OK.
8. Remove the password by completing the following steps:
   a. Click the FILE tab.
   b. Click the Decrypt Database button.
   c. At the Unset Database Password dialog box, type your first and last names in lowercase letters and then press the Enter key.

Viewing and Customizing Database Properties

Each database you create has properties associated with it, such as the type of file, its location, and when it was created, accessed, and modified. You can view and modify database properties at the Properties dialog box. To view properties for the currently open database, click the FILE tab to display the Info backstage area and then click the <u>View and edit database properties</u> hyperlink that displays at the right side of the backstage area. This displays the Properties dialog box, similar to what is shown in Figure 7.7.

The Properties dialog box for an open database contains tabs with information about the database. With the General tab selected, the dialog box displays information about the database type, size, and location. Click the Summary tab to display fields such as *Title, Subject, Author, Category, Keywords,* and *Comments.* Some fields contain data and others are blank. You can insert, edit, or delete text in the fields. Move the insertion point to a field by clicking in the field or by pressing the Tab key until the insertion point is positioned in the desired field.

Figure 7.7 Properties Dialog Box

Click each tab to display additional information about the database.

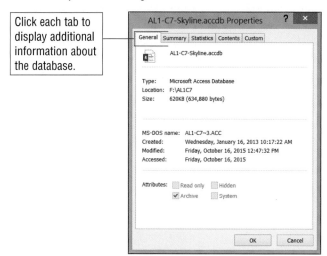

Click the Statistics tab to display information such as the dates the database was created, modified, accessed, and printed. Click the Contents tab and look in the *Document contents* section to see the objects in the database, including tables, queries, forms, reports, macros, and modules.

Use options at the Properties dialog box with the Custom tab selected to add custom properties to the database. For example, you can add a property that displays the date the database was completed, information on the department in which the database was created, and much more. The list box below the *Name* option box displays the predesigned properties provided by Access. You can choose a predesigned property or create your own.

To choose a predesigned property, select the desired property in the list box, specify what type of property it is (such as value, date, number, yes/no), and then type a value. For example, to specify the department in which the database was created, you would click *Department* in the list box, make sure the *Type* displays as *Text*, click in the *Value* text box, and then type the name of the department.

Project 2c   Viewing and Customizing Database Properties   Part 3 of 4

1. With **AL1-C7-Skyline.accdb** open, click the FILE tab and then click the <u>View and edit database properties</u> hyperlink that displays at the right side of the backstage area.

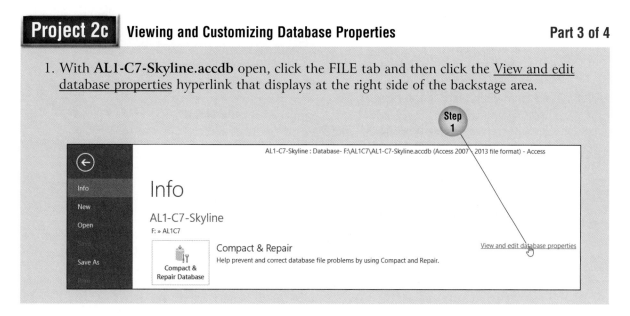

2. At the AL1-C7-Skyline.accdb Properties dialog box, click the General tab and then read the information that displays in the dialog box.
3. Click the Summary tab and then type the following text in the specified text boxes:

Title　　　　AL1-C7-Skyline database
Subject　　　Restaurant and banquet facilities
Author　　　*(type your first and last names)*
Category　　restaurant
Keywords　　restaurant, banquet, event, Fort Myers
Comments　　This database contains information on Skyline Restaurant employees, banquets, inventory, and orders.

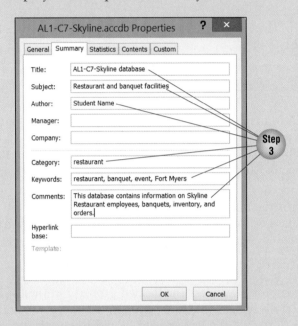

4. Click the Statistics tab and read the information that displays in the dialog box.
5. Click the Contents tab and notice that the *Document contents* section of the dialog box displays the objects in the database.
6. Click the Custom tab and then create custom properties by completing the following steps:
   a. Click the *Date completed* option in the *Name* list box.
   b. Click the down-pointing arrow at the right of the *Type* option box and then click *Date* at the drop-down list.
   c. Click in the *Value* text box and then type the current date in this format: *dd/mm/yyyy*.

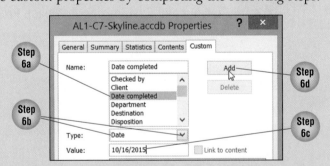

   d. Click the Add button.
   e. With the insertion point positioned in the *Name* text box, type **Course**.
   f. Click the down-pointing arrow at the right of the *Type* option box and then click *Text* at the drop-down list.
   g. Click in the *Value* text box, type your current course number, and then press Enter.
   h. Click OK to close the dialog box.
7. Click the Back button to return to the database.

Saving Databases and Database Objects ■■■■■■■■■■

An Access 2013, Access 2010, or Access 2007 database is saved with the file extension *.accdb*. Earlier versions of Access (such as 2003, 2002, and 2000) use the file extension *.mdb*. To open an Access 2013, 2010, or 2007 database in an earlier version, you need to save the database in the .mdb file format.

To save an Access database in the 2002 to 2003 file format, open the database, click the FILE tab, and then click the *Save As* option. This displays the Save As backstage area, as shown in Figure 7.9. Click the *Access 2002-2003 Database (*.mdb)* option in the *Save Database As* section and then click the Save As button that displays at the bottom of the *Save Database As* section. This displays the Save As dialog box with the *Save as type* option set to *Microsoft Access Database (2002-2003) (*.mdb)* and the current database file name with the file extension *.mdb* inserted in the *File name* text box. At this dialog box, click the Save button.

With an object open in a database, clicking the *Save Object As* option in the *File Types* section of the Save As backstage area displays options for saving the object. Click the *Save Object As* option to save the selected object in the database or click the *PDF or XPS* option if you want to save the object in PDF or XPS file format. The letters *PDF* stand for *portable document format*, a file format developed by Adobe Systems that captures all of the elements of a file as an electronic image. An XPS file is a Microsoft file format for publishing content in an easily viewable format. The letters *XPS* stand for *XML paper specification* and the letters *XML* stand for *extensible markup language*, which is a set of rules for encoding files electronically.

Saving an Object in PDF or XPS File Format

To save an object in PDF or XPS file format, open the desired object, click the FILE tab, and then click the *Save As* option. At the Save As backstage area, click the *Save Object As* option in the *File Types* section, click the *PDF or XPS* option in the *Save the current database object* section, and then click the Save As button. This displays the Publish as PDF or XPS dialog box with the name of the object inserted in the *File name* text box followed by the file extension *.pdf*, and the *Save as type* option set at *PDF (*.pdf)*. Click the Publish button and the object is saved

▼ Quick Steps

Save a Database in an Earlier Version
1. Open database.
2. Click FILE tab.
3. Click *Save As* option.
4. Click desired version in Save Database As category.
5. Click Save As button.

An Access 2007, 2010, or 2013 database cannot be opened with an earlier version of Access.

▼ Quick Steps

Save an Object in PDF File Format
1. Click desired object in Navigation pane.
2. Click FILE tab.
3. Click *Save As* option.
4. Click *Save Object As* option.
5. Click *PDF or XPS* option.
6. Click Save As button.

Figure 7.9 Save As Backstage Area with *Save Database As* Option Selected

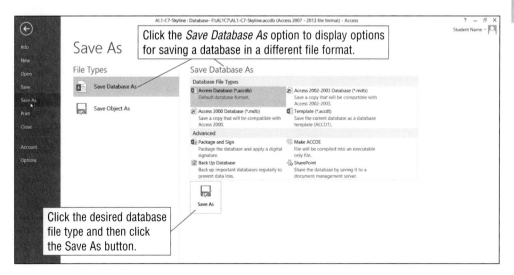

in PDF file format. If you want the object to open in Adobe Reader, click the *Open file after publishing* check box to insert a check box. With this check box active, the object will open in Adobe Reader when you click the Publish button.

You can open a PDF file in Adobe Reader, Internet Explorer, Microsoft Word, or Windows Reader. You can open an XPS file in Internet Explorer, Windows Reader, or XPS Viewer. One method for opening a PDF or XPS file is to open File Explorer, navigate to the folder containing the file, right-click on the file, and then point to *Open with*. This displays a side menu with the programs you can choose to open the file.

Backing Up a Database

Databases often contain important company information, and loss of this information can cause major problems. Backing up a database is important to minimize the chances of losing critical company data and is especially important when several people update and manage a database.

To back up a database, open the database, click the FILE tab, and then click the *Save As* option. At the Save As backstage area, click the *Back Up Database* option in the *Advanced* section and then click the Save As button. This displays the Save As dialog box with a default database file name, which is the original database name followed by the current date, in the *File name* text box. Click the Save button to save the backup database while keeping the original database open.

Project 2d	Saving a Database in a Previous Version, Saving an Object in PDF Format, and Backing Up a Database	Part 4 of 4

1. With **AL1-C7-Skyline.accdb** open, save the Orders table in PDF file format by completing the following steps:
   a. Open the Orders table.
   b. Click the FILE tab and then click the *Save As* option.
   c. At the Save As backstage area, click the *Save Object As* option in the *File Types* section.
   d. Click the *PDF or XPS* option in the *Save the current database object* section.
   e. Click the Save As button.

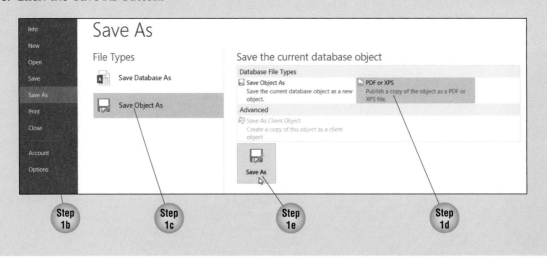

f. At the Publish as PDF or XPS dialog box, make sure the AL1C7 folder on your storage medium is the active folder and then click the *Open file after publishing* check box to insert a check mark. (Skip this step if the check box already contains a check mark.)

g. Click the Publish button.

h. When the Orders table opens in Adobe Reader, scroll through the file and then close the file by clicking the Close button located in the upper right corner of the screen.

2. Close the Orders table.

3. Save the database in a previous version of Access by completing the following steps:

a. Click the FILE tab and then click the *Save As* option.

b. At the Save As backstage area, click the *Access 2002-2003 Database (*.mdb)* option in the *Save Database As* section.

c. Click the Save As button.

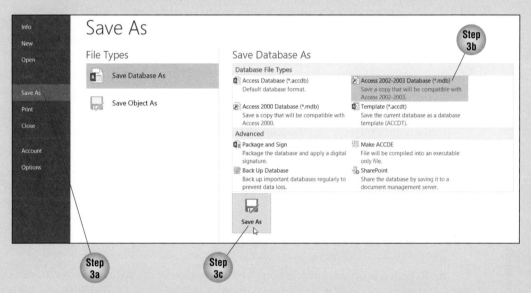

d. At the Save As dialog box, make sure the AL1C7 folder on your storage medium is the active folder and then click the Save button. This saves the database with the same name (**AL1-C7-Skyline**) but with the file extension *.mdb*.

e. Notice that the Title bar displays the database file name *AL1-C7-Skyline : Database (Access 2002 - 2003 file format)*.

4. Close the database.

5. Open AL1-C7-Skyline.accdb. (Make sure you open the AL1-C7-Skyline database with the .accdb file extension.)

6. Create a backup of the database by completing the following steps:

a. Click the FILE tab and then click the *Save As* option.

b. At the Save As backstage area, click the *Back Up Database* option in the *Advanced* section and then click the Save As button.

c. At the Save As dialog box, notice that the database name in the *File name* text box displays the original file name followed by the current date (year, month, day).

d. Make sure the AL1C7 folder on your storage medium is the active folder and then click the Save button. (This saves the backup copy of the database to your folder and the original database remains open.)

7. Close **AL1-C7-Skyline.accdb**.

Chapter Summary

- A set of restrictions called a filter can be set on records in a table or form. A filter lets you select specific field values.

- Filter records with the Filter button in the Sort & Filter group on the HOME tab.

- Click the Toggle Filter button in the Sort & Filter group to switch back and forth between data and filtered data.

- Remove a filter by clicking the Filter button in the Sort & Filter group and then clicking the *Clear filter from xxx* (where *xxx* is the name of the field).

- Another method for removing a filter is to click the Advanced button in the Sort & Filter group and then click *Clear All Filters*.

- Display a list of filter values by clicking the Filter button and then pointing to *Text Filters* (if the data is text), *Number Filters* (if the data is numbers), or *Date Filters* (if the data is dates).

- Filter by selection by clicking the Selection button in the Sort & Filter group.

- Right-click a field entry to display a shortcut menu with filtering options.

- Filter by form by clicking the Advanced button in the Sort & Filter group and then clicking *Filter By Form* at the drop-down list. This displays a blank record with two tabs: Look for and Or.

- Display the structure of a database and relationships between objects at the Object Dependencies task pane. Display this task pane by clicking the DATABASE TOOLS tab and then clicking the Object Dependencies button in the Relationships group.

- Click the Compact & Repair Database button in the Info backstage area to optimize database performance.

- To prevent unauthorized access to a database, encrypt the database with a password. To encrypt a database, you must first open it in Exclusive mode using the Open button drop-down list in the Open dialog box. While in Exclusive mode, encrypt a database with a password using the Encrypt with Password button in the Info backstage area.

- To view properties for the current database, click the <u>View and edit database properties</u> hyperlink in the Info backstage area. The Properties dialog box contains a number of tabs containing information about the database.

- Save a database in a previous version of Access using options in the *Save Database As* section of the Save As backstage area.

- To save a database object in PDF or XPS file format, display the Save As backstage area, click the *Save Object As* option, click the *PDF or XPS* option, and then click the Save As button.

- Backup a database to maintain critical data. Backup a database with the *Back Up Database* option at the Save As backstage area.

Commands Review

FEATURE	RIBBON TAB, GROUP/OPTION	BUTTON, OPTION
filter	HOME, Sort & Filter	▼
filter by form	HOME, Sort & Filter	, *Filter By Form*
filter by selection	HOME, Sort & Filter	▼
Info backstage area	FILE, *Info*	
Object Dependencies task pane	DATABASE TOOLS, Relationships	
remove filter	HOME, Sort & Filter	▼, *Clear filter from xxx* OR , *Clear All Filters*
toggle filter	HOME, Sort & Filter	▼

Concepts Check   Test Your Knowledge

Completion: In the space provided at the right, indicate the correct term, symbol, or command.

1. The Filter button is located in this group on the HOME tab.

2. When you filter data, you can switch between the filtered and unfiltered data by clicking this button.

3. Remove all filtering from an object by pressing the Filter button or clicking this button and then clicking *Clear All Filters*.

4. In the Filter by Form window, these two tabs display toward the bottom of the form.

5. Display the structure of a database at this task pane.

6. Optimize database performance by doing this to the database.

7. Before encrypting a database with a password, you must open the database in this mode.

8. Display the Set Database Password dialog box by clicking this button in the Info backstage area.

9. Data in this dialog box provides details about a database, such as its title, author name, and subject.

10. Save a database object in PDF file format with the *PDF or XPS* option in this backstage area.

Skills Check   Assess Your Performance

Assessment

1   FILTER RECORDS IN TABLES

 **Grade It**

1. Display the Open dialog box with the AL1C7 folder on your storage medium the active folder.
2. Open **AL1-C7-WarrenLegal.accdb** and enable the contents.
3. Open the Clients table and then filter the records to display the following records:
   a. Display only those records of clients who live in Renton. When the records of clients in Renton display, print the results in landscape orientation and then remove the filter. *Hint: Change to landscape orientation in Print Preview*.
   b. Display only those records of clients with the zip code of 98033. When the records of clients with the zip code 98033 display, print the results in landscape orientation and then remove the filter.
4. Close the Clients table without saving the changes.
5. Open the Billing table and then filter the records by selection to display the following records:
   a. Display only those records with a category of CC. Print the records and then remove the filter.
   b. Display only those records with an attorney ID of 12. Print the records and then remove the filter.
   c. Display only those records with dates between 6/1/2015 and 6/10/2015. Print the records and then remove the filter.
6. Close the Billing table without saving the changes.
7. Open the Clients table and then use the *Filter By Form* option to display clients in Auburn or Renton. (Be sure to use the Or tab at the bottom of the table.) Print the table in landscape orientation and then remove the filter.
8. Close the Clients table without saving the changes.
9. Open the Billing table and then use the *Filter By Form* option to display category G or P. Print the table and then remove the filter.
10. Close the Billing table without saving the changes.
11. Close **AL1-C7-WarrenLegal.accdb**.

Assessment

2   SAVE A TABLE AND DATABASE IN DIFFERENT FILE FORMATS

1. Open **AL1-C7-Hilltop.accdb** in Exclusive mode and enable the contents.
2. Create a password for the database (you determine the password), and with the Set Database Password dialog box open, create a screen capture of the screen with the dialog box by completing the following steps:
   a. Press the Print Screen button on your keyboard.
   b. Open a blank document in Microsoft Word.
   c. Click the Paste button located in the Clipboard group on the HOME tab. (This pastes the screen capture image in the Word document.)
   d. Click the FILE tab, click the *Print* option, and then click the Print button at the Print backstage area.
   e. Close Word by clicking the Close button located in the upper right corner of the screen. At the message asking if you want to save the document, click the Don't Save button.

3. Click OK to close the Set Database Password dialog box.
4. At the message telling you that block cipher is incompatible with row level locking, click OK.
5. Close the database.
6. Open **AL1-C7-Hilltop.accdb** in Exclusive mode and enter the password when prompted.
7. Remove the password. *Hint: Do this with the Decrypt Database button in the Info backstage area.*
8. Open the Invoices table and then save the table in PDF file format with the default file name. Specify that you want the object to open when published.
9. When the table opens in Adobe Reader, print the table by clicking the Print button located toward the upper left side of the screen and then clicking OK at the Print dialog box. (If the Print button is not visible, click the FILE option, click *Print* at the drop-down list, and then click OK at the Print dialog box.)
10. Close Adobe Reader and then close the Invoices table.
11. Save **AL1-C7-Hilltop.accdb** in the *Access 2002-2003 Database (*.mdb)* file format.
12. With the database open, make a screen capture using the Print Screen key on the keyboard. Open Word, paste the screen capture image in the Word document, print the document, and then close Word without saving the changes.
13. Close the database.

Assessment

3   DELETE AND RENAME OBJECTS

1. Open **AL1-C7-Hilltop.accdb**. (Make sure you open the AL1-C7-Hilltop database with the .accdb file extension.)
2. Right-click an object in the Navigation pane, experiment with options in the shortcut menu, and then complete these steps using the shortcut menu:
   a. Delete the Inventory form.
   b. Rename the form Equipment as *EquipForm*.
   c. Rename the report InvReport as *InventoryReport*.
   d. Export (using the shortcut menu) the *EquipmentQuery* to a Word RTF file. *Hint: Click the Browse button at the Export - RTF File dialog box and make the folder AL1C7 the active folder.*
   e. Open the *EquipmentQuery.rtf* file in Word, print the file, and then close Word.
3. Close **AL1-C7-Hilltop.accdb**.

Visual Benchmark Demonstrate Your Proficiency

DESIGN A QUERY AND FILTER THE QUERY

1. Open **AL1-C7-PacTrek.accdb** and enable the contents.
2. Create and run the query shown in Figure 7.10.
3. Save the query and name it *ProductsOnOrderQuery*.
4. Print the query.
5. Filter the query so the records display as shown in Figure 7.11. ***Hint: Filter the supplier names as shown in Figure 7.11 and then filter the* UnitsOnOrder *field to show records that do not equal 0*.**
6. Print the filtered query.
7. Remove the filters and then close the query without saving the changes.
8. Close **AL1-C7-PacTrek.accdb**.

Figure 7.10 Visual Benchmark Query

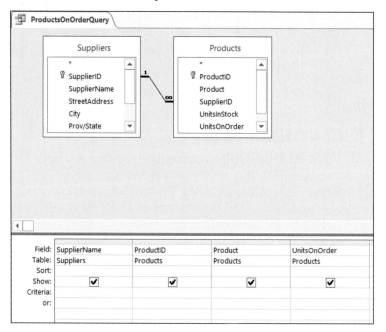

Figure 7.11 Visual Benchmark Filtered Query

SupplierName	ProductID	Product	UnitsOnOrder
Hopewell, Inc.	152-H	Lantern hanger	15
Hopewell, Inc.	155-20	Shursite angle-head flashlight	20
Hopewell, Inc.	155-35	Shursite portable camp light	10
Cascade Gear	250-L	Cascade R4 jacket, ML	10
Cascade Gear	250-XL	Cascade R4 jacket, MXL	10
Cascade Gear	255-M	Cascade R4 jacket, WM	5
Cascade Gear	255-XL	Cascade R4 jacket, WXL	5

Case Study   Apply Your Skills

Part

1

As the office manager at Summit View Medical Services, you are responsible for maintaining clinic records. Open **AL1-C7-SummitView.accdb**, enable the contents, and then insert the following additional services into the appropriate table:

- Edit the *Doctor visit* entry in the Services table so it displays as *Clinic visit*.
- Add the entry *X-ray* with a service identification of *X*.
- Add the entry *Cholesterol screening* with a service identification of *CS*.

Add the following new patient information in the database in the appropriate tables:

Patient number 121
Brian M. Gould
2887 Nelson Street
Helena, MT 59604
(406) 555-3121
Mr. Gould saw Dr. Wallace for a clinic visit on 4/6/2015, which has a fee of $75.

Patient number 122
Ellen L. Augustine
12990 148th Street
East Helena, MT 59635
(406) 555-0722
Ms. Augustine saw Dr. Kennedy for cholesterol screening on 4/6/2015, which has a fee of $90.

Patient number 123
Jeff J. Masura
3218 Eldridge Avenue
Helena, MT 59624
(406) 555-6212
Mr. Masura saw Dr. Rowe for an x-ray on 4/6/2015, which has a fee of $75.

Add the following information to the Billing table:

- Patient 109 came for cholesterol screening with Dr. Kennedy on 4/6/2015 with a $90 fee.
- Patient 106 came for immunizations with Dr. Pena on 4/6/2015 with a $100 fee.
- Patient 114 came for an x-ray with Dr. Kennedy on 4/6/2015 with a $75 fee.

Create the following filters and queries:

- Open the Billing table and then filter and print the records for the date 4/2/2015. Clear the filter and then filter and print the records with a doctor number of 18. Save and then close the table.

- Create a report that displays the patient's first name, last name, street address, city, state, and zip code. Apply formatting to enhance the appearance of the report. Filter and print the records of those patients living in Helena, remove the filter, and then filter and print the records of those patients living in East Helena. Close the report.

- Design a query that includes the doctor number, doctor last name, patient number, date of visit, and fee. Save the query with the name *DoctorBillingFees* and then print the query. Filter and print the records for Dr. Kennedy and Dr. Pena, remove the filter, and then filter and print the records for the dates 4/5/2015 and 4/6/2015. Save and then close the query.

You want to make the Billing table available for viewing on computers without Access, so you decide to save the table in PDF file format. Save the Billing table in PDF file format, print the table in Adobe Reader, and then close Adobe Reader. Close **AL1-C7-SummitView.accdb**.

Your clinic has a manual that describes processes and procedures in the workplace. Open Word and then create a document for the manual that describes the steps you followed to create the *DoctorBillingFees* query and to create and print the two filters. Save the completed document and name it **AL1-C7-CS-Manual**. Print and then close **AL1-C7-CS-Manual.docx**.

MICROSOFT®
ACCESS®

Exporting and Importing Data

CHAPTER 8

PERFORMANCE OBJECTIVES

Upon successful completion of Chapter 8, you will be able to:

- Export Access data to Excel
- Export Access data to Word
- Merge Access data with a Word document
- Export an Access object to a PDF or XPS file
- Import data to a new table
- Link data to a new table
- Use the Office Clipboard

Tutorials

8.1 Exporting Access Data to Excel
8.2 Exporting Access Data to Word
8.3 Merging Access Data with a Word Document
8.4 Importing and Linking Data to a New Table
8.5 Using the Office Clipboard

Microsoft Office 2013 is a suite of programs that allows easy data exchange between programs. In this chapter, you will learn how to export data from Access to Excel and Word, merge Access data with a Word document, export an Access object to a PDF or XPS file, import and link data to a new table, and copy and paste data between programs. You will also learn how to copy and paste data between applications. Model answers for this chapter's projects appear on the following pages.

AL1C8

Note: Before beginning the projects, copy to your storage medium the AL1C8 subfolder from the AL1 folder on the CD that accompanies this textbook and make AL1C8 the active folder.

Project 1 Export Data to Excel and Export and Merge Data to Word

Project 1a

Hilltop Inventory in Excel

EquipmentID	PurchaseDate	PurchasePrice	AvailableHours	ServiceHours	RepairHours
10	01-Sep-10	$65,540.00	120	15	10
11	01-Feb-11	$105,500.00	125	20	15
12	01-Jun-11	$55,345.00	140	10	10
13	05-May-12	$86,750.00	120	20	20
14	15-Jul-12	$4,500.00	160	5	5
15	01-Oct-13	$95,900.00	125	25	20
16	01-Dec-13	$3,450.00	150	10	5
17	10-Apr-13	$5,600.00	160	5	10
18	15-Jun-14	$8,000.00	150	5	5
19	30-Sep-14	$42,675.00	120	20	25

Hilltop Inventory in Excel

BillingDate	Customer	Hours	Rate	Total
01-May-15	Lakeside Trucking	8	$75.00	$600.00
01-May-15	Lakeside Trucking	8	$100.00	$800.00
01-May-15	Martin Plumbing	4	$50.00	$200.00
04-May-15	Country Electrical	16	$75.00	$1,200.00
04-May-15	Able Construction	5	$100.00	$500.00
04-May-15	Able Construction	5	$25.00	$125.00
04-May-15	Miles Contracting	10	$50.00	$500.00
05-May-15	Miles Contracting	10	$35.00	$350.00
05-May-15	Evergreen Painting	8	$25.00	$200.00
06-May-15	Barrier Concrete	8	$25.00	$200.00
06-May-15	Barrier Concrete	8	$25.00	$200.00
07-May-15	Cascade Enterprises	10	$100.00	$1,000.00
07-May-15	Cascade Enterprises	10	$75.00	$750.00
07-May-15	Allied Builders	6	$50.00	$300.00
08-May-15	Martin Plumbing	8	$35.00	$280.00
08-May-15	Evergreen Painting	8	$25.00	$200.00
08-May-15	Evergreen Painting	8	$25.00	$200.00
11-May-15	Able Construction	4	$75.00	$300.00
11-May-15	Able Construction	4	$100.00	$400.00
11-May-15	Miles Contracting	4	$50.00	$200.00
12-May-15	Country Electrical	6	$50.00	$300.00
12-May-15	Martin Plumbing	5	$75.00	$375.00
12-May-15	Lakeside Trucking	6	$100.00	$600.00
13-May-15	Cascade Enterprises	8	$25.00	$200.00
13-May-15	Miles Contracting	6	$25.00	$150.00
14-May-15	Evergreen Painting	6	$35.00	$210.00
14-May-15	Barrier Concrete	4	$100.00	$400.00
15-May-15	Allied Builders	4	$100.00	$400.00
15-May-15	Martin Plumbing	4	$50.00	$200.00
15-May-15	Miles Contracting	8	$25.00	$200.00

Hilltop Customer Invoices Query in Excel

Project 1b

InvoiceID	BillingDate	CustomerID	EquipmentID	Hours	RateID
1	5/1/2015	310	10	8	D
2	5/1/2015	310	11	8	E
3	5/1/2015	267	12	4	C
4	5/4/2015	196	10	16	D
5	5/4/2015	305	13	5	E
6	5/4/2015	305	14	5	A
7	5/4/2015	106	15	10	C
8	5/5/2015	106	16	10	B
9	5/5/2015	275	17	8	A
10	5/6/2015	154	18	8	A
11	5/6/2015	154	17	8	A
12	5/7/2015	209	11	10	E
13	5/7/2015	209	19	10	D
14	5/7/2015	316	15	6	C
15	5/8/2015	267	16	8	B
16	5/8/2015	275	18	8	A
17	5/8/2015	275	17	8	A
18	5/11/2015	305	10	4	D
19	5/11/2015	305	13	4	E
20	5/11/2015	106	12	4	C
21	5/12/2015	196	15	6	C
22	5/12/2015	267	19	5	D
23	5/12/2015	310	11	6	E
24	5/13/2015	209	17	8	A
25	5/13/2015	106	14	6	A
26	5/14/2015	275	16	6	B
27	5/14/2015	154	13	4	E
28	5/15/2015	316	11	4	E
29	5/15/2015	267	15	4	C
30	5/15/2015	106	18	8	A

Hilltop Customer Invoices in Word

CustomerReport

Customer	Equipment	BillingDate	Hours
Miles Contracting	Hydraulic pump	5/5/2015	10
	Trencher	5/11/2015	4
	Scaffolding	5/13/2015	6
	Sandblaster	5/15/2015	8
	Forklift	5/4/2015	10
Barrier Concrete	Sandblaster	5/6/2015	8
	Pressure sprayer	5/6/2015	8
	Tractor	5/14/2015	4
Country Electrical	Backhoe	5/4/2015	16
	Forklift	5/12/2015	6
Cascade Enterprises	Front loader	5/7/2015	10
	Flatbed truck	5/7/2015	10
	Pressure sprayer	5/13/2015	8
Martin Plumbing	Flatbed truck	5/12/2015	5
	Hydraulic pump	5/8/2015	8
	Forklift	5/15/2015	4
	Trencher	5/1/2015	4
Evergreen Painting	Pressure sprayer	5/5/2015	8
	Sandblaster	5/8/2015	8
	Pressure sprayer	5/8/2015	8
	Hydraulic pump	5/14/2015	6
Able Construction	Tractor	5/4/2015	5
	Scaffolding	5/4/2015	5
	Backhoe	5/11/2015	4
	Tractor	5/11/2015	4
Lakeside Trucking	Backhoe	5/1/2015	8
	Front loader	5/1/2015	8
	Front loader	5/12/2015	6
Allied Builders	Front loader	5/15/2015	4
	Forklift	5/7/2015	6

Monday, October 19, 2015   Page 1 of 1

Project 1b, Hilltop Customer Report in Access

CustomerReport

Customer	Equipment	BillingDate	Hours
Miles Contracting	Hydraulic pump	5/5/2015	10
	Trencher	5/11/2015	4
	Scaffolding	5/13/2015	6
	Sandblaster	5/15/2015	8
	Forklift	5/4/2015	10
Barrier Concrete	Sandblaster	5/6/2015	8
	Pressure sprayer	5/6/2015	8
	Tractor	5/14/2015	4
Country Electrical	Backhoe	5/4/2015	16
	Forklift	5/12/2015	6
Cascade Enterprises	Front loader	5/7/2015	10
	Flatbed truck	5/7/2015	10
	Pressure sprayer	5/13/2015	8
Martin Plumbing	Flatbed truck	5/12/2015	5
	Hydraulic pump	5/8/2015	8
	Forklift	5/15/2015	4
	Trencher	5/1/2015	4
Evergreen Painting	Pressure sprayer	5/5/2015	8
	Sandblaster	5/8/2015	8
	Pressure sprayer	5/8/2015	8
	Hydraulic pump	5/14/2015	6
Able Construction	Tractor	5/4/2015	5
	Scaffolding	5/4/2015	5
	Backhoe	5/11/2015	4
	Tractor	5/11/2015	4
Lakeside Trucking	Backhoe	5/1/2015	8
	Front loader	5/1/2015	8
	Front loader	5/12/2015	6
Allied Builders	Front loader	5/15/2015	4
	Forklift	5/7/2015	6

Friday, October 19, 2012   Page 1 of 1

Project 1b, Hilltop Customer Report in Word

October 19, 2015

Miles Contracting
640 Smith Road
Aurora, CO 80041-6400

Ladies and Gentlemen:

Please join us June 1 for our annual equipment sales auction. Some of the choice items up for auction include three forklifts, two flatbed trucks, a front loader, and a bulldozer. We will also be auctioning painting equipment including pressure sprayers, ladders, and scaffolding.

The auction begins at 7:30 a.m. in the parking lot of our warehouse at 2605 Evans Avenue in Denver. For a listing of all equipment available for auction, stop by our store or call us at (303) 555-9066 and we will mail you the list.

Sincerely,

Lou Galloway
Manager

XX
HilltopLetter.docx

October 19, 2015

Barrier Concrete
220 Colorado Boulevard
Denver, CO 80125-2204

Ladies and Gentlemen:

Please join us June 1 for our annual equipment sales auction. Some of the choice items up for auction include three forklifts, two flatbed trucks, a front loader, and a bulldozer. We will also be auctioning painting equipment including pressure sprayers, ladders, and scaffolding.

The auction begins at 7:30 a.m. in the parking lot of our warehouse at 2605 Evans Avenue in Denver. For a listing of all equipment available for auction, stop by our store or call us at (303) 555-9066 and we will mail you the list.

Sincerely,

Lou Galloway
Manager

XX
HilltopLetter.docx

Project 1c, Hilltop Letters

October 19, 2015

Vernon Cook
1230 South Mesa
Phoenix, AZ 85018

Ladies and Gentlemen:

At the Grant Street West office of Copper State Insurance, we have hired two additional insurance representatives as well as one support staff member to ensure that we meet all your insurance needs. To accommodate the new staff, we have moved to a larger office just a few blocks away. Our new address is 3450 Grant Street West, Suite 110, Phoenix AZ 85003. Our telephone number, (602) 555-6300, has remained the same.

If you have any questions or concerns about your insurance policies or want to discuss adding or changing current coverage, please stop by or give us a call. We are committed to providing our clients with the most comprehensive automobile insurance coverage in the county.

Sincerely,

Lou Galloway
Manager

XX
AL1-C8-CSLtrs.docx

October 19, 2015

Helena Myerson
9032 45th Street East
Phoenix, AZ 85009

Ladies and Gentlemen:

At the Grant Street West office of Copper State Insurance, we have hired two additional insurance representatives as well as one support staff member to ensure that we meet all your insurance needs. To accommodate the new staff, we have moved to a larger office just a few blocks away. Our new address is 3450 Grant Street West, Suite 110, Phoenix AZ 85003. Our telephone number, (602) 555-6300, has remained the same.

If you have any questions or concerns about your insurance policies or want to discuss adding or changing current coverage, please stop by or give us a call. We are committed to providing our clients with the most comprehensive automobile insurance coverage in the county.

Sincerely,

Lou Galloway
Manager

XX
AL1-C8-CSLtrs.docx

Project 1d, Copper State Main Document

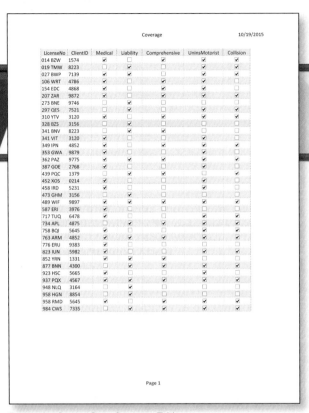

		Coverage			10/19/2015	
LicenseNo	ClientID	Medical	Liability	Comprehensive	UninsMotorist	Collision
014 BZW	1574	✓		✓	✓	✓
019 TMW	8223		✓		✓	✓
027 BWP	7139	✓	✓		✓	✓
106 WRT	4786	✓		✓	✓	
154 EDC	4868	✓		✓	✓	
207 ZAR	9872	✓		✓	✓	✓
273 BNE	9746		✓			
297 QES	7521		✓			✓
310 YTV	3120			✓	✓	
328 BZS	3156		✓			
341 BNV	8223		✓	✓		
341 VIT	3120	✓			✓	
349 IPN	4852	✓		✓	✓	
353 GWA	9879	✓		✓	✓	
362 PAZ	9775	✓	✓	✓	✓	
387 GOE	2768	✓		✓	✓	
439 PQC	1379		✓	✓		
452 XOS	0214	✓			✓	
458 IRD	5231	✓			✓	
473 GHM	3156		✓			
489 WIF	9897	✓		✓	✓	✓
587 ERI	3976	✓				
717 TUQ	6478	✓			✓	✓
734 APL	4875		✓	✓	✓	✓
758 BQJ	5645	✓			✓	✓
763 ARM	4852	✓		✓	✓	✓
776 ERU	9383	✓				
823 IUN	5982	✓			✓	
852 YRN	1331	✓	✓	✓		
877 BNN	4300		✓	✓	✓	✓
923 HSC	5665	✓			✓	
937 PQX	4567	✓	✓	✓	✓	✓
948 NLQ	3164		✓			
958 HGN	8854		✓		✓	
958 RMD	5645	✓		✓	✓	✓
984 CWS	7335		✓	✓	✓	✓

Page 1

Project 1e, Copper State Coverage Table

Project 2 Import and Link Excel Worksheets with an Access Table

Project 2a

PolicyID	ClientID	Premium
110-C-39	0214	$1,450
115-C-41	3120	$935
120-B-33	3156	$424
122-E-30	1331	$745
127-E-67	3164	$893
129-D-55	3976	$770
131-C-90	4300	$1,255
135-E-31	4567	$1,510
136-E-77	4786	$635
139-B-59	4852	$338
141-E-84	4875	$951
143-D-20	1379	$920
145-D-12	5231	$1,175
147-C-10	5645	$1,005
150-C-36	5665	$805
152-B-01	5982	$411
155-E-88	6478	$988
168-B-65	7139	$1,050
170-C-20	7335	$875
173-D-77	7521	$556
180-E-05	8223	$721
185-E-19	2768	$734
188-D-63	8854	$1,384
192-C-29	1574	$1,390

Copper State Policies
Table in Access

Project 2b

PolicyID	ClientID	Premium
110-C-39	0214	$ 1,450
122-E-30	1331	$ 850
143-D-20	1379	$ 920
192-C-29	1574	$ 1,390
185-E-19	2768	$ 734
115-C-41	3120	$ 935
120-B-33	3156	$ 424
127-E-67	3164	$ 893
129-D-55	3976	$ 770
131-C-90	4300	$ 1,255
135-E-31	4567	$ 1,510
136-E-77	4786	$ 635
139-B-59	4852	$ 338
141-E-84	4875	$ 951
145-D-12	5231	$ 1,175
147-C-10	5645	$ 1,005
150-C-36	5665	$ 805
152-B-01	5982	$ 411
155-E-88	6478	$ 988
168-B-65	7139	$ 1,050
170-C-20	7335	$ 875
173-D-77	7521	$ 556
180-E-05	8223	$ 721
188-D-63	8854	$ 1,384
190-C-28	3120	$ 685

Policies Table in Excel

Project 3 Collect Data in Word and Paste It into an Access Table

Project 3

CustomerID	Customer	StreetAddress	City	State	ZipCode
106	Miles Contracting	640 Smith Road	Aurora	CO	80041-6400
154	Barrier Concrete	220 Colorado Boulevard	Denver	CO	80125-2204
196	Country Electrical	12032 Sixth Avenue	Aurora	CO	80023-5473
209	Cascade Enterprises	24300 Quincy Avenue	Englewood	CO	80118-3800
267	Martin Plumbing	1010 Santa Fe Drive	Littleton	CO	80135-4886
275	Evergreen Painting	1045 Calfax Avenue	Denver	CO	80130-4337
305	Able Construction	8800 Evans Avenue	Denver	CO	80128-3488
310	Lakeside Trucking	566 Jewell Avenue	Denver	CO	80125-1298
316	Allied Builders	550 Alameda Avenue	Denver	CO	80135-7643
178	Stone Construction	9905 Broadway	Englewood	CO	80118-9008
225	Laughlin Products	997 Speer Boulevard	Denver	CO	80129-7446

Hilltop Customers Table

You will export a table and query to Excel and export a table and report to Word.
You will also merge data in an Access table and query with a Word document.

Exporting Data ▪▪▪▪▪▪▪▪▪▪▪▪▪▪▪▪▪▪▪▪▪▪▪▪▪▪▪▪▪▪▪▪▪▪

One of the advantages of using the Microsoft Office suite is the ability to exchange data between programs. Access, like other programs in the suite, offers a feature to export data from Access into Excel and/or Word. The Export group on the EXTERNAL DATA tab contains buttons for exporting a table, query, form, or report to other programs, such as Excel and Word.

Exporting Data to Excel

Use the Excel button in the Export group on the EXTERNAL DATA tab to export data in a table, query, or form to an Excel worksheet. Click the object containing the data you want to export to Excel, click the EXTERNAL DATA tab, and then click the Excel button in the Export group. The first Export - Excel Spreadsheet wizard dialog box displays, as shown in Figure 8.1.

▼ Quick Steps
Export Data to Excel
1. Click desired table, query, or form.
2. Click EXTERNAL DATA tab.
3. Click Excel button in Export group.
4. Make desired changes at Export - Excel Spreadsheet dialog box.
5. Click OK.

Excel

Figure 8.1 Export - Excel Spreadsheet Wizard Dialog Box

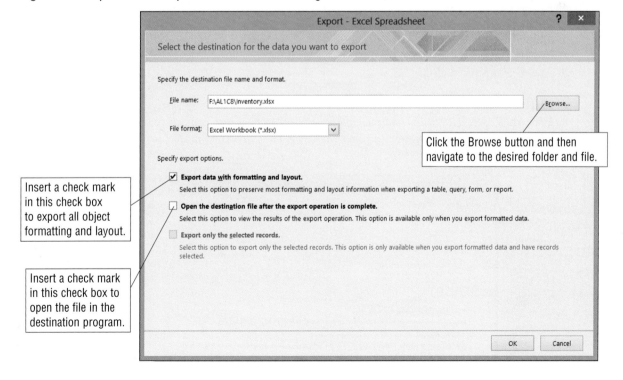

At the first wizard dialog box, Access uses the name of the object as the Excel workbook name. You can change this by selecting the current name and then typing a new name. You can also specify the file format with the *File format* option. Click the *Export data with formatting and layout* check box to insert a check mark. This exports all data formatting to the Excel workbook. If you want Excel to open with the exported data, click the *Open the destination file after the export operation is complete* option to insert a check mark. When you have made all desired changes, click the OK button. This opens Excel with the data in a workbook. Make any desired changes to the workbook and then save, print, and close the workbook. When you close Excel, Access displays with a second wizard dialog box, asking if you want to save the export steps. At this dialog box, insert a check mark in the *Save export steps* check box if you want to save the export steps or leave the check box blank and then click the Close button.

Project 1a Exporting a Table and Query to Excel   Part 1 of 5

1. Display the Open dialog box with the AL1C8 folder on your storage medium the active folder.
2. Open **AL1-C8-Hilltop.accdb** and enable the contents.
3. Save the Inventory table in the Tables group as an Excel workbook by completing the following steps:
   a. Click *Inventory* in the Tables group in the Navigation pane.
   b. Click the EXTERNAL DATA tab and then click the Excel button in the Export group.
   c. At the Export - Excel Spreadsheet wizard dialog box, click the Browse button.
   d. At the File Save dialog box, navigate to the AL1C8 folder on your storage medium and then click the Save button.
   e. Click the *Export data with formatting and layout* option to insert a check mark in the check box.
   f. Click the *Open the destination file after the export operation is complete* option to insert a check mark in the check box.

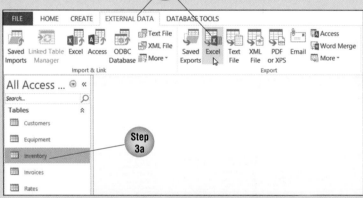

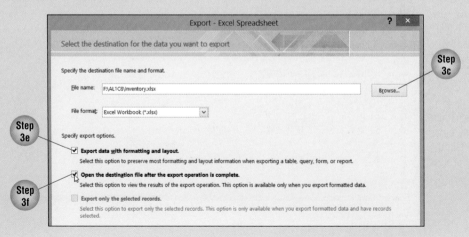

g. Click OK.

h. When the data displays on the screen in Excel as a worksheet, select cells A2 through A11 and then click the Center button in the Alignment group on the HOME tab.

i. Select cells D2 through F11 and then click the Center button.

j. Click the Save button on the Quick Access toolbar.

k. Print the worksheet by pressing Ctrl + P and then clicking the Print button at the Print backstage area.

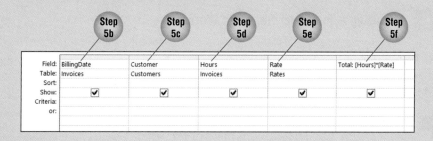

Step 3h

	A	B	C	D	E	F
1	EquipmentID	PurchaseDate	PurchasePrice	AvailableHours	ServiceHours	RepairHours
2	10	01-Sep-10	$65,540.00	120	15	10
3	11	01-Feb-11	$105,500.00	125	20	15
4	12	01-Jun-11	$55,345.00	140	10	10
5	13	05-May-12	$86,750.00	120	20	20
6	14	15-Jul-12	$4,500.00	160	5	5
7	15	01-Oct-13	$95,900.00	125	25	20
8	16	01-Dec-13	$3,450.00	150	10	5
9	17	10-Apr-13	$5,600.00	160	5	10
10	18	15-Jun-14	$8,000.00	150	5	5
11	19	30-Sep-14	$42,675.00	120	20	25
12						
13						

l. Close the worksheet and then close Excel.

4. In Access, click the Close button to close the second wizard dialog box.

5. Design a query that extracts records from three tables with the following specifications:

a. Add the Invoices, Customers, and Rates tables to the query window.

b. Insert the *BillingDate* field from the *Invoices* field list box to the first *Field* row field.

c. Insert the *Customer* field from the *Customers* field list box to the second *Field* row field.

d. Insert the *Hours* field from the *Invoices* field list box to the third *Field* row field.

e. Insert the *Rate* field from the *Rates* field list box to the fourth *Field* row field.

f. Click in the fifth *Field* row field, type **Total: [Hours]*[Rate]**, and then press Enter.

Step 5b   **Step 5c**   **Step 5d**   **Step 5e**   **Step 5f**

Field:	BillingDate	Customer	Hours	Rate	Total: [Hours]*[Rate]
Table:	Invoices	Customers	Invoices	Rates	
Sort:					
Show:	✔	✔	✔	✔	✔
Criteria:					
or:					

g. Run the query.

h. If necessary, automatically adjust the column width of the *Customer* field.

i. Save the query and name it *CustomerInvoices*.

j. Close the query.

6. Export the *CustomerInvoices* in the Queries group to Excel by completing the following steps:

a. Click *CustomerInvoices* in the Queries group in the Navigation pane.

b. Click the EXTERNAL DATA tab and then click the Excel button in the Export group.

c. At the Export - Excel Spreadsheet wizard dialog box, click the *Export data with formatting and layout* option to insert a check mark in the check box.

d. Click the *Open the destination file after the export operation is complete* option to insert a check mark in the check box.

e. Click OK.

f. When the data displays on the screen in Excel as a worksheet, select cells C2 through C31 and then click the Center button in the Alignment group on the HOME tab.

g. Click the Save button on the Quick Access toolbar.

h. Print the worksheet by pressing Ctrl + P and then clicking the Print button at the Print backstage area.

i. Close the worksheet and then close Excel.

7. In Access, click the Close button to close the second wizard dialog box.

Exporting Data to Word

▼ **Quick Steps**

Export Data to Word

1. Click desired table, query, form, or report.
2. Click EXTERNAL DATA tab.
3. Click More button in Export group.
4. Click *Word*.
5. Make desired changes at Export - RTF File wizard dialog box.
6. Click OK.

More

Export data from Access to Word in a similar manner as exporting to Excel. To export data to Word, select the desired object in the Navigation pane, click the EXTERNAL DATA tab, click the More button in the Export group, and then click *Word* at the drop-down list. At the Export - RTF File wizard dialog box, make desired changes and then click OK. Word automatically opens and the data displays in a Word document that is saved automatically with the same name as the database object. The difference is that the file extension .rtf is added to the name. An RTF file is saved in rich-text format, which preserves formatting such as fonts and styles. You can export a document saved with the .rtf extension in Word and other Windows word processing or desktop publishing programs.

Project 1b | **Exporting a Table and Report to Word** | **Part 2 of 5**

1. With **AL1-C8-Hilltop.accdb** open, click *Invoices* in the Tables group in the Navigation pane.
2. Click the EXTERNAL DATA tab, click the More button in the Export group, and then click *Word* at the drop-down list.

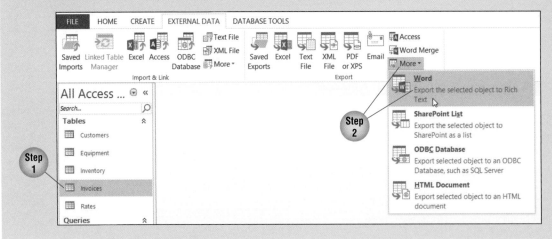

3. At the Export - RTF File wizard dialog box, click the Browse button.
4. At the File Save dialog box, make sure the AL1C8 folder on your storage medium is active and then click the Save button.
5. At the Export - RTF File wizard dialog box, click the *Open the destination file after the export operation is complete* check box to insert a check mark.

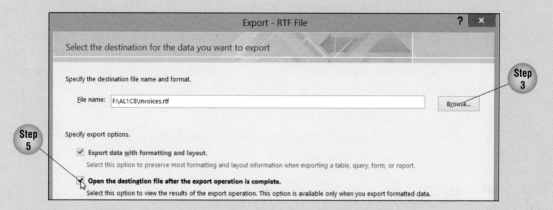

6. Click OK.
7. With the **Invoices.rtf** file open in Word, print the document by pressing Ctrl + P and then clicking the Print button at the Print backstage area.
8. Close the **Invoices.rtf** file and then close Word.
9. In Access, click the Close button to close the wizard dialog box.
10. Create a report with the Report Wizard by completing the following steps:
    a. Click the CREATE tab and then click the Report Wizard button in the Reports group.
    b. At the first Report Wizard dialog box, insert the following fields in the *Selected Fields* list box:

    From the Customers table:
    Customer
    From the Equipment table:
    Equipment
    From the Invoices table:
    BillingDate
    Hours

    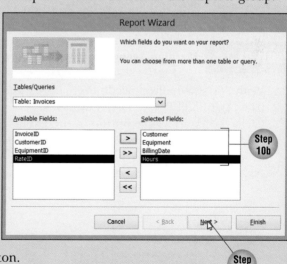

    c. After inserting the fields, click the Next button.
    d. At the second Report Wizard dialog box, make sure *by Customers* is selected in the list box in the upper left corner and then click the Next button.
    e. At the third Report Wizard dialog box, click the Next button.
    f. At the fourth Report Wizard dialog box, click the Next button.
    g. At the fifth Report Wizard dialog box, click *Block* in the *Layout* section and then click the Next button.
    h. At the sixth and final Report Wizard dialog box, select the current name in the *What title do you want for your report?* text box, type **CustomerReport**, and then click the Finish button.

i. When the report displays in Print Preview, click the Print button at the left side of the PRINT PREVIEW tab and then click OK at the Print dialog box.

j. Save and then close the CustomerReport report.

11. Export the CustomerReport report to Word by completing the following steps:

a. Click *CustomerReport* in the Reports group in the Navigation pane.

b. Click the EXTERNAL DATA tab, click the More button in the Export group, and then click *Word* at the drop-down list.

c. At the Export - RTF File wizard dialog box, click the *Open the destination file after export operation is complete* option to insert a check mark in the check box and then click OK.

d. When the data displays on the screen in Word, print the document by pressing Ctrl + P and then clicking the Print button at the Print backstage area.

e. Save and then close the CustomerReport document.

f. Close Word.

12. In Access, click the Close button to close the second wizard dialog box.

▼ **Quick Steps**

Merge Data with Word
1. Click desired table or query.
2. Click EXTERNAL DATA tab.
3. Click Word Merge button.
4. Make desired choices at each dialog box.

Word Merge

Merging Access Data with a Word Document

You can merge data from an Access table with a Word document. When merging data, the data in the Access table is considered the data source and the Word document is considered the main document. When the merge is completed, the merged documents display in Word.

To merge data, click the desired table in the Navigation pane, click the EXTERNAL DATA tab, and then click the Word Merge button. When merging Access data, you can either type the text in the main document or merge Access data with an existing Word document.

| **Project 1c** | **Merging Access Data with a Word Document** | **Part 3 of 5** |

1. With **AL1-C8-Hilltop.accdb** open, click *Customers* in the Tables group in the Navigation pane.
2. Click the EXTERNAL DATA tab.
3. Click the Word Merge button in the Export group.

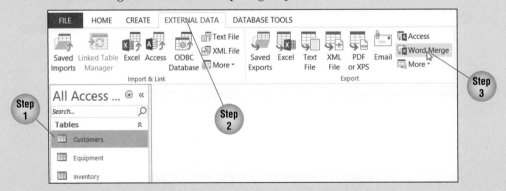

4. At the Microsoft Word Mail Merge Wizard dialog box, make sure *Link your data to an existing Microsoft Word document* is selected and then click OK.
5. At the Select Microsoft Word Document dialog box, make sure the AL1C8 folder on your storage medium is the active folder and then double-click the document named *HilltopLetter.docx*.

6. Click the Word button on the Taskbar.
7. Click the Maximize button located at the right side of the HilltopLetter.docx Title bar and then close the Mail Merge task pane.
8. Press the down arrow key six times (not the Enter key) and then type the current date.
9. Press the down arrow key four times and then insert fields for merging from the Customers table by completing the following steps:

   a. Click the Insert Merge Field button arrow located in the Write & Insert Fields group and then click *Customer* in the drop-down list. (This inserts the *«Customer»* field in the document.)

   b. Press Enter, click the Insert Merge Field button arrow, and then click *StreetAddress* in the drop-down list.

   c. Press Enter, click the Insert Merge Field button arrow, and then click *City* in the drop-down list.

   d. Type a comma (,) and then press the spacebar.

   e. Click the Insert Merge Field button arrow and then click *State* in the drop-down list.

   f. Press the spacebar, click the Insert Merge Field button arrow, and then click *ZipCode* in the drop-down list.

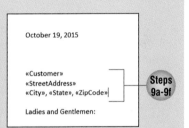

   g. Replace the letters *XX* that display toward the bottom of the letter with your initials.

   h. Click the Finish & Merge button in the Finish group and then click *Edit Individual Documents* in the drop-down list.

   i. At the Merge to New Document dialog box, make sure *All* is selected and then click OK.

   j. When the merge is completed, save the new document and name it **AL1-C8-HilltopLtrs** in the AL1C8 folder on your storage medium.

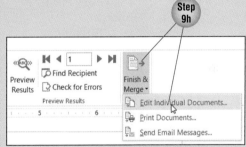

10. Print just the first two pages (two letters) of **AL1-C8-HilltopLtrs.docx**.
11. Close **AL1-C8-HilltopLtrs.docx** and then close **HilltopLetter.docx** without saving the changes.
12. Close Word.
13. Close **AL1-C8-Hilltop.accdb**.

Merging Query Data with a Word Document

You can perform a query in a database and then use the query to merge with a Word document. In Project 1c, you merged a table with an existing Word document. You can also merge a table or query and then type the Word document. You will create a query in Project 1d and then merge data in the query with a new document in Word.

In Project 1c, you inserted a number of merge fields for the inside address of a letter. You can also insert a field that will insert all of the fields required for the inside address of a letter with the Address Block button in the Write & Insert Fields group on the MAILINGS tab. When you click the Address Block button, the Insert Address Block dialog box displays with a preview of how the

Address Block

fields will be inserted in the document to create the inside address. The dialog box also contains buttons and options for customizing the fields. Click OK and the *«AddressBlock»* field is inserted in the document. The *«AddressBlock»* field is an example of a composite field, which groups a number of fields.

In Project 1c, you could not use the *«AddressBlock»* composite field because the *Customer* field was not recognized by Word as a field for the inside address. In Project 1d, you will create a query that contains the *FirstName* and *LastName* fields, which Word recognizes and uses for the *«AddressBlock»* composite field.

Project 1d   **Performing a Query and Then Merging with a Word Document**   **Part 4 of 5**

1. Display the Open dialog box with the AL1C8 folder on your storage medium the active folder.
2. Open **AL1-C8-CopperState.accdb** and enable the contents.
3. Perform a query with the Query Wizard and modify the query by completing the following steps:
   a. Click the CREATE tab and then click the Query Wizard button in the Queries group.
   b. At the New Query dialog box, make sure Simple Query Wizard is selected and then click OK.
   c. At the first Simple Query Wizard dialog box, click the down-pointing arrow at the right of the *Tables/Queries* option box and then click *Table: Clients*.
   d. Click the All Fields button to insert all of the fields in the *Selected Fields* list box.
   e. Click the Next button.
   f. At the second Simple Query Wizard dialog box, make the following changes:
      1) Select the current name in the *What title do you want for your query?* text box and then type **ClientsPhoenixQuery**.
      2) Click the *Modify the query design* option.
      3) Click the Finish button.
   g. At the query window, click in the *Criteria* field in the *City* column, type **Phoenix**, and then press Enter.
   h. Click the Run button in the Results group. (Only clients living in Phoenix will display.)
   i. Save and then close the query.
4. Click *ClientsPhoenixQuery* in the Queries group in the Navigation pane.
5. Click the EXTERNAL DATA tab and then click the Word Merge button in the Export group.
6. At the Microsoft Word Mail Merge Wizard dialog box, click the *Create a new document and then link the data to it* option and then click OK.

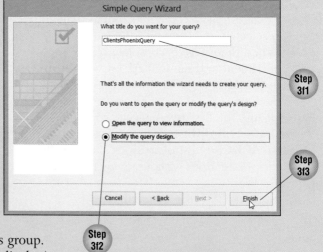

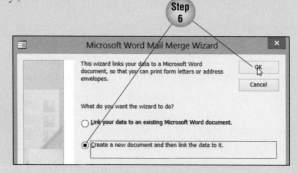

7. Click the Word button on the Taskbar.
8. Click the Maximize button located at the right side of the Document1 Title bar and then close the Mail Merge task pane.
9. Complete the following steps to type text and insert the *«AddressBlock»* composite field in the blank Word document:
   a. Click the HOME tab and then click the *No Spacing* style option in the Styles group.
   b. Press Enter six times.
   c. Type the current date.
   d. Press Enter four times.
   e. Click the MAILINGS tab.
   f. Insert the *«AddressBlock»* composite field by clicking the Address Block button in the Write & Insert Fields group on the MAILINGS tab and then clicking OK at the Insert Address Block dialog box. (This inserts the *«AddressBlock»* composite field in the document.)
   g. Press Enter twice and then type the salutation Ladies and Gentlemen:.
   h. Press Enter twice and then type the following paragraphs of text (press the Enter key twice after typing the first paragraph):

   At the Grant Street West office of Copper State Insurance, we have hired two additional insurance representatives as well as one support staff member to ensure that we meet all your insurance needs. To accommodate the new staff, we have moved to a larger office just a few blocks away. Our new address is 3450 Grant Street West, Suite 110, Phoenix AZ 85003. Our telephone number, (602) 555-6300, has remained the same.

   If you have any questions or concerns about your insurance policies or want to discuss adding or changing current coverage, please stop by or give us a call. We are committed to providing our clients with the most comprehensive automobile insurance coverage in the county.

   i. Press Enter twice and then type the following complimentary close at the left margin (press Enter four times after typing *Sincerely,*):

   Sincerely,

   Lou Galloway
   Manager

   XX (Type your initials instead of XX.)
   AL1-C8-CSLtrs.docx

   j. Click the Finish & Merge button in the Finish group on the MAILINGS tab and then click *Edit Individual Documents* in the drop-down menu.
   k. At the Merge to New Document dialog box, make sure *All* is selected, and then click OK.
   l. When the merge is complete, save the new document in the AL1C8 folder on your storage medium and name it **AL1-C8-CSLtrs**.
10. Print the first two pages (two letters) of **AL1-C8-CSLtrs.docx**.
11. Close **AL1-C8-CSLtrs.docx**.
12. Save the main document as **AL1-C8-CSMainDoc** in the AL1C8 folder on your storage medium and then close the document.
13. Close Word.

Exporting an Access Object to a PDF or XPS File

Quick Steps

Export an Access Object to a PDF File
1. Click object in the Navigation pane.
2. Click EXTERNAL DATA tab.
3. Click PDF or XPS button.
4. Navigate to desired folder.
5. Click Publish button.

PDF or XPS

With the PDF or XPS button in the Export group on the EXTERNAL DATA tab, you can export an Access object to a PDF or XPS file. As you learned in Chapter 7, the letters *PDF* stand for *portable document format*, which is a file format that captures all of the elements of a file as an electronic image. The letters *XPS* stand for *XML paper specification* and the letters *XML* stand for *extensible markup language*, which is a set of rules for encoding files electronically.

To export an Access object to PDF or XPS file format, click the desired object, click the EXTERNAL DATA tab, and then click the PDF or XPS button in the Export group. This displays the Publish as PDF or XPS dialog box with the *PDF (*.pdf)* option selected in the *Save as type* option box. If you want to save the Access object in XPS file format, click the *Save as type* option box and then click *XPS Document (*.xps)* at the drop-down list. At the Save As dialog box, type a name in the *File name* text box and then click the Publish button.

To open a PDF or XPS file in your web browser, open the browser, click *File* on the browser Menu bar, and then click *Open* at the drop-down list. At the Open dialog box, click the Browse button. At the browser window Open dialog box, change the *Files of type* to *All Files (*.*)*, navigate to the desired folder, and then double-click the file.

Project 1e   **Exporting an Access Object to a PDF File**   **Part 5 of 5**

1. With **AL1-C8-CopperState.accdb** open, export the Coverage table to PDF file format by completing the following steps:
   a. Click *Coverage* in the Tables group in the Navigation pane.
   b. Click the EXTERNAL DATA tab.
   c. Click the PDF or XPS button in the Export group.
   d. At the Publish as PDF or XPS dialog box, navigate to the AL1C8 folder on your storage medium, click the *Open file after publishing* check box to insert a check mark, and then click the Publish button.
   e. When the Coverage table data displays in Adobe Reader, scroll through the file and notice how it displays.

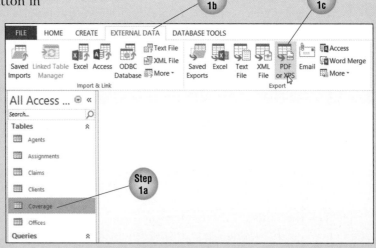

   f. Print the PDF file by clicking the Print button that displays at the left side of the toolbar and then clicking OK at the Print dialog box.
   g. Close Adobe Reader by positioning the mouse pointer at the top of the window (mouse turns into a hand), holding down the left mouse button, dragging down to the bottom of the screen, and then releasing the mouse button.
   h. At the Windows 8 Start screen, click the Desktop icon.
2. In Access, click the Close button to close the wizard dialog box.

Project 2 Import and Link Excel Worksheets with an Access Table

2 Parts

You will import an Excel worksheet into an Access table. You will also link an Excel worksheet to an Access table and then add a new record to the Access table.

Importing and Linking Data to New Tables ■■■■■■■■■

In this chapter, you have learned how to export Access data to Excel and Word. You can also import data from other programs into an Access table. For example, you can import data from an Excel worksheet and create a new table in a database using data from the worksheet. Data in the original program is not connected to the data imported into an Access table. If you make changes to the data in the original program, those changes are not reflected in the Access table. If you want the imported data connected to the original program, link the data.

Importing Data into a New Table

To import data, click the EXTERNAL DATA tab and then determine where you would like to retrieve data with options in the Import & Link group. At the Import dialog box that displays, click Browse and then double-click the desired file name. This activates the Import Wizard and displays the first wizard dialog box. The appearance of the dialog box varies depending on the file selected. Complete the steps of the Import Wizard, specifying information such as the range of data, whether the first row contains column headings, whether to store the data in a new table or existing table, the primary key, and the name of the table.

▼ **Quick Steps**

Import Data into a New Table
1. Click EXTERNAL DATA tab.
2. Click desired application in Import & Link group.
3. Click Browse button.
4. Double-click desired file name.
5. Make desired choices at each wizard dialog box.

HINT

Store data in Access and analyze it using Excel.

HINT

You can import and link data between Access databases.

Project 2a Importing an Excel Worksheet into an Access Table

Part 1 of 2

1. With **AL1-C8-CopperState.accdb** open, import an Excel worksheet into a new table in the database by completing the following steps:

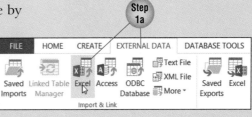

Step 1a

   a. Click the EXTERNAL DATA tab and then click the Excel button in the Import & Link group.
   b. At the Get External Data - Excel Spreadsheet dialog box, click the Browse button and then make the AL1C8 folder on your storage medium the active folder.
   c. Double-click **AL1-C8-Policies.xlsx** in the list box.
   d. Click OK at the Get External Data - Excel Spreadsheet dialog box.
   e. At the first Import Spreadsheet Wizard dialog box, make sure the *First Row Contains Column Headings* check box contains a check mark and then click the Next button.

f. At the second Import Spreadsheet Wizard dialog box, click the Next button.
g. At the third Import Spreadsheet Wizard dialog box, click the *Choose my own primary key* option (which inserts *PolicyID* in the option box located to the right of the option) and then click the Next button.

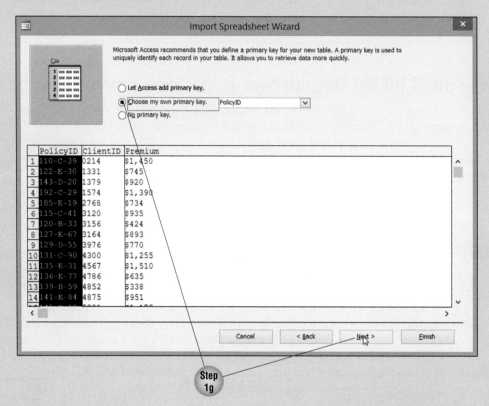

h. At the fourth Import Spreadsheet Wizard dialog box, type **Policies** in the *Import to Table* text box and then click the Finish button.

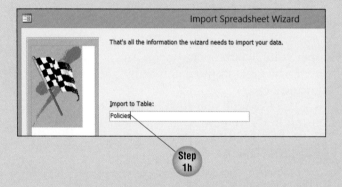

  i. At the Get External Data - Excel Spreadsheet dialog box, click the Close button.
2. Open the new Policies table in Datasheet view.
3. Print and then close the Policies table.

Linking Data to an Excel Worksheet

Imported data is not connected to the source program. If you know that you will use your data only in Access, import it. However, if you want to update the data in a program other than Access, link the data. Changes made to linked data in the source program file are reflected in the destination program file. For example, you can link an Excel worksheet with an Access table and when you make changes in the Excel worksheet, the changes are reflected in the Access table.

To link data to a new table, click the EXTERNAL DATA tab and then click the Excel button in the Import & Link group. At the Get External Data - Excel Spreadsheet dialog box, click the Browse button, double-click the desired file name, click the *Link to a data source by creating a linked table* option, and then click OK. This activates the Link Wizard and displays the first wizard dialog box. Complete the steps of the Link Wizard, specifying the same basic information as the Import Wizard.

▼ Quick Steps

Link Data to an Excel Worksheet
1. Click EXTERNAL DATA tab.
2. Click Excel button in Import & Link group.
3. Click Browse button.
4. Double-click desired file name.
5. Click *Link to a data source by creating a linked table*.
6. Make desired choices at each wizard dialog box.

Excel

Project 2b **Linking an Excel Worksheet to an Access Table**   Part 2 of 2

1. With **AL1-C8-CopperState.accdb** open, click the EXTERNAL DATA tab and then click the Excel button in the Import & Link group.
2. At the Get External Data - Excel Spreadsheet dialog box, click the Browse button, make sure the AL1C8 folder on your storage medium is active, and then double-click **AL1-C8-Policies.xlsx**.
3. At the Get External Data - Excel Spreadsheet dialog box, click the *Link to the data source by creating a linked table* option and then click OK.

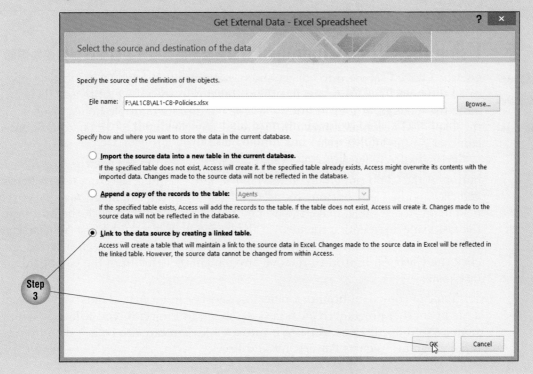

4. At the first Link Spreadsheet Wizard dialog box, make sure the *First Row Contains Column Headings* option contains a check mark and then click the Next button.
5. At the second Link Spreadsheet Wizard dialog box, type LinkedPolicies in the *Linked Table Name* text box and then click the Finish button.
6. At the message stating the linking is finished, click OK.
7. Open the new LinkedPolicies table in Datasheet view.
8. Close the LinkedPolicies table.
9. Open Excel, open the **AL1-C8-Policies.xlsx** workbook, and then make the following changes:
   a. Change the amount *$745* in cell C3 to *$850*.
   b. Add the following information in the specified cells:

22	170-C-20	7335	$ 875
23	173-D-77	7521	$ 556
24	180-E-05	8223	$ 721
25	188-D-63	8854	$ 1,384
26	190-C-28	3120	$ 685
27			

   Step 9b

   A26: 190-C-28
   B26: 3120
   C26: 685
10. Save, print, and then close **AL1-C8-Policies.xlsx**.
11. Close Excel.
12. With Access the active program and **AL1-C8-CopperState.accdb** open, open the LinkedPolicies table. Notice the changes you made in Excel are reflected in the table.
13. Close the LinkedPolicies table.
14. Close **AL1-C8-CopperState.accdb**.

Project 3   Collect Data in Word and Paste It into an Access Table   1 Part

You will open a Word document containing Hilltop customer names and addresses and then copy the data and paste it into an Access table.

Using the Office Clipboard ■■■■■■■■■■ ■■■■■■■■■ ■■

▼ **Quick Steps**

Display the Clipboard Task Pane
Click Clipboard task pane launcher.

Use the Office Clipboard to collect and paste multiple items. You can collect up to 24 different items in Access or other programs in the Office suite and then paste the items in various locations. To copy and paste multiple items, display the Clipboard task pane, shown in Figure 8.2, by clicking the Clipboard task pane launcher on the HOME tab.

Select the data or object that you want to copy and then click the Copy button in the Clipboard group on the HOME tab. Continue selecting text or items and clicking the Copy button. To insert an item from the Clipboard task pane to a field in an Access table, make the desired field active and then click the button in the task pane representing the item. If the copied item is text, the first 50 characters display in the Clipboard task pane. After all desired items have been inserted, click the Clear All button to remove any remaining items from the Clipboard task pane.

You can copy data from one object to another in an Access database or from a file in another program to an Access database. In Project 3, you will copy data from a Word document and paste it into a table. You can also collect data from other programs, such as PowerPoint and Excel.

Figure 8.2 Office Clipboard Task Pane

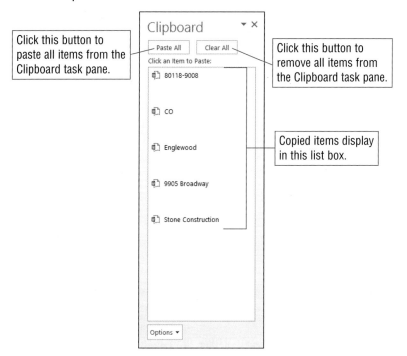

Click this button to paste all items from the Clipboard task pane.

Click this button to remove all items from the Clipboard task pane.

Copied items display in this list box.

Project 3 | **Collecting Data in Word and Pasting It into an Access Table** | Part 1 of 1

1. Open **AL1-C8-Hilltop.accdb**.
2. Open the Customers table.
3. Copy data from Word and paste it into the Customers table by completing the following steps:
   a. Open Word, make AL1C8 the active folder, and then open **HilltopCustomers.docx**.
   b. Make sure the HOME tab is active.
   c. Click the Clipboard task pane launcher to display the Clipboard task pane.
   d. Select the first company name, *Stone Construction*, and then click the Copy button in the Clipboard group.

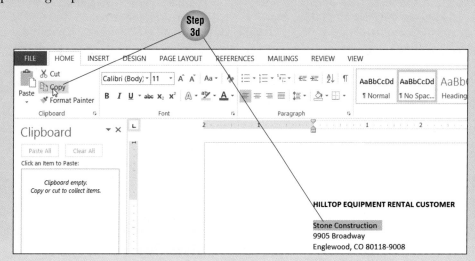

e. Select the street address, *9905 Broadway*, and then click the Copy button.

f. Select the city, *Englewood*, and then click the Copy button.

g. Select the state, *CO* (selecting only the two letters and not the space after the letters), and then click the Copy button.

h. Select the zip code, *80118-9008*, and then click the Copy button.

i. Click the button on the Taskbar representing Access. (Make sure the Customer table is open and displays in Datasheet view.)

j. Click in the first empty cell in the *CustomerID* field and then type 178.

k. Display the Clipboard task pane by clicking the HOME tab and then clicking the Clipboard task pane launcher.

l. Close the Navigation pane by clicking the Shutter Bar Open/Close Button.

m. Click in the first empty cell in the *Customer* field and then click *Stone Construction* in the Clipboard task pane.

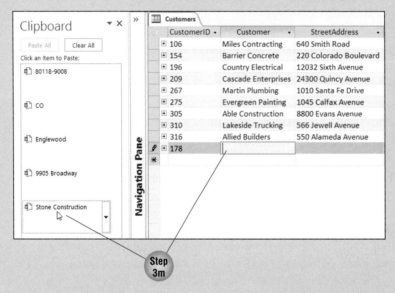

Step 3m

n. Click in the *StreetAddress* field and then click *9905 Broadway* in the Clipboard task pane.

o. Click in the *City* field and then click *Englewood* in the Clipboard task pane.

p. Click in the *State* field and then click *CO* in the Clipboard task pane.

q. Click in the *ZipCode* field, make sure the insertion point is positioned at the left side of the field, and then click *80118-9008* in the Clipboard task pane.

r. Click the Clear All button in the Clipboard task pane. (This removes all entries from the Clipboard.)

Step 3r

4. Complete steps similar to those in 3d through 3q to copy the information for Laughlin Products and paste it into the Customers table. (The customer ID number is 225.)

5. Click the Clear All button in the Clipboard task pane.

6. Close the Clipboard task pane by clicking the Close button (which contains an *X*) located in the upper right corner of the task pane.

7. Save, print, and then close the Customers table.

8. Open the Navigation pane by clicking the Shutter Bar Open/Close Button.

9. Make Word the active program, close **HilltopCustomers.docx** without saving changes, and then close Word.

10. Close **AL1-C8-Hilltop.accdb**.

Chapter Summary

- Use the Excel button in the Export group on the EXTERNAL DATA tab to export data in a table, query, or form to an Excel worksheet.

- Export data in a table, query, form, or report to a Word document by clicking the More button and then clicking *Word* at the drop-down list. Access exports the data to an RTF (rich-text format) file.

- Export an Access object to a PDF or XPS file with the PDF or XPS button in the Export group on the EXTERNAL DATA tab.

- You can merge Access data with a Word document. The Access data is the data source and the Word document is the main document. To merge data, click the desired table or query, click the EXTERNAL DATA tab, and then click the Word Merge button in the Export group.

- Use the Excel button in the Import group on the EXTERNAL DATA tab to import Excel data to an Access table.

- You can link imported data. Changes made to the data in the source program file are reflected in the destination source file.

- If you want to link imported data, click the *Link to the data source by creating a linked table* option at the Get External Data dialog box.

- Use the Clipboard task pane to collect up to 24 different items in Access or other programs and paste them in various locations.

- Display the Clipboard task pane by clicking the Clipboard task pane launcher on the HOME tab.

Commands Review

FEATURE	RIBBON TAB, GROUP	BUTTON
Clipboard task pane	HOME, Clipboard	
export object to Excel	EXTERNAL DATA, Export	
export object to PDF or XPS	EXTERNAL DATA, Export	
export object to Word	EXTERNAL DATA, Export	, *Word*
import Excel data	EXTERNAL DATA, Import & Link	
merge Access data with Word	EXTERNAL DATA, Export	

Concepts Check   Test Your Knowledge

Completion: In the space provided at the right, indicate the correct term, symbol, or command.

1. Click this tab to display the Export group.

2. Click this button in the Export group to display the Export - Excel Spreadsheet wizard dialog box.

3. At the first Export - Excel Spreadsheet wizard dialog box, click this option if you want Excel to open with the exported data.

4. To export Access data to Word, click this button in the Export group on the EXTERNAL DATA tab and then click *Word* at the drop-down list.

5. When you export Access data to Word, the document is saved in this file format.

6. When merging data, the data in the Access table is considered this.

7. To merge data, click this button in the Export group on the EXTERNAL DATA tab.

8. Import an Excel worksheet into an Access database with the Excel button in this group on the EXTERNAL DATA tab.

9. If you want imported data connected to the original program, do this to the data.

10. Use this task pane to collect and paste multiple items.

Skills Check   Assess Your Performance

Assessment

1 EXPORT A FORM TO EXCEL AND A REPORT TO WORD

1. Open **AL1-C8-WarrenLegal.accdb** from the AL1C8 folder on your storage medium and enable the contents.
2. Create a form named *Billing* using the Form Wizard with the following fields:

    From the Billing table: *BillingID*
                                       ClientID
                                       BillingDate
                                       Hours

    From the Rates table: *Rate*

3. When the form displays, close it.
4. Export the Billing form to an Excel worksheet.
5. Make the following changes to the Excel Billing worksheet:
    a. Select columns A through E and then adjust the column widths.
    b. Select cells A2 through B42 and then click the Center button in the Alignment group on the HOME tab.
    c. Save the Billing worksheet.
    d. Print and then close the Billing worksheet.
    e. Close Excel.
6. In Access, close the Export Wizard.
7. Create a report named *ClientBilling* using the Report Wizard (at the fifth wizard dialog box, change the layout to *Block*) with the following fields:

    From the Clients table: *FirstName*
                                     LastName

    From the Billing table: *BillingDate*
                                     Hours

    From the Rates table: *Rate*

8. Close the report.
9. Create a Word document with the ClientBilling report and save it to the AL1C8 folder on your storage medium with the default name. In the Word document, make the following changes:
    a. Press Ctrl + A to select the entire document, change the font color to Black, and then deselect the text.
    b. Insert a space between *Client* and *Billing* in the title.
    c. Position the insertion point immediately right of the word *Billing*, press the spacebar, and then type **of Legal Services**.
10. Save and then print **ClientBilling.rtf**.
11. Close the document and then close Word.
12. In Access, close the wizard dialog box.

2 MERGE TABLE AND QUERY DATA WITH A WORD DOCUMENT

1. With **AL1-C8-WarrenLegal.accdb** open, merge data in the Clients table to a new Word document using the Word Merge button.
2. Maximize the Word document, close the Mail Merge task pane, and then compose a letter with the following elements:
   a. Click the HOME tab and then click the *No Spacing* style option in the Styles group.
   b. Press Enter six times, type the current date, and then press Enter four times.
   c. Click the MAILINGS tab and then insert the «*AddressBlock*» composite field.
   d. Press Enter twice and then type the salutation **Ladies and Gentlemen:**.
   e. Press Enter twice and then type the following text (press Enter twice after typing the first paragraph of text):

   > The last time you visited our offices, you may have noticed how crowded we were. To alleviate the overcrowding, we are leasing new offices in the Meridian Building and will be moving in at the beginning of next month.

   > Stop by and see our new offices at our open house planned for the second Friday of next month. Drop by any time between 2:00 and 5:30 p.m. We look forward to seeing you.

   f. After typing the second paragraph, press Enter twice, type **Sincerely,**, and then press Enter four times. Type **Marjorie Shaw**, press the Enter key, and then type **Senior Partner**. Press Enter twice, type your initials, press Enter, and then type AL1-C8-WLLtrs.docx.
3. Merge to a new document and then save the document with the name **AL1-C8-WLLtrs**.
4. Print only the first two letters in the document and then close **AL1-C8-WLLtrs.docx**.
5. Save the main document and name it **AL1-C8-WLLtrMD1**. Close the document and then close Word.
6. With **AL1-C8-WarrenLegal.accdb** open, extract the records from the Clients table of those clients located in Kent and then name the query *ClientsKentQuery*. (Include all of the fields from the table in the query.)
7. Merge the ClientsKentQuery to a new Word document using the Word Merge button.
8. Maximize the Word document, close the Mail Merge task pane, and then compose a letter with the following elements:
   a. Click the HOME tab and then click the *No Spacing* style option in the Styles group.
   b. Press Enter six times, type the current date, and then press Enter four times.
   c. Click the MAILINGS tab and then insert the «*AddressBlock*» composite field.
   d. Insert a proper salutation (refer to step 2d).

e. Compose a letter to clients that includes the following information:

> The City of Kent Municipal Court has moved from 1024 Meeker Street to a new building located at 3201 James Avenue. All court hearings after the end of this month will be held at the new address. If you need directions to the new building, please call our office.

f. Include an appropriate complimentary close for the letter (refer to Step 2f). Use the name *Thomas Zeiger* and the title *Attorney* in the complimentary close and add your reference initials and the document name (**AL1-C8-WLKentLtrs.docx**).

9. Merge the letter to a new document and then save the document with the name **AL1-C8-WLKentLtrs**.
10. Print only the first two letters in the document and then close **AL1-C8-WLKentLtrs.docx**.
11. Save the main document and name it **AL1-C8-WLLtrMD2**, close the document, and then close Word.

Assessment

3 LINK AN EXCEL WORKBOOK

1. With **AL1-C8-WarrenLegal.accdb** open, link **AL1-C8-Cases.xlsx** into a new table named *Cases*.
2. Open the Cases table in Datasheet view.
3. Print and then close the Cases table.
4. Open Excel, open the **AL1-C8-Cases.xlsx** workbook and then add the following data in the specified cells:

   A8: 57-D
   B8: 130
   C8: 1,100

   A9: 42-A
   B9: 144
   C9: 3,250

   A10: 29-C
   B10: 125
   C10: 900

5. Apply the Accounting formatting with a dollar sign and no decimal places to cells C8, C9, and C10.
6. Save, print, and then close **AL1-C8-Cases.xlsx**.
7. Close Excel.
8. In Access, open the Cases table in Datasheet view. (Notice the changes you made in Excel are reflected in the table.)
9. Print and then close the Cases table.
10. Close **AL1-C8-WarrenLegal.accdb**.

Visual Benchmark Demonstrate Your Proficiency

CREATE A REPORT AND EXPORT THE REPORT TO WORD

1. Open **AL1-C8-Dearborn.accdb** and enable the contents.
2. Use the Report Wizard to create the report shown in Figure 8.3. (Use the Quotas table and Representatives table when creating the report and choose the *Block* layout at the fifth wizard dialog box.) Save the report and name it *RepQuotas* and then print the report.
3. Use the RepQuotas report and export it to Word (to your AL1C8 folder). Format the report in Word as shown in Figure 8.4. Print the Word document and then close Word.
4. In Access, close **AL1-C8-Dearborn.accdb**.

Figure 8.3 Visual Benchmark Report

RepQuotas		
RepQuotas		
Quota	RepName	Telephone
$100,000.00	Robin Rehberg	(317) 555-9812
	Andre Kulisek	(317) 555-2264
	Edward Harris	(317) 555-3894
	Cecilia Ortega	(317) 555-4810
$150,000.00	David DeBruler	(317) 555-8779
	Jaren Newman	(317) 555-6790
	Lee Hutchinson	(765) 555-4277
	Craig Johnson	(317) 555-4391
$200,000.00	Isabelle Marshall	(765) 555-8822
	Maureen Pascual	(317) 555-5513
	Linda Foster	(317) 555-2101
	Catherine Singleton	(317) 555-0172
$250,000.00	Kwan Im	(317) 555-8374
	William Ludlow	(317) 555-0991
	Lydia Alvarado	(765) 555-4996
$300,000.00	Gina Tapparo	(317) 555-0044

Figure 8.4 Visual Benchmark Word Document

Representatives Quotas

Quota	RepName	Telephone
$100,000.00	Robin Rehberg	(317) 555-9812
	Andre Kulisek	(317) 555-2264
	Edward Harris	(317) 555-3894
	Cecilia Ortega	(317) 555-4810
$150,000.00	David DeBruler	(317) 555-8779
	Jaren Newman	(317) 555-6790
	Lee Hutchinson	(765) 555-4277
	Craig Johnson	(317) 555-4391
$200,000.00	Isabelle Marshall	(765) 555-8822
	Maureen Pascual	(317) 555-5513
	Linda Foster	(317) 555-2101
	Catherine Singleton	(317) 555-0172
$250,000.00	Kwan Im	(317) 555-8374
	William Ludlow	(317) 555-0991
	Lydia Alvarado	(765) 555-4996
$300,000.00	Gina Tapparo	(317) 555-0044
	Alfred Silva	(317) 555-3211

Case Study   Apply Your Skills

Part 1

As the office manager at Woodland Dermatology Center, you are responsible for managing the center database. In preparation for an upcoming meeting, open **AL1-C8-Woodland.accdb** and prepare the following with data in the database:

- Create a query that displays the patient identification number, first name, and last name; doctor last name; date of visit; and fee. Name the query *PatientBilling*.
- Export the PatientBilling query to an Excel worksheet. Apply formatting to enhance the appearance of the worksheet and then print the worksheet.
- Create mailing labels for the patients. ***Hint: Use the Labels button on the CREATE tab***.
- Export the patient labels to a Word (.rtf) document and then print the document.
- Import and link the **AL1-C8-Payroll.xlsx** Excel worksheet to a new table named *WeeklyPayroll*. Print the WeeklyPayroll table.

You have been given some updated information about the weekly payroll and need to make the following changes to the **AL1-C8-Payroll.xlsx** worksheet:

- Change the hours for Irene Vaughn to *30*
- Change the wage for Monica Saunders to *$10.50*
- Change the hours for Dale Jorgensen to *20*.

After making and saving the changes, open, print, and then close the WeeklyPayroll table.

Part 2

The center is expanding and will be offering cosmetic dermatology services at the beginning of next month to residents in the Altoona area. Design a query that extracts records of patients living in the city of Altoona and then merge the query with Word. At the Word document, write a letter describing the new services, which include microdermabrasion, chemical peels, laser resurfacing, sclerotherapy, and photorejuvenation, as well as an offer for a free facial and consultation. Insert the appropriate fields in the document and then complete the merge. Save the merged document and name it **AL1-C8-WLDLtr**. Print the first two letters of the document and then close the document. Close the main document without saving it and then close Word.

Part 3

The Woodland database contains critical information and you need to determine how often you should back up the database. (You learned how to back up a database in Chapter 7.) Use the Access Help files to learn more about the backup process and, more specifically, about guidelines for when to back up a database. Search the Access Help files using the phrase *backing up a database* and then read the hyperlinked article <u>Protect your data with backup and restore processes</u>. Since you are responsible for updating the clinic procedures manual, create a Word document that describes how often you think the Woodland database should be backed up and the rationale behind your backup plan. Include steps for creating a backup of the database. Save the completed document and name it **AL1-C8-CS-Manual**. Print and then close **AL1-C8-CS-Manual.docx**.

ACCESS

MICROSOFT®

Performance Assessment

Access
AL1U2

Note: Before beginning unit assessments, copy to your storage medium the AL1U2 subfolder from the AL1 folder on the CD that accompanies this textbook and then make AL1U2 the active folder.

Assessing Proficiency ▪▪▪▪▪▪▪▪▪▪▪▪▪▪▪▪

In this unit, you have learned to create forms, reports, and mailing labels and filter data. You have also learned how to modify document properties, view object dependencies, and export, import, and link data between programs.

Assessment 1 Create Tables in a Clinic Database

1. Use Access to create a database for clients of a mental health clinic. Name the database **AL1-U2-LancasterClinic**. Create a table named *Clients* that includes the following fields. (You determine the field name, data type, field size, and description.)

> *ClientNumber* (primary key)
> *ClientName*
> *StreetAddress*
> *City*
> *State*
> *ZipCode*
> *Telephone*
> *DateOfBirth*
> *DiagnosisID*

2. After creating the table, switch to Datasheet view and then enter the following data in the appropriate fields:

> *ClientNumber:* 1831
> George Charoni
> 3980 Broad Street
> Philadelphia, PA 19149
> (215) 555-3482
> *DateOfBirth:* 4/12/1961
> *DiagnosisID:* SC

> *ClientNumber:* 3219
> Marian Wilke
> 12032 South 39th
> Jenkintown, PA 19209
> (215) 555-9083
> *DateOfBirth:* 10/23/1984
> *DiagnosisID:* OCD

ClientNumber: 2874
Arthur Shroeder
3618 Fourth Avenue
Philadelphia, PA 19176
(215) 555-8311
DateOfBirth: 3/23/1961
DiagnosisID: OCD

ClientNumber: 5831
Roshawn Collins
12110 52nd Court East
Cheltenham, PA 19210
(215) 555-4779
DateOfBirth: 11/3/1968
DiagnosisID: SC

ClientNumber: 4419
Lorena Hearron
3112 96th Street East
Philadelphia, PA 19132
(215) 555-3281
DateOfBirth: 7/2/1987
DiagnosisID: AD

ClientNumber: 1103
Raymond Mandato
631 Garden Boulevard
Jenkintown, PA 19209
(215) 555-0957
DateOfBirth: 9/20/1982
DiagnosisID: MDD

3. Automatically adjust the column widths.
4. Save, print, and then close the Clients table.
5. Create a table named *Diagnoses* that includes the following fields:

   DiagnosisID (primary key)
   Diagnosis

6. After creating the table, switch to Datasheet view and then enter the following data in the appropriate fields:

   DiagnosisID: AD
   Diagnosis: Adjustment Disorder

   DiagnosisID: MDD
   Diagnosis: Manic-Depressive Disorder

   DiagnosisID: OCD
   Diagnosis: Obsessive-Compulsive Disorder

   DiagnosisID: SC
   Diagnosis: Schizophrenia

7. Automatically adjust the column widths.
8. Save, print, and then close the Diagnoses table.
9. Create a table named *Fees* that includes the following fields. (You determine the field name, data type, field size, and description.)

   FeeCode (primary key)
   HourlyFee

10. After creating the table, switch to Datasheet view and then enter the following data in the appropriate fields:

FeeCode: A
HourlyFee: $75.00

FeeCode: E
HourlyFee: $95.00

FeeCode: B
HourlyFee: $80.00

FeeCode: F
HourlyFee: $100.00

FeeCode: C
HourlyFee: $85.00

FeeCode: G
HourlyFee: $105.00

FeeCode: D
HourlyFee: $90.00

FeeCode: H
HourlyFee: $110.00

11. Automatically adjust the column widths.
12. Save, print, and then close the Fees table.
13. Create a table named *Employees* that includes the following fields. (You determine the field name, data type, field size, and description.)

ProviderNumber (primary key)
ProviderName
Title
Extension

14. After creating the table, switch to Datasheet view and then enter the following data in the appropriate fields:

ProviderNumber: 29
ProviderName: James Schouten
Title: Psychologist
Extension: 399

ProviderNumber: 15
ProviderName: Lynn Yee
Title: Child Psychologist
Extension: 102

ProviderNumber: 33
ProviderName: Janice Grisham
Title: Psychiatrist
Extension: 11

ProviderNumber: 18
ProviderName: Craig Chilton
Title: Psychologist
Extension: 20

15. Automatically adjust the column widths.
16. Save, print, and then close the Employees table.
17. Create a table named *Billing* that includes the following fields. (You determine the field name, data type, field size, and description.)

BillingNumber (primary key; apply the AutoNumber data type)
ClientNumber
DateOfService (apply the Date/Time data type)
Insurer
ProviderNumber
Hours (Apply the Number data type, the *Field Size* option in the *Field Properties* section to *Double*, and the *Decimal Places* option in the *Field Properties* section in Design view to *1*. Two of the records will contain a number requiring this format.)
FeeCode

18. After creating the table, switch to Datasheet view and then enter the following data in the appropriate fields:

ClientNumber: 4419
DateOfService: 3/2/2015
Insurer: Health Plus
ProviderNumber: 15
Hours: 2
FeeCode: B

ClientNumber: 1831
DateOfService: 3/2/2015
Insurer: Self
ProviderNumber: 33
Hours: 1
FeeCode: H

ClientNumber: 3219
DateOfService: 3/3/2015
Insurer: Health Plus
ProviderNumber: 15
Hours: 1
FeeCode: D

ClientNumber: 5831
DateOfService: 3/3/2015
Insurer: Penn-State Health
ProviderNumber: 18
Hours: 2
FeeCode: C

ClientNumber: 4419
DateOfService: 3/4/2015
Insurer: Health Plus
ProviderNumber: 15
Hours: 1
FeeCode: A

ClientNumber: 1103
DateOfService: 3/4/2015
Insurer: Penn-State Health
ProviderNumber: 18
Hours: 0.5
FeeCode: A

ClientNumber: 1831
DateOfService: 3/5/2015
Insurer: Self
ProviderNumber: 33
Hours: 1
FeeCode: H

ClientNumber: 5831
DateOfService: 3/5/2015
Insurer: Penn-State Health
ProviderNumber: 18
Hours: 0.5
FeeCode: C

19. Automatically adjust the column widths.
20. Save, print in landscape orientation, and then close the Billing table.

Assessment 2 Relate Tables and Create Forms in a Clinic Database

1. With **AL1-U2-LancasterClinic.accdb** open, create the following one-to-many relationships and enforce referential integrity and cascade fields and records:
   a. *ClientNumber* in the Clients table is the "one" and *ClientNumber* in the Billing table is the "many."
   b. *DiagnosisID* in the Diagnoses table is the "one" and *DiagnosisID* in the Clients table is the "many."
   c. *ProviderNumber* in the Employees table is the "one" and *ProviderNumber* in the Billing table is the "many."
   d. *FeeCode* in the Fees table is the "one" and *FeeCode* in the Billing table is the "many."
2. Create a form with the data in the Clients table.

3. After creating the form, add the following record to the Clients form:

   ClientNumber: 1179
   Timothy Fierro
   1133 Tenth Southwest
   Philadelphia, PA 19178
   (215) 555-5594
   DateOfBirth: 12/7/1990
   DiagnosisID: AD

4. Save the form with the default name, print the form in landscape orientation, and then close the form.
5. Add the following records to the Billing table:

ClientNumber: 1179	*ClientNumber:* 1831
DateOfService: 3/6/2015	*DateOfService:* 3/6/2015
Insurer: Health Plus	*Insurer:* Self
ProviderNumber: 15	*ProviderNumber:* 33
Hours: 0.5	*Hours:* 1
FeeCode: C	FeeCode: H

6. Save and then print the Billing table in landscape orientation.
7. Close the Billing table.

Assessment 3 Create Forms Using the Form Wizard

1. With **AL1-U2-LancasterClinic.accdb** open, create a form with fields from related tables using the Form Wizard with the following specifications:
   a. At the first Form Wizard dialog box, insert the following fields in the *Selected Fields* list box:

From the Clients table:	*ClientNumber*
	DateOfBirth
	DiagnosisID
From the Billing table:	*Insurer*
	ProviderNumber

   b. Do not make any changes at the second Form Wizard dialog box.
   c. Do not make any changes at the third Form Wizard dialog box.
   d. At the fourth Form Wizard dialog box, type the name ProviderInformation in the *Form* text box.
2. When the first record displays, print the first record.
3. Close the form.

Assessment 4 Create Labels with the Label Wizard

1. With **AL1-U2-LancasterClinic.accdb** open, use the Label Wizard to create mailing labels with the client names and addresses and sort by zip code. Name the mailing label report **ClientMailingLabels**.
2. Print the mailing labels.
3. Close the mailing labels report.

Assessment 5 Filter Records in Tables

1. With **AL1-U2-LancasterClinic.accdb** open, open the Billing table and then filter the records to display the following records:
   a. Display only those records with the Health Plus insurer. Print the results in landscape orientation and then remove the filter.
   b. Display only those records with a client ID number of 4419. Print the results and then remove the filter.
2. Filter records by selection to display the following records:
   a. Display only those records with a fee code of C. Print the results and then remove the filter.
   b. Display only those records between the dates of 3/2/2015 and 3/4/2015. Print the results and then remove the filter.
3. Close the Billing table without saving the changes.
4. Open the Clients table and then use the *Filter By Form* option to display clients in Jenkintown or Cheltenham. Print the results and then remove the filter.
5. Close the Clients table without saving the changes.

Assessment 6 Export a Table to Excel

1. With **AL1-U2-LancasterClinic.accdb** open, export the Billing table to an Excel workbook to your AL1U2 folder.
2. Apply formatting to the cells in the Excel workbook to enhance the appearance of the data.
3. Change the page orientation to landscape.
4. Save, print, and then close the workbook.
5. Close Excel.

Assessment 7 Merge Records to Create Letters in Word

1. With **AL1-U2-LancasterClinic.accdb** open, merge data in the Clients table to a blank Word document. ***Hint: Use the Word Merge button in the Export group on the EXTERNAL DATA tab.*** You determine the fields to use in the inside address (you cannot use the *AddressBlock* field) and an appropriate salutation. Type March 12, 2015, as the date of the letter and type the following text in the body of the document:

   The building of a new wing for the Lancaster Clinic will begin April 1, 2015. We are excited about this new addition to our clinic. With the new facilities, we will be able to offer additional community and group services along with enhanced child-play therapy treatment.

   During the construction, the main entrance will be moved to the north end of the building. Please use this entrance until the construction of the wing is completed. We apologize in advance for any inconvenience this causes you.

   Include an appropriate complimentary close for the letter. Use the name and title *Marianne Lambert, Clinic Director* for the signature and add your reference initials and the document name (**AL1-U2-A7-LCLtrs.docx**).
2. Merge to a new document and then save the document with the name **AL1-U2-A7-LCLtrs**.

3. Print the first two letters of the document and then close **AL1-U2-A7-LCLtrs.docx**.
4. Save the main document as **AL1-U2-A7-ConstLtrMD** and then close the document.
5. Close Word.

Assessment 8 Import and Link Excel Data to an Access Table

1. With **AL1-U2-LancasterClinic.accdb** open, import and link **AL1-U2-StaffHours.xlsx** to a new table named *StaffHours*.
2. Open the StaffHours table in Datasheet view.
3. Print and then close the StaffHours table.
4. Open **AL1-U2-StaffHours.xlsx** in Excel.
5. Insert a formula in cell D2 that multiplies B2 with C2 and then copy the formula down to cells D3 through D7.
6. Save and then close **AL1-U2-StaffHours.xlsx**.
7. Close Excel.
8. In Access with **AL1-U2-LancasterClinic.accdb** open, open the StaffHours table.
9. Print and then close the StaffHours table.

Writing Activities ■■■■■■■■■■■■■■■■■■■

The following activities give you the opportunity to practice your writing skills while you demonstrate your understanding of some of the important Access features you have mastered in this unit. Use correct grammar, appropriate word choices, and clear sentence constructions.

Activity 1 Add a Table to the Clinic Database

The director at Lancaster Clinic has asked you to add information to **AL1-U2-LancasterClinic.accdb** on insurance companies contracted by the clinic. You need to create a table that will contain information on insurance companies. The director wants the table to include the insurance company name, address, city, state, and zip code, along with the telephone number and name of the representative. You determine the field names, data types, field sizes, and description for the table and then include the following information (in the appropriate fields):

Health Plus
4102 22nd Street
Philadelphia, PA 19166
(212) 555-0990
Representative: Byron Tolleson

Penn-State Health
5933 Lehigh Avenue
Philadelphia, PA 19148
(212) 555-3477
Representative: Tracey Pavone

Quality Medical
51 Cecil B. Moore Avenue
Philadelphia, PA 19168
(212) 555-4600
Representative: Lee Stafford

Delaware Health
4418 Front Street
Philadelphia, PA 19132
(212) 555-6770
Representative: Melanie Chon

Save the insurance company table, print it in landscape orientation, and then close the table. Open Word and then write a report to the clinic director detailing how you created the table. Include a title for the report, steps on how you created the table, and any other pertinent information. Save the completed report and name it **AL1-U2-Act1-LCRpt**. Print and then close **AL1-U2-Act1-LCRpt.docx**.

Activity 2 Merge Records to Create Letters to Insurance Companies

Merge data in the insurance company database to a blank Word document. You determine the fields to use in the inside address (you cannot use the Address Block button) and an appropriate salutation. Compose a letter to the insurance companies informing them that Lancaster Clinic is providing mental health counseling services to people who have health insurance through their employers. You are sending an informational brochure about Lancaster Clinic and are requesting information from the insurance companies on services and service limitations. Include an appropriate complimentary close for the letter. Use the name and title *Marianne Lambert, Clinic Director* for the signature and add your reference initials. When the merge is completed, name the document containing the merged letters **AL1-U2-Act2-LCIns**. Print the first two letters in the merged document and then close **AL1-U2-Act2-LCIns.docx**. Close the main document without saving it and then close Word. Close **AL1-U2-LancasterClinic.accdb**.

Internet Research ■■■■■■■■■■■■■■■■■■

Health Information Search

In this activity, you will search the Internet for information on a health concern or disease that interests you. You will be looking for specific organizations, interest groups, or individuals who are somehow connected to the topic you have chosen. You may find information about an organization that raises money to support research, a support group that posts information or answers questions, or clinics or doctors that specialize in your topic. Try to find at least 10 different organizations, groups, or individuals that support the health concern you are researching.

Create a database in Access and then create a table that includes information from your research. Design the table so that you can store the name, address, phone number, and web address of each organization, group, or individual you find. Also identify the connection the organization, group, or individual has to your topic (supports research, interest group, treats patients, etc.). Create a report to summarize your findings. In Microsoft Word, create a letter that you can use to write for further information about the organization. Use the names and addresses in your database to merge with the letter. Select and then print the first two letters that result from the merge. Finally, write a paragraph describing information you learned about the health concern that you previously did not know.

Job Study ■■■■■■■■■■■■■■■■■■■■■■■■■■■

City Improvement Projects

In this activity, you will work with the city council in your area to keep the public informed of the progress being made on improvement projects throughout the city. These projects are paid for through tax dollars voted on by the public, and the city council feels that keeping area residents informed will lead to good voter turnout when it is time to make more improvements.

Your job is to create a database and table in the database that will store the following information for each project: a project ID number, a description of the project, the budgeted dollar amount to be spent, the amount of money spent so far, the amount of time allocated to the project, and the amount of time spent so far. Enter five city improvement projects into the table (using sample data created by you). Create a query based on the table that calculates the percentage of budgeted dollars spent so far and the percentage of budgeted time spent so far. Print the table and the query.

Index

opening, 6
pinning to Recent list, 7–8
relational, 22
saving, 6, 281–283
viewing and customizing
database properties,
278–280
viewing object dependencies,
274–275
Database Password dialog box,
277
DATABASE TOOLS tab, 274
Datasheet view, 11
creating split forms and,
210–211
creating tables in, 23–32
assigning default value, 29
assigning field size, 29
changing AutoNumber
field, 29
data types, 23–25
defining the table structure,
23
inserting field name,
caption, description,
27–28
inserting Quick Start
fields, 28–29
renaming field heading, 27
formatting data in table,
148–149
formatting table data in,
148–152
data types, 23–24, 134
Date and Time button, 193
Date Filters, 268
Date & Time data type, 24,
134
Decrypt Database button, 277
default value, assigning, 29,
136–137
Default Value button, 29
defining the table structure, 23
Delete button, 11, 189, 236
Delete Rows button, 143
deleting
control object, 193–194
fields, 13–15
in Design View, 142–147
forms, 187–188

query, 95
records, 11–13
in forms, 189–190
in related tables, 60–61
relationships, 56
report, 236
table, 17
Descending button, 147, 189,
236
Description text box, 27
Design view, 186
creating tables in, 132–136
assigning default value,
136–137
inserting, moving and
deleting fields, 142–147
inserting Total row, 143
overview, 132–136
using Input Mask,
137–138
using Lookup Wizard,
141–142
validating field entries, 141
determining primary key, 47
displaying table in, 47
Properties table in, 132–133
Detail section, 187, 192, 234,
235
dialog box, getting help in,
159–160

E

editing, relationships, 56–59
Edition Relationships button,
56
Edit Relationships dialog box,
50–51
Enable Content button, 8
encrypting database with
password, 277
Encrypt with Password button,
277
Enforce Referential Integrity,
50, 52, 60
Enter Fields Properties dialog
box, 27
entity integrity, 47
Excel button, 295, 307

Excel worksheet
exporting data to, 295–298
Word document, 298–300
linking data to, 307–308
expand indicator, 64–65
exporting
Access object to PDF or
XPS file, 304
data to Excel document,
295–298
data to Word document,
298–300
Expression Builder dialog box,
107
EXTERNAL DATA tab, 295,
298

F

Field List task pane, 207–208
field names, 10
inserting, 27–28
renaming, 27
fields
assigning default value, 29
assigning size, 29
calculated field, 107–108
creating, in Design view,
132–133
data types, 23–25
defined, 23
deleting, 13–15
in Design View, 142–147
filtering on specific field,
268–270
inserting, 13–15
in Design View, 142–147
in forms, 207–210
name, caption and
description, 27–28
in query design grid,
83–84
Quick Start fields, 28–29
moving, 13–15
in Design View, 142–147
primary key field, 46–49
in query
arranging, 92
showing/hiding, 92
sorting, 92–94

printing
    forms, 186–187
    relationships, 53
    specific records, 147
    tables, 17–21
        changing page layout, 19–21
        changing page size and
            margins, 18
        previewing, 18
Print Preview, displaying and
    customizing report in, 236
Print Preview button, 18, 236
Properties dialog box, 278–279

Q

query
    crosstab query, 112–115
    as database object, 8
    defined, 82
    deleting, 95
    description of, 8
    designing, 82–100
        with aggregate function,
            107–112
        arranging fields in, 92
        establishing query criteria,
            84–85
        with *Or* and *And* criteria,
            96–100
        overview, 82–84
        showing/hiding fields in,
            92
        sorting fields in, 92–94
    exporting, to Excel, 296–298
    filtering records in, 268–270
    find duplicate query,
        115–118
    find unmatched query,
        118–119
    inserting calculated fields,
        107–108
    merging query data with
        Word document, 301–303
    modifying, 95–96
    performing
        on related tables, 89–91
        with Simple Query
            Wizard, 100–106
        on tables, 85–88
    renaming, 95

Query Design button, 82
Query Wizard button, 100
Quick Access toolbar, 6–7
Quick Print button, 17
Quick Start fields, 28–29

R

Recent list
    opening database from, 6
    pinning database file or
        folder to, 7–8
Record Navigation bar, 10,
    187, 189
    buttons on, 11
records
    collapse indicator, 65
    defined, 23
    deleting, 11–13
        in related tables, 60–61
    displaying related records in
        subdatasheets, 64–67
    expand indicator, 64–65
    forms
        adding and deleting,
            189–190
        sorting, 189
    inserting, 11–13
        in related tables, 60–61
    modifying record source in
        report, 234
    printing specific, 147
    in reports
        grouping and sorting,
            244–247
        sorting, 236
    sorting data in, 147
record selector bar, 10
referential integrity
    defined, 50
    specifying, 52
related tables
    creating, 45–61
        defining primary key,
            46–49
        deleting records in, 60–61
        deleting relationship, 56
        determining relationships,
            46
        displaying related records
            in subdatasheets, 64–67

editing relationship,
    56–59
inserting records in, 60–61
one-to-many relationships,
    50–52, 62–64
one-to-one relationships,
    61–64
printing relationships, 53
showing tables, 56
specifying referential
    integrity, 52
creating form with, 190–192
defined, 50
performing queries on,
    89–91
relational database, 22
relational database management
    system, 45–46
Relationship Report button, 53
relationships
    creating
        one-to-many relationships,
            50–52, 62–64
        one-to-one, 61–64
        between tables, 45–61
    defined, 22
    deleting, 56
    determining, 46
    editing, 56–59
    printing, 53
Relationships button, 50
renaming, table, 17
repairing, database, 276–278
Replace button, 154
Report button, creating report
    with, 233–235
REPORT LAYOUT TOOLS
    ARRANGE tab, 240
REPORT LAYOUT TOOLS
    DESIGN tab, 233–234,
    240
REPORT LAYOUT TOOLS
    FORMAT tab, 240
REPORT LAYOUT TOOLS
    PAGE SETUP tab, 241
reports, 229–252
    creating
        with fields from multiple
            tables, 251–252

Access 2013 Feature	Ribbon Tab, Group/Option	Button, Option	Keyboard Shortcut
Advanced Filter options	HOME, Sort & Filter		
append query	QUERY TOOLS DESIGN, Query Type		
Application Parts	CREATE, Templates		
close Access			Alt + F4
close database	FILE, Close		
copy	HOME, Clipboard		Ctrl + C
create ACCDE file	FILE, Save As		
create table	CREATE, Tables		
customize Access options or Navigation Pane	FILE, Options		
cut	HOME, Clipboard		Ctrl + X
delete query	QUERY TOOLS DESIGN, Query Type		
delete record	HOME, Records		
Design view	HOME, Views OR TABLE TOOLS FIELDS, Views		
export object to PDF or XPS	EXTERNAL DATA, Export		
export object to Excel	EXTERNAL DATA, Export		
export object to Word	EXTERNAL DATA, Export		
filter	HOME, Sort & Filter		
Find	HOME, Find		Ctrl + F
form	CREATE, Forms		
Form Wizard	CREATE, Forms		
Help			
import Excel data	EXTERNAL DATA, Import & Link		
import Access data	EXTERNAL DATA, Import & Link		

Access 2013 Feature	Ribbon Tab, Group/Option	Button, Option	Keyboard Shortcut
Labels Wizard	CREATE, Reports		
macro	CREATE, Macros & Code		
Make Table query	QUERY TOOLS DESIGN, Query Type		
Navigation Forms	CREATE, Forms		
new record	HOME, Records		Ctrl + +
paste	HOME, Clipboard		Ctrl + V
Performance Analyzer	DATABASE TOOLS, Analyze		
primary key	TABLE TOOLS DESIGN, Tools		
Property Sheet	FORM DESIGN TOOLS DESIGN, Tools OR REPORT DESIGN TOOLS DESIGN OR Tools, QUERY TOOLS DESIGN, Show/Hide OR TABLE TOOLS DESIGN, Show/Hide		F4
Query Design	CREATE, Queries		
Query Wizard	CREATE, Queries		
Relationships window	DATABASE TOOLS, Relationships		
report	CREATE, Reports		
Report Design	CREATE, Reports		
Report Wizard	CREATE, Reports		
sort records ascending	HOME, Sort & Filter		
sort records descending	HOME, Sort & Filter		
spelling checker	HOME, Records		F7
split database	DATABASE TOOLS, Move Data		
Table Analyzer Wizard	DATABASE TOOLS, Analyze		
Total row	HOME, Records		
update query	QUERY TOOLS DESIGN, Query Type		